GAZZA

PUBLISHED MAY '96

EDITION NEW

PRINT No. 8,000

COVER PTR C & W

GAZZA

THE AUTHORIZED BIOGRAPHY OF
PAUL GASCOIGNE

MEL STEIN

BANTAM BOOKS

TORONTO • NEW YORK • LONDON • SYDNEY • AUCKLAND

GAZZA
The Authorized Biography of Paul Gascoigne

A BANTAM BOOK: 0553 40713 9

Originally published in Great Britain by Partridge Press,
a division of Transworld Publishers Ltd, as *Ha'way the Lad,
The Authorized Biography of Paul Gascoigne*.

PRINTING HISTORY
Partridge Press edition published 1994
Bantam edition published 1996

Set in 10/11pt Linotype Sabon by
Phoenix Typesetting, Ilkley, West Yorkshire.

Bantam Books are published by Transworld Publishers Ltd,
61-63 Uxbridge Road, Ealing, London W5 5SA,
in Australia by Transworld Publishers (Australia) Pty Ltd,
15-25 Helles Avenue, Moorebank, NSW 2170,
and in New Zealand by Transworld Publishers (NZ) Ltd,
3 William Pickering Drive, Albany, Auckland.

Reproduced, printed and bound in Great Britain by
Cox & Wyman Ltd, Reading, Berks.

To Big Paul, not so big Paul and Nicky, who all think football is a beautiful game, and Marilyn who doesn't, but can now have her spare room back without the Gazza cuttings.

With thanks to Paul Joannou for the statistics; Neil
Duncanson and all at Chrysalis for their help and
co-operation, Graham Taylor for his frank and
helpful comments; Chris Waddle; Arthur Cox; Glenn
Roeder; Carol and the rest of the Gascoigne family
for the photos; John-Paul King for telling the truth;
Celia Dearing for the trawling through the pictures;
Adam Sisman and Debbie Beckerman for their careful
and constructive editing; Len Lazarus for listening;
and most of all to Gazza himself for not interfering.

THE DAILY TABLOID

GAZZA
BLOWS
HIS
NOSE!

OTHER PAGES | World War 3 Declared

Ken Pyne

GAZZA

I

'ONCE HE'D GOT THE BALL, HE MADE IT TALK'

No life can be lived in the North-East without being coloured by football, by Newcastle United, Sunderland, Middlesbrough, Hartlepool, Darlington or even Gateshead. In the working men's clubs, amidst the smoke, the beer, the darts and the bar billiards, the talk in the 1960s was of Wyn Davies – 'The Mighty Wyn' – Tommy Robson, John McNamee, Dave Elliott and Jim Iley, of whether Alan Suddick should have been allowed to go to Blackpool. For a time Suddick, the young will-o'-the-wisp, was spoken of in the same terms used for Paul Gascoigne some twenty years later; but Suddick's potential was sadly never to be fulfilled. Why did Newcastle always sell their most promising players? Why was it a case of Away the Lads as a response to the Geordie war cry of 'Ha'way the Lad?' If this is Gazza's story, then up to a point it is also the story of Newcastle, both club and city, for Gazza is their child as much as he belongs to his parents.

Paul John Gascoigne was born in Gateshead on 27 May 1967 to Carol and John. Just a few weeks previously Newcastle United, the famous Magpies, had narrowly escaped relegation to the Second Division, only gaining the four points necessary for safety from their last two home matches of the season. Even without a Premier League they had played those matches in front of over 40,000 fanatical Geordies starved of success since the famous cup exploits of the Fifties.

The Gascoigne family lived at 29 Pitt Street, on the first floor of a large converted house where neighbours were friends and friends were neighbours. With John having two brothers and two sisters and Carol coming from an even larger family of six sisters and a brother, Paul was never going to be short of uncles and aunts. His earliest and happiest memories are of Christmas get-togethers, the singing, the laughter and the generous presents despite the eternal lack of money. Perhaps because of that, Christmas is a very special time for him even now.

There were no holidays as such for the Gascoigne family – they were an unknown luxury. By the time the family moved up a notch in Gateshead terms, to Oak Street, then to Pine Street, and finally settled in Edison Gardens, there were four children. Anna-Marie (or just plain Anna as she was usually known) was not only the eldest, but the liveliest. Paul came next, then there was Carl, and finally Lindsay, always to be known to Paul as his baby sister. From a very early age the children, led by Paul, had the ability to entertain, and in one way or another people will pay for entertainment. The elderly neighbours in Edison Gardens would ask them to sing or dance, happy to give them a sweet or chocolate for the performance. Finally the diminutive impresarios, together with some friends from across the road, created a proper street theatre, with a sheet across a washing line in the back garden substituting for a curtain. They then proceeded to put on shows for the old ladies who would pay them twopence for admission.

Paul's ambitions were, however, inevitably greater than those of anybody else. He borrowed an old wind-up record-player and a copy of 'The Stripper'. As the music filled the street, he slowly gave his impression of what he perceived to be a sexy strip-tease, culminating in a streak. Carol Gascoigne arrived home unexpectedly and put an end to the proceedings on a swift and permanent basis. It had not been a great commercial success. Anna recalls, 'When the ice-cream van came round we used to spend all our takings on lollies for the whole audience.' It was typical Gascoigne generosity.

Even before he went to school Paul was a handful. On Parents' Day, Anna's class was giving a demonstration in the gym. Paul, beside his parents, watched with interest and then decided to have a go, only to fall and break his arm. It was his first introduction to the casualty department of Queen Elizabeth's Hospital, but it was certainly not to be his last.

When he was five, Paul was enrolled at Tyne View Nursery, and by the time he'd joined his first proper school, Brighton Junior Mixed infants, there were three passions in his life: his family, his football and his sweets. In particular he looked forward to the visits of his 'Uncle' Ian, Carol's cousin, who never came to the house without a bag of goodies for his favourite honorary nephew.

He was very close to Anna and as small children they shared a room. 'He'd pick the plaster off a wall and throw it at me in bed. The walls were terrible everywhere we lived.'

Food also played a vital part in the life of the young Paul Gascoigne. To get to Brighton Junior School his mother would have to walk Paul and his brother Carl past Kelvin Grove School. To help her work, Carol tried to transfer the boys there as it was nearer to their home. The move lasted precisely one week. Paul came home crying every day, simply because he could not stand the school dinners at the new school. Finally giving in to the pressure of her gourmet son Carol moved the boys back.

Paul returned to Brighton Avenue where he proved

himself to be very bright, particularly at maths. Even today he is incredibly numerate, able to add and check bills in restaurants with alarming speed and accuracy. Now, as then, it is dangerous to underestimate Paul Gascoigne. He was conscientious to an extreme, never missing a day, even dragging himself there when he was ill, and indeed getting a prize for best attendance. Once, after a visit to the dentist when he'd had a gas anaesthetic, he made his mother take him to school, only to be so groggy that the headmaster sent him home.

He was seven when his father bought him his first leather football as a Christmas present. He tried hard to hide the disappointment on his face: he'd wanted and expected a toy, although he enjoyed a kick-about as much as any other seven-year-old. His real interest in football exploded when he got that ball. Even before then when Newcastle had reached the FA Cup Final, Anna and her friends would yell, 'Ha'way the Lasses', while Paul would lead the responsive chants of 'Ha'way the Lads'; but he'd rarely go to matches. He was a player, not a spectator.

Seven years old. The boy and his brother, together, kicking the new football about with their father. And suddenly the boy discovers he can do things with the ball that the others can't, not even his father who'd been no mean player in his day. He tries things, experiments, juggles the ball in the air, hits it with his instep, with the outside of the boot, showing a maturity far beyond his years.

Paul was too young to realize that on many of the occasions that his father had played with him he'd first had to fight through spasms of pain that wracked his head. He'd fallen awkwardly playing football in his teens and the headaches started then, developing into migraine as he got older, migraines that made it sometimes difficult to talk, let alone keep down a job. Eventually, in Paul's seventh year, John collapsed and was rushed to hospital in Newcastle with a brain haemorrhage. The doctors battled for hours to save his life, and after weeks of recuperation they had to tell him the truth – he would never work again.

Carol took any job that was going to protect 'her bairns', never being choosy, yet never losing her dignity. Anything that would bring honestly earned money into the depleted family coffers she took on, often not only working a six-day week but odd shifts at the local glass factory. Instead of coming home to a smiling mother the children most days found themselves returning to an invalid father.

In the playground at school Paul was the organizer, the motivator, the star, despite playing with kids much older than himself. When a pass went astray, when a shot went wide, he'd stand hands on hips in disbelief that something had gone wrong. It was a stance his contemporaries would all remember, a stance that was to be repeated by him a thousand times on pitches all over the world.

In his street Paul also started two teams. His next-door neighbour Kevin Smith captained one whilst Andy Humphrey led the other; but it all had to be done properly, the goals had to be exact, rules had to be precise. It had to be real for Paul Gascoigne, even as a child. At the age of eight he had gone to the trials for the school football team even though it was unheard of for a boy of his age to be selected. Yet his performance on the day left the teacher with no alternative but to pick him, upon the basis that if he was good enough then he was big enough. He became the first child to represent the school at football at the age of eight. Paul was not selected for every match even though his talent merited such selection. Quite properly his teachers wanted to keep his feet on the ground, no easy task even then. However, by the time he was nine he had made a place in the first team undeniably his own.

All the familiar Gazza traits were already in place: the ability to use both feet, the skill to go on long searching solo runs, the deceptive changes of pace, the power to shoot from a distance. It was all so natural that it frightened the coaches. The football became an obsession. Although still too young to join Redheugh Boys Club, a famous footballing source of talent in the area, from the age of seven Paul would climb over the wall just to watch the older boys at play. He accepts now that he probably took more in from watching the more talented youngsters than professionals. In the cold winter nights he would find streetlights to create a floodlit pitch in his mind and then share the image with his friends. There, marathon matches often led parents in pursuit of their missing children, whilst a war of attrition developed between Paul and the local neighbours, whose plants, windows and cars all suffered to some degree or other from being in the line of fire of his lethal shots.

At the age of ten Paul won his first trophy. He scored twelve out of twelve in the Gateshead Primary Schools penalty competition and received a little cup which he took home and kept under his bed, lest it disappear overnight. 'I remember thinking to myself, this is it, this is the start. I really believed I'd be a professional footballer. Somebody gave me a black and white Newcastle shirt and my mum had to peel it off my back to get it clean because I'd hide it on wash days.'

He was desperate to join Redheugh, with its own properly organized teams, properly marked-out pitches, goals with nets – the real thing that Paul had tried so hard to conjure up in his imagination. Time after time he was told he was too young. Finally his father took him down to meet Tommy Leonard. Tommy was, and is, a legend in the area, having run the club for as long as anybody can remember. John's white lie about Paul's age in no way fooled the club leader, but he'd seen the boy play and realized that his talent transcended his age. Paul was therefore allowed to join as an associate member, not to play, but to train alongside the older lads. For Paul it was the foot in the door he so passionately wanted. 'He had no nerves,' Leonard says, 'he just went out, played football and enjoyed it. He had plenty of skill. He might have been a bit more podgy than the other boys, but once he got the ball he'd make it talk. He was always the character in the limelight.'

Once he became really established in the club that was certainly the case. One year, Paul recalls, he won six or seven awards, barely leaving the stage at the annual ceremony before being called back again. Yet his success evoked no ill-will with his clubmates, receiving both applause and laughter as he went on his seemingly endless circuit.

He was always helpful around the club and its older members and was therefore never resented by them. If he wasn't playing, the next best thing was to be allowed to act as a ball-boy or to help put up the nets and the flags. Anything to be involved. At Brighton Juniors he was selected for the Gateshead Under-11 trials. Inevitably he was the youngest trialist, but he let neither his age nor his size hamper him, and made such an impression that he was chosen for a weekend coaching course at Dukeshousewood, a countryside football camp. A young man named Keith Spraggon, playing for a rival school, St Cuthbert's, was also chosen. It was to be the start of a lifelong friendship.

From Brighton Junior School Paul moved on to Breckenbeds Junior High in Low Fell. Naturally he could hardly wait for the football trials that would decide the new lower school football team.

'I was just about the smallest player on the pitch, but it didn't worry me. There were a few kids who knew me, but the rest underestimated me because of my size. Once you're underestimated, you've got an advantage.'

The diminutive figure, in his faithful Newcastle kit, stood out, not only for his size but for his skill, making the right midfield position his own. He loved playing one-twos, and if he didn't get the return pass he'd rant and rave at the offending player whatever his size. He was none too happy with opponents either, always tackling back if he was beaten in a challenge, always seeking retribution for any foul.

By the time he was twelve both he and Keith Spraggon were fixtures at Redheugh. If it wasn't football it was snooker or the juke-box, and the club became a focal point in Paul's social life.

In July 1979 Paul, Keith, another friend called Michael Kelly, and Keith's kid brother Steven went into a local store where they enjoyed annoying a particular lady who served behind the counter. Young Steven ran out of the shop into Derwentwater Road in front of a parked ice-cream van. He could never have seen the oncoming car and was killed instantly.

'I was shattered. I was twelve years old and I'd just seen my best friend's little brother get killed. I couldn't understand why God would want to take a harmless kid like that. It started me asking questions that have never been answered to this day.'

Life had to go on. There was always football to take his mind off things. There was always football to take his mind off everything.

2

'SOME OF YOU WILL MAKE IT AND SOME WON'T.'

At the start of the 1979/80 season the twelve-year-old Paul was picked to play for the Redheugh Under-14 team in a five-a-side tournament at the annual Tyneside Summer Exhibition. There were over a hundred clubs involved and the Redheugh team did well to get through to the final, where they lost to the much older Montague Boys Club. Paul was inconsolable.

'I hated losing, even then. If your best wasn't good enough to win, then you had no right to be out there.'

In the first friendly of the season Paul found himself in the Redheugh Under-12 first team. It was the first time he'd ever played eleven-a-side football on a large pitch, with proper kit and a proper referee. The opposition, Wallsend Boys Club, contained Ian Bogie, Paul Stephenson and Jeff Wrightson, all of whom were later to meet up with Paul in the Newcastle youth side.

Everybody at Redheugh had a nickname, some more unkind than others, but that match day was the first time Paul can remember his team-mates calling him 'Gazza' rather than Paul. A legend had not so much been born as stumbled into existence. Wallsend won 7–3, but all eyes on the touchline were on the little boy who dominated the midfield and spent as much time shouting at his team-mates as kicking the ball.

Paul kept his place for the first competitive match of the season, against Kirkwood. Redheugh won 5–3, although Paul was a bit disappointed he didn't score. 'In those days, if I didn't get a goal, I reckoned I'd had a bad game.'

By the time Paul was thirteen he had created a reputation for himself both on and off the field. The teachers could not cope with him. The disinterest was coupled with boundless energy. 'I couldn't keep count of the number of times I got chucked out of the class, but it meant I could be first out into the playground and bag the best pitch. The worst thing the teachers could do to me was make me stay in the classroom at break to clear up some mess.'

David Lloyd from Middlesbrough was probably the first of the scouts from professional clubs to watch Paul, but following close on his heels were John Carruthers from Ipswich and Peter Kirkley and Jimmy Cook from Newcastle. The manager of Ipswich at the time was Bobby Robson, a Geordie himself, who knew what a breeding ground for talent was the North-East.

Newcastle stumbled upon Paul by accident, even though he was playing right under their noses. Kirkley had actually gone to watch Keith Spraggon who, perhaps because of his size, had generally been considered a better prospect. Paul was playing in a different match but Kirkley stayed to watch and what he saw left a lasting impression. Yes, he was small, yes, he was a little bit slow, but he had an understanding with the ball that went far beyond his years. All the skill was there. It just had to be developed and harnessed.

Yet despite Kirkley's interest Newcastle hesitated. Carol Gascoigne became used to opening the door to scouts from league clubs. Each would ask who else had paid her a visit and in particular would enquire as to Newcastle's interest. When Newcastle did finally pay a visit to the Gascoigne household, they were greeted with the words 'About time and all'.

John Gascoigne, at least, realized the talent he had in the family. 'I'd take him to the park and strangers would watch him do tricks with the ball. "You've a good'un there," one of them said, and he was right.'

At thirteen Paul was, of course, too young to sign on as apprentice, but clubs were still looking to take him as an associate schoolboy. John Carruthers of Ipswich watched him play for Gateshead Boys and was so impressed that he asked Paul's headmaster if he could approach the lad. Paul remembers the match itself clearly.

'My mum had done some overtime and saved up to buy me some Patrick boots. I felt like a king in them and I appreciated them even more because I knew how much effort my mum had put into getting them for me. I scored a cracker of a goal from twenty yards and I was only sorry my mother wasn't there to see it. That one was for her anyway.'

Carruthers's quest took him to Dunston. Paul opened the door himself, looking even smaller than he appeared on the field, and for a moment the scout must have thought he'd made a mistake.

'He asked to see my dad who was out at the club, and then asked to see my mum who was working at a local garage at the time. All he said to me was that he thought I was pretty good and would I like to go to Ipswich for a trial? I didn't really know where Ipswich was but I thought, why not? He said he was going to ask Keith as well, so I knew I'd have company, and when he finally caught up with my mum she was only too pleased to let me have the chance.'

There were about thirty of them there and Bobby Robson took the time to speak to them all in his quiet, well-modulated voice that never lost its native Geordie accent. 'Some of you will make it and some won't,' he said.

Paul was feeling none too sure of himself for the first time in his life. School, the club, they'd been easy. He and Keith had been regularly attending Sunday morning training sessions at Ayresome Park, Middlesbrough, and Paul had also been selected for a series of coaching sessions at Gateshead Stadium after impressing in his performances for Gateshead Youth. But none of that had prepared him for something like this. Looking around he was far and away the smallest boy there and some of the skills possessed by the others were awesome.

Despite his reservations Paul was in seventh heaven at Ipswich, with stars who'd won the FA Cup and played in Europe. Terry Butcher, who was to play alongside Paul for England, John Wark, Mick Mills and Paul Mariner, Paul couldn't stop collecting autographs. Paul Cooper, the goalkeeper, was especially kind.

'I just hope that today's crop of young hopefuls will always say that I was nice to them. I really care about kids. They're the game's future.'

Paul learned a lot in those few days, and not all about football. It was a lesson in how to deal with the world that existed outside the narrow confines of the North-East. Yet he'd missed his family badly, and whatever the outcome of the trial he came home saying he didn't want to go there; it was just too far from home.

On the same day Paul left Ipswich, Redheugh were in a cup final. While the rest of the team warmed up in trainers Paul went back into the changing room and swapped all the boots around. As he watched his team-mates first try and struggle into the wrong-size boots and try to match them up as pairs, he lay helpless with laughter on the floor. On the pitch, though, he was deadly serious. He scored a hat trick and Redheugh won 5–0.

There was only a short gap before he was back at Middlesbrough for official trials. It was to be the first time he'd ever stayed at a proper hotel because at Ipswich he'd been put up in digs. Best of all the Teesside hotel had a snooker table and for Paul it was heaven. Plentiful free food, snooker and football. What more could any teenager desire?

In the middle of the trials he went to see Redheugh play. Although he wasn't available for selection because of his Middlesbrough commitments, he didn't want to let his team-mates down, and decided to support them vocally from the touchline. However, it wasn't enough for Paul just to watch, he had to have a ball at his feet and, while kicking about, some broken glass went straight through the thinning soles of his much-used trainers. Bleeding profusely, he limped off to the nearby Spraggon house since his mother was out at work and would panic if she received a call. Keith's father took one look at his foot and he was back at the casualty department of Queen Elizabeth's Hospital. The cut needed stitches and Paul was unable to complete the trials whilst Keith was offered schoolboy terms. It was the start of the parting of the ways – two roads, one of which would lead Paul to Rome, the other would take Keith to obscurity.

The visit to hospital was not an isolated incident. 'We'd do "duffying", that was dares. Needless to say I'd do all the most dangerous dares. Once I fell while trying to swing from one tree to another and broke my arm. Another time I was sliding down a drainpipe when a huge nail sticking out of it cut through the skin on my leg for about nine inches. It took about sixty stitches in my thigh and I've still got the scar today. We didn't have to fill in admission forms at Queen Elizabeth's, they used to prepare them four at a time and just complete the dates.'

Like Ipswich, Southampton had a Geordie in charge

in the shape of Lawrie McMenemy, who devised the idea of starting a football-skill school in the North-East. Without McMenemy's hands-on control Paul felt it was all too basic and left after a short period. Yet it showed McMenemy too realized the talent there was in Geordieland. It was all coming down to a straight choice between Middlesbrough and Newcastle. Peter Kirkley, the youth development officer at Newcastle, had finally persuaded Brian Watson, the chief scout, to watch Paul play for Redheugh in an International Boys Clubs tournament in Ayr. Paul had been tipped off that the Newcastle scouts were present and did not let himself down.

'You saw skill, just skill, tremendous skill,' Kirkley recalls. 'My job was to pick them up as schoolboys, then hand them over, but Paul had so much before I even got my hands on him, even when he was up against older players.'

It was Watson who visited the Gascoignes, who were only too glad of Paul's opportunity of a trial at Newcastle. Even at nearby Middlesbrough he'd felt terribly homesick, a feeling that was to prevail until well into his Tottenham contract. But for a footballer home has to be not where his heart is but where he plays.

3

'DO YOU REALLY WANT TO BE A FOOTBALLER, GASCOIGNE?'

The Newcastle that greeted the young Paul Gascoigne in the summer of 1980 was a club in turmoil. They were a poor side, even by the old Second Division standards. Bill McGarry was the manager and he was under enormous pressure from the board, supporters and players alike for instant success, and by the end of August he had gone. Rumours as to the identity of the new manager spread like wildfire. Bobby Robson, Brian Clough, Lawrie McMenemy – it would need a big name to rescue Newcastle from the doldrums.

The man they did appoint, Arthur Cox, was not a big name, and more than one supporter asked in all innocence, 'Arthur Who?' Yet the two men who came together in the late summer of 1980, Cox and Chris Waddle (signed for a set of second-hand floodlights from Tow Law), were to be the two biggest influences on the career of the 13-year-old trialist, Paul Gascoigne. In fact Cox's credentials were far better than they appeared at first glance. He had never played football at the highest level, having suffered a serious fracture of the leg when a junior; but he had worked his way up the coaching ladder at Coventry, Walsall, Aston Villa, Halifax and Preston. He had been the Sunderland coach when they'd won the FA Cup in 1973 and achieved promotion, and had also done a good job on a shoestring at Chesterfield where he had just missed out on taking them up. He had a reputation as a disciplinarian with his crew cut and sergeant-major voice and was given a four-year contract, time to turn Newcastle around, time to get to know Paul Gascoigne.

It was a 5p bus ride to the Benwell training ground from Paul's home in Dunston, but it didn't stop him putting in for the maximum £5 worth of expenses. Apart from the convenience of not having to stay away from home, Paul felt immediately comfortable with the Newcastle juniors and the coaching staff. Jimmy Nelson, who was in charge of the schoolboys, made the lads believe in themselves, nurturing their pride in seeking to play for their home town.

Training was every Tuesday evening for two hours, and in the school holidays all day. Just as with school Paul was never late, indeed he was usually so early that he might as well have been given the keys to open up. He did not really stand out for Jimmy Nelson – there were too many other good youngsters such as Ian Bogie and Paul Stephenson. Nelson thought Gascoigne's stamina suspect, that he was still carrying too much weight and, remarkably enough when one looks at him today, also doubted his strength. Cox, though, who regularly attended the schoolboy sessions did see something special in him. As soon as he got the ball he looked complete, 'as if he'd been born with it attached to him.' Cox had seen Chris Waddle and Peter Beardsley demonstrate the same natural ability and now he had Paul Gascoigne. On one occasion training had been cancelled because of a heavy frost. It was just before Christmas and nobody was able to tell Paul. He duly turned up at Benwell to find the ground locked and empty save for the guard dogs. He'd had just enough money on him for the fare to the ground and had been banking on borrowing the return fare from one of his team-mates.

He had two alternatives: either walk six miles home in the cold or think of a way to raise some money. Inspirationally he began carol-singing, knocking door to door, eventually raising enough cash not only for the fare but for a hamburger.

There were many talented schoolboys coming through in the early Eighties, most of them Geordies. 'Somehow it felt right and proper to be playing alongside ten other local lads. I always felt that if we'd kept that youth team together and not seen the intake of expensive outsiders, we could have won anything.'

As a trialist Paul actually got spending money plus expenses, which seemed an absolute fortune in those days. Yet strangely enough he did not spend it on himself. He bought little presents for his mum and dad, brother and sisters, records for his friend Keith. It was another example of the extraordinary generosity that Paul shows today. It is highly dangerous to admire any item of his clothing as he's quite liable to remove it and hand it over.

Peter Kirkley remained a particular fan of Paul's. He'd take all the boys out to lunch at the local hypermarket and pretended not to notice when Paul ate some of his food while queueing, then nipped back into line for a second portion. Even then he realized Paul had to be treated differently.

Whilst playing for Newcastle Schoolboys Paul was picked for a Durham County trial. He duly scored a hat trick and never heard from them again. Whether or not his reputation preceded him, who knew, but the fact is that England's most gifted player of his generation never represented his country or county at any level below the Under-21s, a sad commentary on the national talent-spotting system. Paul himself has never forgotten the agony of rejection.

'Every day I'd dash downstairs to see if I'd been chosen, but all I ever got was a short standard letter saying I'd not made the grade and I'd be kept on the list.'

Paul's schooldays stuttered on their unsteady course. In September 1981 he moved to Heathfield High. 'I was just unteachable. I'd just sit and look at the clock and wonder when I could get out into the playground and kick a ball . . . I remember once during an exam writing my name over and over again when I couldn't answer any of the questions. The teacher asked what I thought I was doing. I told him I was practising because I was going to be a famous footballer. He scoffed at me, "That only happens to one in a thousand." "Yes," I replied, "but I'm going to be that one."'

Although he was mischievous at school he was never dangerously bad, but he was only marking time and very soon the staff came to accept that. He won some swimming certificates, played tennis well enough to be picked at county level, and enjoyed a bit of cooking (mainly because he could eat what he'd made), but that was about it. He was a fine tennis player then and still is now, yet he quickly perceived tennis to be a rich man's sport. He borrowed old rackets, played in football shorts, tatty T-shirts, yet felt no envy for his opponents with their immaculate whites, expensive trainers and brand-name equipment.

On a school tour to Blackpool, Paul got a hat trick in the only match in which he played and was then substituted. Playing the game was more important than getting results, and the teacher wanted to be sure every-body got a game. Yet today the spectre of substitution haunts Paul; he hates the ignominy of being pulled off. It's an accusation, a suggestion that he's playing at less than his best, and often because of that fear he's battled on with injuries long after he should have been lying in the treatment room receiving attention. In his final year at school he would try even harder to get himself thrown out of the class so he could go to the gym and join in with whatever class was there. He was allowed to sit CSE exams and did pass English and Environmental Studies. He was disappointed to fail Maths, but he had an excuse. 'My desk collapsed during the exam after I fiddled with the nuts.'

In May 1983 Paul signed as an apprentice at St James's Park. He was just 16 years old.

Colin Suggett, the Newcastle youth team manager, was a tough, hard-working career professional. Having been born at Washington, just a few miles outside Newcastle, he'd started his career at Sunderland, and ended it at Newcastle in the 1980/1 season, having played in nearly 400 competitive matches. He was Geordie through and through, just the sort of man to be put in charge of a lively bunch of apprentices. There were, and are, no great subtleties about him. He realized at a very early stage that Paul had more natural ability than those around him but was wasting it. Suggett had never had those natural skills; he'd had to work at them long and hard, and he could not believe that Paul was prepared to take a gamble on throwing them all away.

The troubles for Paul started almost from the word go. There was an important schoolboy tournament to be held in Aberdeen, at that time a hot bed of youthful footballing talent. Among the teams invited to participate were Bayern Munich, Rangers, Aberdeen themselves and Newcastle. The tournament went on for some ten days, straddling a weekend, and without any fixtures the Newcastle boys were brought home for a couple of days. With too much time on his hands and too much confidence, Paul decided to try his luck on a friend's 80 cc scrambler motor-bike. Anna Gascoigne had a little 50 cc bike which had to be pedalled and then kick-started. That had been the limits of Paul's motor-cycling experience, but being Paul he could not ignore a challenge, particularly when he believed nothing was

31

beyond him. The scrambler bike was far quicker than anything he'd ever experienced on or off the pitch. He got as far as the first bend before flying off, hitting his shoulder and cutting his knee so badly that he was, yet again, rushed to Queen Elizabeth's Hospital. Even Peter Kirkley, Brian Watson and Jimmy Nelson were scared to tell Arthur Cox about this.

'There was no-one there to deal properly with the injury and they put loads of butterfly stitches in my knee and every time they pulled the skin across it left another hole. Unfortunately one of the first people to see my leg was Arthur Cox . . .'

'Do you really want to be a footballer, Gascoigne?' Cox boomed.

'Yes, sir,' Paul replied, tears already in his eyes.

'Then behave like one. Another incident like this and you're out of here. You understand?'

Paul understood. He was in full flood of tears by now but he understood. Paul missed the semi-final and Newcastle ended the tournament as runners-up. Cox's fury extended beyond the incident.

'It was unnecessary, thoughtless. He injured himself by ignoring the rules of how to live as a professional.'

Cox spoke to Joe Harvey, who'd captained Newcastle in their cup victories in the Fifties. 'I've had enough of him,' he said.

'Steady up, this one's special,' Harvey replied. 'He's got a man's football brain and he's playing with the boys.'

According to Cox, '[Paul] was an ugly duckling. He could control the ball, pass it, shoot, but he couldn't run, but he was learning all the time. He'd play with Keegan, Waddle and Beardsley in the gym in the mornings and he'd learn from them. When he wasn't playing, he'd watch them and copy them.'

The senior professionals would use different-shaped targets in the gym – circles, squares, triangles – the idea being to trap the ball with one touch then hit it through whichever shape the coach called out. Of all the youngsters, only Paul could do it – only Paul was brave and confident enough to try it. Life as an apprentice was never going to run smoothly for someone like Paul – there was too much discipline and not enough football. Every day he would climb aboard the bus at 8.30 a.m. to be at the ground by 9.15. The mornings would be filled with boot cleanings, tea making for the senior professionals, sweeping the dressing-room, cleaning the showers and even the toilets. It was slave labour and when Paul signed for Tottenham he could not believe that they actually employed a lady to come round with the tea.

Paul in his mid-teens was not a prepossessing sight. Chris Waddle was only 22 himself, and having come to the professional game late had just a couple of seasons under his belt.

'I first saw Paul in training,' he says. 'He was doing shuttles or "doggie" as we call them. That involved running from the bye-line to the 18-yard line and back. He was simply the smallest, podgiest and slowest player I'd ever seen in my life. I thought he was some kind of a joke, but then I saw him with the ball and I realized exactly why he was there, he was a different class.'

Paul never regretted his decision to sign for his local club. So many of the players at that time were home-bred Geordies that he could not help but feel at ease with them, and they, for their part, recognized that in Paul himself there was something different. One day Paul had the task of cleaning Waddle's boots, and when Chris complained about his handiwork told him bluntly to do it himself. Chris smacked him in front of everybody. 'I could see he was about to cry but I didn't get any more cheek out of him after that, and indeed that incident seemed to be the start of him looking up to me. He'd always respect anybody that had a go at him provided they were justified.'

Paint fights, destruction of huts with lawn-mowers – fine followed fine and Paul was never too sure how much would be in his wage packet. He would often go home to his mother in tears, plotting all kinds of foul revenge in return for what he (and his family) saw as persecution.

One really hot day in training Paul opened his mouth once too often. Suggett sent everybody else away and had Paul running until he dropped. Finally Paul collapsed on the ground.

'I can't do any more,' he gasped.

'Just one more lap,' Suggett encouraged.

Paul staggered around again.

'You lied to me,' Suggett said, 'now you can do another lap.'

As Paul picked up his weary legs he saw Ian Bogie and Paul Stephenson, his two best mates, leaning over a fence happily sucking ice-lollies.

Paul was hopeless with money in those days. 'Not that I'm much better now,' he adds. He'd got himself a cash card from Barclays and went to get out £20. The card gave him his money and then incorrectly told him he had £200 left. This was news to Paul so he took out another twenty and another.

'It was a bit like winning on the fruit machine.'

Only fruit machines don't ask for the money back as did the bank in a letter that was anything but friendly.

His weight was becoming a problem. He couldn't stop himself eating junk food and the puppy-fat he should have shed from the hours of work and training simply took on a more permanent appearance. He might have skill, he might have vision, but nobody wanted a fat footballer.

4

'DO YOU WANT A MARS BAR, WADDLER?'

It was Jackie Milburn, the Tyneside hero of the 1950s, the man who had spearheaded Newcastle's great FA Cup side, the man who turned the black and white Number 9 shirt into the Holy Grail, who said, after watching Paul in only a handful of first-team matches: 'It's thirty-five years since I saw a lad as good as this. I just cannot believe the skill of him,' and it was Milburn who would pick him up when he was down.

Paul was beginning to play regular competitive football for the juniors in the Northern Intermediate League. It was all very physical and many of his opponents were a couple of years older than him; yet he battled on manfully. He was lifted at the start of the 1982/3 season by the arrival as a player of Kevin Keegan, later to become manager of the club. It set the whole town talking, put a spring into everybody's stride. As Jack Charlton said, 'If Kevin fell into the Tyne he'd come up with a salmon in his mouth.'

Paul was no less excited than any other Geordie. At the age of 15 he believed Keegan was the Messiah, a man who would lead them out of the Second Division. From the first day Keegan arrived at St James's Park, Paul realized he was something special. He made a point of looking over to the apprentices, smiling and waving. Even Arthur Cox had a smile on his face.

Paul could not believe his luck when he was made Keegan's 'apprentice'; but it wasn't luck. Arthur Cox knew exactly what he was doing. If there was one player he felt Gazza could learn from, it was Kevin.

Keegan was as pleasant off the field as he was on it. 'It was hard to believe he wasn't a Geordie at times, he settled in so naturally. I'd have done anything for him. I used to beg to break in his boots for him even though he was at least a size smaller than me and it was absolute agony. He'd just given me a brand-new pair to break in. I was with my mates on the top of a bus and there I was showing them these boots and saying they're Keegan's, and them not believing me, and somehow or other I managed to leave one of the boots on the bus. I got home, realized what I'd done and panicked. My dad took me down to the main bus station and we asked everybody in sight – I think they must have thought we were mad, a grown man and a teenager, looking for one of Kevin Keegan's boots. I was dead scared to tell Kevin and eventually my dad broke the news to him. Kevin just laughed and told me not to worry. However, on another occasion I wore a pair of Kevin's boots in a youth tournament and scored a hat trick.'

That was Paul in those formative years, praised and pilloried, laughing on the outside, worried, confused and tearful inside, eating to compensate, joking to compensate. He needed a lot of time and understanding and fortunately there were enough people at St James's Park in those days to give them to him. Cox knew he had to work hard on the boy. He saw his job not just one of training a footballer, but of making a complete person, fit to take his place in society.

'I'd put the team sheet up the day before a match. I'd write them out by hand, making sure they looked perfect. I saw them as my bond with the players. Once they were up, nobody was to touch them. One Friday I went for a shower and when I returned there were finger-prints all down the sheet as if someone had traced the names one by one with his grimy hand. I called out to Willie McFaul who suggested it might have been one of the kids who'd been getting the boots ready. Colin Suggett rounded up all the youngsters who stood shuffling their feet and looking at the floor. They knew full well it was Gascoigne. Finally he confessed and I said to him, "Don't you ever touch it again, only when your name's on it and then if it is and you do touch it I'll take it off." '

Paul even then was obsessed with becoming a part of the first-team set up. He allowed his imagination to run riot. After a win the players would celebrate with a glass of Harvey's Bristol Cream sherry. It was modest, but it was again Arthur Cox making a statement, trying to impose his personality on the squad. If you won you deserved some reward other than a monetary one. On one occasion Paul was the apprentice designated to clear up the first-team changing room. All the players had left, but from the adjoining coach's room Cox spotted Paul swigging the dregs of the sherry from an abandoned plastic cup, whilst holding a black and white team shirt against his body. He raced into the room, destroying Paul's day-dream of league glory. Paul quickly threw the cup away and began to fold the shirt hoping Cox had not seen him.

'Are you drinking Gascoigne?'

'No Sir.'

'Do you want a glass?'

'No, thank you, Sir.'

'As soon as you get into the first team, then you'll get a glass.'

Arthur Cox then took pity on the lad. The bottle was empty, but he poured what was left in each cup into one glass and gave it to Paul. 'There you are, drink that instead of telling me fibs.'

It took Cox and Keegan two years to get Newcastle promoted in third place at the end of the 1983/4 season, and the success of the first team permeated right the way down to the juniors. In that promotion year another new face joined Newcastle. Glenn Roeder was an unlikely figure and accent for the North-East, as cockney as they came, an experienced professional who'd begun his career with Orient, moved on to QPR, and from there at the age of 28 joined United. Famous for the 'Roeder shuffle' where he'd suddenly change pace, he was probably the best defender of his day never to play for England. Quite why Gazza should have homed in on him is a little difficult to understand unless one knows both men. Glenn is, in a way, everything Paul is not. Married, stable, reliable, serious, yet an hour or two speaking with Glenn sees the dry humour peeking through. Paul saw Glenn as the man he would one day like to be – respected, almost revered by his fellow professionals, a father, a husband with a settled home life that became a second home for Paul when they were both back in London.

Glenn liked expensive clothes and was wearing a full-length sheepskin coat, the like of which Paul had never seen before in his life. 'If I can carry your case will you let me wear your coat?' Paul asked. Glenn smiled. He was over six feet tall and thin as a rake, whilst Paul was small for his age in height if not in width. He humoured him, and somehow refrained from laughing as Paul shuffled along the road looking like an extra from a Marx Brothers movie.

On the field Glenn was an enormous influence, and from his introduction into the side on Boxing Day 1983 in a 1–1 draw at home to Blackburn, Newcastle lost only five of their remaining twenty-three fixtures until promotion was assured.

'The whole town went crazy and even as an apprentice who hadn't played I felt I'd been part of the team success. We had a bit of a drink and a bit of a cry and all I could think of was that I wanted to be playing against the Manchester Uniteds, the Liverpools and the Tottenhams next season. I wanted to be using boots, not cleaning them.'

And so Newcastle United were back in the big time, but as Paul celebrated his seventeenth birthday with dreams of First Division glory two things happened that rocked Tyneside – and Paul personally. Keegan retired and Cox resigned.

Paul, together with most of Tyneside, simply could not believe it when the news of Arthur Cox's resignation was made public. After all he'd done for the club they were only prepared to offer him a three-year contract in the First Division, a year less than he'd been given originally. It was insulting. Paul felt he was not only losing a mentor but a friend.

Once again every big managerial name was linked with the Newcastle job, but this time the hot money was on one of the North-East's favourite sons, Jackie Charlton. He seemed to have everything in his favour. His uncle was Jackie Milburn, he'd been a Newcastle supporter as a child, and then, of course, he had his England World Cup winner's medal from 1966. If he needed any more credentials, then he had twenty years' experience at the highest level of the game, at Leeds United as a player, and then as manager of Middlesbrough and Sheffield Wednesday.

To Paul he'd always seemed pleasant enough when he'd appeared on television. He had a good sense of humour and if he had one fault it was in his direct approach to the game, an approach which sometimes left no room for skilful players in midfield. Charlton was his own man and decided to make his own judgement. He called Paul into his office for a chat.

'I've heard that you're a cheeky chappie,' he said, reaching across and patting Paul's stomach. 'There's a lot of fat there but I'm told that underneath all that you've got a bit of skill. I'm giving you two weeks to get yourself fit and back in the team. If you've not made it by then, well I'll show you the door.'

Paul was in a total panic, but once he'd calmed down he realized that his destiny was in his own hands. Every day he would get home after training, exhausted as he was, put on a plastic dustbin liner to make himself sweat, then run until he could hardly stagger. He pushed himself right up to the bounds of endurance and beyond, just as he was to do in 1991 when he worked with John Sheridan to recover from his knee injuries.

Until Charlton's arrival, Paul had visited The Oven Door Tea Room almost every day, stuffing himself full of chocolate fudge cakes, cream cakes and custard tarts. The counter staff suddenly found themselves under direct instructions from Charlton. He wanted Paul to have the right food in his fight for survival, such as steaks, salads and anything else with high protein. Paul, being Paul, still asked for his fudge cakes, but it was only a hollow gesture.

He began to run in a more disciplined manner and gradually the fat became muscle. As he grew it became clear that his size was his strength and a rake-like Paul Gascoigne would be like Samson without his hair. Within ten days he had lost a stone and his form in training was so irresistible that Suggett had re-instated him in the youth team. The fear that Jack Charlton had put into him at the start of the 1984/5 season was to change his life and there was no looking back. There was no sudden elevation to the first team, but Charlton by now realized the talent there was in the boy. He was beginning to harness his pace to his strength and with sudden bursts of acceleration could cut through the defences of the youth sides against whom he regularly played. He was even made captain of the youth side, a quite remarkable turnaround considering that just a month or so before his career had looked like heading for the scrapheap. In the FA Youth Cup the youngsters beat Coventry, and then Birmingham in a two-legged semi-final to ensure their place in the final. Paul's reward was an appearance for Newcastle Reserves against Sheffield United.

'Jeff Clarke, who'd been brave enough to move from Sunderland to Newcastle, was the captain that day and I learned more in ninety minutes than I'd learned in the whole of my apprenticeship – there's some things you can only see in the heat of battle.'

Paul seemed to be getting nearer and nearer to a first-team début. On 23 March 1985 he was given the chance of travelling with the first-team squad to Ipswich. Chris Waddle had a knee injury and was named as substitute whilst Neil McDonald, who'd been out of the side since the beginning of February, was to take his place. Unfortunately Charlton was never very good with names. At some stage in his managerial career he'd had a player called Gary McDonald in a team. In his pre-match talk in the dressing-room he kept calling Neil 'Gary', whilst telling him to go wide on the right. Paul, sitting next to Neil on the bench, thought the manager was saying 'Gazza' and went to pull on the number seven shirt.

'What are you doing?' Jack asked.

'You just told me I had to play wide on the right. I don't think it's my best position, but I'll have a go,' Paul replied.

'No, I was talking to Gary, not you,' Charlton said, totally oblivious of his mistake.

During the match Paul sat alongside Waddle on the bench, driving him absolutely crazy. Chris liked to watch a match with total concentration. Paul's concentration span was approximately 30 seconds.

The travelling Newcastle fans kept chanting, 'Waddle, Waddle, give us a wave.' Chris waved back and got a cheer and Paul then got Chris to wave every five minutes, just to bring some life into a dull game.

Paul also seemed to have an inexhaustible supply of sweets and chocolates with him. 'Do you want a Mars Bar, Waddler? Do you want a Twix?'

'I may have to go on in a minute, Gazza, leave us alone.'

It was a plea that Waddle was to repeat time and again around the world.

On 8 April, Easter Monday, Paul was named as substitute for the away match against Sunderland. It was every Geordie schoolboy's dream. All local derbies have their blood and passion, but at the time nothing, it seemed, could possibly rival the fervour of Geordies against Mackems. If the idea was to give Paul a taste of the big time, well then, times came no bigger than a visit to Roker Park.

The first team were obliged to wear a suit on match days. This was a problem for Paul because he did not possess one. Off he went to Top Man in the city centre and invested in a garment that he was to wear every match day until he felt able to afford a new one at the start of the 1986/7 season.

As he sat on the bench with the number twelve shirt under his track suit he could hardly contain his excitement. He was almost waiting for somebody to get injured and for him to be called on. Not a serious injury, just a knock would do. Yet when a Newcastle player went down it was little David McCreery, Paul's particular friend, and he suddenly felt guilty, as if his wish had made it happen, then relieved when McCreery got up again. As it was the game finished a goalless draw without Paul getting on to the pitch and Newcastle continued to languish in mid-table, hardly the sort of season their supporters had anticipated with Charlton in charge.

Paul did not have to wait too long to taste the big match atmosphere again. The following Saturday he was named in the squad for the home match against QPR. The more experienced professionals were amused by the youngster's enthusiasm. On his first away trip with the team George Reilly had pretended to be a journalist seeking an interview with Newcastle's new meteoric star. 'Be down at 9.30 in the morning and I'll have a photographer with me.' Gazza got up at the crack of dawn to get himself ready, came bounding down the stairs all prepared for the interview and found himself being greeted by the first-team squad all laughing and cheering.

The match against QPR on 13 April 1985 was a perfect blooding for him. Rangers were a side who were unlikely to raise the temperature on the pitch and were just above United in the League. It was a typical end-of-season fixture with only pride at stake and it says much for the loyalty of Geordie fans that 21,711 turned up to see the match. It was George Reilly who was injured after scoring the only goal, and as he was led off dazed, Paul suddenly realized that Charlton was telling him to go on. There was a big cheer for the youngster. Most of the crowd had read of the youth team's Cup exploits, but those games had been played at the most before a couple of thousand people and now there were ten times that number. There'd been a bigger crowd at Roker Park a few days before, but somehow the noise sounded different on the pitch than from the touchline. It was like being in the eye of a storm.

Paul found himself standing next to QPR's Robbie James, a Welsh international, and a veteran at 28 of over 400 league games.

'Cor, the atmosphere out here is unbelievable,' Paul said. The next thing he knew he was lying on the floor, felled by a meaty challenge. That was his first real lesson that there was no room for the faint-hearted in the professional game. Shaking his head, Paul rose to enjoy the rest of the match, even getting the ball into the net only to see it disallowed.

'I can remember every minute of that day. I thought, this is a start. Brilliant. I wouldn't mind a bit more of this. It was like having sex for the first time. You never forget that either.'

In the final of the Youth Cup Newcastle were to play Watford, whose first team at that time were still riding high in the First Division. Their youth team contained Gary Porter, who had already made his début for the first team and was to become a close friend of Paul's when they met up in the Under-21 squad. In Gary's testimonial year Paul's signed England shirt was handed to him after the victory against Poland at Wembley in September 1993.

Expected to win comfortably at home Newcastle could only draw 0–0. Then at Watford on a Friday night they utterly dominated and ran out 4–1 winners, with Paul and Joe Allon grabbing two apiece. Eight and a half thousand fans filled Vicarage Road, many of whom had journeyed all the way down from the North-East to give the young team their vocal support. It was Watford manager Graham Taylor's first sight of the player who was to play such a crucial and dramatic part in his England managerial career. 'I could see even then he had talent, not just for making but also for scoring goals.'

On the bus travelling home, amidst the celebratory fish and chips, Charlton came to sit next to Paul and offered him a two-year contract, which transpired to contain a two-year option clause in Newcastle's favour. Paul was only too happy to sign and never even thought of trying to renegotiate any of the terms. 'Quite honestly, if they'd told me I had to pay them to play I would have signed.'

44

On 6 May Paul came on as substitute at home to Spurs, who won 3–2 that day. Sitting in the stand was Irving Scholar, the Tottenham chairman and number one supporter, a man who loved Tottenham and football almost as much as he loved life. As the youngster hit a perfect 30-yard pass Scholar looked down at his programme to check the name of the substitute. Paul Gascoigne, a name that was to become not only an obsession, but in many ways his downfall.

5

'HE'S GOING TO BE SOMETHING SPECIAL.'

At 18 years old everything seemed to be going right for
Paul Gascoigne and he had every reason to look forward
to the new season of 1985/6. His three best friends
within the club, Ian Bogie, Paul Stephenson and Joe
Allon, had also been offered full professional contracts,
and with the Geordie Jack Charlton in charge of the
team it looked for once as if there'd be a predominance
of local talent wearing the black and white shirts.

Before the start of the campaign the fans had hoped
that Charlton would have gone out into the transfer
market for one of those dramatic signings that have
awakened the sleeping Tyneside giant from time to
time. But all he'd done was to buy Alan Davies (later
tragically to commit suicide) from Manchester United,
and Ian Stewart, an Irish winger, from QPR. Neither
was able to capture the public's imagination. What was
worse, and almost unforgivable at least to the fans, was
that he'd sold Chris Waddle to Tottenham. That
was a bitter blow to Paul. Waddle had rapidly become
an idol to him. The way he played was exactly the way
Paul thought the game should be played; he made it
seem easy, smooth, even beautiful and Paul admired
him both as a player and as a person.

'It was the close season so he didn't even get a chance
to say goodbye. I couldn't help thinking, here we go

again, we're selling our best players, the club's got no ambition.' It was a thought that was never to be far from Paul's mind in his eventful years at Newcastle.

As the pre-season match against Sheffield United ground to a close the unhappy supporters turned their wrath on the manager. The cry echoed around the ground, 'Sack Charlton, Charlton out.' He was never one to stay where he wasn't wanted and after the game he left St James's Park never to return.

With Waddle and Charlton out of Paul's life a new figure entered in the shape of Alastair Garvie. Garvie was a tall, quiet, chain-smoking Scot who had been the assistant secretary at Newcastle to Russell Cushing for many years. He'd originally trained as an accountant, had come to St James's Park on an audit and had never left. With his gaunt face he always looked permanently worried, yet he was at heart a kind, gentle man. He'd first met Mel Stein when the London lawyer, a fanatical Newcastle United supporter, had followed his team on the FA Cup trails of 1974 and 1976, and whenever Stein wanted a ticket for a match he'd taken to phoning Garvie. Over the years the two had developed a rapport and Garvie confided in Stein that his chances of pro-motion at St James's Park were limited in view of the relative youth, and undoubted efficiency, of Cushing. Almost casually Stein suggested that perhaps Garvie could represent some players as he knew them so well, and was also in a position to spot young talent. Clearly Garvie could not do that whilst employed by the club, and having given in his notice he struck gold first time in the shape of Chris Waddle.

It soon became apparent that, whilst Garvie had little difficulty in discovering talent, and then persuading the players to allow him to represent them, he was not fully prepared for the complex legal, commercial and financial matters that came with success. Consequently a 'team' fell naturally into place with Stein and his best friend Len Lazarus. Lazarus was a chartered accountant and had already gained some experience in football by his representation of Luther Blissett and Ross Jenkins. For a while the association worked most successfully. Garvie would do all the local work, such as personal appearances and obtaining simple equipment contracts, whilst the other two looked after the broader picture. Stein had urged Garvie to seek to represent some of the more talented youngsters at Newcastle and eventually Garvie had persuaded Paul to sign a contract.

Willie McFaul, Newcastle's former goalkeeper, was one of the first to do something positive to harness Paul's star quality. McFaul had certainly served his time at Newcastle. A Northern Irish international, he'd been unlucky enough to be a contemporary of Pat Jennings, but he'd played for United for many years and had acted as youth team manager, coach and assistant manager. Now, with Charlton's walk-out, the Newcastle board for once opted for loyalty and consistency, and appointed him as manager on a caretaker basis. After a few weeks he was offered a contract and within twelve months had secured a three-year deal.

McFaul had his own ideas as to how football should be played. He abandoned Charlton's long-ball approach and reverted to the fluent passing style that the Newcastle supporters so appreciated. He had watched Paul progress through the ranks and for the first match of the season included him in the first team, although he was substituted ten minutes from the end.

'I'd started a match in the First Division and whatever might happen afterwards nobody could ever take that away from me.'

Alan Davies had picked up an injury at Southampton and Paul kept his place for the home match against Luton on 21 August. Neither man then could have predicted what would happen to them in the future. Alan was sadly destined to take his own life, unable to take the pressure of his decline in the game, of impending retirement, whilst for Paul the pressures would be of a totally different nature, the pressures of success, of impossibly high standards, pressures that threatened eventually to destroy him and his relationships with those he loved.

He swapped his number eleven shirt for the number four and was greeted by a huge roar from the home crowd. It was odd, the instant empathy he had with the Newcastle supporters, particularly those standing at either end. It was as if they recognized him as one of their own, their representative on the pitch. He even had a nickname they could understand, Gazza. Paul Gascoigne could stand with them, drink with them, perhaps even fight with them, any time he liked.

Newcastle were unbeaten after five matches, including a 2–2 draw against a Liverpool side containing Kenny Dalglish, and were fourth in the First Division. Yet it was to be another false dawn for the team, and also in a way for Paul. After a 3–0 hiding at Old Trafford by Manchester United, McFaul decided his young star had received enough exposure and named him as substitute for the visit to Spurs on 7 September. Chris Waddle was the decisive influence on the match as Spurs raced into a 5–1 lead. At that point McFaul took off young Rob McKinnon, who'd been given a torrid time at full back against Waddle, replacing him with Gazza. Paul was in no way overawed and with one or two telling passes gave a clear message to his manager as to what might have happened if he'd played him from the start. Irving Scholar and Stan Seymour, the Newcastle chairman, were seated together in the Tottenham directors' box. Seymour pointed at Gazza: 'See that lad, you want to watch him, he's going to be something special. It's not just me saying that, Jackie Milburn thinks the same.' Scholar watched and waited.

McFaul was determined to take a softly softly

approach with Paul. He saw how easily he'd flare up in training, and was also concerned about his eating habits. The days of steak and salad seemed to have been forgotten and he'd reverted to junk food. He had too much time on his hands and time is so often the enemy of the young professional. Relieved of his tiring duties as an apprentice he suddenly finds the days stretching ahead of him, long and empty once training is finished, and a day off, so long awaited, can be purgatory. Paul had kept to his old mates. Although he'd not been at school with Jimmy Gardner he'd known him from around the town for many years. He was fat, jolly, game for anything – a perfect foil for Paul's jokes and often the butt of them. It was Jimmy Gardner that Paul invited to Italy to keep him company when he moved villas and who became a folk hero in his own right when he was dubbed 'Five Bellies' by the national press. As time was to tell Paul could not have wished for a better or truer friend. When he was taken to hospital with his fractured knee-cap after the night-club attack, Jimmy cried down the phone to Mel Stein, 'I wish it could have been me.'

Against Oxford, again coming on as a substitute, Gazza scored his first league goal but also picked up his first injury after a real battle in midfield with Ray Houghton. Not for the last time in his career he pushed himself to come back too early, this time against Barnsley in the Milk Cup on 25 September. It was a drab goalless draw, but it was of interest for one thing. In the players' lounge afterwards Garvie introduced him to Mel Stein for the first time. Gazza stood there unprepossessing off the pitch, his hair still wet from the shower, a drink in his hand, a small blonde girl – Gail Pringle, a local lass and his then girlfriend – on his arm. The two men shook hands.

'You're Waddler's lawyer, aren't you?' Gazza asked.

Stein made some polite comments about Paul's performance.

'Nah, I was crap,' Gazza said. 'Anyway, if you're good enough for Waddler, you're good enough for me. Will you be my lawyer?'

'Sure.'

'Top man. Look, I've got to get away to my lass and the family. I'll see you—' and he was gone with one of his vanishing tricks that were to become so much his trademark as the pressures of fame began to weigh down his young shoulders.

McFaul rested him again for the next match against West Ham, but he was back to play against Barnsley in the second leg of the cup game, where after extra time Newcastle went through on the away goals rule after a 1–1 draw.

'It was the first time I'd ever played one hundred and twenty minutes in my life. I was gone on my legs, but I knew if I looked at the bench the Gaffer would take me off.'

After that experience Paul was left nursing his wounds and did not return until 26 October when, against Aston Villa, for the first time he wore the number eight shirt that he was to make his own. He scored as well and received rave reviews as Newcastle ran out 2–1 winners. But yet again the season and his career were to travel together on a roller-coaster ride. Oxford knocked the Geordies out of the Milk Cup 3–1 on 30 October and Paul limped off to be replaced by Alan Davies.

His profile, his fame and reputation were beginning to spread, not just in the North-East but around the country. Newcastle had another hot property in the young Paul Gascoigne, but he was troublesome, he had a temperament problem, he could be wound up easily by an experienced professional, and once rattled he'd be off his natural game. On the credit side, Paul collected the North-Eastern Young Player of the Month awards for both August and November.

His stop-start season continued. Substituted in a 1–0

defeat at Maine Road against Manchester City, injury saw him sitting out late November and early December before he finally returned to face a Liverpool side at Anfield who had by now climbed to second place in the League. 'All the other players told me what it was like to play at Liverpool. There's this sign as you go out of the tunnel on to the pitch. "This is Anfield," it says. I joked with them – I'll take a black marker pen and write "This was Gazza".' United got a point in a 1-1 draw and Gazza lasted the whole 90 minutes to gather praise from all quarters.

On New Year's Day 1986, Everton were the visitors to St James's Park and Paul scored his third goal of the season. Again, however, the result was a draw and Newcastle's fine start to the campaign was forgotten as they slipped to eleventh place. Although Paul was about to embark on a run of seventeen consecutive league matches, the club was still unhappy about his weight and threatened to fine him a pound for every pound he put on. In fact he lost half a stone in a week by fasting, running and sweating, and the new slimline Gascoigne felt his game improving. The improvement had a knock-on effect and suddenly, from February onwards, Newcastle really began to put things together. After four straight league wins they travelled to Oxford once more on 19 March for a mid-week match. Gascoigne's performance that night was simply breathtaking. On a wet, slippery pitch he made the ball talk, and the comparisons with George Best were immediate, inevitable and accurate. Newcastle won 2-1, with Paul scoring the first and making the second for Peter Beardsley. Then just as suddenly as the team had found their form they lost it again and won only one of their next five matches.

Pressures and frustrations were beginning to build up for Paul both in his footballing career and his personal life. He accepted he'd signed his first contract of his own free will, but that was before he'd become a regular in the side and he felt entitled to believe that, after some thirty appearances and many fine performances, the club should have come to him with an improved offer. That wasn't greed, it was just a basic fact that many other clubs would have done the right thing. But Newcastle wasn't any other club and the Newcastle board of the time had tunnel vision, and a very narrow tunnel at that.

Despite being named Young Player of the Month yet again, the season ended in disarray both for Paul and for Newcastle. At home to Birmingham he was fouled once too often, the thin veneer of self-restraint cracked and he reacted by throwing a punch at Robert Hopkins. The referee promptly sent him off and a red-faced Gascoigne ran back to the bench close to tears, even though United ran out 4–1 winners.

'I was only angry with myself. Who wasn't to say that while I was suspended somebody wouldn't take my place and play out of their skin.'

6

'WHO KNOWS WHERE HE'LL BE IN FOUR OR FIVE YEARS?'

A few weeks into the 1986/7 season Willie McFaul called Paul into his office. Inevitably Paul wondered what he might have done wrong. 'I've got a present for you,' McFaul said.

Could this be another improved contract? But no, it was in fact a copy of *Rothman's Football Year-book*, soccer's equivalent of cricket's *Wisden*. There on the front cover was a photograph of Paul tangling with Liverpool's Mark Lawrenson during the previous season's match. The publication of Rothmans was a bright spot in what was otherwise a difficult year for Paul both on and off the pitch. He actually worked hard during the close season, disciplining himself over both food and drink.

McFaul had gone on record as saying, 'Self-discipline is what Paul needs most of all. With it the world can be his oyster. Without it, who knows where he'll be in four or five years?' As evidence of his faith, in August, he'd given Paul a new, improved contract for three years which was intended to take him through until June 1989. Garvie had negotiated it on his own and the sums involved were still fairly derisory. So derisory that Paul has no problem in disclosing that the signing-on fee was a massive £3,000, i.e. £1,000 per annum.

Paul's enthusiasm was dampened before he could

kick a ball in a competitive match. In the first half of a friendly in the Isle of Man he damaged his knee and was back on the treatment table. Again he convinced himself, a specialist and the physio that he was fit and he started in the opening match of the season against Liverpool.

'I realize now it was stupid, but I still felt that if I didn't kick off the season I wouldn't be certain of my place in the team for the rest of the season. I never thought I might do myself even more damage by playing. I was young, and believe it or not I was nervous.'

In any event Paul started the match, broke down, and was replaced by Neil McDonald. This time the hex that Newcastle appeared to have had over Liverpool the previous season was nowhere in evidence. Liverpool had gone on to win the League and began against Newcastle like true champions, seeing them off at St James's Park by two goals without ever really raising a sweat.

Newcastle had hardly ventured into the transfer market in the close season. Money was tight even then, and they were largely relying upon the squad which had finished in mid-table, plus a few of the youngsters who, like Paul, had come through the junior system.

Paul's early-season injury meant he missed the trip to White Hart Lane, but he played in the next four matches which brought three defeats and a draw and only two goals. It took until 20 September for United to get their first win, a narrow 1–0 victory over Wimbledon with Paul scoring the goal. Worse was to follow. They lost 2–0 at Second Division Bradford City in the Littlewoods Cup, and by the time they visited Norwich at Carrow Road at the end of the month Paul had been relegated to the substitutes' bench and Newcastle were rock-bottom of the League.

Depressed and miserable, Paul spoke to both Garvie and Stein about the prospects of a transfer. They both explained that he had nearly three years of his new contract yet to run, and that having signed in August it was just too early to change his mind. 'Look, Paul,' Stein said, 'just keep playing well whenever you get the chance and in a year or two you'll be able to have your pick of clubs.'

Within the club it was Glenn Roeder rather than Willie McFaul who first cheered up Paul, then calmed him down and got him believing in himself again. You didn't become a bad player overnight, he was told; everybody in the game went through a difficult patch at some time or other in their career. Gail Pringle was also very supportive. Paul was not the easiest person to be with when his football wasn't going right.

On 11 October it looked as if the corner was being turned with a 3–1 win at home to Manchester City. Paul scored his second goal of the season and immediately felt brighter. 'It was amazing what one good win could do for you. I went out on the town that night and the whole place was buzzing. You could see the people walking just that little bit taller and I thought, these folk deserve better than what we're giving them, so I suppose I tried that little bit harder.'

In fact he tried too hard, and after losing 2–1 at home to Arsenal he was dropped. The nightmare came to a head against Oxford, the same Oxford he'd demolished almost single-handed just a few months before. He'd hurt his groin in training a few weeks before but had said nothing lest he fall off the tightrope he felt he was walking. Now, in the match, the groin was agony from the first few minutes, but instead of signalling to the bench to take him off he decided to battle on. The fans saw only what was apparent, a young man they'd thought was going to be the greatest running sluggishly about the pitch. After a while every time he got the ball they booed, and as the barracking rose in volume so his confidence fell. Eventually he came off, not realizing he would not pull on a black and white shirt for the first team until the following March.

He struggled manfully to get back to fitness but the injury persisted, and with so much time on his hands he began to fall back into his bad ways, eating, drinking and generally becoming troublesome around the town. He bought himself a car before he'd passed his test and drove so recklessly that even the boldest of his team-mates refused to get into the vehicle with him. He became a familiar figure to the local police who, as soon as they saw it was Gazza driving, tended to put away their notebooks, disarmed by his grin and an effusive apology.

However, just before Christmas he had an accident for which no apology could excuse him. Inevitably Jimmy Gardner, from whom he had become virtually inseparable, was with him, when a man suddenly stepped into the road straight in front of Paul's Renault. He did his best to avoid him but he still gave him a glancing blow sufficient to knock him over. Paul pulled up in a panic, got out, looked back, saw the man was relatively unscathed and, instead of reporting the incident, just drove off at speed. 'I was dead scared, but if I'd have really hurt him obviously I'd have called an ambulance. Somehow, I didn't think as a learner I'd be believed. I realized as soon as I got home it was wrong and I would have to pay for it.'

Pay for it he did, with a £150 fine for failing to stop after an accident, £100 for failing to report it and £10 for not displaying 'L' plates. Even Jimmy was fined £10 for aiding and abetting.

On the field things were not going too well either. He turned out for the reserves against Everton, but realizing something was still wrong he was pulled off before the end. The injury was particularly frustrating as, for a change, Newcastle seemed to be getting a bit of a Cup run together. They'd beaten Northampton 2–1 in the third round and got what seemed like an easy home tie in the next round against struggling Preston. However, by the end of January Paul was still not back in training and had to sit and watch as his club won 2–0.

The league situation was becoming ever more critical. By mid-January they were rooted to the foot of the table, having lost six consecutive matches. 'It was hell sitting and watching them lose week in, week out.'

By February Paul was back in training, determined to make the team for the fifth-round cup match against Spurs at White Hart Lane on 21 February. It is hard to explain or describe what the FA Cup means to Tyneside. If Newcastle won the Premiership three years running, questions would still be asked as to when they were going to triumph at Wembley. But in 1987 mere determination was not enough for Paul and yet again he was a spectator as Spurs luckily won through a much-disputed Clive Allen penalty. It made Paul re-double his efforts, but once more he pushed himself too hard and broke down in training.

The England Under-21s had already played three matches in the season and their next fixture was to be at the end of April against Turkey, but Paul's dream of playing for his country at any level was fast turning into a nightmare. 'It was bad enough that I'd not done myself justice at the start of the season but now I wasn't on display at all. All I could think was that if I didn't get fit, and get fit soon, that I'd be forgotten.'

Eventually Newcastle strung a few good results together, and when they beat Southampton 2–0 in May Paul scored one of them, just days before his twentieth birthday. 'I ran towards the crowd at the Gallowgate end. I could feel them sucking me in and I wanted to leap over the fence. I treasure that goal. It told me I could still do it, and more than that it told the fans I could still do it as well.'

Newcastle moved off the bottom and were on a roll

that virtually guaranteed them First Division status for the following season. When they beat Manchester United the season was almost complete. At the end of the campaign there was good news for Gazza. After all the ups and downs of the season he was named in the Under-21 squad to travel to Toulon for the end-of-season international tournament. Against Forest in the last match of the season Paul scored when United were 2–1 down, a consolation goal for the team but a declaration of intent for the player. On 9 May the curtain fell on yet another disappointing season for Tyneside.

Toulon was heaven for Paul. At the age of twenty it was his first real trip abroad, and wandering around, looking at the high-rise hotels and the expensive shops, it was an eye-opening experience. Typically he had arranged for his dad and a couple of friends to come out at his expense to watch the games and to do a little fishing. It had been a Christmas present of a fishing-rod when the family had lived at Edison Gardens that got him interested in the sport, and he'd been quite content to sit for hours by the side of the lake in Saltwell Park.

To his absolute delight Paul was named in the squad for the first match of the tournament against Morocco on 7 June. The vagaries of football are best illustrated by the comparative fortunes of Paul and young Gus Caesar of Arsenal, who also made his début in that match. Whilst Paul has gone on to fame and fortune, poor Gus's reputation never recovered from one nightmare performance he had against a Chris Waddle at the very top of his game. Gus went from Arsenal to Bristol City, then to Scotland and then to obscurity, one of the few players to represent his country at any level and then to be given three free transfers.

It was typical of Paul to score the first goal of the tournament from a brilliant free kick and England went on to win 2–0. The team followed that up with a goalless draw against Russia in which Paul had another fine match, but he then went down with flu, probably caught while fishing. It hurt him to sit out the next game against France which England lost 2–0, but the defeat only illustrated and underlined his contribution to the team.

An England side and its management had their first taste of Paul's eccentricity. He found it difficult to sleep, impossible to sit down. He'd wander into anybody's bedroom at all times of the day and night and drive them crazy. When he went off on his fishing trips the rest of the squad would breathe a sigh of relief until he returned to regale them at length with stories of the one (or the dozen) that got away. He was back for the last game against Portugal but not fully fit, and England could only play out a goalless draw to finish a disappointing fifth. Not for the first time, without realizing it was happening, a team had become totally dependent upon Paul Gascoigne.

Paul's return to Tyneside signalled the start of the silly season for the newspapers. In the summer of 1987 the journalists could not get enough of Gazza. In late July it was rumoured that Manchester United and Sheffield Wednesday had made offers for him. After the Waddle débâcle the pressure was on the club not to let him slip through their clutches, particularly as Newcastle were about to lose another of their favourite sons with Peter Beardsley on his way to Liverpool. There was no way the board could permit a further controversial departure, and so for Paul the only destination was the St James's Park pitch.

7

'HAVEN'T YOU FORGOTTEN TO ASK FOR THE TYNE BRIDGE?'

At 20 Paul was still largely felt to be unproven outside the North-East where he already had his cult following. His contract was not due to expire until 1989 but, almost before the season started, McFaul declared he'd like him to sign a new five-year contract which would tie him to the club until 1992. McFaul was taken aback when Paul said he wanted to discuss matters with his advisers, but when Newcastle learned that he was contracted to Alastair Garvie they relaxed. They knew Alastair was a gentle, honest man, unlikely to be unreasonable – he had after all been their assistant secretary for years and had rarely shown any sparks of ambition, innovation or indeed aggression. Garvie arranged a confidential meeting with Newcastle officials at a hotel in Durham, but also arranged for Mel Stein and Len Lazarus to come up and conduct the negotiations. This was the first time that Lazarus was to meet the man who was to play such an important part in his life. Paul arrived from training wearing a clean white sweat-shirt, his curly hair and round chubby face giving him the look of a cheeky school-boy. Offered something to eat he patted his stomach, muttered about a diet and said he wasn't hungry. After a moment's reflection, he then said he might have a steak, and finally added that he'd have chips and a glass of beer with it. He then saw an unfinished plate of canapés and polished them off as well. Lazarus couldn't quite believe what he was seeing.

As Stein ran through the proposals he intended putting to Newcastle it was Paul who could not believe them. He was receiving a pittance under his existing contract and had still to come to terms with his real worth. Yet not in his wildest dreams did he think it was anything like the figures that were now being bandied about.

'One thing I have to ask you Paul,' Stein said. 'If the offer's right do you want to stay, or is this just an exercise to see how much they'll go to, so we can see what we have to beat elsewhere?'

The reason for the question was important. If Paul had really decided he was going to leave whatever the offer, then it was simply a matter of putting the figures to the Newcastle contingent and sticking to them. If, however, he would stay if the deal was right then everything was negotiable.

'No, I'd like to stay, but they've got to pay me what I'm worth,' Paul replied.

'So if they accept these proposals you're happy to sign?'

Paul grinned. 'Oh aye, if they accept the proposals, I'll sign all right.'

They didn't accept the proposals, although in March they came very close to doing so. By then, however, it was too late.

Newcastle fielded a strong team: Russell Cushing, the experienced secretary, who was later to become chief executive under Sir John Hall, Gordon McKeag, the chairman, a well-respected local solicitor, and Stan Seymour, Mr Newcastle himself, who'd served the club as player, manager and director.

'Let us hear your proposals first,' McKeag said.

'Why don't you tell us what you have to offer?' Lazarus asked, just in case the Gascoigne suggestions were being pitched too low.

He needn't have worried. By the time Stein had read through his shopping list, against the background of a stony silence broken only by the sound of Gazza picking his teeth with a ring and the occasional intake of breath, it was apparent that there was an enormous gap between the two sides.

It was Cushing who broke the ice. 'Haven't you forgotten to ask for the Tyne Bridge?' he asked.

After a couple of hours of negotiations Newcastle had improved substantially from their first offer, but nowhere near enough. It was about ambition as well as money. Paul was still concerned that he was regarded as 'the boy' by the club; there was positive evidence of this. Newcastle had a history of negotiating more lucrative deals with incoming players than youngsters who'd come up through the system.

In some ways that early meeting with Newcastle was conclusive. At that moment, if they'd been generous, there was every possibility Paul would have committed his long-term future to the club. But they weren't, and from then on Paul knew that sooner or later he would be plying his trade away from the North-East. He wouldn't be playing to get away, but in some ways the love affair was over.

The 1987/8 season itself had started badly for Newcastle with a 3–1 defeat by Spurs at White Hart Lane on 19 August. Although they beat Sheffield Wednesday 1–0 at Hillsborough three days after that, they then lost 0–1 at home to Forest. With only three points and two goals from their first three games the board realized they had to do something dramatic. Back in 1971 it had been Malcolm Macdonald who'd arrived in a white Rolls-Royce; in 1982 it had been Kevin Keegan, conjured up by Arthur Cox; now it was Francisco Erandi Lima da Silva – better known as Mirandinha – who arrived from Brazil, the first Brazilian international to play for an English club. Mirandinha had scored against England in a 1–1 draw at Wembley in May 1987, and had received some very complimentary reports for his performance that night.

Gazza and Mira (as he came to be known) homed in on each other like soul mates, to the consternation of everybody, and particularly Glenn Roeder, the club captain. The very first time Mira was introduced to his new team-mates, Paul stood second in line, and then as Mira moved along he nipped along the back and popped up again at the end of the queue. As Glenn Roeder says, 'One Gascoigne was bad enough, but two . . . '

Mira simply couldn't handle the English winter and wore black tights and gloves even when the other players were sweating. Gazza waged a one-man war on his protection, cutting off one leg of his tights or the fingers from his gloves whenever he had the chance. He also assumed the unlikely role of teaching Mira English.

Mirandinha's first match was away at Norwich. Thousands of Geordie fans travelled the huge distance, and toy shops in the town did a roaring trade in drums whilst Brazilian hats and the national team shirt were begged, borrowed or stolen wherever they could be found. As Paul said to Mira as they ran out on to the pitch, 'You're sure you're Mirandinha, not Maradona.'

Unfortunately, one of the English words that Paul had clearly failed to explain to his little Brazilian friend was 'pass', and although he put the first game down to a desire to please the fans, Paul became more and more frustrated playing alongside him.

Paul had been selected, as he'd expected, to play for the England Under-21s against West Germany on 8 September. What he didn't disclose as he travelled was that he'd picked up a knock the previous Saturday. Looking back now, Paul realizes that what he did was irresponsible, not just to himself but to his club and country; but then he truly thought the injury would just go away – a belief that has in some ways carried him through the pain barrier when other lesser players would have been limping to the treatment couch. It was, however, a bad decision in every sense of the word. As if to compensate for the injury, Paul totally hyped himself up for the game, and those who saw both that match and the 1991 Wembley Cup Final say that they saw the same Paul Gascoigne, a young man obsessed with making his mark on the game, chasing lost causes, flying into tackles, losing his position – a clockwork creature wound up to its very limits. A goal down at half-time, Dave Sexton, in charge of the squad, had seen enough and pulled Gazza off.

Willie McFaul was not a happy man when Paul reported back for training with a pronounced limp and was unable to play against Manchester United. Indeed, if the result in the following game against Liverpool had not gone so badly, Paul might have found himself struggling to regain his place. However, by 23 September he had shrugged off the injury, which it had been feared might actually require a cartilage operation. He confounded the doctors by his speed of recovery and, perhaps more than that, his will to recover, his all-consuming desire to play football.

Although the club were not setting the First Division alight, Paul was still steadily building his reputation. He won the *Newcastle Chronicle*/Hennessy Cognac Player of the Month for August, the first of several awards that were to come his way that season, although by the end of September it was already looking as if honours were again going to be thin on the ground for Newcastle. They'd travelled to Third Division Blackpool in the Littlewoods Cup and found themselves played off the park, with the only goal being scored for the Seasiders by Geordie reject, Tony Cunningham.

Against Southampton Newcastle won 2–1 with Mirandinha and Goddard both scoring from Gascoigne passes, and that was followed by another good game for Paul in a 2–2 away draw against Chelsea. Not for the first time he became the butt of the opposing fans and he drew continuous boos and jeers from 'The Shed', and taunts of 'Fat Boy'. At the end of the game, in which he'd played a decisive part, he ran to his tormentors, pulled up his shirt, patted his non-existent paunch and turned jeers to friendly cheers.

On 7 October Blackpool visited St James's Park to defend their narrow lead before a huge crowd of over 20,000. They had not contemplated meeting Paul Gascoigne in full song. They'd subdued him at Bloomfield Road, but Gazza in front of his own following was irresistible, making a couple of goals, then scoring himself, to enable United to win 4–1 and give the hungry crowd a taste of a Wembley cup run. Yet his performance wasn't enough to save his Under-21 place and for the first time in his international career he found himself dropped because of form rather than injury. He was stunned and hurt. He felt that, rather than being punished for playing against the Germans with an injury, he should have received some credit for wanting to play. The same old worries crept into his mind: somebody would pull on his England shirt and turn on a virtuoso performance. But that was not to be: England got a drab 1–1 draw at Bramall Lane, before a miserable crowd of only 5,800, and a midfield of Keown, Clough and Rocastle (all of whom were to earn full England caps) was very disappointing. Dave Sexton was the first international manager to discover that a side without an available Gascoigne was no side at all, and if he didn't realize that, then the fans were likely to object with their feet.

Newcastle continued their steady recovery with a 1–1 draw on 17 October against Everton. Mirandinha scored again but was still regarded, not just by Paul but by the rest of the team, to be less than a team player. When he got the ball – and with Paul servicing him that was an awful lot of times – he far too frequently ran at goal, oblivious to what was going on around him. Paul and he nearly came to blows in dressing-room post-mortems, but the little Brazilian just nodded as if he understood and then continued in exactly the same way.

Off the field Mirandinha was delightful, although always seemingly short of money, always borrowing. On one occasion he invited the whole team round to partake of some Brazilian culinary delights. The brave ones, including Gazza, accepted but as they approached the house a most terrible smell was drifting out of the windows. They were greeted by Mira, stirring a giant metal dustbin, the epicentre of the smell. Mira heaped generous spoonfuls on to Gazza's plate. Paul, who would normally eat anything, looked around in desperation. There was the springer spaniel he'd bought for the Brazilian's sons and named 'Gazza' by the boys. He coaxed the dog outside, emptied his plate into its bowl and then watched with dismay as the dog turned up its nose and walked away, leaving the food clearly in view for anyone to see. As they left the house Paul put his arm around Mira's shoulders. 'Don't give up the day job,' he said.

In Newcastle's next match Paul tried to send a message to Dave Sexton in the best way he could, not just by making a goal for Paul Goddard, but scoring himself in a 3–1 victory against Coventry, to push United up to twelfth place, their highest position so far that season. Although they rounded off the month by losing unluckily 0–1 at home to Arsenal, Paul's contribution was recognized by the award of the Barclay Young Eagle of the Month.

A heavy 4–0 defeat at Luton did not stop Paul's recall to the Under-21 side for the match against Yugoslavia at

Zemun on 10 November. As he has done so often since, Paul rose to the occasion to prove a point, scored twice, and generally ran amok in a 5–1 victory against strong opposition. Finally he ran out of steam and was substituted by Martin Allen of QPR. Gazza was back and the message was clear, 'I don't like being dropped.'

He returned to England to face Derby County. He has always hated playing against any team managed by Arthur Cox. It's not so much the players or the style of play but the sound of his voice booming across the pitch that still sends a shiver of fear down his spine. Yet whatever the outcome the two of them were always to be seen in close, almost secretive conversation after any match – a father and son relationship that neither time nor distance had ever threatened. Wherever Paul plays, Cox phones him or those around him to ask about his progress and his happiness. To Cox, Paul will always be one of his 'babies', perhaps the most troublesome, without doubt the most talented, but the link is still there. Paul was heartbroken when he heard the news of Arthur's premature retirement in the autumn of 1993 through persistent back problems and was delighted when Arthur was invited to rejoin Newcastle in May 1994. On this occasion honours were even, a 0–0 draw.

Against QPR he received his marching orders after a rash tackle and made the headlines for all the wrong reasons. The newspapers began to hype him up as, one by one, he was linked with other major clubs, and at the end of November, with Newcastle slipping down the table, Stein and Lazarus were invited to Irving Scholar's office in Maddox Street, in London's West End. The parties had first met at the time of the Waddle transfer and had become friendly. Scholar had started to instruct Stein's firm on a few matters and he and Lazarus were regularly invited to be the chairman's guests in Tottenham's directors' box. Lazarus was a long-time Arsenal supporter but still admired Scholar, who had achieved every fan's dream – he had bought the club he supported. It had been at the time of Waddle's transfer that Stein had first mentioned Gascoigne to him as a potential bargain who would then have cost under £100,000.

However, once Stan Seymour had mentioned his name as one for the future, Paul was a target for Scholar. He seemed to have reached some sort of understanding with Seymour: the player wasn't for sale, but if the situation ever changed then Tottenham would have first option. There was never anything in writing but the two men had both been in football a long time, were scrupulously honest, and it never occurred to either to break that agreement.

'Let's be perfectly honest about it,' Scholar said (one of his favourite expressions), 'Gascoigne's not on good money at Newcastle. He won't win anything there. What will it take to get him down here?'

Paul's advisers carefully explained that it was unlikely Newcastle would sell him just like that, and particularly to Spurs, given the supporters' reaction to the Waddle transfer.

'Don't worry about that. I know Stan Seymour well. What does Paul actually want in life?'

Stein and Lazarus explained that Paul was desperate to get enough money together to buy his parents a house. They were living in council accommodation and he was still at home, and in his mind was the desire to reward them for all the sacrifices they'd made for him. Scholar had never met Paul at the time, but the fact that his family were uppermost in his mind rather than his own financial situation impressed him greatly. As Scholar himself says, 'Some players are Tottenham players, others are not, however skilful they might be.'

It was largely in theoretical terms that the three men spoke of Gascoigne joining Tottenham. It was possible that Newcastle would come through with a serious offer, possible they would have an FA Cup run, possible that Liverpool would come in for him. Paul himself had always said that if he ever left Newcastle it would be to go to Liverpool, a team that had not only got into the habit of winning but believed in its divine right to win. Any of these events could have stopped him joining Tottenham – and, of course, Newcastle could just have flatly refused to sell him until the end of his contract. Scholar would have none of these negative thoughts, and brushed them aside as if Paul was already on the train heading down to London. By the end of the meeting he had also almost persuaded Stein and Lazarus that there was an inevitability about Paul joining Tottenham Hotspur.

They reported back to both Garvie and Paul. Garvie was the more excited of the two; Paul still did not want to go south. At the time he had an inherent suspicion, even dislike, of anything or anybody born south of Gateshead. But of course Waddle was at Tottenham, Waddle his friend and mentor. He was at least beginning to think of the prospect.

'Let's wait and see if Liverpool come in for me,' he finally said.

Dalglish was interested but had a problem – he simply didn't have the money. When Stein spoke to him his plan was simple. 'Let the lad stay on for another year. I'll buy him then.'

The principle was fine if one had been talking about a mature experienced player who would wait and play out his time patiently, in the knowledge that what he really wanted was just twelve months away. But Paul was young and impatient for success, and if he couldn't find it with Newcastle, then he felt he couldn't wait. Dalglish was persistent, speaking to Stein regularly.

Meanwhile Newcastle had already lost their way on the road to glory in one cup competition. Wimbledon

seemed to be their bogey team and had seen them off
2–1 on 28 October in the third round of the Littlewoods
Cup, and again Paul had a quiet, disappointing match.
So as they headed into December, mid-table and out
of the Littlewoods Cup, the FA Cup represented their
only real hope of a trophy that season. As United were
drawn out of the hat at home to Crystal Palace in
the Third Round it was the match upon which all
eyes turned. Mirandinha kept scoring, he got a great
goal against West Ham, but Newcastle still lost 2–1.
Paul still felt it difficult to play alongside him and his
frustrations caused him to give away a free kick by
a more than robust tackle on the 41-year-old veteran
West Ham defender, Billy Bonds. Bonds looked at him
in astonishment. He had a reputation for being a hard
man and kids like Gazza did not usually take him
on.

'Are you all right, Billy?' Gazza asked cheekily.

'It's my ankle,' replied Bonds.

'Oh, that's OK then. I thought it might be arthritis.'

Brave, but also foolish because Bonds recovered to
mark Paul out of the game. There was never any
substitute for experience.

Probably Newcastle's best performance of the season
was on Boxing Day in front of their biggest league home
gate against Manchester United, a team who were flying
high and waiting to pounce on the title from a handy
fourth place. But in the first half Roeder scored what
proved to be the only goal of the game, and Paul
did enough to impress Alex Ferguson and the watching Manchester United directors. Maurice Watkins,
another solicitor and a member of the Manchester
board, remembered that Stein had told him about the
lad a year or two before. Ron Atkinson had been in
charge then and had taken the tip no further. Ferguson,
however, was a different kettle of fish. He too had
decided to target the young Geordie, and early in

the New Year Watkins telephoned Stein and enquired about Gazza's current position.

Paul was again nonplussed. 'What about Liverpool?' he kept asking.

His advisers explained the problem to him and at that stage he seemed almost prepared to accept Dalglish's advice and tough it out at St James's Park. Stein and Lazarus had come to know Paul well and felt such a course of action would lead to problems. He was a primed hand grenade on the pitch and potentially explosive off it. If he came under pressure during a year of contractual contrition, they felt there was every chance he would crack. If Liverpool wanted Paul as badly as he wanted them, then they would have to find the money.

On 28 December 1987 Newcastle crashed to earth against that very Liverpool side for which Paul yearned to play, Liverpool consolidating their lead at the top of the First Division. Paul was convinced that both Liverpool and Dalglish were winners whilst, try as he might to lift them, he was contracted to a club which was at the time destined to lose.

New Year's Eve 1987 was spent with the team in Nottingham. As the old year was chimed out Paul felt a surge of excitement: 1988 – he'd be 21 years old and he was sure this was going to be a year of destiny for him. In that positive frame of mind he turned on one of his best performances of the season in a 2–0 defeat of Forest at the City Ground, scoring one goal and making the other, inevitably for Mirandinha.

As 9 January and the third round of the FA Cup approached, the town began to buzz and the excitement spilled over on to the players. There was enormous pressure on them to bring back a trophy which had last graced the Newcastle boardroom over thirty years before. No team relished an away day out at St James's Park, but despite their Second Division status Palace were unlikely to be push-overs. They were lying second in the table at the time and looking favourites for promotion, although they later tailed off and came sixth. Their rising star was a certain Ian Wright, destined to play alongside Paul for England. Gazza scored the only goal of a tight match and United were through to the Fourth Round and another home fixture, this time against Swindon Town, a match that was to be memorable for more than one reason.

Newcastle's next home fixture was even more important as far as Paul's future was concerned. Tottenham were the visitors, a Tottenham side which was to be eliminated from the FA Cup by Third Division Port Vale, a bitter disappointment for the previous season's losing finalists, and a result that was to bring more pressure on Terry Venables for a big name signing. Scholar needed no convincing that Gazza was his man, but Venables had never seen him play before. As Scholar says in his own book, *Behind Closed Doors*:

> At one moment in the first half Gascoigne collected the ball just on the arc of the centre circle in his own half and strode forward. Terry Fenwick went in very forcibly to try and dispossess him, but Gascoigne with just a shrug of his shoulders shook him off and Fenwick literally bounced off him . . . Terry and I looked round at each other. We didn't need to say anything, our eyes did the talking. Terry was astonished at the sheer power and strength of a player who was still only twenty and I am convinced that at that moment Terry decided that Gascoigne was the signing we both felt the club badly needed.

Gascoigne ignored all the pressure of playing against a club he knew wanted to sign him, and scored a goal in each half to ensure a 2–0 victory. Chris Waddle, who returned to his native North-East to play against him that day, describes his mood: 'He was supremely confident, almost arrogant. Yet he was totally in control, there were no crazy tackles, no running around and following the ball. He ran the midfield with a maturity way beyond his years and anybody watching would have wanted him in their side.'

In the month of January 1988, Gazza's 'mensis mirabilis', Paul still continued to sparkle and astonish despite bitterly cold weather. Even before the cup-tie against Swindon Paul was awarded the Barclay Young Eagle of the Month. He could have been forgiven for resting on his laurels, but instead, backed by a vociferous Geordie choir, he orchestrated a 5-0 defeat of Swindon Town. Some time later the game was the centre of a scandal that, together with tax infringements, led to the team's demotion. However, there could be no detraction from Paul's performance which would have bemused any team.

Peter Kirkley remembers that game in particular: 'He started out on the left, then switched the ball to the right and brought it back to the left again for his goal. He'd have had a hat trick if he hadn't put one over the bar. It was an all-round performance, the first time he'd had ninety minutes where the whole attention was on Paul.'

Bobby Robson had watched the match and was later to describe Paul as a 'little gem', quickly defusing press suggestions that for Paul to win a full cap he would have to leave Newcastle. As it was he did leave United uncapped, but who could seriously believe that he would not have been selected for England if he'd stayed there.

January was a month that Paul wished never to end, a month that saw Newcastle edge into the top half of the table for the first time, a month in which the name 'Gazza' edged its way into the public consciousness.

By February it was etched there, but for all the wrong reasons.

There seemed to be no way Newcastle could avoid Wimbledon. They'd lost to them in the League and the Littlewoods Cup, now they were drawn against them in the fifth round of the FA Cup and also had to play them again in the League on 6 February. Vinny Jones had begun his career at Wealdstone, had honed his talents in the Southern League whilst still earning his living as a bricklayer, and had then entered league football with, perhaps, the only possible club at that stage – Wimbledon. At 23 he belonged to a bygone era of short back and sides, knife-like partings, metal-toed boots and laced-up footballs. Although the future, with the likes of Leeds and Chelsea, was to prove he could play a bit, he was making no admissions as to his footballing talents back in 1988. He was a destroyer of men, a destroyer of reputations, and proud of it. He'd only secured his place in the Wimbledon side against Manchester United in November, but since then the Dons had lost only two of their ten matches and had risen to sixth place in the First Division. In a way the press built up the confrontation. It was a gunfight by invitation between the kid and the town villain. They already had their kid and Jones was manna from heaven.

It all began in the tunnel. Jones turned to Paul and kicked him. 'I'm Vinny Jones. I'm a gypsy. I earn a hundred quid a week and I'm going to bite off your ear and spit in the hole. It's just you and me today, fat boy, just you and me.'

Paul looked at him in dismay. He was built like a navvy and swore like a stoker. Even Colin Suggett who had rarely treated Paul with kid gloves had never spoken to Paul like that. In the first few moments Paul got the ball, balanced himself for a run, and found himself flat on the floor. Along had come Jones. All afternoon he came along, so close to him at times that he could feel his breath, hot like a dragon. 'I don't mind being tackled, but this was pure aggression, pure physical threat. At one point I felt his spit on my face and a voice in my ear saying, "I'm just going to take this corner, fat boy, but I'll be back—"'

The photo of the two of them, with Jones backing into Paul and squeezing his private parts, has passed into Football's Hall of Fame whilst making both of them a few pounds. Afterwards Paul was able to smile about it, and indeed to send Jones a red rose from a bunch he'd been given by a fan before the game. In return, sentimental soul that he was, Vinny Jones sent him a toilet brush. Eventually the two formed an unlikely friendship, sharing a particular mutual interest in shooting – guns rather than footballs.

Paul left to join up with the England Under-21 side for the match against Scotland, although a few writers had called for his inclusion in the full England party who were playing a friendly in Israel the same week. The seniors drew 0–0, whilst the youngsters won through a single Gary Porter goal. Players always talk about money and the relative merits of their agents, and as Paul met up with players from other big clubs he felt like a poor relation.

On 20 February it was Wimbledon again. Two defeats and a draw – surely Newcastle were due for a win and as this was the road to Wembley they would cheerfully have conceded the other matches to the Dons in return for a ticket to the next round. Many people, both in and outside the North-East, were tipping Newcastle to go all the way, and as long as they were in with a chance of a trophy there was no possibility of Paul leaving. It wasn't to be. Jones did another tough, but fair, marking job on Gazza and Newcastle had no answer to Wimbledon's long-ball technique, an aerial barrage aimed at the battering ram that was the controversial head of John Fashanu. Fashanu scored one of the Dons' three goals and all Newcastle could manage in reply was a Neil McDonald effort. So it was Wimbledon who would progress towards the twin towers, and indeed went all the way, finally as underdogs bringing off one of the surprises of post-war Cup history with a well-deserved 1–0 win over Kenny Dalglish's mighty Liverpool. It would be the workmanlike Jones who would climb the steps to the royal box to receive his medal, not the artistic Gascoigne. If ever there was a final nail knocked in the coffin of Gazza's Tyneside ambitions, it was that defeat in the Cup. Now it seemed there was nothing for which to stay.

Paul felt he had to do something and spoke to his advisers about his future. Newcastle were still keen to sit down with him to develop the new contract and indicated they could improve considerably on their first offer, which raised the question as to why they had put such a disappointing deal to him in the first place. Garvie spoke to Sheffield Wednesday, Stein to Scholar, but Paul still wanted to go to Liverpool. Dalglish was adamant that he wanted him, but equally firm that he could do nothing until the following season – clearly he had to sell to buy. Newcastle refused permission for Paul to talk to anybody directly. They might have been out of the cup competitions and out of the title race, but they did not regard themselves as out of the battle for Gascoigne.

The supporters, meanwhile, were not happy. Nearly 29,000 had turned up for the cup-tie, whereas the following week only 17,000 saw them beat Chelsea 3–1, with Paul scoring one and helping Mirandinha to the other two. If Gascoigne was to be lost to them, it was likely there would be public protests of dramatic proportions.

He was saddened and puzzled by Newcastle's attitude. 'If they want to keep me, why don't they give me what I want?' It was, indeed, hard to understand. At the end of the day Spurs were to give him what he'd sought from Newcastle and more. Both were First Division clubs who could count upon huge support if they were even mildly successful, but one was ambitious, the other at the time was not. It was not difficult to predict Newcastle's decline and relegation, and to shudder as to what might have happened if Sir John Hall and Kevin Keegan had not forged their successful partnership.

It was with a troubled mind that Paul went to Nottingham to play the return fixture with Scotland's Under-21s. Problems and uncertainty followed him on to the pitch and he found himself substituted yet again. Throughout his life Paul has found it hard to deal with problems or unpleasant decisions. He has often found a way to get others to decide for him, and then to implement the decision while he remains in the background, but this was one decision he had to make for himself, and there was no doubt it was playing on his mind.

The following year at Tottenham he was simply not performing in training. His concentration was miles away and it showed. Venables spotted this at once, took him aside and asked what the problem was. Paul said it was his bath, which had been wrongly installed. Venables rang Stein, who promptly sorted out the problem with the plumber. But if something as inconsequential as the mispositioning of Paul's bath could blow his mind, heaven only knew what turmoil was going on in there over his footballing future. He wanted it sorted out for him, and fast. For the sake of expedition he was even prepared to give up his immediate ambition to play for Liverpool.

On 4 April the pressure finally got to Paul. In a 2–1 defeat at Derby he was sent off for the second time in the season. He stormed off, kicking over the physio's bucket of water in his rage, and soaking a female member of Derby's office staff, and then proceeded to take out his temper on the dressing-room door. Arthur Cox was less than pleased with his behaviour. Although Paul was no longer his responsibility, what went on at Derby County's Baseball Ground *was* down to him. He also felt that Paul's attitude reflected badly on his training and he told him so in no uncertain terms. He was made to apologize to the woman and pay for the damage. He returned to Newcastle in a very subdued frame of mind. A few days later he wrote to Arthur Cox, '. . . I want to win things and . . . I want to become the best player in the country and I promise I won't let *you* down . . .'

Paul had not scored in the League since February. Mirandinha had suffered a persistent injury, and the partnership which had started the season with so much promise had disintegrated. In mid-March Paul's advisers, without the player on this occasion, had met again with Newcastle's representatives on the neutral ground of The Post House at Derby. Russell Cushing, Gordon McKeag and Willie McFaul attended and put forward formally a much-improved package compared to that tendered at Durham.

One of the key issues as far as Paul himself was concerned was the pressure that was falling on his young shoulders as the perceived star of the team. To ease that burden Paul was concerned about who else Newcastle might intend to sign to signal their ambitions. McKeag's response was not encouraging. 'We're after John Robertson of Hearts. We see him as linking up with Paul.' Paul himself was less than impressed.

It was McFaul who broke first. Shortly after the meeting he rang Stein to ask whether or not Paul had made a decision. 'Somebody's got at him,' he said bitterly. 'I know that for sure.'

Suddenly Manchester United became more positive. Maurice Watkins phoned Stein again and told him that Alex Ferguson was at last interested in pursuing Gascoigne. Would he and Len Lazarus come up to

Old Trafford for a meeting? It was not an easy situation. Scholar's understanding with Seymour meant that Tottenham effectively had first option as and when Newcastle gave the green light to direct talks with the player. Paul himself did not fancy a move to London. Could United, with its glorious past and hopeful future, tempt him away from his obsession with Liverpool, and if they could, would Newcastle be prepared to sell him to another northern club? Would Scholar and Tottenham see that as a double betrayal, by both Newcastle and Paul? Newcastle clearly felt there would be less of an uproar from supporters if Paul went south rather than north. But Stein and Lazarus felt they would be failing in their professional duty if they did not listen to what Manchester United had to say. So they flew up, to be given the full public relations treatment by United.

However, it seemed the club had a wage structure they were not prepared to break for Gascoigne or anybody else. Paul's advisers had gone to the meeting convinced that Ferguson saw Paul as the natural successor to Bryan Robson, but to their surprise Ferguson told them that to get Paul he was prepared to agree an exchange deal with Newcastle involving any player *except* the then England captain. He saw Paul and Bryan forming a partnership in midfield, with Robson as Gazza's mentor.

Martin Edwards, Maurice Watkins and Ferguson took them through into the impressive boardroom. There was no denying the tradition of the club, nor its ambition, yet something just did not feel right for their client, even before they got down to discussing terms. The lawyer and the accountant explained what they had sought from Newcastle, and Edwards shook his head. 'We've got full England internationals here on less than that.'

There was no doubting that Ferguson really wanted Paul and clearly saw him as the last part in the jigsaw of the all-conquering club he was trying to create. As Stein and Lazarus were taken on a tour of the stadium and its facilities, they could not help but be impressed by the miracle that was Old Trafford – the superb catering facilities, the private boxes, the trophy room with its gleaming silver, the perfect playing surface, and everywhere the ghosts of the greats of the past – of Tommy Taylor, who they had both seen as schoolboys scoring a hat trick at Highbury a few days before he was to perish at Munich, and Duncan Edwards, with whose precocious talent Paul's had so often been compared.

Martin Edwards suggested that the yawning gulf between them on personal terms was not important, that if Paul came he would be part of a winning team, that the bonuses he'd receive would more than compensate for any shortfall in the guaranteed salary and the other commercial advantages they sought. History was to prove him right.

Stein and Lazarus were then asked to wait in an ante-room while the proposals were discussed. When the discussions resumed there was a marked improvement on the original offer, but it was still some way short of the figures put forward on behalf of Paul. It was agreed that the two Londoners would talk to Paul and would then put forward some compromise proposals in writing. If some accommodation could be reached on the salary structure, then Ferguson wanted to meet Paul personally. He was convinced that in face-to-face discussions he could sell his club more effectively than any bland figures on paper, however high they might be.

When Paul was told of Manchester United's interest he agreed to meet Ferguson informally. He was, however, still concerned as to the reaction of the Tyneside fans if he joined Manchester, and his first question was, as ever, 'Have you heard anything from Liverpool yet?'

Arrangements were duly made for Paul to come down to London, the idea being that, as Manchester United had a friendly against, of all clubs, Spurs, Ferguson would come to Mel Stein's house on his way to the match and meet with Paul. The arrangements proved chaotic. Paul was travelling down to London with Garvie and had insisted on bringing Gail Pringle with him. Neil McDonald was also unhappy at Newcastle and had similarly decided to take the chance to come and have a chat with Stein and Lazarus about his future. He brought his wife Lynn with him, which meant there was no possibility of everyone travelling in Garvie's modest car, and nobody was volunteering to be driven by Gazza. Consequently Neil Ramsay, a trusted insurance broker who was later to become an agent himself, was roped in to bring half the Newcastle contingent.

Ferguson duly arrived on time, but there was nobody to greet him except Stein's wife, Marilyn, who was totally confused as to who was who. Stein had been called away from work to collect his elder son Nicky from Putney after an exhausting charity walk. Lazarus was also stuck in traffic driving from his office. It began to assume the proportions of a classic French farce. Marilyn made Ferguson cup after cup of tea, as he anxiously looked at his watch and she desperately tried to keep up her end of the conversation with a very limited knowledge of football. Finally Stein arrived but there was still no sign of Paul, by now also delayed in traffic. Ferguson began to relax, and showed a human side to his character that does not always come across in public. He gave Nicky a donation to his school's charity, and Stein, who had strong misgivings as to how Paul would react to the dour Scotsman, began to think that perhaps, after all, it might work.

Eventually everybody arrived and split up into separate meetings in different rooms. Ferguson and Paul went up to Stein's tiny office, Stein and Lazarus sat with Neil McDonald and Neil Ramsay, Gail Pringle and Lynn McDonald were left on their own, and Marilyn Stein tried to get on with the business of making supper for two hungry schoolboys while continuing the tea service to the three meetings.

In the office, Paul sat on one side of a desk, Ferguson on the other, the Scotsman leaning forward, his face just a few inches from Paul's. He did most of the talking, explaining just how he saw Paul slotting in to the Manchester United set-up. Paul merely listened. He felt tired and confused; it had been a long drive down and all he really wanted was a meal and a drink. It was unfortunate for Ferguson that, although he'd got his meeting with his man, it was the wrong time and the wrong place. As he was leaving Stein asked him how it had gone. 'It went well, I thought. He's a nice lad. He'll do fine with us.'

With hindsight it was clear that Ferguson went away thinking he had got his man, which might well explain why he was so upset when Paul finally signed for Spurs. However, to be fair nobody on Paul's side made any promises, and no further progress was made to bridge the gap on the financial proposals until it was too late.

That meeting was the first time the sort of money that was being sought on his behalf for his services actually sank into Paul's mind. At the original meeting in Durham he'd not really taken it all in, and he'd not been present at the Derby hotel for round two of the negotiations, nor indeed at any of the discussions with Scholar. Now Paul listened and asked if Lazarus could write it down for him. The accountant duly obliged and Paul read and reread the figures. Then he smiled, 'Right, let's go and eat.'

They went as a group to La Fondue, a smart local restaurant. Paul asked what was good and was told to try the fondue speciality. The waiter duly brought the fondue flames and prongs followed by the uncooked meat. Gazza looked at it with horror.

'It's raw,' he said.

'It's meant to be,' somebody gently explained to him.

'What's the fire for?' he asked.

'To cook it,' was the reply.

'Blimey, I thought that was what you paid the restaurant for.'

8

'VENABLES MAY BECOME THE ENGLAND MANAGER ONE DAY.'

By May 1988 even Newcastle were coming to terms with the fact that Paul would soon be on the move. By their own standards it had not been a bad season: a mini Cup run, three consecutive wins at the end of the season pushing them up to eighth place, and even a brief moment of unexpected glory at Wembley in the Mercantile Credit Centenary Tournament over the weekend of 16–17 April. It was almost a quiz question: who beat Liverpool and lost to Tranmere on the same day? The answer was Newcastle United, but at least Paul had enjoyed the brief experience of winning a match at Wembley. 'It was the first time I'd played there and even in a minor competition I could feel it had a special atmosphere. I just couldn't wait to get back.'

If he was to return then it would not be with Newcastle. On 7 May Paul pulled on the number eight for United for the last time in a competitive match. Although he'd neither signed nor committed himself to anybody else, he knew in his heart of hearts that this was goodbye to the St James's Park faithful, all 23,731 of them. When West Ham took the lead and kept it at half-time, it looked as if the farewell was to be muted; but that would not have been typical Gascoigne. O'Neill equalized and then Paul got the winner, his eleventh goal in all competitions for the season but the one he savoured the most. For the crowd it was as if he'd scored the goal that had won the Championship. At the end of the match he ran first to the Gallowgate end and applauded the fans, appreciating the applause they'd given him so generously over the years. He went from side to side, with even the West Ham supporters sensing the emotion of the moment and clapping him. By the time he got back to the dressing-room he had tears in his eyes, but there were more to be shed before the transfer would finally go through. No transfer involving Paul was ever to be easy. 'I had to get away. It was as if I'd been baby-sat at Newcastle. I wanted to win things and at the time it felt as if I'd have a better chance elsewhere.'

Scholar had kept his cards close to his chest and had disclosed nothing of his discussions with Stein and Lazarus. When he finally got a reluctant Gordon McKeag to quote a figure, he was told that Newcastle wouldn't contemplate a sale at less than £2.5 million, plus a share of any future transfer dealings. It was astonishing. There had never been a deal between British clubs in excess of £2 million, and here Newcastle were seeking far more than that for a player who had not yet won a full England cap, and who would not be 21 until 27 May.

Paul took the easy way out, removing himself from the firing line by going away on holiday. He didn't enjoy his vacation. Normally he would have been able to dismiss all footballing problems from his mind, but this time he was concerned about his future. He'd thought long and hard about the Manchester United situation and had finally decided that if Liverpool did not come through he would join the Lancashire club in preference to Spurs, simply because he wanted to stay within easy travelling distance of the North-East. And so throughout his break he was short-tempered, finally deciding to return home early. Hanging around beaches in the sun, actually doing nothing, relaxing as other people might see it, simply did not come easily to him. What he wanted to do was get back to England and start kicking a football again for whoever might be signing him.

A meeting was arranged between Stein and McKeag and Cushing the morning after Paul last pulled on a Newcastle shirt, in an end-of-season friendly with Whitley Bay. It took place in a darkened boardroom, as dusty as Newcastle's own trophy cabinet. Stein knew that Paul was still contracted to play for the team whenever requested, but Paul was determined not to go on a Far Eastern tour with the club. As a lawyer Stein felt uneasy about entering a meeting with only pragmatism on his side, but there was no beating about the bush. He told them Paul was not only not going on tour, but was not prepared to accept their offer of a new contract. McKeag pointed out he was still under contract and they could keep him for another year, but as he spoke he must have realized the words were hollow. Stein left the meeting feeling uncomfortable. As a fan he'd felt bad when he'd been involved in the negotiations which led to Chris Waddle leaving, but with Gazza it was somehow worse.

As it was, before Paul had made his final decision John Hall (later Sir John) phoned Stein. 'I'm close to doing something up here. If I get control will Paul stay?'

It was tempting. Hall was a man with admirable qualities and first-class credentials, a man who almost always succeeded in what he set out to do. Against all the odds he'd turned wasteland into the hugely successful Metro Centre shopping mall, and at the same time turned himself, a miner's son, into a millionaire. Paul agreed to see him and was enormously impressed. Afterwards he phoned Stein to tell him, 'What a man! If he'd been running the club there's no way I'd have wanted to leave.' But Hall wasn't running the club, and far from being 'close to doing something', it would take a lot more boardroom bloodshed and another four years before his power struggle would be resolved.

Paul left again for Toulon with England for the European Under-21 tournament with his future still in the balance. On 28 May he had started and scored in a 1–1 draw with Switzerland in a friendly, but Toulon was much more meaningful. Their first game was against Mexico, and an England side containing Paul, Nigel Clough, David Rocastle, Nigel Martyn and Michael Thomas (all to win full caps) won 2–1, with both goals coming from Clough. No substitutions were made and Paul felt he'd done more than enough to retain his place. He was devastated when he found himself on the bench against the USSR two days later, although he did come on for Samways after Vinny had scored the only goal of the match. The semi-final was against Morocco and, with Samways' injury persisting, Paul was in the starting line-up. As he'd done so often in the past and was to do so often in the future, he pulled out all the stops, turning in a superb all-round performance which he topped with a typical Gazza goal. England won 1–0 and were through to the final against France, for which Paul kept his place. But the French had not forgotten a magnificent effort by Paul against them in April at Highbury, including a stunning goal, and set out to man-mark him out of the game. The tactic rebounded on them because Michael Thomas, given far more space than usual, scored twice, and after ninety minutes it was 2–2. However, in extra time the English team tired and the French scored twice to take the trophy.

It was with some regret that Paul turned his back on France and football to return to England and transfer speculation. Something had to happen, and had to happen soon so that he could achieve some peace of mind. Tottenham's persistence had finally paid off. McKeag offered a hard bargain – £2 million and 10 per cent of any future profit. If that was agreed then Tottenham could talk to Gascoigne officially and directly. When Paul heard the price tag that had been put on his head he blew his top. Newcastle had signed him for nothing, paid him next to nothing, and now sought not only to make a massive fortune out of him but to keep a stake in him for the future. 'I'm not going unless I get something out of the transfer fee from the club,' he told Stein.

It wasn't a question of greed but of principle. Nobody who has ever met Paul in any depth would accuse him of greed, nor of being motivated by money. Many have said that left to his own devices he would play for nothing. McKeag was immovable: Newcastle wanted to see £2 million net out of the transaction; Paul would have to do his own deal with Tottenham. The moral issue did not sway him. Newcastle were unwilling sellers, he claimed, and if Paul wanted to stay their offer was still on the table.

Things began to come to a head. Alex Ferguson had gone on holiday, as indeed had Kenny Dalglish, but both had left their hotel telephone numbers with Stein. Paul gave him strict instructions: 'Tell Kenny that if he makes an offer for me now and we can agree terms, I'll sign for him.'

This was bound to cause problems because Newcastle had only consented to Paul speaking to Spurs, but if he turned down Tottenham and Liverpool offered the same money, McKeag was hardly likely to say no. Dalglish was regretful, but firm. 'Tell the lad, I really want him, but it has to be another year.'

Stein explained that was just not on and the reason why, and the two men parted on amicable terms. Ferguson was more difficult. In his absence Stein had been talking to Maurice Watkins, but United and Paul were still some way apart on financial terms. It was beginning to look as if Spurs were the only really viable alternative to staying at Newcastle, but Paul was still not keen on moving to London and had not even wanted to talk to Venables. However, Stein and Lazarus persuaded Paul at least to meet with him. 'Look, Paul, you're a long time dead in football. Venables may become the England manager one day. Do you want to be remembered as the kid who refused to talk to him?' It was a prophetic comment.

It was around the time of Paul's twenty-first birthday that the meeting had been set up, at Stein's office in the heart of Mayfair. Stein and Lazarus had bought him a giant 'Teddy Ruxpin', a toy bear with a cassette in its back which enabled it actually to conduct a limited conversation. Paul was very taken with his new toy, and when Venables arrived at the office he found him more concerned with the bear than any footballing matters. Venables couldn't believe that Gazza was for real.

Yet Paul had made him laugh, and had recognized something in the Cockney that he'd not seen in Ferguson, and had certainly not been there in any other manager for whom he'd played, a willingness to give him a long leash. The two of them got on incredibly well, and when Venables explained his football philosophy Paul understood exactly what he was saying. From that moment onwards Tottenham was a serious alternative to Liverpool and Manchester United.

On a sunny morning in early July, Paul visited the City of London School, where both Stein's and Lazarus's sons were pupils, to sign autographs and raise money for their charity fund. The school is situated overlooking the Thames, at the foot of a steep flight of stairs leading directly down from St Paul's Cathedral. It was a beautiful and dramatic setting for some of the final scenes in this particular transfer. Whilst Paul mingled with the schoolboys, his advisers took a portable phone and began their round of calls.

First of all Maurice Watkins. He told them United could not meet all of Paul's terms, but even more important Newcastle were still refusing to consider any offer from them. The men sitting by the river agreed to explain the situation to Paul, but they told Watkins they had doubts. Then Irving Scholar, the Tottenham chairman, who was as optimistic as ever. 'Terry's away,' he explained, 'but bring him down to White Hart Lane. We'll show him around without any commitment on either side.'

The groundwork had already been done. The previous Sunday Chris Waddle had been in the North-East. 'Terry had spoken to me before he went on holiday,' Chris recalls. 'We both agreed it would be great for Spurs if Gazza came down. He asked me to speak to him and tell him what it was like to be a Geordie at a London club. I rang him up in Newcastle and we met up at a pub. I'd told him to come at noon and he turned up incredibly enough with all his mates. At first he told me he was going to Man. United. I gave him the spiel about Spurs and within three pints of lager he told me he had to go to the Dunston Excelsior. His parting words were, "Right, tomorrow I'll sign for Spurs."'

Over lunch with his advisers he was told of Scholar's proposals, Dalglish's difficulties and United's financial offer. They'd tried to phone Ferguson at his hotel, but unfortunately (or perhaps symbolically) the battery had run down on the mobile phone. Paul agreed to go with them to White Hart Lane. They drove there in Stein's car, ignoring Gazza's pleas to be allowed to take the wheel, and arrived without any fanfares or publicity.

Scholar greeted Paul like the fan he was and Paul was taken aback. He was used to chairmen demanding respect, even reverence, but all Scholar wanted to do was to talk football and demonstrate his knowledge of the game. Eventually Alan Harris, the assistant manager, came to the rescue and showed Paul around the ground, whilst Scholar, Stein and Lazarus tried to put the finishing touches to the financial package. By the time Paul returned the three men were almost in agreement on money. It was now down to Paul. For his part, he had been impressed. White Hart Lane made St James's Park look like a Victorian workhouse.

Scholar left so that Stein and Lazarus could go through the proposals in detail, and within five minutes Paul had made up his mind to join Spurs. However, his obsession with Liverpool refused to disappear. Eventually it was agreed to suggest a clause whereby, if Liverpool made an offer for him equal to the cost of his acquisition by Spurs during his first season with them, then the London club would be obliged to sell him if he still wanted to go. Scholar was not happy with the condition, but felt sufficiently confident that Paul would become so committed to Spurs once he'd joined that he wouldn't want to leave. Consequently he agreed to its inclusion in the contract.

By the time Stein visited Paul at the West Lodge Park Hotel that evening, Gazza and some newly summoned Geordie friends, including Jimmy Gardner, were at dinner. They seemed to have worked their way through every delicacy on the menu, topped off by a bottle of champagne per head per course. Paul was a very happy boy. He was about to earn a salary beyond his wildest dreams, little knowing that the Lazio deal in a few years' time was to make the Tottenham contract seem as insignificant as the Newcastle one did then.

On the following day Julia Masterson, Scholar's personal assistant, telephoned Stein at his office. She was less than amused. 'You have to do something about Paul and his friends. I've had the manager of the hotel on the phone.'

The lawyer groaned and asked what they'd done.

'They were running up and down the corridors in the small hours of the morning letting off fire extinguishers, they kept the other guests up half the night, the fat one [Jimmy] was seen locked outside wearing only a sheet and was then sighted swimming across the duck pond without the sheet . . . ' – the litany of offences continued, but it was hard for the two of them to stop themselves laughing.

'I'll talk to them,' Stein said.

They were all suitably apologetic: it wouldn't happen again. As it was, the lads had to be kept otherwise amused while Paul had to be present at the continuing transfer arrangements. Manchester United had now come back and agreed to the final requests of Paul's advisers, but it was too late. Paul was simply not prepared to create a Dutch auction and now felt morally committed to Spurs. Stein explained the position to Maurice Watkins, who was nonplussed.

'But we're prepared to give him what you asked for.'

'Yes, but Spurs gave it first.'

Alex Ferguson, still on holiday, was furious even though Stein did his best to explain the position from his car on a very bad line. He'd really felt he'd got his man and could not understand how Paul could have chosen Tottenham in preference to his own side. Yet no promises had been given and somebody had to lose out. It was just that not many players said no to Manchester United.

Alastair Garvie, who was still involved as Paul's agent, came down to join his professional advisers. Paul by then was already growing disillusioned with the whole concept of an agent earning commission on his back. There was no doubt, although Garvie would see it otherwise, that by the time Paul signed for Spurs he was relying principally on advice from his solicitor and accountant rather than his agent. Tottenham had now reached a final agreement with Newcastle, and although Paul still felt bitter about the amount of money his former club were earning from his talents, he was sufficiently satisfied with his own package to proceed with Spurs. Unlike some other players who had left or were to leave Newcastle, Paul did not want to make his fight public and leave a bad taste in the mouths of the best supporters in the world.

The final signing session took place at Stein's offices. Half-way through, Paul suddenly asked about 'the Liverpool clause', referring to his right to join the Merseyside team if they wanted him. 'I've changed my mind. I'm happy just to sign for Spurs.' It was an enormous tribute to Scholar's personality and enthusiasm which had clearly got across to the player.

The *Sun* photographer duly arrived to take some pictures. Scholar and Paul together – a photo the Spurs chairman used on the front cover of his book – Paul (looking fat in his Brooks track-suit, with a Tottenham rosette purchased on the way pinned to him) posing on the steps outside with Stein, Scholar and Garvie, after which the photographer looked for a suitably smart car against which Paul could lean. A passing taxi driver, obviously a Spurs supporter, recognized him and gave him a thumbs-up.

The question on the lips of the media was how he would live up to the price tag that dangled around his neck like an albatross. His answer was simple. 'I didn't fix the price – but believe me, Spurs got a bargain.' His self-confidence in public, his ability to make a statement that without his charm would appear conceited, was astonishing for one so young.

It was to be his last night in the West Lodge Park. The revelry had continued unabated and Jimmy Gardner's bare posterior was too much for the most hardened hotelier. Tottenham were politely but firmly told that the future custom of P. Gascoigne Esq. & Associates was not welcome.

Stein and Scholar hauled the miscreants down to Scholar's office just before they were due to return to the North-East. They were lined up at the top of the stairs to receive their lecture. Heads bowed, still proudly wearing their new track-suits, they all humbly apologized and admitted to having had the time of their lives.

9

'HE WAS A BIG KID RUNNING RIOT.'

Paul Gascoigne joined up with his new Tottenham team-mates for pre-season training in July 1988 under enormous pressure to live up to the reputation that preceded him. A British record signing, only 21 years old and voted the PFA Young Player of the Year. Who could blame Spurs supporters if they were going to be disappointed that he did not walk on water?

After his brief flirtation with the West Lodge Park and an even briefer stay at the Hendon Hall Hotel, Paul found the Swallow Hotel, just off the M25 near Waltham Abbey, welcoming him with open arms. With its proximity to Chris Waddle's home in Broxbourne, good fishing, its swimming pool, leisure facilities and understanding staff, it became home from home for him, although he would still go across to the Waddles to eat on Friday nights. 'Almost every time he came,' Chris says, 'Lorna would make spaghetti bolognese. Maybe she knew something he didn't. Paul was very superstitious. He'd convinced himself that when he'd eaten Lorna's spaghetti bolognese he'd score the next day.'

Even after Paul acquired his own house in Dobbs Weir he continued to use the Swallow, sometimes moving out when family or friends filled his house, and staying at the hotel for weeks on end. As Chris Waddle puts it, 'He held court at the Swallow. He'd bring his karaoke machine in at night and entertain the other guests, and on one occasion even sat in on an interview for a new receptionist. I remember one particular night when Gazza, Paul Stewart and I went back to the Swallow and Gazza ordered champagne. He then got his karaoke machine out and started singing to Elvis, Elvis and more Elvis. I'd had enough and put the ice bucket over his head. For Gazza that was the signal for battle to begin. He got an extinguisher, I ducked and Paul Stewart got soaked. He was never one not to retaliate and also armed himself with an extinguisher. The manager came running out to see what was left of his hotel. He just had time to yell out "Gazza" when his legs went from under him on the slippery wet floor and he literally took off before landing flat on his back. It was like a scene from a Carry On film.'

Yet Paul still missed Newcastle and took every opportunity to dash up the motorway to the North-East, to his familiar and comforting surroundings. Eventually Chris Waddle had to have a word with him. 'I told him not to keep running home. We'd be somewhere like Southampton away and he'd get Jimmy Gardner down to take him home. Then he'd have to get up at the crack of dawn to get back for training. They'd sleep in the car, but I lost count of the number of times he'd be fined for being late for training. He wanted to feel free, but he also wanted to see Gail, his mates and his family on weekends. For him London was a kind of holiday place.'

It did not take long for the problems to start. At the end of July there was an alleged incident of drunken and offensive behaviour at a London night-club. Paul was puzzled. He'd behaved no differently from a hundred such nights at the Dunston Excelsior and nobody had ever complained about him up there.

Everything was new to the starry-eyed youngster, and as he jetted off with Tottenham on their pre-season tour of Sweden he revelled in what he perceived as his new-found freedom and luxury. As he ran out on to the pitch for the first friendly in Sweden in Trelleborg, he made the mistake of patting the head of one of the pretty girls who lined the path from the tunnel. It was innocuous, a typical Gazza gesture. The girl obviously thought otherwise. By the time the Tottenham team had reached Jönköping on the next stage of the tour, there was already a passionate letter and pin-up photograph of the girl waiting for Paul. He thought it was just a laugh and showed the rest of the team the photo, which somewhat the worse for wear eventually disappeared out of the coach window, in very much the same way that Paul had dismissed the girl from his mind. Yet the situation began to take on the more sinister proportions of *Fatal Attraction* when a bunch of roses from the same girl was delivered to the room he shared with Chris Waddle.

Then came the phone calls. The first Paul took himself. It seemed churlish to refuse to talk to somebody who appeared to be a devoted fan, but when the girl said she had booked a room in the hotel and was intending to travel the 200 miles to be near him, Paul panicked. He asked Waddle to talk to her if she called again.

The girl did call again, this time claiming she was actually in the hotel and would be delighted if Paul would join her in her room for a drink. Waddle told her to get lost, but whether or not his accent was too broad Geordie for her to understand, she still persisted until Paul was reduced to a nervous wreck. Finally he told Venables what was going on. A check of the hotel register did not reveal her presence, and with the phone calls, flowers and letters all drying up Paul thought the incident was closed. Not a bit of it. A few weeks later a Sunday paper ran the story that the girl had spent a night of passion with Paul. For the first time, although not for the last, Paul had to instruct his solicitors to take the necessary action to protect his name.

Back in England and back to football. For the first time the Makita pre-season tournament was being played at Wembley and Paul was looking forward to his English début for Spurs against Arsenal in front of a big crowd. It was an enormous disappointment. Arsenal beat the much-vaunted Spurs side 4–0 and that was that. Instead of leaving Wembley with a medal Paul departed with the taunts and chants of the Arsenal supporters ringing in his ears: 'What a waste of money', interspersed with 'You fat Geordie bastard'.

Alastair Garvie also felt insecure. There were 400 miles between him and the player, and even when Paul came up to the North-East he did not make contact with him. Not that there was anything sinister in that. Months can go by without him phoning even his sister and brother-in-law, but then suddenly out of the blue they'll receive a call inviting them to Rome to stay as if he'd spoken to them only yesterday. It is all part of the Gazza character that if you're out of sight you're usually out of mind. Garvie did not see it that way and more and more found himself having to communicate via Paul's parents or Stein and Lazarus; and he liked neither route. Without consulting Paul he began to talk to other agents with a view to sharing his asset, and even received an offer from Dennis Roach at PRO to buy out his contract for the massively generous sum of £1,000. Needless to say the offer was rejected.

The 1988/9 season got off to a farcical false start when Tottenham's new stand failed a safety inspection, leading to the first match against Coventry being postponed. So on 3 September Paul made his league début for Spurs against the club which had bred, groomed and sold him, Newcastle United. He received a mixed reception at St James's Park. The true fans have always stayed loyal to Gazza, but there was an element who felt he had betrayed his roots, a feeling which persisted until he won over the hearts of the nation in June 1990. Going to take a corner at the Gallowgate end, Paul found himself pelted by sweets, including a particularly nasty knock from a frozen Mars Bar, his former trademark. Paul understood their feelings and tried to bring a little humour to the situation by pretending to take a bite from the chocolate. Yet although he understood he was still hurt, and almost relieved when the game finished in a 2–2 draw, with him being substituted.

There was no let-up on the footballing pressure. On 10 September Spurs were at home to Arsenal. In the build-up to the match wherever he went he was urged on by Spurs supporters, jeered by Arsenal fans for whom the memory of his disappointing Makita performance was uppermost. But then something happened to take his mind off the match. He was selected for the full England squad to play Denmark on 14 September.

The Arsenal game was not the perfect build-up, with tackles flying in from all directions. Played at 150 miles an hour, Arsenal went into a 3–1 lead with Waddle getting Spurs' goal. Then Allen passed the ball from the left into the Arsenal penalty area to Waddle, who stroked it to Gazza who'd just lost his boot after a tackle. Without hesitation, with his stockinged foot Paul put the ball into the net to score his first goal for his new club. It wasn't enough. Arsenal held on in the second half.

Paul went off to join up with his new England team-mates. Neither they nor Bobby Robson knew what they were letting themselves in for. New boys in the England squad are usually quiet, shy, retiring, knowing their place and not speaking out of turn. There was never any chance of Paul fitting into that mould. The Bobby Robson squad was visibly ageing, and after the disasters of the European Championships in Germany all the pressures were on him to introduce new talent.

Chris Waddle was secretly pleased to have Paul in the squad, but not so thrilled when he found out that he'd been assigned his young Geordie friend as a room-mate. 'Paul loved it with England, even the hardest of training sessions. He was a big kid running riot. I'd just not get any rest while he was around. He always had to be doing things even at two in the morning. He'd have the light on and the TV blasting out all night long until he'd finally fall asleep, leaving me to turn everything off.'

The announcement of the team itself for the match was disappointing to press, public and Paul alike. Only Rocastle of the named eleven, at 21, could be considered a fresh young face, and that despite the success of the Under-21 side in Toulon compared to the performance of the seniors in the European Championships. However, with only five minutes left Peter Beardsley was called off and replaced by Paul Gascoigne. One North-Eastern career appeared to be nearing its twilight whilst another was just dawning. Yet, as so often is the case in football, nothing is truly what it appears. Beardsley in inspirational form for Newcastle in 1993/4 aged 33 played his way back into the England team.

The Paul Gascoigne who made his England début seemed not to have a care in the world. Given his few moments of glory he dashed around wildly, tackling back everywhere, screaming for the ball to be given to him by his more experienced team-mates. It would have been nice to relate that he'd breathed new life into a dying match, but apart from breaking the record for the number of touches by a substitute in five minutes he did nothing that was memorable or remarkable. But he had arrived, he was an England international. There could be no going back now.

Four games into the 1988/9 season Spurs got their first win at home to Middlesbrough, and again Paul felt reasonably pleased with his performance. At long last it seemed to be taking shape, both for him and the team. However, Spurs were not to win another league match until mid-November. By then they'd slumped to twentieth in the table, the lowest they'd been since their relegation year. Another cup run, though, seemed to be gaining momentum, this time in the Littlewoods Cup. On 27 September they looked down and out in the first leg of their second-round match away to Notts County when Samways equalized after eighty minutes to make things look easier for Spurs in the home leg.

Before that match could take place, however, as a bit of light relief Paul turned up at Osidge Primary School in North London to conduct a training session with the children. He was an instant success, organizing a twenty-a-side match and then running rings around anybody who tried to tackle him. One 10-year-old slid in on a tackle and dispossessed him; Paul stopped in disbelief and then chased back to recover the ball as if it were a Cup Final. At whatever level he hates to be beaten. Jimmy Gardner came with him and he and Paul decided to take some pot shots at a series of ambitious goalkeepers. One of them was bespectacled and all of four feet tall. Gazza encouraged Gardner to have a go, and Jimmy let fly with his full, not insubstantial weight behind the ball. Unfortunately the diminutive keeper got his hands and body right behind the shot, took off as if he'd been hit by a cannon ball, and landed against the back stanchion of the goal, sliding down like a cartoon character. It was a different face to Gazza. The kids loved him, he loved them back, and as he patiently signed autograph after autograph on everything from scraps of toilet-paper to tennis balls, the teacher in charge said, 'He's just a big kid himself, isn't he?'

Two draws in the League, against Manchester United and Charlton, still left Spurs in deep trouble towards the foot of the table, and even in the second leg of the Littlewoods Cup Spurs had to battle against Third Division Notts County to win 2–1. Paul scored the vital second goal, the first of many cup goals in his years at Tottenham. However, the miserable run continued with three league defeats and a struggling home draw in the Littlewoods Cup against Second Division Blackburn Rovers, in which Paul was substituted.

Then – and most painful of all for Paul – came another league defeat, against Derby. Paul was clearly trying too hard, almost attempting to impress the opposition manager to the exclusion of everyone else. In fact, as Arthur Cox recalls the game, it was he who saved Paul from being sent off. 'He was clearly hyped up, going in for tackle after tackle, running about everywhere on the pitch. I yelled out, "Gazza, behave yourself." He obviously heard me because he was as good as gold after.' But this defeat was just about Paul's blackest hour at Tottenham – in the relegation zone, looking as if they couldn't beat anybody, destroyed by his old mentor.

Inevitably he turned to Chris Waddle for advice. 'If Spurs go down I'm out of here,' he said, having already spoken to Stein to see if there was a break clause in his contract in the event of relegation. Waddle calmed him down. He too had not experienced instant success when he'd come to Spurs, and it had taken him over a season to win round the fans. The supporters were not yet getting on Paul's back in the way he'd experienced at Newcastle, but there were still rumblings that Scholar might have paid too much for a player who had it all to prove at the highest level.

On 12 November it was Paul Gascoigne v. Vinny Jones, although the fixture list described the match as Tottenham against Wimbledon. Spurs won 3–2 although Paul was substituted when it seemed things might be getting out of hand. It was a turning point in his season, and as Vinny stayed behind with the rest of the 'Crazy Gang', Paul joined up with the England party for his first visit to the Middle East to play against Saudi Arabia on the 16th. Ironically, in 1994 it would be the Saudis catching the plane to the World Cup rather than the English.

This time Paul had plenty of Geordie company as the squad included Bryan Robson, Peter Beardsley and Chris Waddle. None of them could quite believe the luxury and opulence, with palaces and houses which could contain the whole humble streets in which they'd been raised. Everything seemed to be made of either marble, gold or both, while the people there were football crazy and, apart from their dress of traditional flowing robes, very westernized and very knowledgeable about the game. The national coach was also knowledgeable, too knowledgeable for Bobby Robson. The Saudis took the lead in the fifteenth minute and held it until half-time. Tony Adams did what a strike force of Lineker, Beardsley and Waddle could not achieve and equalized after 54 minutes, but that was as good as it got.

Paul replaced Chris for the last ten minutes, but it was too late in the day for him to make any impression, other than that he should have been brought on earlier. Back in England it was the nadir of Robson's fortunes as the cruel headlines greeted his homecoming: 'Desert Storm', 'For the Sake of Allah go now', or 'What a load of camels'. The underlying message was that if England were to have any chance of qualifying for the 1990 World Cup it should be under the guidance of somebody other than Robson and without the likes of Waddle and Beardsley. Paul was pleased to have been awarded another international cap, but sad that it had been Waddle he replaced. The two men had never been closer. If Chris Waddle's England career was coming to an end, the one person who did not want to benefit from that decline was Paul Gascoigne.

10

'YOU PLAY WHERE YOU'RE BLOODY WELL TOLD.'

Paul felt the media focus on him once again. 'I knew they were dying to label me a two million pound flop, but I wasn't going to give them the pleasure. If I showed what I could do week in week out, then England couldn't ignore me. I've always reckoned I'm a bit difficult to ignore anyway.'

As he began to feel more at home he began to form his own social circle, largely gathered from the young single players at the club such as Steve Sedgley, John Moncur, Paul Moran and Philip Gray. Paul Stewart was the exception. He'd found it harder than Paul to settle in London; his wife simply hated it and moved back to Blackpool, which pushed him more and more into the company of Gazza, not always a good thing.

As the two Pauls began to click on the pitch, Gazza was substituted in the victory over Sheffield Wednesday on 20 November. It was the start of an ankle injury that was to disrupt his season, but typically he did not complain immediately, in case he missed a match just when he felt it was coming right. In the mid-week match that followed Stewart scored again in a 1–1 draw with Coventry, but it was Gazza who started the move with a free kick. Spurs followed that up with virtuoso performances from the Geordie duo of Gazza and Waddle in the second half against QPR: 2–0 down at half-time, Paul then drove a free kick past David Seaman, who not for the last time when facing Gascoigne simply stood and watched. Then Waddle seized on an Ossie Ardiles mistake to get the equalizer, leaving Rangers happy to hang on for a point.

Spurs were rising in the League, Paul was settling down, and he looked forward to the fourth-round Littlewoods Cup match away to Southampton with some confidence, Spurs having beaten Blackburn in the replay. But it ended 2–1 in the home team's favour and yet again the road to Wembley had turned out to be a dead end.

Paul was now looking for a house in the South, in an attempt to bring to an end his vagabond ways. Having spent so much time with the Waddles, he had in mind a place just like theirs and eventually found it in Dobbs Weir in Hertfordshire. It was perfect for him, newly built and so without any decorating problems, near enough to several other Spurs players to enable him to scrounge lifts when necessary, and also conveniently situated for fishing and the pleasures of The Fish and Eels pub, which was to become both his local and his refuge.

Without sufficient rest his ankle was beginning to be troublesome. On 10 December he made the first goal against Millwall for Waddle, who struck home from outside the box after 'nutmegging' the referee, then scored himself with a cheeky free kick to the left of the keeper. Spurs then beat West Ham by the same 2–0 margin but Paul was substituted in some pain, and then again failed to complete the goalless draw against Luton on Boxing Day.

When John Sheridan, one of Tottenham's physiotherapists, and the club doctor looked at his injury they shook their heads, wondering how he'd played on for so long and guessing he might well be out for a month. Yet, as he was to do so often, he confounded their expectations and was back as substitute for the game against Forest on 15 January. What he missed in between was both heartbreaking and disastrous for him. On New Year's Eve he was forced to sit out the return fixture at White Hart Lane against Newcastle. It was not the same club that he'd left. Willie McFaul had not survived Paul's departure and, after a brief caretaker period under Colin Suggett, Jim Smith, 'the Bald Eagle', had arrived to try and arrest the slide. David McCreery and Glenn Roeder were still there but the heart had gone out of the side, and even without Gazza Spurs ran out easy 2–0 winners.

In the third round of the FA Cup Spurs had been drawn away to Bradford City, lying seventeenth in the Second Division. Paul sat with the substitutes on the touchline in a tightly packed stadium containing over 15,000 people and was shattered when City took an early lead through Mitchell, incredulous when they held on to that lead to see Tottenham out of the competition. This time Paul was not able to lift his team-mates' spirits, nor indeed his own. The season that had started with such high hopes had crumbled into mediocrity, embarrassment and the fears of a niggling injury that refused to mend.

Named as substitute against Forest, he saw the fickleness of the Tottenham following compared to the fanatical north-eastern support: 27,739 had come to see them beat Newcastle while they were still in the Cup; just 16,903 turned up a fortnight later after the ignominy of the Bradford defeat. Chris Waddle ploughed a lone furrow and scored again, but still Spurs lost 2–1 despite Paul's second-half arrival. He was very down. Everything seemed to get to him, and when Newcastle director Stan Seymour went public on the back of a rumour of a Christmas drinking binge at the Swallow Hotel and called Paul 'George

Best without brains', it was all more than he could take.

In the only way he could, he hit back at Seymour through the tabloids, and in the *Sun* said that, if he was Best without brains, then Seymour was 'brainless' for selling him at a bargain price while Newcastle struggled against relegation. If he was fat, then Seymour was fatter. He did not help the relationship with the board of his former club by saying on 26 January, 'If the directors genuinely cared they would let John Hall take over now.' To his utter astonishment the Football League intervened and charged Paul with bringing the game into disrepute. The fact that Seymour, a director of a league club, had fired the first shot seemed irrelevant to them.

The hearing took place on 24 February and the Tribunal, impressed by Paul's defence, was about to dismiss the case when Paul's honesty got him into trouble. He admitted he'd given the quotes to the newspaper even though he'd not been paid for them. At that point to save everybody's face (except Paul's) they found him guilty but let him off with a reprimand, whilst at the same time agreeing to write to Seymour for his explanation. Whether or not they received an answer, Paul never discovered.

Still slightly troubled by his ankle, Paul had done enough in training to convince Venables that he should be given ninety minutes in the fixture against Middlesbrough on 21 January. Inevitably, after his public and much publicized dispute with the board at Newcastle, a fair number of United supporters turned up at Ayresome Park to demonstrate to their former hero just where their loyalties lay. Paul was determined to defuse the situation. He ate a non-frozen Mars Bar tossed at him and then ran to a bespectacled supporter, took his glasses for a moment and then did a fair impression of Mr Magoo walking into a lamp-post. Soon the jeers turned to cheers and Paul was at one with the world.

Brooks, the boot company, had faith in Gazza's national popularity. Mel Batty was their managing director at the time, a plump, myopic individual with a ready smile, but whose permanent breathlessness made it difficult to believe how gifted an athlete he'd been. It was, at the time, Paul's first major contract outside his club and he took to stardom well, handling the media with remarkable maturity. When asked at the press launch if he'd actually tried the boots he said, 'No, I'm leaving that to Nora Batty.' Batty smiled, a strained smile, the sort of smile that was to appear on the faces of many long-suffering sponsors over the years.

Lack of match fitness caused Bobby Robson to omit Paul from the team for the friendly international against Greece on 8 February. Waddle was out of favour as well, and the international rejections seemed to affect their performances for Tottenham in the League. Both players were very muted in a 1–0 defeat at Old Trafford by Manchester United. Alex Ferguson must have viewed the result with some pleasure as the side he was creating moved into the top three without Gascoigne.

Robson gave himself a few more inches of life-line when England won 2–1 in Athens, but the manner of the victory was not convincing. Neil Webb played in Gazza's position and did quite well, so well in fact that from that match until his untimely injury he seemed likely to be first choice for the forthcoming World Cup.

Paul was ill at ease with himself and it showed. In a 1–1 draw against Charlton he was booked for swearing and arguing with the referee, a booking which took him to twenty-one disciplinary points and a two-match ban. It was a situation hardly likely to gain him favour with the England management. Venables dealt with him in the best possible way, a verbal kick up the posterior and then a cuddle to show he still loved him. Even then it seemed to the footballing *cognoscenti* that Paul Gascoigne was walking a tight-rope without the benefit of a safety-net.

The Venables approach seemed to work. On 21 February Paul gave one of his best performances in a Spurs shirt in a 2–1 win against Norwich. Nayim was a new face in the side, a young Morocco-born Spaniard who'd come on trial from Barcelona. For reasons best known to the Tottenham management Gazza was given the responsibility of teaching Nayim English. Maybe it was because of the rumours of his success with Mirandinha, or perhaps it was simply because he volunteered, but the unsuspecting young man was entrusted to his untender care. It did not take long to realize it had been a big mistake.

'What day is it Nayim?' Paul would ask, as if talking to a performing parrot.

'Ees Wankday,' the poor kid would reply on a Wednesday.

Two Tottenham wins without Paul against Southampton and Villa enabled some of his critics to suggest that perhaps he was a luxury that Spurs could not afford. When he returned to face up to Arthur Cox's Derby, the sound of knives being sharpened was audible from the terraces. With a goal that went in off the post from a free kick he seemed to have stifled his critics and then proceeded to run the show, drawing the comment from Arthur Cox, 'Like all good players he makes it look as if the ball belongs to him.'

Although he was substituted again against Coventry, Bobby Robson did at least take Paul in the squad which travelled to Albania, just about the worst place that Paul had visited in his footballing career. There was some doubt as to whether Chris Waddle would be allowed into the country with his long hair and Gazza was for ever encouraging him to get it cut or else he'd be thrown into gaol. However, despite the hard-line communist regime the fans were incredible, with thousands of them turning up even for the training sessions. Paul became the centre of attention of what seemed like the entire school population of Albania, not just for his shooting skills but for his mimicry of the goalkeepers in the squad. Even without Paul making an appearance, England won 2–0, with goals from Barnes and Robson.

On 29 March Paul turned on all his old skills in a 3–1 defeat of Luton at Kenilworth Road. The third goal belonged entirely to him. He collected the ball in his own half and began his run. He had Walsh to his left, Stewart to his right but ignored them both. The experienced Steve Foster fell victim to a perfect dummy, Les Sealey was drawn off his line, and before he could turn Gazza was already celebrating his goal.

It had happened late in the season but it was better late than never. Gazza and Tottenham were finally in tune. With a 3–0 victory against West Ham, Spurs were suddenly sixth in the League; the thoughts of relegation and Paul's departure were a bad and distant dream. It was no great wonder that 28,000 turned up at White Hart Lane on 22 April to see the revitalized side beat Everton 2–1 and climb into the top five. 'Why couldn't we have played like this earlier?' was the question on the lips of most supporters. Indeed, if they had they must have been challenging for the title.

It was on a real high that Paul set off the next day to join up with the England party for the return World Cup qualifier against Albania to be played at Wembley later in the week. Despite the fact that Neil Webb, David Rocastle and, of course, Bryan Robson seemed to have a grip on the midfield, he was full of optimism. He was at least named as one of the substitutes and felt that, provided England took command of the game as they should, he had a good chance of making his World Cup début. In fact England were 3–0 up with a goal from Lineker and two from Beardsley, but seemed to be losing their way in a match where goals were vital. After 67 minutes Bobby Robson pulled off Rocastle, and to a huge, expectant roar from the crowd the Crown Prince came on to claim his kingdom. Robson's instructions to Paul were to keep to the right-hand side, but he was so excited that he forgot them the moment he ran on to the pitch – that is if he'd even listened in the first place. Waddle was operating down the left and Paul knew he'd get service there, was certain to receive the sort of return balls that would enable him to show his virtuoso skills.

Robson screamed at him from the bench but it made no difference, and it was on that night that Robson privately, although not yet publicly, coined the phrase 'daft as a brush'. Within a few minutes of his arrival, Paul played a perfect pass for Waddle to score and then hammered one in himself to make it four out of five for the Geordie Brigade.

After the game Robson berated him for playing almost anywhere on the field except where he had been told. Gazza replied that he was not a right-sided midfield player. 'When you're picked for England you play where you're bloody well told.'

Chris Waddle has clear memories of the night. 'Paul was always on a high, but after the Albania match he went into space. He was very emotional. That was probably one of the best moments of his career even if he doesn't see it that way. He and I always had a great understanding. He loves one-twos, loves dribbling, just like me. We both want to play football and on that night I hope we both gave a lot of people something to admire. If there was one game you could point to and say Paul Gascoigne had arrived on the international stage then that was it.'

It wasn't so much Paul Gascoigne who had arrived as Gazza. When he rejoined Spurs his confidence was brimming over. He was no longer the new boy. Alongside Waddle he was the only current England international in the team. He had nothing to prove any more. The freedom in his mind gave him freedom on the pitch and Spurs ran riot in a 5–0 defeat of Millwall at The Den. One goal in particular lives in the memory. Gazza getting the ball in his own half, drifting past two men, passing to Stewart, on to Nayim and then to Samways to finish it off. It was vintage Tottenham and perhaps it was no coincidence they should have chosen to turn on the magic in front of Bobby Robson.

He was substituted in the final 0–1 away defeat against QPR; but by the end of the 1988/9 league season, Paul had reason to feel contented with himself and his move, despite the eight bookings and the suspensions he'd collected. Spurs had finished sixth in the League, a position that some years earlier, before the ban on English clubs, could well have given them a place in Europe. He'd scored seven goals, several of them memorable; he'd established himself in the England squad, if not the team, and scored his first international goal; he had a nice house, had Chris Waddle to father him on and off the field, a manager in the shape of Venables and a chairman in Scholar who both idolized him. And he was only 22 years old. The best was yet to come.

For Paul Gascoigne, however, the 1988/9 season never really ended. Within three days of trooping off the pitch at Loftus Road he was in Switzerland playing for the newly created England 'B' team. There he was determined to show the English management and the media that he could add discipline to the steel and skill that were obvious parts of his game. Dave Sexton, the Under–21 manager had already said publicly, 'He knows if he gets into trouble, he'll be off.'

With three bookings at Under–21 level he could be forgiven for being nervous, but told to hold his position on his less comfortable right side of midfield he obeyed the instructions to the letter in the first half, tackling ferociously and distributing with pin-point accuracy. In the second half, rather than fading as he'd done so often in the past, he simply stepped up a gear and also stepped past a whole procession of Swiss defenders on a 40-yard run that ended with him selling the keeper a dummy and tapping the ball into an empty net. He waved to his manager as if to say, 'There you are, I can play it both ways, and I can play for ninety minutes.' An own goal completed a 2–0 England win and the party, lifted by the victory but still tired from a long and exhausting club season, moved on to Reykjavik in Iceland. 'How can I play in a place I can't even say?' Gazza asked plaintively.

As his career progressed he was to play in places with even more unpronounceable names. Again Paul played the whole of the match, and although he didn't score he set up a goal for Steve Bull after Hurlock had given England the lead. Another 2–0 win and the circus left town for Norway – without Gazza who had returned to England for higher things.

England had arranged, and then been obliged to enter, a meaningless tournament at Wembley called the Rous Cup, also involving Chile and Scotland, in the vague hope of generating some interest. Presumably it was intended to pay lip-service to those who bemoaned the loss of the old Home Nations end-of-season matches, but when only 15,000 turned up for the first match and 9,000 for the last, perhaps even the organizers had second thoughts as to its viability.

For the players, rather than the spectators, it did have some importance. The World Cup finals were just a year away, and it was quite clear that if England qualified Bobby Robson would be looking to firm up the hard core of his squad within the next few matches. The more games that were played, the nearer the tournament they got, the more difficult it would be for any new player to come into the reckoning.

After his goals against Albania and the Swiss 'B' team, the media were virtually shouting Paul into the team, and it was no surprise when he actually started the match against Chile and played the whole 90 minutes. Robson experimented with John Fashanu as a target man, with Clough playing further forward and Waddle wide. It simply didn't work. Fashanu waited for the high balls that didn't come, whilst the two Geordies looked for the quick one-twos and movement up front. Eventually, in the seventy-first minute the theory became more ridiculous with the entry of the diminutive Tony Cottee. He fared no better and the game ended goalless.

Paul was less satisfied with his performance than the fans and the press. He'd given the crowd that *frisson* of excitement that so few players bring to the game, the thought that at any moment they might do something remarkable, something memorable, a fear to leave your seat lest the unrepeatable is achieved in your absence.

Robson clearly did not want to push him too hard and Paul started the match against Scotland on 27 May, his twenty-second birthday, on the substitutes' bench. Perhaps Robson felt Hampden Park with 63,000 hostile Scots (no tickets having officially been made available to the English supporters) was just the sort of melting-pot to bring Gazza to the boil. The Scots were unlikely to take prisoners against the old enemy and Paul was always liable to react to both a physical and a verbal battering.

England went 1–0 up through Chris Waddle, who was as determined as Paul to book his ticket to Italy. With twelve minutes to go the game still hung in the balance. Tony Cottee's brief international career came to an end as he was signalled off in favour of Paul. It was Denmark all over again. Fresh legs, despite the tiring 'B' tour, eager to impress, he was all over the place and within two minutes his influence and vision saw Steve Bull score and put the game beyond Scotland's reach.

The curtain had finally descended on the season and now Paul could reveal the secret he'd tried to keep to himself throughout the thirty-six games he'd played for Spurs, the travels to Albania and Saudi, the tour to places he could not pronounce – the ankle that had first troubled him as early as November needed surgery and he finally entered hospital to bring an end to the pain that would have stopped almost anybody but Paul Gascoigne. Whatever might be his faults, a lack of courage was not one of them. On 3 June England faced Poland in a crucial World Cup qualifier. Neil Webb scored in a 3–0 win, and David Rocastle did well when he came on as substitute. The success of his rivals for one of the midfield berths was not good news for Paul. Despite all the good work he'd done in an England shirt, despite his efforts to break the pain barrier, despite the praise heaped on his youthful head by the media, the sunshine of Italy seemed further away than ever.

11

'HELLO GARY, AU REVOIR CHRIS.'

With Gary Lineker's arrival from Barcelona, Tottenham seemed to be stating their intentions of making a serious challenge for the league title in 1989/90. There was mutual excitement. Lineker had been attracted to White Hart Lane for several reasons: he liked the idea of playing under Venables as both of them had achieved so much at Barcelona; he felt, quite correctly, that Scholar was the sort of chairman who would always put his money where his mouth was; and perhaps most important of all, Spurs already had in Gascoigne and Waddle two of the most skilful players in the world, ready to provide the bullets for his lethal weapons. They would be, as Scholar said, 'a holy trinity'. Of Gazza Lineker said, 'He's without doubt as good a natural as I've seen.'

Paul had fully recovered from his operation and he and Waddle had talked at length about Lineker, reaching the conclusion that with him on their side they would actually win something. Both the Geordies felt in their prime. Paul had worked hard after his operation and looked as slim as he had ever been.

The bombshell came before Lineker had even kicked a ball in anger for Spurs. Olympique de Marseille had made a bid of £4.2 million for Chris Waddle, the club had accepted it, and he had decided to go. Both Paul and Lineker were upset, not with Waddle, for who could blame him taking such an opportunity, but with the club itself. No sooner had they declared their intentions to the players and the fans alike than they had unilaterally withdrawn them. The supporters were probably the most unhappy. They'd bought or renewed season tickets on the back of the opportunity of seeing three superstars play together.

As one father figure left Tottenham, another familiar face joined in the shape of Steve Sedgley from Coventry. When Paul had been younger he'd actually stayed over in Steve's mother's house when the two of them had played together in the Under–21 side. Sedgley was in many ways the cockney equivalent of Gascoigne, full of humour, personality and with a penchant for practical jokes. The thought of them in the same hotels and dressing-rooms was horrendous. Gazza would always be taking the rise out of Sedgley because of his looks, 'You'll never get booked, Sedge, you're too ugly,' but despite all the insults the two of them became close friends. After Paul's departure Steve matured so rapidly that, when Gary Mabbutt was injured in November 1993, he was actually made captain, a challenge to which he responded with surprising success.

The loss of Waddle left a big gap in Paul's life, and off the field he was also making changes. Alastair Garvie was beginning to annoy him, suggesting investments in such ventures as garden centres and night-clubs, and finally Paul told Stein and Lazarus he really did not want Garvie to bother him directly again, but wanted everything to go through them.

A pre-season friendly at Ibrox against Glasgow Rangers proved to be anything but friendly. Paul was kicked up in the air on every occasion and eventually could take it no longer and retaliation earned him a booking. It was no way to start, and things got worse when he and Lineker went for the same ball, clashing heads and leaving Lineker dazed and bleeding.

The season proper started on a muted note: a 2–1 home win against a weak Luton side with Gazza, out of sorts with himself and his team-mates, finally being substituted. Worse was to follow. In mid-week they travelled to Everton, lost 2–1, and Paul was booked and lucky not to be sent off. It happened as early as the fifth minute when he went into a reckless challenge on Mike Newell. Newell decided to take revenge and made the mistake of knocking Paul to the floor in a bruising tackle. Paul reacted immediately and went for Newell. Gary Stevens, Paul's own team-mate, tried to intervene but Paul turned on him as well.

Another away fixture followed at Manchester City where Paul, on a hat trick of league bookings, seemed to be making a definite effort to keep himself under control. Venables also appealed to referees not to crucify him, feeling that he was being preceded by his name and reputation. He got through the match without another yellow card and also scored, drawing a comment from Mel Machin, the City manager, that he was a 'one-off'.

If Tottenham brought back no points from Goodison, they did at least bring back Pat Van den Hauwe, a tough, uncompromising defender whose tackling made anything Gazza had to offer seem positively ladylike. But the acquisition of two defenders in the unlovely shapes of Sedgley and Van den Hauwe was unlikely to pacify the Tottenham fans who were still looking for someone to replace Waddle's silky passing and dribbling skills. Even if success could be achieved on the field, for the customers to be satisfied it had to be achieved in a particular way.

Glenn Roeder had moved back to London, having left Newcastle on a free transfer for Watford. That at least was good news for Paul, who used Glenn and Faith as a surrogate southern family in place of Chris and Lorna Waddle. The Roeders at the time also had a daughter,

Holly, who loved playing with Paul, and when their son William was born, it was no great surprise when Paul was asked to be his godfather.

Paul was predictably included in the full England party for the World Cup match in Sweden. With the two qualifying places in the group being contested by Sweden, Poland and England, Bobby Robson could not afford to take chances. Bryan Robson was injured, and while Paul would have seemed to be the natural replacement, the manager settled for the experience of Steve McMahon rather than the unpredictable flair of Gascoigne. Yet, with the score at 0–0 after 72 minutes, Paul did come on to replace Neil Webb, and demonstrated his maturity by holding his position firmly and doing nothing that could in any way be criticized. He hadn't liked being chastised in public by Robson suggesting he should grow up, but if it meant getting a game he was prepared to tolerate it. Anyway, it was hard to be angry with Bobby Robson. He was not exactly a disciplinarian, and many of the players actually laughed to his face, particularly when he failed to remember the names of even his most senior professionals. But Gazza's was a name he was hardly likely to forget, and as he put his arm around the boy at the end of the hard-fought goalless draw, he just said, 'Well done.' It was all one Geordie had to say to another.

Yet if Paul had tasted success with England, what he was to return to with Tottenham was pure disaster. September 1989 was a bad month for both club and player until its very last day. They lost 2–0 at Villa and then were humiliated at home by Chelsea, 4–1. Paul scored but it was scant consolation for an unhappy night. The club sank to nineteenth in the League, and with no Waddle to turn to for comfort, Paul was left to his own miserable nightmare vision of relegation. He spoke of his worries to Glenn Roeder who quietly explained to him that he had to do it for himself. An untidy win against Southend in the first leg of the Littlewoods Cup gave no great encouragement.

Heeding Roeder's advice Paul really buckled down and against Norwich at Carrow Road Spurs raced to a 2–0 lead by half-time, with Paul scoring the first and making the second for Lineker. It was his first goal for the club in his sixth match and helped to ease the pressure that was beginning to weigh heavily on his shoulders as well. Had Spurs bought him just past his sell-by date? In the second half Lineker took a knock and was substituted, and Norwich pulled back to 2–2, but the Gascoigne-Lineker partnership had worked sufficiently well for the first 45 minutes to give Venables hope. It took just seven days for hope to turn to reality. Against QPR Paul was irresistible and Lineker benefited by getting a hat trick in a 3–2 victory.

Paul felt that despite Tottenham's poor club form he had personally done enough since Sweden to keep his place in the England team. He was bitterly disappointed and hurt not to be named in the side that was to play against Poland in Chorzow on 11 October. A goalless draw was enough to guarantee England a place in the Italian sun the following June.

It was going to be a tense few months, not made any easier by the cruel decision to allow Robson to select an initial twenty-six players, and then discard four on 21 May 1990 when he would announce his final twenty-two. 'I was determined not only to be in the squad but also not to be one of the rejects. Yet I couldn't help feeling that I needed at least one more good performance in an England shirt to be a part of whatever was going to happen in Italy.'

The goals began to come freely. Both Gazza and Lineker scored in a 3–1 win at Charlton, and then Paul got his first sweet taste of victory in a local derby when Spurs beat Arsenal 2–1. On 25 September, with Paul sidelined yet again by suspension, Spurs turned in their best performance of the season by beating Manchester United 3–0 in the Littlewoods Cup. There were a few murmurings inside and outside the club as to whether his skills were worth the price that had to be paid for by his disciplinary record and the adverse publicity that tended to follow him.

Without Gazza Spurs could not beat their Anfield hoodoo and lost 1–0, but a week later he was back and scoring in a 1–1 draw at Southampton. He knew that wherever he played he was being watched, if not by Bobby Robson himself, then by Dave Sexton, Don Howe or Mike Kelly. Robson was to admit later that he'd put the microscope on Paul far more often than any other player in his time as manager. He knew the talent was there, but so was the unpredictability, and whilst he would normally rely upon managerial reports and recommendations – particularly from someone as experienced as Venables – he felt in the case of Gazza he had to see for himself how his skills, and more important his temperament, were progressing.

In mid-November there were two international fixtures against Italy, one a full game, the other a 'B' match. Paul was shattered when he learned he'd been selected for the 'B' game. There would be 75,000 at Wembley on the Wednesday night, Waddle was coming back from France for the first time, and Lineker was of course in the side. Paul played before 16,000 at the Goldstone Ground in Brighton, a decent crowd for an unlikely venue. The Italians had obviously been told all about him. Trips, dives, niggles, kicks, spitting, they were all part of the Italian tactics. It ended 1–1, with Paul taking a free kick to make the goal for Tony Adams. As he swapped his shirt at the end he said to his uncomprehending marker, 'You've tried to take it a dozen times in the last ninety minutes – you only had to ask.'

If Robson was looking for Paul to consolidate the demonstration of his restraint on the pitch then Crystal Palace was not the place for him to be on 18 November. Even before the kick-off Paul's sense of humour threatened to get him into trouble. As he came on to the pitch to warm up, three young men dressed as Postman Pat, Jess the Cat and Yogi Bear were having a game of mock football to entertain the fans. The Cat went to shake hands with Gazza, whereupon Paul began to wrestle with Yogi and in the mêlée gave The Cat a friendly kick up the posterior. Incredibly enough the lad inside the cat suit claimed he'd been hurt and his boss demanded an apology.

The kicking did not stop when the match began in earnest. A wild tackle by Paul on Eddie McGoldrick was the spark that lit the fire in what was already a stormy match. A whole group of Spurs and Palace players squared up to each other, and although Paul was not involved in the fracas he spoke out of turn to the referee and got booked yet again. Now he was on the brink of a suspension that would eliminate him from the reckoning for the next England game. Once more he had pressed the self-destruct button. 'It was the worst tackle I'd ever made and I even went and apologized to Steve Coppell, the Palace manager, after the match.'

Controversy followed controversy, incident followed incident. At Tranmere in the next round of the Littlewoods Cup, whilst warming up, Paul hit a ball straight at a cameraman, breaking his glasses. It was a pure accident but neither the media nor the photographer saw it that way.

There was always somebody waiting in the wings to cause Paul trouble. The cameraman made no complaint, and when Paul later learned what he'd done he offered not only to buy him a new pair of glasses but to meet him for a drink. However, a professional do-gooder in the crowd actually wrote to Tottenham to complain about the player's behaviour, presumably ensuring that the media found out all about his good citizenship. Then there was the publication of an unpleasant little book called *Daft as a Brush*, which had been organized by a PR company working with Garvie. Due to a lack of copy control it contained all sorts of crudities, swear words and attacks on referees likely to bring upon Paul a charge of bringing the game into disrepute. Paul speedily disassociated himself from it and donated all of its proceeds to charity.

With his nerves already stretched, a match against Derby County and Arthur Cox was what he least needed. There was a certain inevitability in Spurs losing the lead given to them by Paul Stewart, and going down to two second-half Derby goals. After the match Arthur sought out Paul. He wasn't trying to interfere with Venables but felt the boy needed advice from an outside party, somebody he respected, feared and trusted. By the time Tranmere visited Tottenham in the replay on 24 November Paul had got his head together and was irresistible in a 4–0 win. Yet again what he did with his feet on the pitch made the worldly problems disappear.

Once again he was disappointed to be included in the 'B' side against Yugoslavia rather than the full team to play at Wembley. Robson doubtless thought he was nursing him along gently, but the inconsistency in selection was doing nothing for Paul's self-confidence. He still preserved his sense of humour. On 7 December the BBC filmed him as the mystery celebrity for *A Question of Sport*, for which he decided to make himself available at his lawyer's office in Park Street. They filmed him to the tune of 'Money, Money, Money', and as Abba sang about a rich man's world Paul's fingers were to be seen counting £20 notes. As he finally revealed himself he stuck the notes to his forehead, grinning broadly at the camera. This was Paul at his most self-deprecating, assuming Harry Enfield's Loadsamoney image rather than that of the Geordie yob, Bugger All Money. He was bridging the North–South divide, perhaps without even realizing it.

The previous day there had been some ominous writing on the wall in the real world of finance and big business. At Tottenham's AGM Scholar had been forced to admit that the club had no money to spend. The failure of Hummel and other subsidiaries, the escalating cost of the new stand – they were all taking their toll.

12

'HE CAN DO THINGS ON A FOOTBALL PITCH NO-ONE ELSE CAN.'

Paul warmed up for the England game in style by helping Spurs to a 2–1 win at home to Everton on 9 December. Lineker got his eighth goal of the season and was firmly slotted into his role of goalscorer, whilst Paul was beginning to feel more comfortable with Lineker and Paul Stewart in front of him. The contrasting strengths of these two enabled him to revel in his midfield role whilst allowing him to conserve his strength for those bruising attacking runs that could panic defences.

The England 'B' match was at Millwall's ground, The Den. There was no doubt Paul ran the game from midfield, but even more meaningful was that he stayed cool and calm, following Dave Sexton's advice. It was not only the England manager who thought Paul was man of the match. The press were full of praise with such headlines as 'Razzle, Dazzle, Gazza', and Robson was under enormous pressure from that night on to include him as an automatic choice in his first team, but the most pertinent thing he had to say was 'He behaved himself.'

'I was going to ask if I could play the next night as well because I'd enjoyed myself so much, but even I thought that was a bit cheeky. So I just said "Thanks" and let what I'd done on the pitch speak for itself.'

Yet once again Bobby Robson fell into the traps set for him by the tabloids. He'd given a perfectly reasonable post-match statement, not wishing to go overboard about Paul, thus putting more strain on his young protégé. 'The man who plays alongside Bryan Robson has to have a brain and discipline. He has to be able to work out when to go and when to stay, when to take chances. I'm not saying Gascoigne hasn't got a brain, but he still has to learn when to use it.' In tabloid-speak that became 'Gazza has no brain', or 'I can't trust Gazza', as the *Sun* put it.

Paul, who rarely read beyond the headlines, had yet to discover the full depths of media troublemaking. He was hurt. What more did the England manager want from him? 'I'm just twenty-two,' he said, 'I need encouraging, not knocking.'

Venables too was fooled by what he read. He was in a position to have spoken to Robson and cleared the air, but instead he took his usual route and hit back through his own tame journalists. 'I trust Paul Gascoigne completely and if Bobby Robson doesn't, why is he still in the squad? Every other game seems to be Gazza's last chance. By now he should either be in or out.'

Paul's future prospects received a boost when the England side scraped home 2–1 the following night, with Bryan Robson scoring both goals. If Paul was to be seen as his ultimate successor he was being set high standards to maintain. The following Saturday the league fixture list played one of its timely jokes and brought Gascoigne and Bryan Robson together under the same spotlight as Spurs visited Old Trafford. Tottenham got the only goal, inevitably through Lineker, and Paul received all the plaudits. Spurs, almost invisibly, had moved up to fifth place and for the first time in the season began to be spoken of as serious championship contenders. Still in the Littlewoods Cup, and with the FA Cup beckoning,

Paul felt he had finally arrived in a winning side, a side genuinely capable of giving him success.

Yet at home to Forest on 30 December, when Spurs could have expected to continue their progress to the top, he simply did not perform and the team lost 3–2. Forest manager Brian Clough had devised a system to contain Paul and he was engulfed by midfield mêlées every time he threatened. Whatever the criticism and allegations against Clough off the pitch, Paul has nothing but praise for him as a manager. 'You have to admit it. He's done everything, achieved everything, except a cup-winner's medal. He says what he thinks and sometimes that hurts, but at least you can't accuse him of being two-faced.'

Within ten minutes of the first fixture of 1990 Paul had been booked and fractured a bone in his left arm in a wild tangle with Lloyd McGrath of Coventry. He ended up in hospital, returning to London with his arm in a plaster cast. It was a frustrating time to have such an injury as he saw Spurs exit from the FA Cup and the Littlewoods Cup. Without him kicking a ball, in the space of a few short weeks his season had been reduced to tatters.

Tottenham and Venables were desperate to get him back. Only by his absence had his irreplaceability been demonstrated. It wasn't just what Paul did, it was what the opposition thought he could do that was of equal value. Some sides tried man-to-man marking, others actually designated two players to watch him, and both tactics gave the rest of the talented Spurs side more space in which to work. If Gazza was on song then so were Tottenham, a litany echoed by every club or national side in which he has ever appeared.

At first it seemed as if he'd be sidelined for a couple of months, but on 26 January he played 70 minutes in a testimonial match, and then, fitted with a light-weight cast, he was rushed back to play at home to Norwich in a televised match on 4 February. The gamble paid off. The referee took a good look at the protective covering before allowing him to play, but once given the go-ahead Paul was superb, Lineker grabbed a hat trick and Spurs won 4–0. If any further proof of his value to the side was needed, that was it.

If Paul was Jekyll against Norwich he was Hyde when Spurs played Chelsea. As fate would have it Bobby Robson chose to watch him at Stamford Bridge rather than at White Hart Lane. Fouled, fairly brutally, by John Bumstead, he actually struck out at him. There was no doubt that if the blow had connected he would have been walking off the pitch in front of the England manager, his World Cup dreams inevitably shattered. Bumstead was perplexed: 'Gazza said he was sorry five times, apologized twice to the ref, patted me on the head and shook my hand.' Robson was concerned, wanting to see no more of that sort of behaviour.

Paul had acquired his *eighth* booking of the campaign and was beginning to feel persecuted. 'It got so bad that I began to hold back from tackles and there was no doubt it was affecting my game. I was also much younger then, much less in control. Nowadays I try and smile straight away, shake their hands, pat them on the head. It drives them crazy.'

At the Football Writers Lunch in February 1990 the England manager stated quite categorically that he regarded David Platt and Paul Gascoigne as alternatives and they were scrapping over one place. Platt would play against Brazil on 3 March and Paul against Czechoslovakia on 25 April. Quite why Robson did not feel then he could play them both together when not only had they played together in the Under–21 side, but he himself was to use them so successfully in tandem in Italy, is simply not clear. It placed an intolerable burden on both players, a burden that was made even heavier by the media into whose ruthless hands Robson had inadvertently pushed his two talented young midfielders. Graham Taylor, already tipped as the next England manager, was more positive. 'He can do things on a football pitch no-one else can. I'm sure he'll be in the World Cup squad.'

Paul rose to the occasion as Spurs actually beat table-topping Liverpool and was outstanding throughout the match, outshining McMahon, one of the other main midfield candidates. In every game from then on it was Gazza rather than Spurs who grabbed the headlines. No player before or since would ever have come under closer inspection and analysis. Spurs were the only team to beat Liverpool in the last twenty-two games of the season, and although they were no higher than ninth in the League the victory did wonders for the confidence of both the club and Gazza. If he could take the champions-elect apart, who could doubt that he could do the same to any other team in the world? For a person as impatient as Paul 25 April seemed an eternity away. He was a player once more on the top of his form; he just had to make sure he could sustain it until then.

As he sat on the bench at Wembley on 28 March nobody could have blamed him if he'd had mixed feelings about the success of England, and David Platt in particular. As it was, and as it was always to be, he became immersed in the game, screaming encouragement as England came under pressure from a young and largely unknown Brazilian side. Platt and McMahon both played well in a 1–0 victory over what were clearly more talented opponents. Although Paul came on as substitute for the last few minutes to replace Beardsley, Bobby Robson was minded to keep Platt in the team for the match against the Czechs. He'd always said he regarded Gazza and Platt as alternatives, but he'd promised Paul his chance of a game against Czechoslovakia, and if Robson had his faults dishonesty was not one of them. Paul did not look likely to let him down. He'd been on top form for his club as they went on a run, leaving Scholar and Venables wondering what might have happened if Gazza had been available for the vital cup matches earlier in the season. However, at The Den against Millwall in a 1–0 victory his Under–21 performance was totally forgotten by a hostile crowd. They really got at Paul, and as if he had to prove something to them he went wild, fouled Ian Dawes and was substituted for his own protection a few minutes after receiving a caution for the incident. It was, by then, his tenth yellow card of the season in just over thirty games, a strike rate which if converted into goals would make any centre-forward proud. 'I was beginning to think if I got many more cards I wouldn't have to buy any at Christmas.'

On 21 April, just four days before the England –Czechoslovakia game, Manchester United were the visitors to White Hart Lane. Ferguson was in charge off the field, Bryan Robson on, two men who were likely to test Paul's skill and temperament to the full. Once again Paul had the last laugh and left the United manager grim and unsmiling. He virtually took the star-studded Manchester side apart single-handed, drifting past players at will, spraying 40-yard passes as if he were in a training session. He scored a brilliant individual effort (his first league goal since November) and helped Lineker to a second before half-time. Neither he nor Spurs could keep up the pace in the second half, but they held on to win 2–1 and move into the top three for the first time in the season. Although the title was beyond them they were finishing in style. Rob Hughes wrote in the *Sunday Times*, 'What joy in performance. We have too few artists in our game to deny ourselves the wonder of this one.'

As Paul joined up with the England squad, assured of his place in the starting line-up against Czechoslovakia, he felt a fully paid-up member of the exclusive club of England internationals. In the first few minutes he ran around everywhere, chasing the ball, eager to please, quick to dispute every decision with the referee. When the Czechs scored through Thomas Skuravy, who was later to play in Serie A in Italy, it looked as if the game was going to be too much for him. However the goal, rather than firing him up, calmed him down, settled him to his task. After 17 minutes he played a perfect through pass for Steve Bull to run on to and crack into the net. It was an old-fashioned English goal with a touch of continental brilliance. Seven minutes later Paul raced to take a corner – he hurried to most corners and throw ins – and found the head of Terry Butcher perfectly, who nodded it back for Stuart Pearce to score.

There was more to come in the second half as Paul returned to the field to thunderous cheers. This was his audience, his people, no matter who they supported on a Saturday afternoon. After 55 minutes Paul went on another mazy run down the right-hand side, beating two Czech defenders and pulling another couple out of position. He got to the bye-line like an old-fashioned winger and then pulled the ball back for Steve Bull to get his second and England's third. Against the run of play the Czechs brought it back to 3–2, but Paul was to have the last word as was fitting for the man who had written the script. He latched on to a long through ball from Dorigo, beat a defender, then blasted a shot past the advancing goalkeeper. It was a superb goal that sent the crowd home with only one name on their lips – Gazza.

After the game he was physically exhausted yet psychologically high. The post-match interview was virtually incomprehensible and even Bobby Robson, a Geordie himself, had difficulty understanding him. When he claimed a hand in all four goals Robson suggested he'd only made three.

'Nah,' said Gazza, 'what about my corner?'

'Any bugger can take a corner,' Robson responded.

'Yeah, but not like me.'

It wasn't arrogant, merely factual. Paul knew for certain after that match that he could compete at the highest level. Publicly Robson now appeared to agree. 'He could do for us what Maradona does for Argentina.'

Tottenham's season came to an end the following week with a 2–1 win at home to Southampton and for the first time under Venables Spurs had finished above their North London rivals, Arsenal, in third place. Three days earlier Paul had paid his personal tribute to the great (and now sadly late) Danny Blanchflower by playing in his long-overdue testimonial match against an Irish XI. He took a cheeky penalty, dragging his right foot behind his left and flicking the ball past Newcastle's Tommy Wright in goal. It was the sort of magic Blanchflower must surely have appreciated.

There was no real doubt about Paul's inclusion in the short list of twenty-six for Italy. However, that list would be reduced to a final twenty-two and, although those closest to Paul felt confident of his ultimate selection, there was still a chance he'd blot his copybook before the final selection on 21 May. Before that there was one more friendly – against Denmark. It was hard to see how Robson could omit Gazza after what he'd done to the Czechs, but it had similarly been difficult to make a case for Platt's non-selection after his performance against Brazil. Just because Paul's game was fresher in the mind was no justification to select one rather than the other. Before that, and irrespective of any risk of injury at such a crucial time, Paul played in the Dean Horrix testimonial match at Millwall. Horrix was a young professional who'd been killed in a road accident before his career had ever had the chance of maturing. Paul had never met him, never even played against him, but still he motored down from the North-East to take part without payment or reimbursement. He even dug deeply into his own pocket for a £50 note by way of a personal contribution.

On 15 May it was Paul, rather than David Platt, who made the starting line-up against Denmark. In the pre-match introductions Paul was introduced to the President of the Danish Football Federation, who said hello. Gazza did a passable impression of the Swedish chef from *The Muppets* and said, 'Hello, how's your family?' as if he'd known him for years. Lineker scored the only goal, Paul performed adequately and sensibly, holding his position, tackling back, doing nothing really sensational, but nothing irresponsible either. If the Czech game proved his skill, the Danish match proved his temperament.

Robson kept his twenty-six together at Burnham Beeches. Whoever was not chosen, it was going to be cruel. In fact Robson had told the four already: Beasant, Alan Smith, Rocastle, but perhaps the most surprising omission was Tony Adams, to make up an Arsenal trio of rejects. As the quartet packed their bags and left there was an embarrassed silence which even Paul was not insensitive enough to break.

So that was that. Robson had shuffled his pack, dealt the cards, and after all the waiting and heart-searching Paul was in the team. There were elements of luck, of him being in form at the right time, of Neil Webb's injury, David Rocastle's mysterious loss of form, but Paul was there. The world's stage beckoned and he could not wait to make his appearance.

13

'HE'S GOING TO BOOK HIM . . .'

England's first entry into the World Cup arena had been arranged for 11 June in Cagliari, Sardinia, which was felt to be a venue where some control could be exercised over the English fans. However, before then Robson, amidst much criticism, had organized two friendlies, one at home to Uruguay on 22 May and the other in Tunisia on 2 June, the latter to try and get the players acclimatized to playing in severe heat. Despite all the insults thrown at him, Robson had established a sequence of seventeen matches without defeat. If it had continued against Uruguay would England have gone to Italy over-confident?

They began well enough against the skilful Uruguayans but the South Americans ran out 2–1 winners. The press response was fairly mild. England had not played badly and at least they had rid themselves of the pressure of achieving the record unbeaten run. However, if they were kind to Robson about his team's performance on the field, then the following day they were cruel about his personal performance off it. An alleged mistress was about to write a book about their affair and it was disclosed that he had accepted the job of manager of PSV Eindhoven, with a commitment to start straight after the World Cup whatever the result for England.

As if that were not enough to fill the headlines, Paul himself was in the middle of another potential conflagration. He'd gone up to Newcastle to say his goodbyes and when leaving a bar had been accosted by a young man in the car park. He'd never seen him before in his life, but the youth seemed to know Paul and told him he was going to get him. Paul tried to joke him out of it, but the lad was having none of it. Paul said he would not hit anyone wearing glasses, so the other man took them off, put them down on the bonnet of Paul's car and made to hit him. Gazza, in self-defence, turned round, punched him once on the nose, and the lad ran away in tears. That was it.

His old friends at the *Sun* wrote a banner headline, 'World Cup Wallies', with pictures of Paul and Bobby Robson side by side. It was not the most auspicious start to the campaign, but it did have the effect of bonding the team together, placing them firmly behind their comic genius and their forgetful manager. It also drove Robson and Paul further into a father–son relationship that was to be so vital in getting the best out of Paul.

If the Tunisia match had been arranged to restore the team's confidence it failed miserably. Firstly it poured with rain, which rather ruined the acclimatization aspect. Then Tunisia scored and it took Steve Bull, coming on as a substitute for Lineker, to grab an equalizer. Paul played the whole 90 minutes but was to blame for the goal. 'It was strange. It wasn't that I wasn't trying. I just didn't feel motivated. The game was meaningless, the country was worse. Paul Parker summed it up when he said, "Worst country in the world, that is," but then he'd not played in Albania.'

On 27 May Gazza had been 23. It was incredible to think he was still the baby of the party. Some baby, but at least his youth put a lot of other things into perspective. At an impromptu, belated birthday dinner in Italy he rose to give a speech. 'I was great at seven . . .'

there were cheers, he signalled for silence, 'by the time I was ten I was brilliant. At seventeen I went to Newcastle and showed them how to play. . . They offered me a grand a week and I said I wasn't going to take a drop in salary for them . . . At twenty I was the greatest player in the league . . . At twenty-one I was earning £7,000 a week. Now I'm a millionaire. What have I got?'

Only Waddle muttered the reply, 'Loads of money – and a big mouth.'

Chris Waddle had, as anticipated, drawn the short straw of sharing a room with him at the Ismola Golf Hotel in Sardinia. 'He'd be up before eight, off to the pool, have a game of table tennis, take a sauna and then be raring to go for training. Even when that was finished he'd be down to the beach for a pedalo race, or dragging somebody out of bed to play tennis with him. He couldn't sit still for a minute.'

Paul made friends with everybody – the security guards, the soldiers, the children who could not get enough of the English team. He gave away so much kit (not just his own) that he had to be restrained lest the England side be forced to play their first match in underwear. Nobody could get on the table-tennis table while Paul was about, and if anybody had the temerity to beat him he'd simply play them again and again until he finally won. He had to have the last word, had to end up on top. It was his way of life.

Golf has never been his strongest or favourite sport. It takes far too long and involves walking long distances before anything actually happens. In the tournament organized amongst the players, there were some serious scratch golfers and nobody wanted to pair up with Paul. Waddle finally volunteered, but because of the numbers a third was needed, and the dubious honour fell to the tournament favourite, Tony Dorigo. Paul believes this was engineered by the bookmakers in the team – usually Lineker, Robson and Butcher – who thought Paul might be the downfall of a good thing. Paul actually controlled himself and got through to the last six, but once the TV cameras arrived on the scene he went wild, lying flat on his stomach and pushing the ball along with his nose, dancing and singing with Chris, swinging the club upside down. Give Paul an audience and he simply cannot help performing.

The team, and Paul in particular, thought they were safe from media lies whilst they conducted their lives in the spotlight of Cagliari. They were lulled into a false sense of security. One of the Italian hostesses, a girl called Isabella, was suddenly dismissed. As if at a given signal the English journalists roused themselves from the local bars and got to work on their normal hotchpotch of innuendos and quarter-truths. Clearly if she had been sacked she must have been caught in the sack with at least half a dozen of the players, including Paul. The official line was that she had been removed because her English was not good enough, but the players for their part had genuinely liked her friendly smile and helpful attitude. A delegation, Paul amongst them, sought to get her reinstated. It never occurred to him not to meddle, that it might give some strength to the lies; he just felt sorry for a young Italian girl with a nice smile. It was naïve but it was Paul.

By 11 June when England took the field against Jack Charlton's disciplined Irish regiment, Paul was fitter and leaner than he'd ever been and was first choice with Bryan Robson in midfield. The papers homed in inevitably on how Big Jack would counteract Paul, a player he knew better than most. It soon became apparent that Charlton had told his team to hustle Gazza, upset him, his rhythm, and the rhythm of the team. But within 8 minutes Lineker scored from a superbly timed Waddle pass: 1–0 up inside of 10 minutes of the World Cup. The impossible dream now seemed to be within their grasp.

But try as they might the second goal would not come. Paul was doing everything right, pushing precise passes around the midfield, holding things together, not leaving the gaps that his forward runs sometimes created, but as the game went on it became clear that he was almost on his own in terms of creativity. Waddle was not yet at his best, Barnes was non-existent, still relying on his past glories. McMahon replaced Beardsley, promptly lost the ball to Kevin Sheedy, who equally promptly scored with his clinical left foot. The rest of the England team were shell-shocked but it was Paul, the youngest of them, who stuck out his barrel chest, dug deep into his resources of energy and kept coming forward. A Gazza free kick a minute after Sheedy's goal just escaped Butcher's head, and then the other face of Gascoigne threatened to show. Brought down by Chris Morris, he clenched his fist, pulled the Irishman towards him to facilitate the punch, then fought himself rather than the opponent, hugged Morris and shook his hand. He turned towards the bench as if seeking a nod of approval, as if to say, there you are, I'm a big boy now.

It wasn't the result England had been looking for, but it wasn't the national calamity some made it out to be and for once nobody could justifiably use Paul as the fall guy. It was just one game, one point and all to play for, but a long, long way from the semi-finals.

For the next match, against Holland, Robson took a gigantic gamble and for the first time as an international manager chose to play a sweeper in the shape of Mark Wright. Paul revelled in the extra freedom it gave him as the two full backs, Parker and Pearce, were able to strike down the wings themselves, safe in the knowledge that Wright was there to tidy up if they could not get back in time.

Just on the half-hour Paul gave a hint of the greatness that was to come. Gian Marco Callieri, president of Lazio, was later to declare it was that mazy dribble that first attracted him to Gazza. He got the ball on half-way, was then brought down by a professional foul that would have seen an immediate red card in domestic football. At half-time it was 0–0, but Gazza was looking confident.

Paul was impressed by the fact that most of the Dutch players spoke perfect English. He'd already gone public with his views on Gullit's hair-style, but now he turned to Koeman after a delightful chip and said, 'Blimey what do they pay you then?' Rijkaard replied for his team-mate, 'A hell of a lot, and more than you.'

After 65 minutes Robson limped off and on came Platt to play alongside Paul, the impossible pairing, and for the last 35 minutes they put Holland on the rack. Paul combined the Roeder shuffle with the Cruyff turn, almost mimicking the Dutch hero, then hit a hard, low cross that just evaded the onrushing Bull and Lineker. A minute to go and he was off again on a dazzling, weaving run, then obstructed on the right he fell to the floor and earned an indirect free kick. Pearce hit it so hard and accurately that unfortunately it touched nobody as it flew into the net. England had won the battle of the tactics but had drawn the game. Two matches, two points, the group was going to be tight.

The papers were kinder the next day, but none of the team was prepared to talk to the English press, so disgusted were they by the reporting of the Isabella affair. 'Whatever we'd have said they'd have written whatever they'd have wanted, so what difference did it make?' Paul maintained his vow of silence for longer than any of the other players. When asked why he simply said, ''Cos I hate them.' He delighted in interfering in anybody else's interview, not realizing that he was providing material just by his disruption, his speciality being to hold a copy of *Playboy* open at its centre spread just out of camera range, while pointing to strategic features.

Nobody was laughing at the Egyptians any longer. The make-weights in the group had drawn 1-1 with Holland and 0-0 with Ireland, and if they drew with, or beat, England they had a great chance of going through to the knock-out rounds at the expense of one of the more fashionable footballing countries. On 21 June, with the need to score goals against them, Robson gave Steve Bull his chance for a full game after two appearances as a substitute. Gazza always rated Bully: 'There was something dead English about Steve. I reckon he could just as easily have played in the Fifties as the Nineties. I always thought we had a bit of an understanding, and with due respect to Wolves, if they'd been a bigger club at the time he could have had a regular England place. Maybe now that Graham Taylor's taken over it'll be good for everybody.'

Paul was an automatic selection, looking more comfortable with every minute both on and off the pitch. The night before the match he was still begging for an opponent in a table-tennis match, and that after winning £800 from Lineker the Bookmaker on the filmed races that entertained the team night after night. The win just about put him ahead on the trip, or on the holiday as he now regarded it. World Cup pressure? For Paul it was a myth, he was having a whale of a time. He'd even bribed the waiters to serve him bottles of fizzy water topped off with a generous amount of wine. He was with footballers, making people laugh, ignoring journalists when he wasn't taunting them, taking part in all sorts of sports, and best of all playing football. Whether it was in the world arena, or on the grass of the hotel with the local kids, it was all he really wanted to do.

Although Wright played against Egypt, this time it was in a flat back four. Paul was disappointed that the sweeper system had been abandoned, even though Robson had made it clear it was just for one game against particular opposition. By half-time it appeared as if he'd made a mistake. Paul was still beating players at will, even at the edge of the area, but he was getting little or no support. His frustration showed when Barnes was brutally fouled, as he raced up to the referee demanding retribution and protection. Fortunately the official did not speak Geordie and he avoided a yellow card – for the moment.

The news at half-time with the score at 0–0 was not good. Holland were beating Ireland 1–0 and if the scores stayed the same the Dutch would win the group, Ireland would be bottom and England and Egypt would have to draw lots between second and third places. Gazza decided to do something about it. In the fifty-eighth minute he took a free kick and floated it over the watching defence for Wright the erstwhile sweeper to turn attacker and head the ball into the net. And that was it. Quinn equalized for the Irish, so after their stuttering start England actually topped the group, just ahead of Ireland, with four points.

In the bath the team sang 'World in Motion', their own World Cup song that had reached the top of the pop charts back home. The squad members who weren't playing also launched themselves into the rendition and into the bath (some reluctantly and fully dressed with the help and encouragement of Gazza).

It was farewell to Cagliari and on to Bologna. Bryan Robson, the unfortunate Captain Marvel, having dragged himself back to fitness to get to Italy now found himself unable to maintain it, and had been flown home with an inflamed Achilles tendon. Gazza had lost his supposed protection in midfield, but by now Paul felt he'd served his apprenticeship and come of age. He didn't need a minder and was happy to play alongside whoever the manager chose.

England were based at the Novotel in Castenaso. Paul's advisers bought him a belated birthday present – Union Jack swimming shorts, bright socks and underwear. Somebody at the hotel must have seen the handover of the gifts because a birthday cake promptly appeared at the side of the pool. With the cameras there Chris Waddle could not bear to miss the opportunity. 'How many birthdays are you going to have?' he asked, then without waiting for a reply slammed the cake straight into Paul's face with all the dexterity of a silent movie comic. Gazza sat there, the cake dripping down his face; then, as he licked his lips like a satisfied cat, said, 'Lovely, chocolate.'

Before the match against Belgium for a place in the quarter-finals there was a siege atmosphere in the ancient city, one of the great Italian seats of learning, under perceived threat from the English vandals who had allegedly decimated nearby Rimini. Tanks lined the streets to the ground, armed police searched even the most respectable of visitors. Gazza and the rest of his team-mates seemed oblivious to the atmosphere. He ran out on to the pitch, looked up into the stand, spotted his fan club and waved.

For once it was to be Waddle's night. 'I was dead pleased for Chris. I knew there were knives out for him, but I also knew he was a great player. He can do things I only dream of. Somehow he was never fully appreciated when he played for England.' Yet after 90 minutes it was still all to play for. Even Waddle was fading after his heroic efforts. Paul, though, seemed to be getting stronger and stronger, each penetrative run taking him marginally further into enemy territory. A minute to go of extra time, the players trying to remember in which order they were to take dreaded penalties. Then, suddenly, the chest stuck out, the absurd legs began to pump up and down, and there was Gazza running with the ball from the edge of his own penalty area. The Belgians stood back and watched him as if he were insane, a man who'd been wandering through the heat of the desert, speeding towards a mirage. He was breaking the rules, with so little time left he should accept there would be penalties to decide the outcome.

Almost as an afterthought a Belgian defender raced across midway in their half and cynically brought him down. He was on his feet immediately, wildly signalling that he was going to take the free kick long. Platt was on for McMahon, Bull for Barnes, the Belgian penalty area was like Harrods on the first day of its sale. Somebody from the bench shouted, 'Knock it in,' and Paul resisted the temptation to go straight for goal. He hit the ball with sufficient curve to take it over the Belgian defence, Platt with his back to goal somehow swivelled, almost pushing Bull away, and struck it with deadly finality into the net. It was just 30 seconds from the end of extra time. Gazza and Bobby Robson embraced. The prodigal son had done it for the patient father. The manager, suddenly remembering where he was and who he was, pushed Paul back on to the field. The Belgians were down and out, and as the final whistle blew it was hard not to feel a little sorry for them. Waddle and Butcher, shirts off (Waddle had swapped his with Nico Claesen, his old Tottenham team-mate) were dancing to the background of the English fans' choir, 'Let's all have a disco'.

Paul, not knowing quite where to go first, finally ran to join them, then forgetting the media blackout, even gave a TV interview to Jim Rosenthal which ended in an emotional embrace of Mark Wright. It was that sort of night, a night when grown men needed to feel the company of each other, where there was no shame in tears, where nothing done or said could seem stupid or ridiculous. 'We've got a big heart in the England camp, we've done it now, and we'll do it again in the next round.'

Cameroon, their quarter-final opponents in Naples, had other ideas. They had come to Italy as an unknown quantity and in the first match, on 8 June, had shocked the footballing world by beating the holders, Argentina,

1–0. Yet amidst the flair and the excitement their football had a dark side, an element of raw aggression. Gazza was fascinated by Roger Milla's antics when he scored – a whirl around the corner flag, followed by a wiggle of the bottom. By the time of the match he'd perfected the technique himself, ready to give an accurate impression if he got the ball into the net.

But Cameroon had not come to Naples just to make up the numbers. Even with *four* players suspended they still came out to play, and like mighty Vesuvius that overshadows Naples they looked as if they might be ready to erupt. Platt for McMahon, a reward for his goal, was the only English change. Clearly Robson had long forgotten his reservations about Platt and Gazza playing together in midfield. The team started as brightly as they'd finished against Belgium. Paul seemed to have the legs on anybody in the opposition, but the frenetic pace was something new to them in the tournament. Cameroon were totally unpredictable, probably because they themselves did not know what they were going to do next. Gazza could empathize with that.

On 1 July, in the heat of the early evening, the game slowly swung towards the lithe men from Africa who, unperturbed by yet another booking, still pushed forward. Paul began to get involved in the wrong way, despite all his good intentions. Fouled on the edge of the area after beating four men, he got up with all the danger signs on his face. He began to complain to the referee, but Platt scored after 25 minutes and gradually Paul got himself under control – or so it seemed.

As Cameroon came out for the second half they'd made the substitution the English camp had dreaded. Roger Milla, the veteran, was on and despite his indeterminate age (there were rumours he was pushing 40) he could still play a bit, if not for 90 minutes. Quite what Gazza was thinking of in the sixty-third minute, even he can't recall. Why was he back in his own penalty area, why didn't he leave the last line of defence to the defenders? Milla turned him and as he did Paul put out a foot, thought he'd won the ball, but instead found the man. Milla went down and the referee pointed to the penalty spot.

'I wanted the ground to swallow me up. I could feel my face burning. To come all this way and then give away a stupid penalty. I just felt I'd let everybody down. I prayed, I really did, that he'd miss it, but no luck. Two minutes later that bloke Milla again, unbelievable he was, chipping the ball through and one of the other substitutes – he'd only been on the field five minutes – runs on to it and we're 2–1 down. We've drawn with Holland, beaten Belgium and we're losing to bloody Cameroon. Right I said to myself, don't get angry, get even.'

He did his best, splitting the defence wide open with a stunning pass, but Platt just missed. Lineker was brought down in the penalty area, the referee gave the spot kick, and Lineker coolly scored.

Full time, 2–2. Another 30 minutes in the unrelenting heat and humidity. It was like kicking a ball in a sauna. Then 16 minutes from the end it was Belgium all over again. Paul somehow got his tired limbs working and ran 20 yards before putting Lineker through with an inch-perfect pass. Only he could have looked so calm. No hesitation, past the keeper, England 3–2 up. And then it was over, Paul racing over to the travelling fans, applauding them as they had applauded him. He took off his dripping shirt and swapped it with an opponent, and then back at the hotel, and only then, realized he was part of a team that was in the semi-final of the World Cup.

Turin was not the most appropriate place for an ever growing horde of English supporters to visit. Heysel was still too fresh in the memory, and there was a nasty undercurrent of violence that might erupt if the English started to celebrate too vociferously. Gazza clenched his fists, tensed up for the game of his life. 'If I'd had any doubts, the minute we got out on to the pitch I realized it was going to be something special. The Gaffer hadn't messed with the team. Why should he? The more we played together the more we understood each other, and those waiting patiently for a game were understanding as well. The English fans seemed to be outnumbering, outshouting and outsinging the Germans and we knew we couldn't let them down.'

From the very start England were on top, determined to break the German jinx that had continued in meaningful matches since 1966. Paul put in a volley in the first few minutes that he thought was goal-bound, when Illgner in the German goal just managed to push it aside. Brehme tried to tackle him and came off worst, then most satisfying of all he nutmegged Matthäus, which increased his confidence if that was possible. Neither Gazza nor Waddle were scared to try anything, they were men inspired, playing at the very top of their form. It was all England. Then a man Paul was to come to know very well as a Lazio team-mate came on to replace Rudi Voller – Karl-Heinz Riedle – and from then on Germany looked a better side with Paul forced to operate in a more defensive role. On 44 minutes he and Brehme tangled again. Paul tousled the German's hair and fortunately both men parted smiling. At half-time it was 0–0 and nobody could recall a dull moment.

Then in the fifty-ninth minute Germany got the most incredible stroke of luck. From a free kick Brehme received the ball, shot and saw his tame effort deflect upwards off Paul Parker and over Shilton, caught in a no man's land: 0–1 down and there was no justice in the score–line. Again it was Paul lifting the side, urging everybody on, running here, orchestrating there. He shot a free kick just wide, sprayed passes around only to see wave after wave of attack break against the German sea-wall of a defence. Ten minutes to go and suddenly Lineker found space to score the goal that has been shown on television almost as often as Geoff Hurst's 1966 hat-trick goal.

Extra time yet again, for the third consecutive match. How much could these young bodies take at the end of what had itself been an exhausting season? Paul ran over to the English fans, conducted them, waved to them, as if to say, come on, it's up to you. We'll do the business on the pitch, you do it for us on the terraces. Ten minutes into extra time, and after two promising moves and passes, he saw Berthold pick up the ball on the right touchline. Right in front of his own manager Paul went in for the fatal tackle.

'I've looked at it hundreds of times and it becomes clearer and clearer that I didn't touch him.' It was true. Berthold went into a theatrical fall, rolling over and over in mock agony. The German bench rose to their feet in anger and the combination of the actions brought the Brazilian referee walking towards the incident. Who knows what might have happened if Paul had left well enough alone?

'The Boss had told us, any trouble pat them on the back, say you're sorry and shake hands. I did just that, even helping the bugger to his feet, gave him a smile and then I saw the ref. I held up my hands, half in surrender, half in disbelief. Then he did it. It seemed like slow motion. He took out the yellow card and with the booking I'd already received I knew at once I was out of the final if we got there. We'd been told two yellow cards and it's a one-match ban, the next match, only when I'd been told that I never thought the next match could be the World Cup Final.'

Lineker turned to the bench, mouthing at them to have a word, signalling that he thought Paul's head would go. As the card was held up, Paul looked towards Bobby Robson for support in a wordless appeal. In the past there'd always been someone to come along and bail him out, and if not then the tears had worked, winning over whoever might be angry with him. But the tears that came were to have no effect on the referee only on the rest of the watching world. The game had to go on and to their eternal disgrace not one of the German players attempted to intervene on Paul's behalf, to try and persuade the referee of his innocence. The TV commentator John Motson caught the drama of the moment. 'He's so involved. Oh dear, oh dear me. He's going to book him. He's going to be out of the final if England get there.'

The gloom spread around the world. Terry Venables said, 'I wanted to cry as much as he did. It'd have broken his heart.' Glenn Roeder felt it just as badly, 'He knew at that moment he wouldn't be there – everybody's ambition. The whole nation cracked up with him.' Arthur Cox, as ever, was more demanding. 'I felt he was unprofessional. That would have been the first thing I'd have said to him. He knew, before the match, that if he got another booking he would miss the next game – the final itself. The German was going nowhere, but Paul still had to try to get stuck in. The emotion, though, that came from what he thought he was going to miss – it means so much to him to play football.'

There were thirty million viewers that night, and only the Germans could have failed to feel anything. Paul felt like walking off the pitch there and then, going back to the hotel, packing his bags and heading home. 'I thought at twenty-three I'll never get another chance. I wanted to be anywhere but on that pitch.'

Robson, too, had a dilemma. Did he pull him off to save him from the threat of a red card, or did he give him a few minutes to get his head together? Paul's eyes were glazed over, he was running on automatic, there was noise, colour, the ball, twenty-one other players, a referee who'd done this terrible thing to him, but Paul

Gascoigne was trapped in a world of his own. Waddle was one of the first by his side. 'I said to him, "Come on, Gazza, get on with it," but he just kept saying, "I'm going to miss the final," over and over again. All he could think about was that he was certain to miss the biggest game in the world. As it was we all missed it, but I don't think that made Paul feel any better.'

Butcher had a word, so did Lineker, and suddenly Paul was back in the land of the living, wiping his nose on his shirt, rubbing his eyes clear with a clenched fist like a small, grubby child. Brehme fouled him cynically. This time it was the English bench who were horrified.

Would Paul react? Somehow he kept his cool, got up, shook himself, and then reached for the German's hand, smiling ruefully. The referee booked Brehme, but that was no consolation.

One hundred and twenty minutes gone: 1–1 and it was down to penalties, down to the wire and beyond. On the pitch there was chaos, players wandering on shaky legs like survivors of a nuclear attack, officials running up and down with little pieces of paper and clipboards, and there in the midst of it all Bobby Robson consoling Gazza, who was now crying heartbrokenly, unashamedly.

The rest is history, almost too painful to recount. Three all. Then Stuart Pearce, the safest of all penalty-takers, shoots straight at the keeper, the German scores and it's all down to Waddle who, sick as the proverbial parrot, shoots the ball high over the bar, high over the moon, and England's dream is as dead as the ball falling to earth at the feet of some distant and anonymous spectator. Pearce is crying now, Waddle too, and Butcher is left to comfort Gazza, holding him tight without any feeling of shame or embarrassment. For England, for Paul Gascoigne, the World Cup ended in Turin. For Gazza life began there.

The image persists in the mind's eye of Paul Gascoigne standing, red-faced, arms raised, applauding the fans, holding his tear-stained shirt in front of him and kissing it. The portrait painted by no less a person than Giovanni Agnelli, president of Juventus: 'The Dog of War, with the face of a child.'

Some half a dozen of the other players were crying too, and by the time they were back in the dressing-room, with the cheers of the fans still echoing around the stadium, Paul was inconsolable, but then so was everybody else.

For some five or ten minutes there was total silence on the coach back to the hotel. Then Lineker said, 'It's gone, we can't bring it back.'

Someone else began to sing their own World Cup song, and Gazza's voice, at first a little trembling, then as loud and raucous as ever joined in. In less than an hour he'd put adversity behind him. Chris Waddle says that people have asked how they could sing and drink within a few short hours of losing the chance to bring the World Cup back to England, but as he comments, 'Life goes on.'

Paul himself just felt numb. 'I've been asked over and over again, would it have been worse for me if we'd won and I'd had to sit out the final. The answer is no. I wanted us to win even if I couldn't play – and maybe we could have appealed then. It wasn't just me who'd lost, it was all of us, not the team, the squad, but the country, including my family. We just felt gutted, but we also couldn't let the Boss, or the journos, see how badly we were taking it deep inside.'

Back at the hotel he made straight for his room and got on the phone to his parents. He had to tell them he was fine, knowing the way they would have felt watching his grief exposed in front of millions of viewers. He had no idea that those millions viewing were now his fans, many of whom would idolize him through thick and what was to become more than a little thin.

After the largely irrelevant third-place match (which they lost to Italy) there was a big party. As a tribute to their manager, the players threw him into the hotel swimming pool still wearing his suit, and missed killing him through collision with a concrete wall by centimetres. The partying continued throughout the night. The athletes who had been tightly coiled for so long were finally given the chance to unwind. They were like little children on the day school broke up. They played silly games, going round the table saying 'Good Morning Vietnam' in different ways, singing the England song about fifty times. To the casual onlooker it would have appeared infantile, but for the players it was a time to laugh at anything, including adversity. Sunday 8 July was the final, a bitterly disappointing and ill-tempered affair that the Germans won 1–0, leaving the neutrals in the crowd cruelly mocking Maradona of Argentina, 'Diego, Diego, Ha, Ha, Ha.' Four years later, Maradona would be sent home from the USA in disgrace for drug-taking, but who would have predicted that just a few days later, Gazza would bare his soul to the British nation, only this time as he confessed to the violent side of his nature, his tears would win him nothing.

But all English eyes were firmly fixed on Luton Airport. The players were utterly stunned by their reception. On the plane back Paul asked Beardsley, Shilton and Waddle what sort of crowd had gathered when they'd returned from Mexico in 1986. 'Pretty good,' said Waddle, 'around 10,000 people.'

Nothing prepared them for the multitudes that met their eyes as they got off the plane. Estimates ranged from 200,000 to half a million, cheering their heroes home, recognizing their gallantry in defeat. 'Cor, you'd think we'd won the war,' Paul said and promptly donned a pair of false boobs, presented to him at the airport.

They struggled through the crowds on an open-topped bus, singing, waving, popping champagne corks, with Paul happily drenching anybody who came near him. Yet, throughout the slow progress, throughout the cheers, one word rose above all others, 'Gazza, Gazza'. It was the first public demonstration of Gazzamania.

They finally reached the hotel and Paul sought a comforting, friendly face in the crowd, his dad. Inevitably, amidst the crowd, they found each other and embraced long and hard. Once more Paul felt the tears rising in his eyes.

'You should have been there,' Paul said.

'I was,' his dad replied. He was right. Everybody had been there, everybody had lived through the drama from its beginning to its incredible end.

The main problem now was how to get out of the hotel in one piece. Paul said his farewells to the rest of the team, and his final goodbye to Bobby Robson, then he and Waddle were smuggled out to the camper he'd bought his father as a present. They lay down in the back, and the cheering crowds ignored the vehicle that contained the man they most wanted to see. With curtains drawn, the two men fell asleep as they headed north up the M1 towards their home.

It was ten at night when John reached Tyneside, but the Dunston Excelsior was buzzing. They had waited a long time to welcome their own lad and they were determined to do it in true Geordie style. The roar that went up when Paul entered the room rivalled anything he'd heard in Italy. Everybody wanted to buy him a drink, to pat his back, to feel a part of the success he'd brought home with him, to have a little touch of Gazza in the night.

14

'GAZZAMANIA.'

At 8 a.m. on Monday the telephone began ringing in Lazarus's West End office. Stein had stayed over in Rome to see the final and the two men did not talk until Monday night. By then it was already getting out of control. Everybody now wanted their little touch of Gazza and they did not mind if it was day or night. Paul himself was due to go on holiday and his advisers realized they had to sit down with him before he left, at least to establish the ground rules. They felt as Brian Epstein must have done when The Beatles first charted; they were on the brink of something totally unknown in the world of football. They have both come under much criticism from the ill-informed and the jealous since then, but the fact of the matter was that nothing was done without Paul's consent, no contracts or appearances were ever foisted on the player. The number of offers rejected far outweighed those accepted and Paul's own interests were always paramount. They took no percentages, but merely professional fees for their respective firms based upon time, as with any other client. This ensured that there was never any conflict, yet despite that they were accused of greed, of putting Paul's off-the-pitch activities before his football, of manipulating a young, immature lad who trusted them implicitly. It all pained them, particularly as they both regarded Paul as a son and would as soon have hurt their own children than cause him any harm.

On 12 July 1990 Stein and Lazarus flew to Newcastle to see Paul before he departed for his well-earned break, and to report on the innumerable meetings they'd had since his return. It had been the hardest job in the world keeping people at bay, but they had refused to commit Paul to anything without his consent. On their way to the airport the *Mail on Sunday* rang the car phone seeking an exclusive interview, the first exclusive Paul would have given since his triumphant return. Wondering what to charge, as Stein drove, Lazarus threw what he thought was an outrageous figure at the negotiating editor, who said he would have to come back to them. 'He didn't say no,' Lazarus commented in amazement.

They met Paul and Chris Waddle in a bedroom at the Gosforth Park Hotel. Paul stretched himself out on one bed, Chris on the other. Paul was asked if he was happy to discuss everything in front of Waddle. 'No problem. I've no secrets from Waddler, I've roomed with him often enough.'

They had already met with several prospective licensees and began to go through the list with Paul. Even at that stage it was enormous and the two of them had done little of their normal work in the preceding week. Television and radio interviews, newspapers and magazines, a substantial clothing deal, lunch boxes, books, bedroom rugs, curtains, duvet covers, greeting cards, footballs, a new boot deal – as Paul listened to the seemingly endless list his mouth opened in disbelief, and for once his boredom threshold remained uncrossed.

They then asked him what he would and would not like to do. A few items immediately disappeared – a pin-up cheese-cake topless calendar, a stream of media interviews, anything that required too many personal appearances. Then the policy decisions were taken.

Stein and Lazarus were to be given complete financial control. Anything interesting would be pursued by them, but the final decision whether or not to proceed would be left with Paul.

They went off to dinner as it was Stein's forty-fifth birthday the next day, and from the moment they sat down to eat Paul realized there was going to be a price to be paid for fame. The management sent over a complimentary bottle of champagne, but thereafter there was a constant stream of autograph hunters, all politely wanting a moment of his time, yet not realizing he just wanted some peace and quiet to be able to eat his meal. He dealt with them all, signing obediently, posing without fuss, the smile always there for the cameras.

Throughout the meal the phone in the restaurant rang and rang. The *Mail on Sunday* was trying to negotiate the price down for the interview. Stein left the table to take each call, and every time he did so Gazza spiked his drink. Somehow or other the lawyer kept his feet and the cocktails devised by Paul gave him the confidence to hold out for the wishful figure first floated by Lazarus. Finally the newspaper surrendered: they would pay the price and give copy control. It was a watershed in the affairs of Paul Gascoigne. He didn't like doing interviews. Now he'd seen the price he could command if he made himself unavailable. From then on that was to be his minimum figure; if people didn't want to pay it that was fine by him. It wasn't greed, he simply didn't enjoy doing them, and he was beginning to understand he didn't have to do anything he didn't enjoy.

Back in London Paul's advisers tried to bring some order to the situation, but it was becoming too much for the pair of them, even working flat out from morning to night. Each day was devoted to a whole stream of meetings regarding Paul and it got to the point where the press, unable to secure sufficient access to Paul himself, would settle for members of his family, or even Jimmy

Gardner. Stein and Lazarus themselves were in constant demand for interviews and despite their desire to keep a low profile were having the legendary fifteen minutes of fame thrust upon them. It was a kind of fame for which at least one of them would pay dearly in time.

It did not all come easily. Paul's boot deal with Brooks had been terminated amidst threats of legal proceedings made through the pages of the popular press. Paul's advisers were virtually interviewing companies to see what they could do for him. Mizuno, Lotto, Diadora, Umbro, Nike and Puma's representatives all filed through the solicitors' offices, Finers, where Stein was a partner; it was the worst-kept secret in the world. All they had to do was to read the signatures in the visitors' book in reception to see with whom they were in competition. Finally it boiled down to a straight fight between Umbro and Puma, both fine companies with whom Stein and Lazarus had, and have, enjoyed the best of relationships. In the end it wasn't a question of a Dutch auction. Paul actually preferred Puma Kings to the Umbro range, and it was he who had to wear them. Puma got their man.

Perhaps the biggest tribute of all to Paul's marketability was Kelvin Mackenzie, ebullient editor of the *Sun*, insisting on a personal breakfast meeting with Stein and Lazarus. They'd never met him before, but to their enormous surprise they actually got on extremely well. Kelvin was direct and to the point and ate no babies at the table. He wanted Gazza exclusively, not just for a series of articles but for TV advertisements and a series of promotions. By now the lawyer and the accountant knew the value of their product. Kelvin was at first shocked, then amused, and finally agreeable. He too had his man.

The *Sun* started Gazzamania officially with their constant use of the phrase, but Harry Harris in the *Mirror* had probably been responsible for coining the phrase almost a year before. All the *Sun* was doing, as it did so often, was reflecting public opinion.

It became obvious that Stein and Lazarus needed help. First of all they decided to establish a fan club to deal with the mail that was arriving in sackloads at Tottenham, their offices, even at the FA headquarters at Lancaster Gate. Paul had definite ideas as to who he would want to run it – his mother and his younger sister, Lindsay. He wanted no outsiders pushing their way into the tight circle. Next they needed someone to weed out the wheat from the chaff, the possible from the improbable. They needed someone to keep Paul's diary, to liaise with licensees, a personal assistant with enough brains to operate independently when the need arose. Lazarus's sister-in-law Renée Menir was a qualified solicitor who had become disenchanted with private practice; she had the time, the temperament and the intelligence to deal with Paul and she was on board by the end of the summer.

By August 1990 Paul Gascoigne Promotions Limited had its own office within the Finers building, and a telephone line that rarely stopped ringing. A contract was signed for three books with the publishers Stanley Paul – a picture biography, a book on the 1990/1 season, and a soccer skills book to tie in with a forthcoming Channel 4 TV series. A video biography was also on the drawing board. Irving Scholar, as much as anybody else, saw the possibilities of marketing Paul and did not want to be left out of the money-making opportunities. He invited Stein and Lazarus for another of his avuncular chats and the outcome was three joint ventures between Paul Gascoigne Promotions Ltd and one of Tottenham's subsidiaries, Cockerel Books, for a Gazza calendar, a Gazza poster magazine, and most ambitious of all a Gazza video of his life – *Gazza, The Real Me*.

Scholar came up with a brilliant idea. He was often doing that, the only problem being that he was two brilliant ideas ahead of those trailing in his wake still trying to put his earlier ideas into operation. This time, however, he actually pulled it off on his own. Woolworths would be given the sole and exclusive rights to sell the video in return for committing themselves to a massive order. The video itself worked perfectly and the real moment of inspiration was when Danny Baker was asked to do the voice over and the linking interviews. At that time Danny was relatively unknown, his fame limited to the South-East where he'd appeared sporadically on London Weekend's Friday-night sports programme; but the combination of Baker and Gascoigne was irresistible and since then they've become firm friends, often meeting for early morning saunas when Paul was still in England. Even more ambitious was the record. The concept of a footballer making a pop record was not new: at the height of his fame Kevin Keegan had charted briefly, whilst there'd been innumerable team or national successes, and 'World in Motion', the England World Cup song, had actually got to Number One in the charts. But very few records by footballers had actually been taken seriously. Paul had clearly become a pop figure with his photographic appearances in the pop culture publications even before he'd sung a note in anger – so why not a record? Again the critics sharpened their knives. It was cashing in, crass, commercial; but Paul enjoyed making it. The public had the opportunity to make up their own minds and it sold in its thousands. Lindisfarne had long been Geordie heroes in their own right, but their 'Fog on the Tyne', the unofficial anthem of the North-East, had never been released as a single. They took little persuasion. For Paul it was a long way from singing for pence to little old ladies in their street.

Gazza products continued to pour on to the markets: key rings, watches, shell-suits joined the list of the licensed goods all bearing the cheeky little caricature created by Paul Trevillion at the request of Stein and Lazarus. They had already faced the problem of the pirating of Paul's name and the label signified an authorized product. The demands on his time were neverending, but he did not surrender to the temptation.

At a very early stage Paul's advisers discussed the matter with Terry Venables, who seemed less than overjoyed at his young player's commercial success. Perhaps there was an inevitable hint of jealousy that the opportunities had not been around when he was young, particularly as he had a better singing voice than Paul. What was agreed, without any fuss, publicity or acrimony, was that Paul would accept no commercial engagements for forty-eight hours before a match. This meant that if Spurs had one game on a Saturday, in theory Paul would be available Sunday through to Thursday afternoon; if they had a midweek game on a Wednesday, then he would only be available on Sunday or Thursday. However, since Paul disliked working on a Sunday, personal appearances were fairly limited, contrary to the allegations and criticisms that were being levelled.

It might seem that football was beginning to play a relatively small part in Paul's day-to-day life, but he had slipped back into the routine of training, although the crowds that were drawn to the Spurs training ground had changed in numbers and in sex. There was to be another footballing change in Paul's life. On 14 July Graham Taylor was appointed England manager, an individual known throughout the game to be his own man, a manager who with Watford and Aston Villa had achieved success with long balls aimed at the heads of tall strikers such as Luther Blissett and Ross Jenkins, a man, according to the media, not renowned for his appreciation of individual skill and flair. Taylor in charge of England, Gazza in charge of Gascoigne. Whatever the 1990/1 season had in store it was unlikely to be dull.

As Paul continued his pre-season training at Tottenham there was to be no escape from the headlines. AC Milan had allegedly bid £19 million for him and Lineker; Fiorentina, Genoa, Sampdoria were all about to pounce. 'It was a bit odd coming back to the daily grind. I mean, although Italy was hard work, it was also a bit of a holiday. You'd wake up, you'd see the sun, the sea, the beach, the pool and you'd think, this is all right. I can live with this. But I was glad to get back to the lads at Spurs. They didn't treat me any differently and it got my two feet back on the ground.'

Tottenham went to Norway for their pre-season tour. Whether it was the aftermath of Italy, whether it was the expectations that he would always make things happen, or whether it was simply that he'd needed a longer rest than he'd had, Paul did not play especially well and was both booked and substituted. There was an element of staleness in his game, and with hindsight perhaps Tottenham should have excused him from the trip. But there was the commercial aspect of things and there was no doubting that his drawing power was immense. The more palatable reason was that it had to be in everybody's interest for him to be immersed in the normality of club life as soon as possible. The pressures were beginning to tell, and before he returned to France Waddle had noticed it: 'At first it was all unbelievable and he loved it, but after about two weeks he got bored. He wanted it to stop dead, not just fizzle out. I warned him it would all turn to bad press. That had to be typical of the English journalists. They'd build you up to be a hero, then knock you down and get the boot in while you're still on the floor. Gazza belches, everybody laughs; then he does it again six months later and everybody says "What a pig."'

Back in Britain Spurs went to Scotland and played Hearts in another friendly. Again the crowds flocked

into the ground in unprecedented numbers. Like pilgrims to Lourdes they were waiting for a miracle –
it did not come. After a mere 12 minutes Paul was
booked, and thereafter the game deteriorated into an
untidy series of niggling incidents that belied the word
friendly. Paul was at a loss to understand why he'd been
booked and gave an interview to the *Sun* claiming he'd
received the caution for smiling. In accordance with
the copy-control clause the article was sent to Lazarus
for approval as Stein was holidaying in France. The
accountant anticipated a problem and asked for the
comments about the referee to be deleted. The London
editions carried the expurgated version, but the amend-
ments did not filter through to Scotland where the *Sun*'s
headline read: 'He Booked Me For Smiling!'

The Scottish FA reported him to the English FA
asking that they charge him with bringing the game
into disrepute. It was the fault of the *Sun* and they
were big enough to admit it, joining with Paul's lawyers
in writing a letter of explanation to the FA which
was finally accepted. It was a warning shot as far
as Paul was concerned, to show him how thin was
the line he was expected to tread, how much of a
target he was now likely to be.

Gordon Taylor, Chief Executive of the Professional
Footballers Association, went public on Paul's behalf
and pleaded with referees and players alike to treat
him fairly. He was a national treasure, the one player
in England who could bring English football back to
the heights it had achieved in the Sixties.

White Hart Lane on 25 August 1990 was to be
the stage upon which Paul was set to prove that his
greatness was not merely a flash in the pan, set to
disappear in a matter of seconds. A huge banner outside the ground proudly proclaimed 'Welcome back,
Paul and Gary' for the game against a Manchester
City team that had championship aspirations of its

own. The two of them were used to writing their own scripts, and when Lineker put Spurs ahead the match already had a carnival atmosphere. Played in hot sunshine, the short-sleeved crowd in holiday mood rose to their hero, only to be silenced before half-time by a Niall Quinn equalizer. The second half, though, was to belong to Tottenham, and Gazza and Lineker in particular. Lineker scored again, and then Paul showed exactly why he was the cause of such excitement with a brilliant goal: 3–1 to Tottenham, Gazza was in heaven and all was right at the Lane – for the moment.

The North-East was not the friendliest place to visit for Spurs' next match. The Sunderland fans were certain to make it clear that they were not fooled by Gascoigne. To them he was still a Geordie, and perhaps even worse a Geordie reject, a man who'd turned his back on his home town. Yet 30,214 of them still assembled to see him, 4,000 more than were to turn up the following Saturday for the visit of Manchester United. To the unconcealed delight of the many Mackems Paul looked anything but the best player in England and was marked out of the game which ended in a goalless draw. Yet at the end there was still enormous public clamour from the young fans to get a glimpse of Gazza, a scribbled autograph, even a smile, and finally for his own protection he had to be smuggled out of the ground in the boot of a car. It was an escape route to which he was to become accustomed and which tested his claustrophobia to its very limits.

Local derbies are never easy and the one against Arsenal on 1 September, in front of a packed Highbury with 40,000 partisan fans, was even less so. Arsenal fans had still not forgotten how their trio of Adams, Rocastle and Smith had been despatched from the hotel when the England squad had been reduced to twenty-two. Although they may have supported England on the day, the semi-final team had contained no Arsenal players and the two England heroes now wore the hated colours of Tottenham. Gazza was given the full Highbury treatment, and as the game gathered pace, so he faded and was finally substituted in what turned out to be another goalless draw.

Paul had complained to Venables of being tired before the match. It might therefore be asked why he played him. Inevitably his off-the-pitch activities got the blame as did his advisers, but that was all nonsense and Venables knew it. Paul had hardly made an appearance in support of his various licensees and those tasks he had undertaken were hardly strenuous. The trouble was that they appeared to be to the gullible readers of the tabloids. As an example, his photograph appeared on the front cover of *Radio Times*, with an interview inside to launch Radio 5. It looked like a major project, but the interview had taken place at the Swallow Hotel to suit Paul and the whole thing had taken less than an hour. Paul went on to the *Wogan* show on BBC television. Again he got extremely nervous beforehand, and calmed himself down à la Best with a few brandies in the hospitality lounge. Outside the BBC Television Theatre in Shepherds Bush the crowd's depth rivalled that of the Oscar awards, and as Paul arrived a scream issued from thousands of teenage throats. A doorman commented that it was the worst they'd had since David Cassidy. Again the comparisons with the world of pop fanaticism were irresistible.

On air Paul's sense of comic timing was totally professional as he did a double-take in reaction to Wogan placing his hand on his knee. Wogan himself was moved to turn to the audience and almost with surprise say, 'What a nice lad,' as if he'd half-expected him to vomit on air. That was always the problem: wherever Paul went he was prejudged. If he behaved impeccably the response was one of surprise; if he let himself down, which he did at times, then nobody was disappointed.

Although what Paul said on *Wogan* could not have been clearer, the journalists still chose to write what they had wished to hear rather than what was actually said. According to them Venables had put a stop to his commercial appearances, there had been a wholesale cancellation of contractual commitments. It simply wasn't true. Gazzamania showed no sign of letting up and nothing was cancelled.

Graham Taylor was by now sounding warning notes. The first England match under his management was on 12 September and from this very early stage he felt able to speak freely with the press, perhaps too freely. Openness was his style, but all too often his own words were unfairly, and often inaccurately, used against him, even to write his final obituaries.

George Best climbed unsteadily on to the bandwagon. 'He'll be a goner inside two seasons. One reason is that he's just not good enough.' To which Paul responded, 'I don't want to end up like him. I'm Paul Gascoigne, not the new George Best.' It was interesting that he did not claim to be 'Gazza'; but whichever face of the Janus mask Best was criticizing, the press ensured the dispute rumbled on until November when the *Sun* carried the headline 'Let's be pals'. Even the tabloids had run that story into the ground by then.

Paul, as usual, came bouncing back on the Saturday after the Arsenal game with the best answer he could give, a hat trick against a Derby side still managed by Arthur Cox, and with Shilton in goal. Peter Shilton may have retired from the international scene, but he was still arguably the best keeper in the world. It was not so much that Paul scored three goals just a week after his alleged exhaustion, but the manner of them – two stunning free kicks, one solo effort – and an ability to orchestrate the game such as had not been seen in English football for many years. 'Tired?' Paul said. 'You want to see me when I'm fully awake.'

On 9 September, the morning after the Derby game, the headlines were not so much about Paul's hat trick as Robert Maxwell's bid for Tottenham. Paul's reaction was immediate: 'I'm not playing for that fat bastard. If he takes over then I'm off.' He knew the appalling way Maxwell, when owner of Derby, had treated Arthur Cox, knew that football to him was an ego trip rather than a passion, and wanted no part of it.

Harry Harris of the *Daily Mirror* phoned Stein on behalf of his newspaper's proprietor to ask if there was any chance of a photo of Gazza with Maxwell if the deal went through. 'No chance' was the reply.

It appears that Maxwell had said he would like a photograph with 'Gaza' (pronouncing it like the Middle Eastern province), perhaps perceiving that as a short cut to the hearts of the Tottenham faithful. But from the moment the Maxwell bid was disclosed the odds were tilted in favour of the departure of both Gascoigne and Scholar, although Scholar believed that the offer guaranteed both their futures and indeed the future of the club. 'We didn't really understand what was going on in the boardroom. It was all about this Act and that Act, and the nearest most of us had got to the Stock Exchange was applying for BT shares. Gary Mabbutt seemed to have a better idea of it all and we tended to rely on him for a potted version every day.'

Despite all the furore in the press, Graham Taylor made few changes to the England squad he had inherited from Bobby Robson for a friendly against Hungary. The whole team had been to Italy and only the omission of Waddle from the starting line-up raised a few eyebrows. The crowd, still filled with World Cup euphoria, had come ready to cheer anything – particularly from Gazza. A corner, a throw-in whipped them into frenzies of excitement, but it was a disappointing match, and although England won 1–0 through a Lineker goal it was against a team in decline, and

Taylor must have realized for the first time that the job was not going to be easy.

Back with Tottenham the players had to concentrate on the task for which they were being paid and after eight league matches they were unbeaten, riding high in third place behind Liverpool and Arsenal, while on 25 September Paul ran riot against Hartlepool in the newly renamed Rumbelows Cup, scoring four out of five goals.

Clearly the High Court judge Mr Justice Harman did not read the sports pages. On 12 October he refused to grant an injunction being sought by Paul's lawyers to stop an unauthorized biography using the name 'Gazza' as its title. His decision was made upon the grounds that he'd never heard of Paul Gascoigne and doubted if he was sufficiently well known to have acquired any proprietorial rights in his own nickname as far as the book was concerned. 'Isn't there an opera called *La Gazza Ladra*?' he asked, managing even to get the translation wrong. His musical knowledge seemed as poor as his sporting awareness.

Graham Taylor, meanwhile, named his squad for the European Championship qualifier against Poland on 17 October and it contained few surprises. Again Waddle was on the substitutes' bench but Paul was on the field, and played well, if not sensationally, in a comfortable 2–0 victory. The goals came from Lineker and a last-minute effort from Beardsley, who had come on as a substitute. Waddle had also entered the fray half an hour from time, and had done enough in linking up with Paul, and then with Beardsley, to satisfy most neutrals that the three Geordies should be automatic choices for the team.

Again Venables suspected Paul needed a rest. The Hartlepool game was already won in the first leg and he left him on the bench for the return match. He might just as well have played him as he expended as much energy running up and down the touchline, chatting to the crowd and teasing the ball-boys. At one stage he had them all doing press-ups alongside him, until he disappeared without them noticing, tip-toed up behind them, and then flattened them one by one with a well-aimed kick to the posterior.

In the League the Tottenham run continued, 4–0 against Sheffield United on 20 October, with Paul substituted (feeling his groin injury again) and dubbed a 'buffoon' by United manager Dave Bassett. 'If my kids behaved like that they'd get a good smack.'

If Paul had to pick one match where he realized something was really wrong with his groin then this was it. Yet a 2–1 victory at Forest followed, in what was to be a Cup Final rehearsal, bringing the unbeaten run to twelve games. What was even more relevant was that Spurs had only used thirteen players. 'I reckoned it was because we couldn't afford to put any more on the payroll. Playing in a settled team, particularly a winning one, is a great help. You get to know what your team-mates are going to do before they do it.'

On 29 October Scholar took the first step on his long, lonely road to exile, resigning as director of the public company that owned the football club, but still remaining as chairman of Tottenham Hotspur Football and Athletic Club Ltd. There was no doubt that it appeared to the public that his wings had been clipped. Paul meanwhile, on the 30th, went proudly to 10 Downing Street with other members of the England World Cup squad to meet Mrs Thatcher. When he put his arm around her and pronounced the iron lady 'cuddly' it was a headline writer's dream. 'Gazza Meets Magga' was the best of them. 'I talked to her about fishing,' he said.

Tottenham continued to fly as high as ever, taking their unbeaten run to thirteen with a 2–1 win over Bradford City in the third round of the Rumbelows

Cup. Paul scored again to take his season's total into double figures. He'd actually bet Glenn Roeder he'd get twenty for the season and here he was with a quarter of the season gone, half-way there. Maybe, though, Roeder knew something Paul did not, because injuries would ensure he added just nine to that tally in all competitions, leaving him one goal short.

If Spurs were riding high in the League and Cup, Paul was still on the crest of the wave of his own popularity. Madame Tussaud's asked him to model for a waxwork and he had to endure hours of sitting perfectly still while they re-created his face. He was awarded the Panasonic London Sports Personality trophy, and then received an even more unlikely award in the shape of The Best Dressed Man of the Year at the London Men's Fashion Exhibition. 'I don't know to this day how I got that one – maybe Worzel Gummidge was the only other entrant.'

Brut was the only Gazza endorsee to be approached by Paul's advisers. Henry Cooper had endorsed the product successfully for years, but they perceived he was now of a different generation to those at whom it was aimed. Sales of the product had declined and they saw Paul as a natural successor. After a series of meetings he signed an agreement to advertise Brut on television and through the media generally. A press launch had been arranged for 18 September to bring the good news to the great British public. Paul was shown a script of what Brut wanted him to say. He just laughed it off, confident that whatever he said off the cuff would be far more effective than any words that could be put into his mouth. It was an unmitigated disaster.

'How long have you been using Brut, Paul?' somebody asked.

'I don't.'

'What aftershave do you use?'

'None. They bring me out in a rash.'

Brut and Gazza got the headlines the next day, but for all the wrong reasons. But the headlines and Gazza were seemingly permanent bedfellows. He took a Geordie girl called Heidi Shepherd out to dinner once. She was local born, the daughter of Freddie Shepherd, a successful scrap-dealer. Somebody at the restaurant decided to phone a newspaper and by Sunday every tabloid was suggesting this was the great romance of the twentieth century. Whether or not they ever wanted to meet again the pressure on the poor girl made that impossible. The papers even tracked down Heidi's former boyfriend to see how he felt about 'losing her to Gazza'.

Paul never forgot his old loyalties. John Hall was trying to take over Newcastle United and, although he is one of life's natural gentlemen, he is also not one to take defeat easily. To raise funds, Newcastle, deeply in debt, had sought to go the Tottenham route and float the company that owned the club. Paul was asked if he would go up to Newcastle for Hall and launch the appeal. He readily agreed to do it for nothing and at the Metro Centre there was, unfortunately, more attention on Paul than on the shares. It was, with hindsight, the wrong time. Newcastle were fifteenth in the Second Division and looking as if they'd struggle to stay there, let alone get back to the First. Paul did his best but the failure of the share offer at the time at least demonstrated that both Gascoigne and Hall were only human.

After the launch there was a lunch at a smart Newcastle hotel. One of Hall's associates had the misfortune to sit next to Gazza, a mistake when Paul has an audience. The man went off to make a phone call and returned to tuck into his custard trifle dessert, which had by now been generously laced with pepper. As he spluttered Paul just sat innocently staring into space as if he could not have had anything to do with it in a million years. Paul's services on this occasion may have come free, but there was always going to be a price.

On Sunday 4 November third-placed Spurs played the leaders, Liverpool, at home in front of a sell-out 35,000 crowd, which despite the match being televised live was to prove their biggest gate of the season. The media as ever had built the game up out of all proportion, calling it 'The Championship Decider' – and this in November with eleven matches played out of thirty-eight. Paul was incredibly hyped up and Kenny Dalglish, then the Liverpool manager, was intelligent enough to pick his team accordingly, choosing David Burrows to do a man-to-man marking job. He did it to such good effect that Paul's frustration finally erupted into violence when he lashed out at Burrows and was fortunate not to be sent off. Spurs lost 3–1, their first defeat of the season, leaving Paul and his team-mates to bemoan their fate, and Paul to nurse a bloody nose, courtesy of a collision with Steve McMahon.

On the following Wednesday Paul had two commitments, neither of which was going to help pay his mortgage. He'd been invited to be one of the star celebrity guests at the Champion Children of the Year awards in aid of Barnardo's to be held at the Savoy Hotel. What had particularly excited him was that the awards were to be made by HRH the Princess of Wales, Diana. Paul had always had a soft spot for the Princess and was happy to accept the Barnardo's invitation. Renée Menir was shocked to receive a telephone call from Buckingham Palace. The message was cold and crystal-clear: 'Hands Off Diana'. Any repetition of the Thatcher cuddle would not be welcomed, and generally speaking it would be preferable if Paul not only kept his distance from the Princess, but was not even in the same room as her.

As it happened they need not have bothered. Paul had to go training first and then had a crisis – he'd forgotten to bring a suit. Renée was well used to the situation and not only had his suit size but details of his requirements for shirts and shoes. She raced out to buy him a couple of new suits to add to the Moss Bros dimensions of his wardrobe. Paul turned up, suited, in the middle of the lunch, with Diana already on the podium. His reception committee consisted of a gaggle of journalists who had been leaked the story of Paul and the Princess. Paul took refuge in a bedroom, kindly and thoughtfully provided free of charge by an understanding management accustomed over the years to the demands of movie and pop stars. For them a sporting star was a novelty but they saw no reason to treat him any differently.

In the room overlooking the Thames, now alone with his advisers, Paul burst into tears. He simply couldn't understand why the Palace were so concerned. 'What do they think I am? Some kind of thug?' He was deeply hurt, refused to be photographed with his *Spitting Image* puppet, and had to be persuaded to continue with his other engagement for the day. Anybody peering into the room would have seen a frightened, tear-stained boy totally unable to cope with the world around him. Gradually he brightened up enough to be smuggled out of the back entrance to a waiting car.

Every personality waits for the call to switch on the Christmas lights in Regent Street, and this year Paul had been an obvious choice. He arrived in a limousine at the rear entrance to Liberty's store, where a crowd of young girls had gathered, pushing forward in a frightening surge, and was taken up to the reception area behind the balcony upon which the ceremony was to take place. The room was smoky and crowded and he was shaken by his greeting and traumatized by his day. Nearly five months on from his tumultuous welcome at Luton and he still could not get used to it, still could not shake off his fear of crowds in enclosed spaces. Looking for air he went out on to the balcony. The throng on the opposite pavement was already six or seven deep, and as he was spotted a buzz went through them. Paul waved and they waved back. A cry went up from the street, a cry from female throats who had doubtless bought Paul's record to enable it to make its chart entry the following week. 'Gazza, Gazza, show us your chest.'

Paul grinned. This was much better, this was his kind of audience, he'd let them see what Diana had missed. Unbuttoning his shirt he flashed his torso at the crowd, oblivious to the freezing conditions. The screams got louder and Mel Stein encouraged him to do it again. Paul repeated the exercise some half a dozen times with similar results, then became bored. Within minutes, to the consternation of the organizers of the event, he had vanished. He'd clambered out on to the neighbouring balcony and was happily toying with the electronic equipment, risking a fall of several hundred feet against the alternative of electrocution.

By 6.45 when the lights were to be switched on, Paul with the help of a few drinks was totally relaxed and accepted the adoration of the crowd with all the panache of a Roman emperor receiving his due tributes. In the course of one short day, Stein had seen Paul Gascoigne, the working-class kid, hurt and reduced to tears, and then Gazza, the pop star, the property of his fans, flaunting himself without restraint. Where did the dividing line begin or end? Did even the young footballer know the answer to that question?

A week is a long time in football, and there were only six days between the Liverpool defeat and the visit of Wimbledon to White Hart Lane. A story had broken in the press that an unnamed Italian club had bid £7 million for Gazza. Given what was to follow it is a little difficult to surmise from where exactly the story emanated. Was it just a wild stab in the dark or was it more likely that the source was an agent called Majid Mohamed? There is no doubt that Mohamed was trying to do business in Italy, and indeed in February 1991 he attempted to involve himself in the Lazio deal. But at some time prior to that, perhaps even as early as November, he'd approached Scholar and put in an offer on behalf of an anonymous Italian club for Gascoigne and Lineker. Scholar had rejected it out of hand, and as far as Paul himself was concerned he was totally unaffected by the newspaper rumours and turned on a match-winning display in Tottenham's 4–2 defeat of Wimbledon. His old conflicts with Vinny Jones were forgotten as he faced up to a new-look Wimbledon side trying to play football and live down their long-ball image.

A few days later Paul's future shifted to the international arena as on 14 November England had a crucial European Championship qualifier against the Republic of Ireland. Graham Taylor had two victories under his belt against Hungary and Poland, both achieved without conceding a goal. Ireland too had started well, having beaten Turkey 5–0 to add to the euphoria of their quarter-final position in Italy. Jack Charlton had already proved his raggle-taggle side could match the best in the world by playing to a system they could understand and achieve. He also understood Gascoigne and no doubt felt he'd kept him relatively subdued in the group match in Cagliari.

Taylor still appeared to be keeping faith with the Robson school, but there was at least one interesting name in the squad he chose to travel to Dublin. Gordon Cowans had last played for England back in 1986 against the USSR when he'd been a midfielder for Aston Villa, but in 1990 at 32 years of age he must have felt his international future was limited. The night before the match Paul was in a terrible state, his face red, his eyes puffy. Taylor had told him that he would not be playing and that Cowans, of all people, was taking his place. He was lying on his bed in despair, as if his international career was at an end. He'd taken enormous pride in making the national side, and not only had that pride been hurt but tomorrow the pain would be exposed to the whole footballing world.

'Look, Gazza, it's only one game. There'll be lots of other chances for you,' Chris Waddle said, at that stage sure of his own place. Beardsley joined them (probably because nobody but the two other Geordies could understand a word Peter was saying) and sat on the bed to watch himself on *A Question of Sport*. Gazza's humour began to return; 'I don't know how you can bear to watch yourself, Beardo.' Players drifted in and out, but as his audience finally disappeared Paul's mood of despondency returned. He lay on the bed, unusually still for him, inconsolable, and the following day the papers were left to speculate on the reason for his omission.

In fact the truth never came out. 'It was only the third time I'd met him and he turned up in a state,' Taylor recalls, 'telling me a long and largely incomprehensible story about making a hole in his neighbour's fence and wanting to escape *them*. I'd also heard on the football grapevine that if he'd played he wouldn't last on the pitch for more than twenty minutes. I decided he wasn't in the right mental state and that we could beat the Irish without him. I got Bryan Robson to have a word and by the time we got on the plane Paul sat beside me and told me he understood.' Was this the start of the paranoia and decline that would take nearly four anguished years to fester and finally cast a long dark shadow over the sunny personality that won over almost everybody who was exposed to it?

It was, in fact, to be the only time that Taylor did not select Paul when he was available. Waddle also had to pull out at the last minute when a knock he'd taken on the leg during training suddenly blew up. Thus when Taylor announced his team Cowans was in for Gazza and McMahon for Waddle. Nobody seemed to believe, or wanted to believe, that Waddle's injury was genuine:

as far as they were concerned Taylor had just ditched two flair players who he did not believe were up to what was likely to be a tough and physical battle. As it was they were well out of a dreadful match, played on a pitch that would have been criticized in the English Fourth Division. In wind and rain the teams slugged out a 1–1 draw. The honeymoon was over and to the very end of Taylor's period of control, whenever the papers sought to create or comment upon any alleged rift between Taylor and Gascoigne they would still refer back to his Dublin omission.

Throughout November, some five months after Italia '90, the headline writers would have been virtually unemployed without Gazza. Even television's *This Week*, normally more concerned with heavyweight political matters, decided to dedicate a whole programme to him. It was time for his advisers to step back and look at Paul as others saw him. There were some interesting comparisons. Ian Botham's advice was perhaps the most pertinent as the comparisons between the two sportsmen were irresistible. 'You become a target. If you do well, then you become open prey. The following day it can be just the opposite. I've stopped reading the papers, good or bad.'

Paul accepted that advice, and just as Ian had become involved in charity by his Leukaemia Research walks, so Paul established the Paul Gascoigne Charitable Trust. He was modestly grateful for everything that was happening to him. 'I know I'm only getting this because I love football. If I stop loving it, everything will disappear. Football's my life.'

It was Dennis Tuohy, the presenter, who best summed up the situation. 'How long before the music stops? Impossible to say. The heartbeat that gives life to Paul Gascoigne Unlimited is the heartbeat of Paul Gascoigne the Footballer. As long as he does it on the field why shouldn't he continue? He's no longer just the kid that cried but images, shimmering pictures, not a statistic. He can cause a deep intake of breath at the bar twenty years later.'

As the winter set in Tottenham's autumn form began to fall away like the leaves on the trees, and it was no coincidence that Paul, too, began to struggle. On the surface everything seemed set fair for the run up to Christmas, with only one defeat in eighteen matches, but the manner of the last few successes had not been convincing, and there were unsettling rumours of a joint Real Madrid bid for Venables and Gascoigne to ease Tottenham's financial worries.

December had its bright moments, with Paul collecting the most prestigious award for any British sportsman or woman, the BBC Sports Personality of the Year. Voted upon by the viewing public, it was an enormous endorsement of his personality as he won by a landslide from Stephen Hendry in second place and Graham Gooch in third. It fell to another Geordie, Bobby Charlton, to make the award and he spoke, with obvious sincerity, of the pride that England had taken in the performance of their team in Italy and in particular their receipt of the Fair Play Award. He then made a slight gaffe by suggesting that he wanted to 'nominate' Paul for the award, rather than present it to him. 'Aye, aye, I thought, it's a bit late for that. What happens if he doesn't get anybody to second him?'

Gazza took the award with unexpected modesty, as if he himself felt that he should have done more to get there, and as he made his speech the tears once more were rising in his eyes. 'I'm speechless really. I'm so pleased and honoured, to get this from such a great man as Bobby . . .' he threw a backward glance, gave a half-grin ' . . . I was going to say Jackie. I haven't won much in the game as yet, but what I have won is a World Cup medal and I'm very proud of that. We helped to put football back on the map in this country . . .'

It was a speech he'd written himself and it came straight from the heart. If anybody watching was waiting for him to embarrass himself they were sorely disappointed, and as the cameras closed in on him he kissed the trophy and finally broke into a smile. Gazza was forgotten and he was once again the little boy next door who'd just been given a sweet. If his tears had won the nation over in June, in December it was his smile.

But on the field the *attitudes* in English football were getting him down. 'Whatever we did wasn't good enough for some of the journalists. I kept thinking how beautiful the game had been in Italy, and what it had been like to get up to sunshine every day.' He was booked yet again against Manchester City in a 1–2 defeat, giving rise to further speculation about his temperament and how he would fare if he went abroad. He accepted the booking, but what he could not accept was an allegation that he had sworn at a young autograph hunter as he and Gary Lineker made their way to the team coach. 'I always try to sign an autograph if it's possible, but on that day there was an enormous mob and if I remember correctly this kid had his book or programme knocked out of his hands. Somebody may have sworn, but it wasn't me and indeed I stopped to help him pick it up. But if somebody heard a swear-word and I was in the neighbourhood, you could bet your life I'd get blamed.'

The cynicism was already beginning to take root amidst the natural love of life.

By 23 December there was even more news to keep the press boys happy. Venables now appeared to be making a bid for the club with the help of an unknown backer. Publicly Venables neither confirmed nor denied the rumours, and indeed it was not until early March that he introduced a certain Larry Gillick to Scholar.

In a 2–0 defeat at Coventry on Boxing Day Paul aggravated the hernia problem that had been niggling at him for weeks, and which also kept him out of the 3-0 thrashing by Southampton three days later. At that stage he was not the best of patients. He felt a mixture of helplessness, anger and frustration as he sat and watched. With his glorious year drawing to an end he could little imagine how many games he would be forced to watch over the long, bleak months ahead.

15

'YOU WOULDN'T WANT THAT TALENT TO BE LOST TO ENGLAND.'

For Paul 1990 had been incredible. Chaotic, the sort of success story that only features in novels and Boy's Own comic books. His love affair with the British sporting public had been a Mills and Boon of football. He had been built up by the press and public alike to such dizzy heights that he was terrified to look down. But it had to end somewhere.

Tottenham's bankers had made it clear that the club must appoint a full-time executive chairman acceptable to themselves. With an overdraft of £10 million who could blame them? The name of Nat Solomon was eventually put forward. He was a popular figure in the City, a neat, dapper man with impeccable manners, a former public company chairman; but perhaps more important than that he was a fervent Tottenham supporter. Within a few days of his meeting Scholar in the first week of January, Solomon's appointment was made public.

The New Year's Day match against Manchester United was once again live on television, as if the cameras were scared to miss any twist or turn in the soap drama that was Paul's life. Spurs had been playing attractive football and catching the public imagination before they lost their way, whilst United were always value for money. Spurs took the lead with a penalty and it looked for a while as if they were back on the right lines but before half-time they conceded a penalty themselves and the teams went in for the break on level terms. Then at the start of the second half Paul began to show off his skills and Tottenham were moving confidently forward in search of the winner. Paul put Lineker through with a precision pass but he was tackled by Brian McClair and the whole home crowd screamed for a penalty. Even Lineker, who had never received a booking in his life, was complaining to the referee, Kit Callow. Paul, unfortunately, was the most vociferous, and as Callow waved him away Paul swore at *himself* in temper. To this day he maintains his comments were not addressed to the referee, but in front of 30,000 spectators in the ground and 10 million viewers in England alone, Paul Gascoigne, hero of Italy, the BBC Sports Personality of the Year, received a red card and was sent off for the first time in his Tottenham career. It was a long, lonely walk to the tunnel for The Man Who Fell To Earth.

With Spurs down to ten men McClair grabbed a last-minute winner for United and Tottenham tumbled to sixth place in the League, the highest they were to be for the rest of the season. The vultures were waiting and they smelled blood. 'Gazza's Shame' was one of the mildest headlines. Paul was driven to apologize to his team-mates, both privately in the agony of the post-match dressing-room, and publicly in the press. 'I let myself down and the rest of the lads. I'm sorry.'

Venables tried to come to his rescue, stating he'd been the victim of two bad fouls where the referee had done nothing, and pointing out that swearing was common on the pitch. The football pundits happily wrote Spurs off for the title and dug in for a long, hard winter of discontent. The troubles off the pitch, it was alleged, had finally come home to roost on it. The growing murmurs of the transfer speculation and his commercial activities had also got to Gascoigne.

It did not take long for the smile to be restored to his face. He still had the FA Cup to look forward to – a trip to the seaside, the first step on the path that would take him to Wembley – and tragedy. But on 5 January Blackpool resembled Antarctica. The pitch was muddy, the rain freezing, the wind a cold howling gale, churning the sea to a fury before sweeping across Bloomfield Road. Paul Stewart returned to his old club, scoring the only goal. Wherever Gazza went two or three Blackpool players would follow, yet despite their close attention he still stamped his own inimitable class upon the game. The players, the board, the manager and the creditors all breathed an enormous sigh of relief that the first hurdle towards a lucrative Cup run had been safely negotiated, and were even happier when Fourth Division Oxford were drawn out of the hat to visit Tottenham in the fourth round. As the team coach made its way back from Blackpool, Paul summed it all up when, on sighting a night club called 'Rumours', he said, 'Let's face it, there's plenty of those going about Spurs at the moment.'

Tottenham's public line, via Scholar, was that Gazza was not officially for sale, that he did not want to sell him, and that if he were sold, then he, Scholar, would also leave. In his autobiography, *Behind Closed Doors*, Scholar discloses that he did not know at the time that a pre-condition to the appointment of Nat Solomon was that Gascoigne had to be sold; but from the day of his arrival the potential sale of Paul was an item that featured regularly on board-meeting agendas.

Although Scholar had resigned as a member of the public company board after the Maxwell problems, he was still invited to attend some meetings and was still a director of the football club. On 15 January, three days after a goalless local derby with Arsenal, Scholar was told by a fellow director that if he wouldn't go along with preliminary steps on the sale of Gazza, then his resignation would also be demanded from the football club board. It was then that Scholar appears to have conceived the idea of introducing Dennis Roach to handle the sale, in the knowledge that at the time Stein and Lazarus had fallen out with him and would not even sit in the same room. Scholar's action might be regarded as strange, looked at objectively. He was after all a director of the company, and was from the inside hoping to sabotage a majority decision of the rest of his board; but that was always Scholar's problem. He thought like a fan and not like a director.

Whatever might have been the case, without any information being given to Paul and his advisers, without any discussion as to whether or not Paul wanted to leave Tottenham, the club, through Roach, made plans to sell the player. It was outrageous. If Paul *had* been asked at the time he would have said he did not want to leave, for despite everything he was very happy. He had his house, he had his friends down regularly from Newcastle, he had good social mates at the club, and he'd regularly go fishing with the likes of Paul Allen. The fact that there had been no prior consultation with him was one of the prime reasons for Paul's decision to leave. Whilst the belief that he was saving Spurs was high on his list of priorities, there is no doubt that his view of Lazio would have been seen through very differently coloured glasses had Tottenham, as his employer, behaved in a gentlemanly manner. If a player whilst under contract talks to another club without the permission of his present club, then that is a breach of the League Rules. So why should it be any different when a club talks to another club about their player without his permission?

By the middle of the week the papers had other news of which to write. On the eve of the Rumbelows Cup tie against Chelsea, for which Paul was suspended, the

Evening Standard reported a statement by Nat Solomon that Gascoigne 'might' be sold. The blow to the supporters was obviously going to be given to them softly. The tie was drawn and Paul returned to the fray for the replay very much fired up, but neither he nor the team in any way started to play, and Chelsea romped home easy 3–0 winners. Venables was, to say the least, upset and told the team what he thought of their performance, or lack of it, in no uncertain terms.

With Spurs out of the title race and out of the Rumbelows Cup (two of the three routes to Europe and potential financial safety) Paul did not think it the moment to tell them that his groin was really giving him cause for concern. He took off for a few days at a health farm, but inevitably his presence was leaked to the press who hazarded a variety of guesses at the reason for his stay – he was being treated for an injury, having a secret operation, even that he was drying out from a drink problem. It was all fantasy.

It soon became apparent that there was no way a double hernia operation could be avoided. It was just a question of timing, and what was decided for him was that Paul would keep match fit by training as hard as it was safe to do, play in the occasional league game to sharpen him up, and go all out for glory in the Cup with pain-killing injections. If Paul had been an animal it is likely that the RSPCA would have come to his rescue. Immediately before the Oxford cup match Paul filmed his Soccer School series for Channel 4, to be produced by Neil Duncanson of Chrysalis and then made into a video. Involving a mixture of children of both sexes and aged from 10 to 15, Paul was very keen on the concept as he not only liked working with children, but it gave him the chance, once again, to play at Wembley where the series was to be filmed. Everybody involved breathed a sigh of relief when Paul came through it without serious injury, particularly as it was virtually impossible to get him off the pitch once he started. It was when he began diving about to demonstrate his goal-keeping skills that he was forcibly removed from the field. He took one look at the proposed script, ignored it completely and ad-libbed his way through the whole programme like a seasoned professional broadcaster. Indeed, the way Paul handled the cameras sowed the seeds of the idea for Channel 4's Saturday morning Gazetta Football Italia in Duncanson's mind. The finest moment in the programme was when each of the children was allowed to pick up the FA Cup – when it came to Aron Lazarus (Len's son) he dropped the lid with a resounding clang.

There was no such fall in standards when Tottenham faced up to Oxford United in the fourth round of the Cup on 26 January. Paul had a superb match and Spurs were two up with goals from Mabbutt and Lineker; however, their complacency was jolted a little when the visitors pulled one back just before half-time. A Gazza effort seemed to put the match beyond Oxford. He robbed his own player in the shape of Fenwick, passed to Walsh, moved to receive the return pass, then, seemingly having gone too wide, scored brilliantly from the narrowest of angles. Still Oxford were not dead and came back to 3–2 before Paul scored his second four minutes from the end, a superb left-footer after a typical Gazza dummy. He just made it all seem so easy. It was the beautiful game played beautifully. Venables waxed lyrical about Paul to anybody who would listen, comparing him to Dave Mackay and Maradona, whilst Oxford's manager, Jim Smith, was similarly overwhelmed. 'We needed twelve men out there, but even if we'd put someone on him he'd still have done his own thing. He's a special player and you wouldn't want that talent to be lost to England.'

Yet the Oxford game was a catalyst in his move abroad. Forces were moving inexorably towards a sale that the player still neither dreamed of nor desired. Roach having touted him about Europe had achieved but one concrete lead and that one where the seeds had already been planted by the club president himself. Soon after the Oxford match Roach telephoned Scholar to tell him that Lazio of Rome were very interested, having been impressed not only by his World Cup performances but by his remarkable games for Tottenham in the Cup. A meeting was to be arranged for around the first week of February. Willingly or not Gascoigne was about to be sold.

16

'WHERE'S LAZIO?'

As far as Paul himself was concerned it all began with a phone call from Rome on the 28 February. Stein was told that a Mr Manzini was on the line about Paul Gascoigne. Just before Manzini, Scholar himself had called Stein. Information and questions were given and posed reluctantly.

'Paul wouldn't want to go abroad, would he?' Scholar had asked.

'Why?' Stein had queried. 'Do you know something specific?'

'No, not really. I wouldn't sell him anyway. You know that.'

'I think it's a bit too early to talk about Paul playing abroad. I'd like to wait another year or so, Stein commented, not knowing that he was, in time, to get his wish.

Within the game of verbal chess, what Scholar did not disclose was that he and Roach had already met a delegation from Lazio on 20 February at London's White House Hotel. In his autobiography Scholar says that he went unwillingly and quoted £10 million in the hope it would see them off. The Italians at that stage offered £5 million, but Scholar clearly thought they'd be back and presumably that was the reason for his call to Stein. The conversation had petered out into small talk although as soon as Stein got off the phone he called Lazarus to tell him he thought something was afoot. Indeed, on the same day as Manzini's call Alex Henderson of the *Sun* had called Stein to check out a story about AC Milan showing an interest.

Paul himself rang Stein and told him he'd been approached by a certain Jane Nottage, who had also heard transfer rumours in Italy. Nottage had worked as a liaison officer for Italia '90 and claimed to have a good inside knowledge of the mechanics of Italian football. Paul simply passed her number on to Stein and asked him to phone her. She seemed to think that Juventus would be the club to be most interested, but in any event Stein arranged a meeting with her to see whether there might be any interest in, or indeed any need for, her services.

By the time she actually came to visit Stein, he had completed his conversation with Manzini. Maurizio Manzini was an interesting character. He'd been a lifelong Lazio supporter, and although for many years he'd been employed by American Express, he'd given up his career and taken a substantial drop in salary just to be employed full-time with the club he adored. There could never have been a more devoted servant to the club. His official position was general manager although that covered an enormous range of sins, from shepherding the players in their hotels to sitting on the bench at matches with Dino Zoff, the coach, and signalling the numbers for any substitution.

Manzini told Stein that Lazio were very interested in Paul, had made a preliminary approach to Spurs and would like a confidential meeting. Stein and Lazarus were already going to Italy the following week to watch Chris Waddle play for Marseille in the European Cup quarter-final first leg against AC Milan. If the San Siro Stadium beckoned, then why not a quick diversion to Rome? They spoke to Nottage, who was still pressing her cause with dogged persistence, and when she agreed to be sworn to secrecy about the trip they were happy to take her with them as an interpreter. The three of them then planned a route that would take them first to Milan to see Waddle and then the match, followed by an overnight stay and a morning flight to Rome. There they had arranged a secret rendezvous with Manzini and the Lazio officials at the offices of an Italian carpet importer known to both of Paul's advisers. They were about to discover, however, that in Italy there is no such thing as a secret.

Even before they left London RTI television phoned Finers' office and asked Stein if Paul could be made available for a live TV chat show with Maradona and Ruud Gullit. The caller said that there was an enormous interest in Paul throughout Italy, particularly as he was about to play there!

They arrived in a cloudburst that actually threatened the match and Italy could rarely have seemed less welcoming. Yet, they did receive a warm welcome from the scores of journalists staying at their hotel, all of whom appeared to know Nottage. She seemed to be all for holding a press conference there and then. 'You have to deal differently with the Italian press. You can't charge for interviews, but you have to talk to them. They've got a lot of pages to fill,' she said referring to the many daily papers devoted entirely to sport, and largely to football.

Stein and Lazarus pointed out to anybody who asked that they were in Italy to watch Waddle, but none of their interrogators seemed very convinced. 'Which club is Gascoigne joining?' one persistent journalist asked, then answered his own question. 'We know it is Juventus.'

At the Marseille team hotel Bernard Tapie, the French club's president, was none too welcoming. He had not met Stein or Lazarus during the negotiations for

Waddle's transfer, and once told who his guests were, viewed them with caution, suspicious they might be negotiating the sale of Waddle to Italy. How the papers heard of the encounter is anybody's guess, but a few days later at least one of the tabloids reported that, rather than going to Italy, Paul was about to join up with his old friend Waddle in France, and Paul's advisers had already had one lengthy meeting with Tapie. Some length. The conversation consisted of 'Bonjour. Ça va?'

The Roman part of the trip began in some confusion. Stein, Lazarus and Nottage arrived at the carpet warehouse where their friend had thoughtfully laid on a buffet lunch. Nowhere could they have been more guaranteed of privacy and confidentiality. The friend was totally uninterested in football and had not even heard of Gascoigne. His warehouse was on the poor side of the city, the most unlikely venue for a high-power meeting of this nature. Yet when they arrived there was Manzini advising them that the president had arranged lunch for them in a restaurant in the centre of Rome, and the trio got into Manzini's car and sped off through the lunchtime traffic of the ancient city.

At the restaurant they were led through to a section at the rear and for the first time were brought face to face with the larger-than-life figure of Gian Marco Callieri. Callieri and his older brother George had lived and breathed Lazio, having acquired control a few years previously when it was at its lowest ebb, infamous in England for the street brawling of its players with Arsenal fans, and in Italy for the various scandals which had rocked the club under previous ownership. Callieri himself owned a powerful security company which numbered Madonna amongst its clients, and which not only provided security to visiting celebrities, but was responsible for the security in the Olympic Stadium itself. Callieri had seen Gascoigne play in the World Cup and had fallen in love with the young man's image. Like Martin Luther King, Callieri had 'dreamed a dream', and in it Paul Gascoigne wore the famous blue and white of Lazio. He had already spent millions on the club, was prepared to spend more, and Gazza was to be the spark to light the fire amongst the fanatical supporters, many of whom had become disaffected with the club over the years. For some little time Roma had been the dominant club in Rome and Callieri was determined to bring an end to that situation. Unfortunately George Callieri had died from cancer just a few weeks before, but Gian Marco had decided to make the rebirth of Lazio his memorial.

Manzini made the introductions – Callieri, Carlo Regalia, a grizzled ex-player who made an important contribution to the management team, and a notary called Giadoni, who was the spitting image of Harry H. Corbett. Seven people seated around a table adjoining an open restaurant, with waiters buzzing around or standing by listening to every word. It was hardly the most confidential of environments.

Callieri was a huge man, who'd played football himself and had obviously been schooled in the university of life. After a few minutes Stein whispered to Lazarus, 'He's just like Irving.' Later they both agreed that if Callieri and Scholar were ever to meet they would be immediate soulmates. That was not exactly how it was to pan out as no room was ever big enough to contain their two egos, and in any event, although Stein and Lazarus did not know it at the time, a meeting had already taken place.

Callieri seemed puzzled by the absence of Roach. Stein and Lazarus expressed surprise that his name was even being raised, given their difficulties in bringing themselves to talk to him. They told Callieri of their feelings, at which point he asked them why Tottenham had asked Roach to sell Gascoigne. Their mouths fell open in disbelief. Scholar was well aware of their feelings towards him. Callieri must be mistaken. No, Callieri assured them, Roach was a real player in the game, and rustling in his file he produced a letter which left both Stein and Lazarus dumbfounded. It was from Tottenham to Roach's company, authorizing him to seek a purchaser for Paul Gascoigne amongst European clubs, although stopping short of giving him any authority to conclude any deal. In other words he could seek, but he could not bind Tottenham. The two Englishmen were furious. They regarded the letter as an absolute betrayal of their relationship with Scholar.

What Callieri did not disclose was that he had not only already met with Scholar, but after that had had a further meeting with Solomon at the latter's office, with Roach and Scholar in attendance. There he'd felt he'd struck a deal, having improved his initial offer of £5 million to £7.2 million. As was so often to be the case throughout the long-running saga, there was an enormous gap between wish and fulfilment.

So as the men sat around the table, that Thursday 7 March 1991, not all the cards were on the table, nor did they fully comprehend that they held not just Gazza's destiny in their hands, but the future of Tottenham Hotspur Football Club. That first meeting reached no final conclusions. Stein and Lazarus agreed to report back to Paul the general impression they had gleaned about the club and its ambitions, while Callieri would see if he could pin Tottenham down to a written agreement as to price. If there was mutual progress then they would meet again with a view to discussing terms.

It was possibly the worst-kept secret of all time. The following day newspapers in Italy and England reported the meeting down to the fine details of who had actually been present. Manzini telephoned Stein very upset and accused Nottage of having told the Italian press. Stein expressed complete confidence in

Nottage, but Manzini did not seem to be satisfied and told Stein that they would not want her at any meetings where money was being discussed. Given her betrayal of Paul's privacy in writing her book about her year with Paul, it would appear that Callieri was a better judge of character than Stein.

Scholar was on the phone to Stein like a shot. 'Did you meet with Lazio in Rome yesterday?'

'Did you give Roach a letter of authority to sell Paul?'

Neither of them would admit anything to the other but clearly this was to be the start of a jockeying for position that would continue right up to the finishing line some eighteen months later.

Stein and Lazarus reported back to Paul on the meeting. 'Where's Lazio?' he asked. Neither of his advisers had been too sure of that either, until Manzini had explained that it was the area of Italy which contained Rome, a little like Manchester being part of Lancashire. They told Paul that Callieri was his number one fan and was probably prepared to pay a considerable sum of money to maintain that pole position. Paul seemed satisfied, although he did ask whether Juventus or AC Milan were interested. However, he made it clear there was no question of him leaving Spurs before the end of the season. He had good vibes about their FA Cup run and was most concerned he should not let down the fans.

Brian Woolnough in the *Sun* had no doubts on the situation. 'Gazza will go', he wrote on 9 March, quoting Stein as saying, 'Paul will play in Italy. There is no doubt about that. When, is up to Spurs. They have to agree a deal.'

Meanwhile Paul's groin was beginning to become a major problem, and nobody, whether it be Tottenham or Lazio, was going to want a player who couldn't play. Reluctantly he realized John Sheridan had done as much for him as he could and it was time to turn to the doctors. He agreed to enter the Princess Grace Hospital for what was to be the first of a seemingly endless series of visits.

There was still a whole world of football going on outside the enclosed world of restaurants, hotels and boardrooms. By the time Spurs had been drawn to play Portsmouth in the fifth round of the FA Cup on 16 February, Paul's injury was already such that any normal player would have cried off, but Tottenham's season was falling apart around their ears, and with the flood tide of their financial problems up beyond their eyebrows a good Cup run was vital for players, officials and supporters alike.

There was a collective sigh of relief when Spurs came safely through their potentially difficult match against Portsmouth, at Fratton Park, and again it was Paul, playing through the pain barrier, digging deep into his reserves of energy, who saw Tottenham home with two goals, the second a typical individual effort, after Pompey had gone ahead.

By the time Spurs had to play Notts County in the sixth round – a Sunday match for the benefit of television – Paul knew the 'when' of his operation. He was to go into hospital as soon as the final whistle blew. A double hernia had been diagnosed by the specialist and the idea was that if he had the operation performed immediately then, assuming Spurs won, there was a chance, given his extraordinary strength and speed of recovery, that he'd be fit for the semi-final.

The question must be asked as to whether Venables was expecting too much from Paul, and whether Tottenham as a whole was putting his whole future at stake in exchange for their own financial security. If that were so then Paul was a willing accomplice. The game plan from a very early stage of the season was to ease him through and the club had been assured there was no danger in playing. However, from Christmas

1990 Paul's football was shrouded in a grey mist of pain that at times bordered on agony. Despite the criticism he took in the press, which could easily have been deflected by the truth, he never once went public about his problems. It was all part of the game.

On the morning of the Notts County match the *News of the World* carried an article under the headline 'Lazio Chief Flies In For £7m Talks'. Callieri now admitted that talks had taken place with both the club's and the player's representatives, and that he was, 'counting on agreeing terms for Gascoigne to sign for us'.

From the kick-off on a grey afternoon, the pitch slippery under foot, it was obvious that Notts County were not going to have to cope with much running from Paul. Pushed up front, he was more a talisman than a participant. His midfield role abandoned, he looked for much of the game what he was – a man who had played too long with a serious injury.

Just before half-time it looked as if the Tottenham tactics were going to fail. County went ahead and Paul's main contribution had been a bruising conflict with Paul Harding, the County full-back. The papers next day made much of that encounter, showing full lurid illustrations of Gazza elbowing Harding in the face and causing an injury which required extensive treatment. 'I didn't mean to elbow the guy. I was just trying to get away from him.'

Six minutes into the second half Spurs equalized and then, fanning the dying embers of his strength, Paul scored a delightful winner. The crowd were ecstatic and if Paul had leapt in amongst them he would probably never have been seen again.

Stuart Jones in *The Times* on 11 March summed it up when he wrote the headline, 'Gascoigne Remains The Golden Asset', and then went on to say, 'Almost single-handedly he has led them along a lucrative path in the FA Cup to the semi-final.'

The rest of the papers were euphoric about Paul's performance and Stein had his office fax them across to Italy. Callieri's reaction was immediate. He could see the price rocketing and stated that, although his £7.2 million bid stood, he would pull out if other clubs became involved in a public auction.

Spurs were through to the semi-final, their bank manager was at bay temporarily and Paul was in a bed at the Princess Grace Hospital. There were five weeks between the sixth round and the semis. Whatever happened after the operation it was going to be tight. For the first time in the Gazza saga the press camped on the pavement opposite the hospital, zoom lenses aimed up at the window, hoping to catch a shot of the injured star. They did, in fact, start off by positioning themselves beneath the window, but a few well-aimed water bombs soon saw them beating a hasty retreat.

The hospital staff must have breathed a collective sigh of relief when Paul was discharged. As soon as the operation was over his hyperactivity triumphed over the effect of the anaesthetic. Chrysalis delivered to him a whole stock of football videos, including 'Gazza's Soccer School' which was just about to be released. Paul persuaded the hospital to slot it into their central video system, which meant it was compulsory viewing for everybody else in the hospital tuned to the video channel. Impatient as ever, Gazza made them interrupt the film then showing, Eddie Murphy's *The Golden Child*, right in the middle so that he could have his own première screening. This meant the rest of the patients suddenly found the black Hollywood star dissolve into a shot of a crew-cut Geordie teaching a bunch of kids how to take free kicks at Wembley. Some of them are probably still trying to work out the plot of what had become a very avant-garde movie.

Paul's departure from hospital was carefully planned. John Coberman, the ultimate Spurs fan and soccer groupie extraordinaire, a man with a heart of gold who would walk through fire for Paul, and often did, was sent into the front line. Disguised as Paul he dashed into a large waiting car, pursued by hordes of photographers, whilst Paul himself quietly sneaked out of the back with his father. As he said good-bye to the staff he had no idea how swiftly he was to resume their acquaintance.

After his few days in hospital there was just over a month to go to the semi-final. At the time Tottenham employed two full-time, top-class club physiotherapists in the shapes of Dave Butler and John Sheridan. When it came to match-day injuries it was Butler who ran on to the field, but Sheridan's quiet and unassuming manner with the long-term injured at the Mill Hill training ground was equally important.

Sheridan is an ex-sailor, softly spoken, well man-nered, pipe-smoking, with a noticeable limp that Gazza mimicked to perfection by the time Sheridan had fin-ished with him. Yet the gentle exterior hides a grim determination that dares any patient to ignore his advice and sometimes agonizing therapy. The therapy he gave Paul for his groin strain was simple compared with the treatment he was later to give him, but thereafter it was down to Paul's natural powers of recovery. He therefore took himself off, quite happily, to the South of France to stay with the Waddles. Behind him he left tumult and intrigue.

Lazio pressed on apace with their negotiations. Scho-lar now openly admitted Spurs were talking to the Italians, although he denied any firm agreement had been entered into, and still maintained that if there was to be a sale of Gascoigne it would not be his decision. Both Stein and Lazarus made it absolutely clear to him that there was no point in agreeing *anything* with Lazio until Tottenham had agreed the terms with Paul upon which he was prepared to leave the club. He had a contract with Spurs, it worked both ways, and it was they who wanted to sell him.

These 'exit terms' or 'demands' as Tottenham described them, became a matter of great controversy as Spurs tried to paint a picture of a greedy footballer throwing a spanner in the works of a concluded deal, a player holding to ransom a club which had treated him generously. Nothing could have been further from the truth. Scholar ducked the issue by delaying any substantive negotiations with Stein or Lazarus, although it may well be it was no longer within his power to agree these in any event. He knew full well the bank were expecting an agreed net payment, but it appeared he was hoping that Lazio would give Paul such a remunerative contract that he'd forget all about Spurs' obligations. Either that or Micawber-like he was praying something would turn up to get Spurs out of the hole and make the sale of Paul avoidable.

Paul's injury problem in no way affected Lazio's interest in him, and Stein and Lazarus were invited to another meeting in Rome on 17-18 March. Lazio were clearly out to impress them. They were met at the airport by Gianni Zeqireya, their first encounter with 'Johnny', the gentle giant who was to become such an integral part of Paul's life. He had a senior position with Callieri's security company, and one look at him left one in no doubt as to the reason why. It was also the English pair's first experience of his driving, which swung wildly between the irrational and the insane. Gianni stressed that their visit was to be treated as highly confidential, yet taking them first to a public restaurant for lunch and then flaunting them around the Olympic Stadium before the Lazio-Cagliari match did not seem to place confidentiality very high on the list of priorities. The fans certainly knew they were there as the famous Curva carried a huge picture of an English beer mug and placards proclaiming one word, 'Gazza' .

It is one of life's little tricks that Paul's nickname should actually be a real Italian word meaning, of all things, 'Magpie', the nickname of Newcastle United. It certainly did no harm to the love affair between Paul and the Lazio fans that was about to start. When the team ran on to the pitch, the spectators miraculously orchestrated a giant flag in Lazio colours, simply by waving individual favours in rehearsed positions. Stein turned to Lazarus. 'I thought the Geordie supporters were special, but this is something else. Paul could be a hero here.'

In the pre-Gazza days of 1990/1 the patience of the Lazio faithful had been sorely tested. In almost every match they would lead, only to surrender a point in the closing minutes. The game against Cagliari was no different, and having been 1-0 up, the visitors equalized with two minutes to go.

It was not until nearly 9 p.m. that Callieri finally met Paul's representatives at the Hassler Hotel. He got straight down to business, asking what it would take to bring Paul to Lazio. Stein and Lazarus explained that Paul had not yet discussed, let alone agreed, any exit terms with Tottenham and therefore any agreement reached with Lazio would have to be conditional upon that. Callieri was as dismissive of that problem as Scholar and simply waved his hands, carving the air like joints of meat. Had Lazio reached an agreement with Tottenham? Again Callieri was dismissive. They would. Tottenham were being difficult, even greedy, but it would be resolved. Would the English gentlemen please get on with their list of requirements. It had been a long day and he would like to get to bed.

The Italians were coy about making an offer. Stein and Lazarus had anticipated this and had decided to go for broke, on the basis that they could always go down but they couldn't go up. It was Newcastle all over again as they saw the variety of emotions flitting across Callieri's expressive face – disbelief, amusement, annoyance, frustration, and perhaps a flicker of admiration. Finally Callieri said quite bluntly that what had been asked for was quite impossible; Paul would be earning more than Maradona, more than any other player, Italian or foreign, had ever earned in Italy.

Callieri, Regalia and Manzini adjourned for private discussions. Stein and Lazarus felt on firm ground. They had decided that Callieri was desperate to get Paul and had dug himself into a deep hole by publicly declaring he would bring Paul to the club, whatever might be the cost. As the night wore on Stein and Lazarus held firm, gradually the gap narrowed, Callieri's eyes began to droop and it was finally agreed that they would adjourn until the morning.

It was during this first meeting that a note of high comedy was reached in relation to a trout farm. When the whole issue had been discussed with Paul, they'd asked him whether there was anything in particular that he wanted. He told them that he was happy to leave the financial arrangements to them, but he'd like a house with some private fishing facilities, as well as some English company for the duration of his stay. Callieri had showed utter disbelief when the question of fishing had been raised; there was no trout fishing in Rome, he said. Very well, let's create some, was the reply, albeit tongue in cheek. Paul's house is to be in grounds sufficiently large for him to install a trout farm where he can fish to his heart's content and be sure of a catch. Callieri, to their astonishment, agreed. The trout farm was to be an item in the contract.

As far as company was concerned, eventually an idea instigated by Paul began to develop. One of his idols and mentors from his Newcastle days, Glenn Roeder, appeared to be coming to the end of his playing career at Watford. His first-team appearances were infrequent and he had been made reserve team manager, responsible for bringing through youngsters into the senior side. Paul's suggestion was that he and his family should accompany him to Italy, and serve not only as English-speaking company but as a ready-made family and calming influence. In every way it was perfect. Lazio needed very little persuasion. However, Roeder himself was not prepared to come out just to baby-sit Paul. He saw an opportunity for himself to learn the game at the highest level in preparation for managerial responsibilities.

Callieri, meanwhile, had never met Paul and wanted that omission rectified as soon as possible. Stein and Lazarus felt there ought to be some agreement between club and player in principle, as well as agreement between Spurs and Lazio, before such a meeting took place. Callieri was both impatient and insistent; he was like a child banging on the door of the sweet shop with his 10p piece in his hand some five minutes before opening time. It was agreed that the parties would meet the following day. If that went well, then while Paul was in France with Waddle he would be going to watch the return leg of the Marseille-AC Milan European Championship quarter-final. With an Italian team involved that would be a perfect excuse for Callieri to be in France. Stein and Lazarus had been contemplating a trip to visit Waddle and watch the match and this was also reason enough for them to firm up the arrangement.

The whole cloak of secrecy that Lazio had wanted thrown about the transaction had been blasted away. Everybody in Rome seemed to know that the meeting was taking place and it was hard to see how, short of a fatal accident, Callieri could not finalize the transaction. He'd promised the fans Gazza and now he had to deliver.

The meeting began with a formal exchange of compliments in the bright spring sunshine on the terrace of the hotel. The entrance hall began to fill with journalists as the news of the venue of the 'secret' meeting began to spread. By lunchtime in the panoramic rooftop restaurant, there were still some financial differences but all the important points of principle had been agreed. Over their pasta the parties tried to bridge the gap. Stein put it to Callieri that they should try and meet half-way, to which Callieri replied with a broad grin, 'Ah, but we started in the cellar and you started on the moon.'

Callieri, not unreasonably, wanted to hear from Paul's own mouth that he, in turn, really wanted to play for Lazio. Consequently it was agreed that the parties would all meet up again on 20 March, just two days later. The bandwagon was rolling and there was no time for anybody to get off.

17

'SURELY HE'S NOT GOING TO SHOOT FROM THERE?'

Back in England the papers seemed to know more about the meeting than the participants themselves. The *Mirror* claimed that Paul was to receive a £1 million signing-on fee and a five-year contract worth a basic £2 million tax free. The *Sun* went even further as they engaged the services of three of their leading writers, Woolnough, Richardson and Samuel. Clearly three heads were better than one as they trumpeted that Paul was to get £6.5 million from a six-year deal, whilst Spurs were to receive £8.5m. The one consistent theme running through the stories was that Callieri was already declaring he had got his man.

Scholar phoned Stein. He sounded anxious and more than a little rattled. 'If, and I say if, we were prepared to sell Paul, how quickly can you finalize the deal with Lazio?' It was the first time Scholar had actually admitted the reality of the situation, namely that Spurs' financial situation was so dire that without the income from the sale of Paul the club might well fold.

The lawyer was a little reticent. 'We're well down the line with Lazio, but there's still a lot to do. We're meeting them again next week. But I've got to make two things clear. Paul won't leave Spurs while they're still in the Cup and he won't sign for Lazio until we've agreed our exit terms.'

Scholar did not see that as a problem, but what was a problem was that he rarely listened because his mind was always on what he was going to say next. Events had been moving swiftly, perhaps too swiftly as far as Scholar and Tottenham supporters were concerned. On 26 February at their long-postponed AGM they had disclosed a financial position that was critical. The shareholders were told that the sale of *both* Gascoigne and Lineker could not be ruled out if that would bring in £10 million.

On 13 March Terry Venables had declared his intention of bidding for the club. The shares of Tottenham Hotspur Plc had been suspended after the Maxwell débâcle and Scholar had little room in which to manoeuvre. The Tottenham supporters themselves were becoming disenchanted. Stein and Lazarus could go nowhere socially without being berated by angry fans. Lazarus in particular got the rough end of the stick as he was an Arsenal supporter.

For Paul to leave was unthinkable for the hard-line Spurs supporters. Yet the thought was fast becoming reality, not least of all for Paul himself. He had taken his long-suffering father and one of his friends off to France. Using the Waddles' house as his base Paul conquered the Marseille region. Waddle's favourite watering hole was the Café de Paris run by two young Armenians, David and Marcel, both of whom lived and breathed Olympique de Marseille. It had taken Waddle the best part of a year to settle in France, but it took Paul all of five minutes, and that without any attempt at the language.

'He took up court at the Café de Paris,' Waddle recalls. 'David and Marcel were a couple of quiet lads, wrapped up with working for their parents. Gazza got them drinking concoctions they'd never heard of, and they had been running a bar for years. At 6 a.m. one morning David was still flat out from Gazza's attentions the night before. The pair of them had never drunk before Paul got at them, and in fifteen hours with Gazza they'd probably consumed more alcohol than in their entire lifetimes. Their mother found the younger one still flat out in the morning and screamed "Look at my baby", but Gazza just stood there laughing his head off.'

On 20 March, the day of the match, Callieri and Regalia arrived in the afternoon, unfortunately without Manzini, their normal translator. Stein, Lazarus and Callieri conversed in French as best they could and then everybody withdrew to the garden, leaving Callieri and Paul without a common language between them. It did not seem a problem as in pidgin English Callieri told Paul how everybody in Rome was looking forward to seeing him. The Englishman replied slowly, in the odd lilting Geordie accent he adopted when speaking English to foreigners, professing his desire to pull on the blue shirt with which he'd been presented. Although neither could really have understood very much, the body language obviously spoke volumes. The meeting ended with a huge embrace between the two men, and Paul saying, 'I think he fancies me.'

The financial bargains that had been knocked out by his advisers had now become an emotional bond, a bond so strong that it would survive all the traumas that lay ahead. Callieri and Regalia went off to watch the match well pleased with the man they now regarded in all respects as their player, leaving Stein and Lazarus to prepare and submit some Heads of Agreement as soon as possible.

Paul arrived at the ground simultaneously with the Marseille team coach. The photographers moved in, not to snap the team but to grab pictures of Paul. With his close-cropped hair, his smart brown jacket on top of a dazzling white leisure shirt, he looked every inch the star as he happily smiled at the mob milling around him. Chris Waddle appeared mildly embarrassed. As Paul wished him good luck all Waddle could find to say was, 'Behave yourself, Gazza, I have to live here.'

Paul was taken to a VIP box in the tightly packed, slightly old-fashioned stadium and there to his surprise met up with Graham Taylor and Lawrie McMenemy, who'd come to watch Waddle. Paul took a glass of champagne into the box and McMenemy promptly removed it from his hand. 'There's long range cameras out there. Can you imagine what they'd make of you sitting boozing alongside the England managers?'

Waddle scored a wonderful goal to put Marseille one up after 74 minutes, and then as a reward was rabbit-punched on the back of the head by one of the Milan players. As soon as he was brought round he was fouled again. Like a punch-drunk boxer he staggered to his feet, headed the ball and went down for a third time. Perhaps Marseille should have thrown in the towel for him, but he rose yet again to set off on a long mazy run, twisting one way, then the other, dropping his shoulder to cut inside, leaving defenders trailing in his majestic wake. It seemed certain to end in one of the most spectacular goals of all time when he was cynically fouled. Paul could not believe what he was seeing. 'If they try that with me they'll be sorry,' he paused, 'but then they won't get near enough.' It was another challenge to which he was eagerly looking forward.

The Marseille crowd, meanwhile, were incensed, and then the floodlights failed a couple of minutes from the end to add to the confusion ('Must be an Italian electrician,' Paul said). Even when they were partially restored Milan rushed off the field, claiming they could not see. The referee thought differently, got the French team back on the pitch and awarded them the match. As the whole stadium was clearly visible, even from the highest point in the stands, there was no doubting the justice of the European ban imposed on the Italians for their churlish behaviour.

Encapsulated in one match Paul had a foretaste of the best and worst of Italian football. Gullit's skill and strength were still amazing, yet the brutal fouls and the cynical attempt to rescue a lost match by seeking a replay were warnings that Paul's temperament was likely to be tested to breaking point.

Leaving behind the crowd of singing Frenchmen, many of them carrying Union Jacks, the Gascoigne/Waddle party trooped off to the plush restaurant adjoining the ground. The tables were laid out beautifully, the club having hired an internationally famous French chef to prepare a twelve-course gourmet meal. Each table came filled with bottles of wine bearing the label, 'Vin de Pays des Côtes de Gascoigne'. 'Nice of them to bother,' Gazza said.

Waddle's old friend and fellow songster Glenn Hoddle was also in France to see the match, nursing a long-term injury from which he was eventually to recover to the surprise of many doctors. He too joined the table, thoughtful, reflective, showing all the qualities off the pitch that made him so successful on it, and which he was later to bring to his management of Swindon and Chelsea.

As each of the Marseille heroes came up to the restaurant from the dressing-room and endless post-match interviews they were greeted with a cheer. One by one they filed in, joining their respective tables. Only Waddle was absent and the first course had already come and gone. Eventually he arrived to a tumultuous welcome, but hardly seemed to notice. He took his place at the table and as a worried Lorna put her arm around him he said, 'It's all right. I've just got a bit of a headache.' He was absolutely ashen, his face drawn with pain. Suddenly he slumped forward on the table, head buried in his arms. Gazza still thought it was all wildly funny. 'Bloody typical,' he said, 'you invite all these people out to dinner and you can't even be bothered to talk to us.'

Waddle struggled on for another course, then asked Lorna to take him outside for some fresh air. He sat miserably on the steps of the now deserted stadium, Gazza, Lorna, Stein and Lazarus by his side. Stein said they should get him a doctor. 'Nah, he doesn't need a doctor, he just needs a few drinks,' said Gazza; but the club doctor had arrived in any event and immediately called for an ambulance.

Waddle could not stop being sick and was clearly concussed. Marseille's sophisticated solution to this was to bring a bed out of their treatment room and place it at the top of the stairs, in the open air. 'Get up on the bed, Waddler,' Gazza said, 'pose for a few snapshots, it'll be a laugh.' Waddle was not laughing, he was groaning and retching, but as the ambulance came into sight he still managed to mumble, 'Don't let Gazza come with me to the hospital.' Then he was gone.

By the time Gazza returned to England at the end of March the future of Tottenham Hotspur and the sale of Paul Gascoigne were publicly and inextricably intertwined. There were many questions in the air. Would the present Spurs board sell Gazza or would it be left to a receiver? Would Scholar survive if Gazza went? Would Venables succeed in getting together his finances to buy out Scholar? And would Scholar ever sell to the man he perceived as having betrayed him? The footballing issue of whether or not Paul would be fit to face Arsenal in the semi-final became almost secondary.

On 22 March Stein faxed the draft Heads of Agreement to Manzini. On the same day the Venables bid, which at the time was backed by the unlikely Larry Gillick, collapsed. It seemed, from Tottenham's point of view, that nothing could stop the Gascoigne sale proceeding within a matter of days.

On 26 March the storm clouds drifted towards the Royal Lancaster Hotel in West London. By now Solomon was firmly at the helm of Tottenham and had met with Stein and Lazarus, listening politely and attentively as they explained to him the history of the Gascoigne–Tottenham contract, and precisely what Paul was seeking in accordance with its terms. With that information in mind he met with the Lazio contingent and Roach, who was still battling to retain his place in the midst of the transaction. Scholar, on the other hand, was almost on the outside looking in.

Lazio and Tottenham were closeted together for the first two days whilst Paul and his advisers patiently waited for a call to tell them that the parties were ready to meet with them. Each time they asked they were told there was no point in them attending a meeting that was nothing to do with them. Nothing to do with them! A player under contract was being sold at a club's behest. A player under contract was seeking confirmation that the club would honour its contract – and it was nothing to do with his advisers!

Eventually on the 28th they received the summons. They had finally pinned down Scholar who, whilst not being in control of the negotiations, was still regarded by Paul's team as crucial. He knew better than anybody the flavour of the negotiations that had brought Paul to Spurs. Stein and Lazarus arranged to meet Scholar before they attended the joint Tottenham/Lazio meeting. It was all a bit like 'Deep Throat' in *All the President's Men*. Scholar came up to the rooftop car park at the hotel, looking around him to make sure nobody was watching him consort with 'the enemy'. The three of them climbed into Stein's parked car and began to talk. Scholar was his usual amiable self, although obviously a little nervous, less self-confident than usual. There was no doubt that as a naturally gregarious man his isolation within the club was beginning to get to him. After the usual chit-chat, and his repeated assertion that he did not want Paul to leave and that if he did he himself would resign, he finally got down to the point. The 'point' was that the club was prepared to offer only a derisory sum compared to that to which his advisers thought he was entitled. Stein and Lazarus reminded him that this meeting should have happened long before. If the club had gone this far down the line without, in effect, even talking to the player and formally asking him if he wanted to leave, then it had only itself to blame.

By the time the three had joined the main meeting, making sure that they did not arrive together, it was clear that the parties were at loggerheads. Part of the problem was that Tottenham wanted all of the money deposited immediately, whilst Lazio was nervous about the club's financial position. The actual figures were now taking shape. Lazio would pay just over £7 million, payable as one-third when Paul passed a medical and the balance when he actually moved at the end of the season. Scholar and Solomon calculated that to be worth £8.5m in true terms, with the benefit of the use of the money and the saving of interest. The meeting still finished inconclusively. There was no agreement between Gascoigne and Tottenham, and because of Scholar's continual intervention no agreement between Tottenham and Lazio.

Paul himself was just setting about the task of getting himself fit for the semi-final against Arsenal, which it had been decided would be played at Wembley, given the enormous demand for tickets for the North London confrontation. The player demonstrated his enormous powers of recovery, was back in training after a fortnight, and actually playing by 10 April when he started a league match against Norwich. Before the game John Sheridan made Terry Venables promise that, however well Paul was playing, he would take him off at half-time. He already knew his patient. Left to his own devices Paul would play 90 minutes in agony.

Gazza's presence in the line-up against Arsenal in the semi-final was psychologically vital. There could be no doubting the respect in which he was held by the Highbury players and supporters alike, who in a begrudging way appreciated the pride he had re-established in English football. Then there was the financial aspect. If the club got it together on the field, Scholar hoped the bank might be persuaded to stay its hand. He was whistling hopefully in the dark. The bank's patience was already wearing wafer-thin and they had looked long enough at the Tottenham accounts as a football club. Now they had to be looked upon as a business.

By 14 April, the Sunday of the semi-final, there was still confusion over the future of Tottenham, their sale of Gascoigne, and Paul's own fitness. On 28 March the Italian delegation had come to London for another five-hour meeting with Stein and Lazarus. From there they had moved on to meet with the Tottenham executives who were still frantically trying to beat up the price to the region of £8.5 million, when Lazio believed they already had a deal at a little over £7 million. Tottenham were seeking short-term salvation by the quickest route possible, the sale of their most valuable asset. That asset, a month after leaving hospital, was about 70 per cent fit, and under normal circumstances would not have been considered for selection. But a semi-final at Wembley against deadly rivals could hardly be considered normal.

This was in a way the Cup Final itself for both clubs and their supporters, but at the end of the day it seemed Spurs wanted to win more than Arsenal, and Paul wanted to win more than anybody. Although he was still relatively young at 24, he still felt he'd won nothing in the game and this burning desire to win a Cupwinner's medal with Tottenham, this intuitive feeling that this was to be Tottenham's year, was to cost him dear. Arsenal were the bookmakers' favourites – they were on course for the League title, and Spurs fans were unlikely to be able to swallow easily another Highbury double. It was rumoured, perhaps by a Spurs insider, that the Gunners had already recorded their Cup Final song. It wasn't true, but that coupled with the smart Cup Final-style lounge suits that the Arsenal team affected for Wembley was almost enough to give Spurs a goal start.

In fact it was Paul who actually scored it, a goal that will live for ever not only in Tottenham memories, but in the nightmares of David Seaman. When they bury the poor goalkeeper he will have two names inscribed on his tombstone, those of Gazza and Koeman. The free kick was awarded after 5 minutes, about 30 yards out and slightly to the right of goal. Throughout the filming for the Gazza Soccer School programme on Channel 4, Paul had been regularly finding the net from that exact position in demonstrating free kicks; but that had been against Spurs' youth team keepers and this was against the man who was arguably England's number one goalkeeper. Paul never considered for a moment any alternative to having a shot at goal. The commentator queried the sanity of it, 'Surely he's not going to shoot from there? He is, you know. . .' Seaman leapt in vain, the ball was in the back of the net and one-half of North London went mad. Arthur Cox, watching the game on television, permitted himself a quick smile. He'd seen Paul do it all before as a lad on the training ground, dozens of times before. He, at least, had known Paul was going to shoot.

Paul had first met John-Paul King back in January 1991. John-Paul, with his gingery mop of hair, was immediately designated 'Ginga' (pronounced with two hard 'g's). He had been appearing in pantomime with Paul's sister Anna, and was developing a career in scriptwriting for Bobby Davro, whilst at the same time gaining a favourable reputation for his own act, mixing comedy and magic. John-Paul's marriage was on the rocks and he began a close relationship with Anna, which was at first looked upon by Paul with suspicion. He takes a close proprietorial interest in his sisters' affairs of heart, wary in case somebody is sneaked into the inner circle of whom he does not approve. Darren, Lindsay's boyfriend, has over the years of his 'walking out' with Paul's younger sister become an accepted part of the entourage; but Ginga was different, more mature, more experienced, potentially more dangerous. He would have to be looked at carefully.

After a charity football match at Gateshead Football Stadium, Ginga and Paul went back together to the Gosforth Park Hotel and Gazza began the examination. 'I didn't even realize I was being tested,' John-Paul recalls. 'I love an audience, and when I had one like Paul I just couldn't stop telling jokes. Anna had some auditions and I spent most of the week with Paul and Darren. The days passed, for me, in an alcoholic daze. Paul fed me about twenty Long Island cocktails, which consisted of iced tea with four different spirits, a total of some eighty measures.'

There is quite often a cruel streak in Paul's humour which in a more sophisticated setting would be called black comedy. He knew full well that Ginga was terrified of swans and geese, yet one day whilst out fishing on a boat he deliberately lured a swan over by feeding it crisps. John-Paul turned his back, and then felt himself attacked by something he thought was Gazza. It was, in fact, the swan, which Paul had picked up and placed on his 'mate'. John-Paul turned round, screamed, 'Get it off! Mum!' and then actually jumped into the water.

Ginga was good for Gazza, there was no doubt of that, but whether Gazza was good for him was another matter. Yet John-Paul is a useful witness to the rise and fall and subsequent resurrection of Paul Gascoigne. He was able to view it initially from the outside and then within. He was able to see its effect on Paul and those around him, to see the agony and the ecstasy.

'My first taste of Gazzamania was at a pub in Cheshunt. I went there for a quick drink with Gazza, Stewey and Sedge. There was one old guy propping up the bar, another playing solitaire, and a third practising darts. Within twenty minutes of Paul's arrival you couldn't move in there. They had to turn the lights on because the kids looking through the windows had blocked out the sun. I called Anna to get a cab down but she didn't arrive. The police had blocked off the roads. Eventually we had to climb out the back way via the cellar. But thinking about it, that was nothing unusual. Most days I spent with Paul were like that.'

As part of his effort to get fit from his hernia operation Paul dragged Ginga and Anna up to the Springs Health Farm in Leicestershire. Whilst Anna took herself off to the beauty parlour Paul subjected his future brother-in-law to non-stop torture in the gym, the pool and then on the tennis courts, where Paul discovered a mechanized cannon that would fire the ball at 120 mph from all angles. It was like playing Sampras, Becker and Courier all at once. When it came to the archery, John-Paul gave a sigh of relief. This looked more relaxing, a gentleman's sport straight from the old village green. Paul went up to the lady in charge who gave them both a bow and arrow. 'I'll point you to the targets,' she said. 'Don't bother,' Gazza replied, 'Ginga'll go out for ten minutes and I'll go and look for him.'

On the eve of the semi-final Venables had given the players a few hours off and Gazza had come back to his house to pick up his wash-bag. 'Darren, Lindsay's boyfriend, was with us,' John-Paul recalls, 'and Gazza suddenly said, "Come on, let's have a game of football." He put on a pair of Bermuda shorts, and off Darren and I toddled with several million pounds of footballing talent. We went to the green by the Fish and Eels pub and used the trees as posts. Gazza decided we had to see who could score from the furthest free kick. It was barmy. There could only be one winner, but he knew that, which was why he'd thrown down the challenge. Gazza started firing them in from forty yards and wanted me to try and save them. I saw a glimpse of one within reach, stuck out my hand and I'd never experienced such pain. It was like getting the strap from a sixteen-stone schoolmaster. It was back to Paul's roots. He was playing football for fun with a couple of mates on a Saturday afternoon. He then put me on the line, and made me try and head his crosses past Darren. And he was arguing whether or not a ball had crossed the line. The greatest player in England, maybe the world, and he is arguing over a pub kick-around. Yet the following day at Wembley, the free kick was a replica of those he'd been putting past me. I could have made a fortune from David Seaman, if I'd called him the night before and told him that Gazza was putting them to the left.'

The Gazza semi-final comeback show was not yet complete. He played a one-two with Paul Allen, one of Tottenham's unsung heroes, and there was Gary Lineker to score in typical fashion. Just before half-time the Gunners pulled one back, but the Spurs defence then held firm and it was no great surprise when Lineker broke away 15 minutes from the end to score a third. Paul had already been substituted, exhausted and aching, his job done. He was on the bench, then off it, playing every minute with the rest of the team, urging them on with as much verbal enthusiasm as Venables and his assistant Duggie Livermore. At the final whistle, the three 'managers' embraced each other, then Paul, forgetting his hernia, raced on to the pitch and lifted his close friend Paul Stewart.

Gazza was gracious in victory, shaking hands with every Arsenal player and giving them a consoling pat. BBC TV got to him first. He told them how he'd been unable to sleep the night before. Then, with a quick jibe at Arsenal, he excused himself by saying that he had to be off to get himself measured for his new Cup Final suit.

18

'THE SPAGHETTI WILL HAVE TO WAIT.'

Whilst Paul was delighted to get Spurs to Wembley he
did not necessarily realize the full implication of their
success. Solomon and Scholar met the day after the
match and, according to Scholar, Solomon felt that the
financial position had been so changed by their victory
that they might not need to sell Gascoigne. In any
event they would not sell before the Cup Final and the
price of £7 million plus seemed ludicrously low. What
nobody knew was that crucial talks between Scholar
and Venables were creating a rift between them that
was ultimately to turn into a bloodbath.

They all seemed to have forgotten the player and his
feelings. They'd set him off down the road, at first
reluctantly, but he was now committed to follow that
road all the way to Rome. Tottenham's bankers, having
appointed Solomon with the aim of selling Gascoigne,
clearly saw that as just the beginning. They felt exposed,
and with the overdraft much reduced *they* would feel
much happier, even if their customer was much weakened in the real world it inhabited. The football once
again had become a side issue.

On 29 April Stein and Lazarus prepared for yet
another flight to Rome. A meeting had been called at
the offices of Giadoni, the notary who had been present
at the very first meeting. At long last Tottenham were

about to grasp the nettle and open tripartite negotiations to clear the way for Paul's exit from the club.

In fact, after some delays with their flights, Paul's
advisers did not arrive at the notary's office until nearly
five in the afternoon. To their astonishment a meeting
was in progress, from which they were once again
excluded. They had asked Solomon if he had wanted
to fly with them and he had declined. Now they knew
why. The office was situated in a typically beautiful
Roman building, dating back to the sixteenth century
and surrounded by a high-walled garden. The entrance
hall was dark and cool, hung with oil paintings of the
notary's family dating back to the 1400s. A historical
setting for a historic meeting.

Manzini apologetically showed Stein and Lazarus
into an office adjoining the main boardroom, and
asked them to wait. Tottenham and Lazio had not
yet resolved their differences. Patiently, as they had
done so many times before, they cautioned that Paul's
requirements had to be taken into account in any deal.
Therefore what was the point of the meeting next door
proceeding unless they were to be involved. Manzini
shrugged. It was not his decision.

The lawyer and the accountant waited and waited.
Then something happened that made their patience
snap: they heard an all too familiar voice in the corridor
– it was Roach. As soon as Stein and Lazarus realized he
was there they called Manzini into the room that they
were fast regarding as home and made it clear that they
were not prepared to discuss Paul's terms in front of the
agent. Maurizio toddled back inside with the message.

It was not until nearly eight o'clock that they were
invited to join the meeting. By that time they were
tired, hungry and very angry. Roach left as required,
and Paul's advisers settled down in a smoke-filled room
to begin the long night of negotiations. As far as they
were concerned they had nothing of real substance

to discuss with Lazio. They felt they had an agreement with them, albeit conditional upon both parties reaching agreement with Spurs. That, as it proved, was to be a major stumbling block.

As the meeting began a huge, salivating dog appeared at the French windows, snarling and baring its teeth. Stein both hated cigarette smoke and was terrified of dogs. He jokingly asked whether or not the animal would only be brought into the room if a deal could not be struck. Nobody smiled. Apart from Roach, Solomon brought with him a solicitor, James Perry from Ashurst Morris, who in the course of the transaction became known to Stein and Lazarus as 'Jimbo'. Within his restraints he dealt courteously, taking the jibes about his devoted support of Torquay United with good grace.

By midnight the parties were no nearer an agreement than when the meeting started. Cold pizza and boiled sweets were the best that could be mustered for supper. As the hours passed, as the smoke thickened and the dog in the garden became ever more frantic, it became clearer and clearer to the experienced negotiators that it had to be resolved in favour of Tottenham. Lazio had weakened their own position by their positive promises that they would bring Paul to the club and that did not help, but although the pincers tightened, still Stein and Lazarus would not yield. The parties had reached that point in the night where they knew that sleep was not on the agenda, but with the adrenaline pumping through their bodies sleep would not have been possible. Finally, just after midnight, Stein and Lazarus played their trump card. 'If you don't believe us,' Stein said to Solomon and Callieri, 'phone Paul yourselves.'

Incredibly enough, before the conversation started Paul and Solomon had to be introduced over the telephone. Here was the man who'd been given the task of rescuing one of England's most famous clubs, and he'd never met the asset that was intended to be its salvation. The two men exchanged a few pleasantries down the line, and then Solomon, anxious by now to get to his bed, came to the point and asked Paul to confirm his own position.

Paul's reply was unmistakably clear. 'I've two years left on my contract. I didn't ask to be sold. I'll only go if the terms are right.'

If Paul did see his contract through, assuming that by some miracle Tottenham were in existence at the end of the 1990/1 season, then he would be a free agent, and the most they could expect to receive for him under UEFA rules would be £1.5 million. Solomon was convinced; he would sell Gascoigne. Together Tottenham and Lazio would somehow agree their terms. At 3.30 a.m. Stein and Lazarus staggered back to a nearby hotel, theoretically for three hours' sleep. But sleep would not come. Although they appeared to be coming to the end of the road there was still a gnawing feeling that around the corner, through the hairpin bends, there was an accident just waiting to happen.

On 4 May the fixture computer played one of its regular practical jokes. Tottenham were to entertain their Cup Final opponents, Nottingham Forest, in a fairly meaningless league match. Paul played his first 90 minutes of football since the derby with Arsenal on 12 January. Uncommitted observers felt that Forest had deserved to win by a large margin, but Spurs carved out a 1–1 draw thanks to a goal from Paul Walsh. Gazza was out on his feet at the end, but at least he had come through without any adverse reaction to the injury.

Venables's position was that he knew nothing about the deal and that if he took over the club then Paul would not be leaving. Callieri was more than happy to take him on in the media. 'If Venables is so good at saving clubs from drowning he should become a lifeguard,' he said.

Paul still refused to be drawn on the battle raging for the club, and after discussion with his advisers he gave the *Sun* his one and only quote: 'Right now all I care about is winning a Cup medal for Spurs. The spaghetti will have to wait.'

The final outcome of the Rome meeting was that Solomon had returned with a firm agreement to be signed when Lazio's bank guarantee was in place for the full amount of the transfer fee, which now appeared to have been agreed at £6.7 million. It was, of course, also conditional upon Paul signing his contract of employment with Lazio. With that end in mind yet another appointment in Rome was arranged.

One major problem was that Paul was obliged to sign the agreement between Tottenham and Lazio. Although Lazio had no objection to his advisers seeing it, Tottenham were none too keen and seemed to expect that he would be prepared blindly to put his name to anything that was placed in front of him. By signing the agreement Stein and Lazarus felt it could be construed that Paul was bound by its terms, and they could hardly commit him to some unknown obligations. When the contract was finally and reluctantly produced, their suspicion was proved to be totally justified as it did, indeed, contain a clause that was totally unacceptable. Lazio had given Tottenham first option on Paul if he was ever to return to the United Kingdom. That, it appeared, had been one of Scholar's contributions to the deal. However, it is one thing for clubs to agree and quite another for that agreement to be binding on the player. Paul was always willing to listen to any proposals for him to rejoin Spurs if he came back to England, but he was certainly not going to have them imposed on him. Finally a compromise was reached. He would sign the Spurs/Lazio contract to satisfy the Italian League requirements, but the Tottenham option clause would specifically be declared as non-binding upon him.

Callieri's attention was brought back to the meeting when Stein and Lazarus introduced their Rome lawyer, Carla Vissat, for the first time. Carla was a delightfully pretty, bubbly woman, half American, half Italian, who'd decided to make her career in Rome rather than her native New York. Callieri always had an eye for a pretty girl and Carla was no exception. The first dinner engagement was offered almost immediately and Callieri was in no way dissuaded when Carla announced she was engaged to another lawyer from her firm.

By the end of a lengthy meeting, it was agreed that Stein would return to England to redraft the contract. Manzini would translate it and the Italian version would be sent to Vissat for approval, as would the final form of the playing contract. Even a timetable was optimistically prepared for the conclusion of the deal, with the intention that by 24 July 1991 Paul would be a fully-fledged Lazio player.

The timetable did not last long. Vissat duly received the draft agreement and Manzini got his copy on 3 May. Everything seemed resolvable and everybody seemed to accept that Paul was on his way to Italy. Yet there was still an element at Spurs who for one reason or another appeared to wish to spike what was certainly a moral, if not a legally binding, agreement with Lazio. There were by now two separate parties seeking to buy Scholar's shares and thus Tottenham – three if one did not discount the shadowy figure of Robert Maxwell still looming in the background. Baltic had long flirted with the possibility of taking an interest in the club, but they not only wanted Scholar, Bobroff and Berry out, but also desired to have Venables's involvement limited to playing matters. Venables, on the other hand, was still banking on Gillick coming good as his backer and at a board meeting on 7 May it was suggested that if the Venables offer was accepted then Spurs would not need to sell Gascoigne.

Somehow or other the players still had to go through the motions on the field for the sake of the paying customers, of whom Tottenham needed every one, whilst off it Paul tried various methods of relaxation in the April and May of 1991. He went to the leisure club at the Swallow Hotel in Waltham Abbey every day with Stewey and John-Paul, and found a big green football in the pool. 'Let's see who can head the ball the most against the wall. Whoever heads it the least the others get to punch on the arms.'

John-Paul never stood a chance. He went home with his arms black and blue. The next day at the pool he faced up to Gazza.

'Paul, we're not playing the punching game.'

'Nah, that's all right. We'll lay down by the side of the pool . . .' he paused ' . . . and the others can throw the ball at the stomach of the one lying down.'

On 9 May Scholar came to the Finers' offices first thing in the morning. The very fact that he'd agreed to a 9 a.m. meeting illustrated how important it was to him, for he was a notoriously late riser who groaned at the thought of what he considered early morning meetings. He launched straight into things with the minimum of his usual preliminaries. 'Right,' he said, 'just tell me what you want for Paul to stay and I'll see if I can do it.'

Stein and Lazarus were almost embarrassed by the question. 'It's very difficult,' Lazarus explained. 'If we tell you what Paul would want, we'd be telling you what he's got on offer in Italy and that's a breach of professional confidence.'

Scholar was nonplussed. 'Come on, be reasonable' – a favourite phrase of his – 'we've known each other a long time. He loves it at Spurs. I know it. He must be prepared to stay for less than he'd get abroad. You know I can't match it.'

The advisers were still reluctant to put any figures on the table. 'Look, Irving,' Lazarus said, 'give us your best shot, no messing about, and we'll take instructions.'

Scholar had obviously expected this. He scribbled away on a notepad and then told them the offer. It was good, but the Lazio offer was excellent. They told him so. Scholar paused; knowing with whom he was dealing he had clearly kept something in reserve. He increased the signing-on fee to what surely would have been a British record. He also offered Paul an increased share in the value of his own contract and a break clause after four years to allow him to go abroad then. Still Stein and Lazarus were not enthusiastic. They knew Paul better than most, and there was too much jam tomorrow about the offer.

'You've signed, haven't you?' Scholar said rather than asked.

'No. Paul won't sign anything until after the final, and anyway we've still got a few things to agree.'

Scholar was never a great one for listening and as far as he was concerned their hesitation in saying no to him was tantamount to agreement. 'OK. Give me till Thursday. I'm not sure I can do it, but I think I can.'

Stein and Lazarus nodded. It seemed only fair that if Scholar could come up with a package such as he'd put to them, that they in turn should at least put it to Paul. From everybody's point of view it was an unusual build-up to a Cup Final. Instead of the directors enjoying themselves, arranging dinners, deciding who'd sit in the royal box, here they were scrabbling for survival.

On the Thursday morning a meeting was called at Solomon's offices without the Italians. There were still the joint ventures instigated by Scholar between Tottenham and Gazza's company, which Stein and Lazarus wanted resolved before the transfer. Scholar was also invited to the meeting and, feeling this might well be D-Day, Stein cornered him alone on the stairs. 'Irving, you said you'd come back to us by today.

Have you got it together? We need to know if your offer is actually on the table.'

Scholar shrugged and gave a weary smile. 'To be perfectly honest' – another Scholarism – 'I haven't.'

'You realize then we have to go ahead,' Stein said.

'I understand.'

Stein felt a sudden overwhelming sadness for him. He'd lived and breathed Tottenham since he was a kid. He'd brought Waddle, Gascoigne and Lineker to the club almost single-handed. He'd sunk his own money and time into the rescue operation. He'd seen Hoddle and Waddle go, he'd been pilloried in public for the Maxwell fiasco, and now the one principle he'd stuck to was about to vanish – Gascoigne would be sold.

He stayed only briefly at the meeting, a sad and disillusioned man, and by the time Solomon asked whether Paul would sign for Lazio that day, he'd already gone. Solomon explained that Tottenham were under extreme pressure from the bank and Lazio for Paul to sign. Stein explained that Paul did not want to sign before the final as he felt that if he did he'd be letting down the fans. Whatever the legality of the situation, he wanted to play the final in a Tottenham shirt as a Tottenham player.

Finers would send one of their trainee solicitors to Paul's house with all the documentation. Paul would sign everything and it would be kept in escrow until the Monday, assuming there was to be no replay. It was not totally satisfactory but everybody parted with handshakes, believing the deal had been struck.

Venables, meanwhile, had also been busy. He called Stein and asked him if it was worth his while coming to see him. Stein was non-committal, but it seemed odd to him that the Tottenham board did not seem to be keeping their manager fully informed, notwithstanding his dual position as a potential buyer of the club. Venables asked the same question as Scholar. 'Has he signed?'

'No,' Stein replied truthfully, having not yet despatched his trainee.

'Can I come and see you then?'

Stein agreed, and Venables arrived about lunchtime in a hurry. Trying to keep his star player was not his ideal preparation for a Cup Final. Venables's approach was less concise than that of Scholar. 'You know I'm trying to buy the club,' he said. 'We're very close. If I buy then I don't want to sell Paul. What will it take to keep him?'

'OK, Terry. Paul does like you personally, there's no doubt of that. I appreciate you can't match what's on offer from Lazio, but just give me your best shot.'

Venables made a vague offer which seemed to be less than half the figure mentioned by Scholar. Stein believed that no matter what public stance Venables took, he reluctantly accepted that one day Paul would have to be sold to a big foreign club such as AC Milan or Juventus. He made his offer even vaguer with talks of bonuses, trying to convince Stein that if Spurs were successful Paul's value would soar, and when it came to the point of a move to a really big Italian club, then he would not stand in his way. If Scholar's offer had been jam tomorrow, then this was jam next year.

'Sorry, Terry, that's way off.'

'You've got to be realistic. The boy either wants to stay or he doesn't. The club's in a terrible mess and that's what we can afford.' In typical Venables fashion, he had tried to turn the situation around. The guilt was being loaded on to Paul and his advisers.

Finally Stein agreed to take instructions, although both men knew it was a mere formality. It just wasn't on. He wished Venables good luck for the match and then left the office.

19

'WILL LAZIO STILL TAKE ME NOW?'

It was of little interest to Gazza, while he was driving his team-mates crazy the night before the Cup Final at the Royal Lancaster Hotel, that Venables was trying to finalize his deal with Scholar's solicitors. He had been told of Venables's offer and had felt, as did his advisers, that he was much too far down the Lazio road to turn back, particularly for something that might or might not happen.

Everybody was billing the final as Gascoigne v. Clough, when in fact the day would belong to neither of them. In a BBC interview Brian Clough had maintained that he was not obsessed with Gazza, but that he'd asked the team's coach driver to try and knock him down if he saw him in the Wembley tunnel. In fact Paul was feeling so strong, so hyped up, that the coach would probably have come off second best. Who would have predicted that within a couple of years both would be lost to English football?

In Paul's mind, bar a replay, this was to be his last game for Spurs, and he wanted the fans to remember it for ever. That wish at least was about to be fulfilled.

'Go out there and get stuck in,' Venables said – not, perhaps, the best advice to a player who had never needed any encouragement to get stuck in, and whose efforts in that respect have ended all too often with a yellow or red card. In the tunnel Paul threw the ball ferociously and repeatedly against the wall, his gaze distant and glassy. He was in another world.

As the crowd exploded in the moment the two teams took the pitch, Paul was jerked back to reality, seeking his family in the stands as he always did, waving madly to them, clenching his fists at the Tottenham fans in a gesture of anticipated victory. It was Paul's demonic instability, fuelled by the media, that came to the fore on 18 May 1991. He had waited a long time to get near to the Princess of Wales, and as he was introduced to her before the game he asked if he could kiss her hand, whilst affecting a mock curtsey. She blushed, he asked again, and he duly bestowed the kiss he'd been denied the previous year. Then it was down to business.

On their last visit to Wembley the Tottenham directors had invited ridicule by parading around the pitch with the players, waving to the fans as if in some way they had been responsible for the team being there. Now there was no such demonstration. They sat grim-faced in the royal box, divided into their warring factions, hardly talking to each other. The tension spilled out on to the field of play and within minutes of the kick-off Paul was at the centre of the fray. He went in for a 50-50 ball with Gary Parker, his leg out before him, straight and high. He connected with the ball, but his follow through also connected with Parker's chest. Paul cheekily turned to referee Roger Milford, and asked why he'd given a free kick when he'd played the ball, but Milford tolerantly, perhaps too tolerantly, smiled and waved him away, seeming not to want to disturb the carnival spirit so early in the day.

Unfortunately neither Paul nor the match were given any opportunity to settle down before Gary Charles, the Forest full back, received the ball wide on a right-side overlap and cut inside across the edge of the penalty area. Paul was stranded deep in his own half, unaware that he had any cover from the defence and Pat Van den Hauwe in particular. He believed that he, and he alone, stood between Charles and what seemed a certain Forest goal. Defence is not one of the strongest qualities in Gazza's game. Having seen the incident time and time again Paul still cannot believe it.

'I thought I'd get to the ball, I really did; but he was quicker than I expected and my tackle became a lunge. At first it was him I was worried about, a young defender, playing his first match at Wembley, and I was about to put him out of the game. Then Charles was up on his feet. I knew the referee had given a free kick and even from the ground I looked at him hoping he had nothing worse in store for me. Dave Butler got me to my feet after what seemed a lifetime. I put some weight on the leg and it held. "I'm all right," I said, "I'll run it off." Dave was looking grim; he exchanged a glance with the referee and shook his head. None of it was sinking in. I got up, seemingly to everybody's surprise, and took my place in the Tottenham wall. I was working on automatic. Stuart Pearce, their captain, my England team-mate, took the kick almost apologetically. As he hit the ball, I knew I couldn't keep upright and I toppled over again like a rag doll. The ball whistled past me, past Thorstvedt our keeper and into the net. It was far worse than the World Cup booking. There I'd only hurt myself, here I'd let everybody down. I got to my feet once again and began to hobble towards the centre circle for the kick-off. I never made it. Dave Butler, who'd been poised by the touchline, was at my side again. I wasn't in any pain. I think I was numb with shock and fright. I looked up and saw Terry looking solemn and it was at that moment I knew it was serious.

'They put me on a stretcher and I felt I was falling into a deep, black hole. I thought of silly things. Who'd collect my medal, winner's or loser's? Where had I parked my car? Words echoed in my head. Mel and Len saying to me when I went mad spending, "It won't last for ever." I'd known that, of course, but I couldn't believe it wouldn't last beyond that May afternoon, couldn't accept that "for ever" had already come to an end. I wanted to start all over again, to press the rewind button and wipe out the nightmare of the last twenty minutes. I wanted someone to make it better for me. I wanted my mum and dad, I wanted to speak to Mel and Len, to ask them just one question. Will Lazio still take me now?'

As Paul lay waiting to be taken to the Princess Grace Hospital he heard the roar for Paul Stewart's equalizing goal. He'd then listened to the commentary on a radio in the ambulance and actually arrived in his hospital bed in time to see the last few moments of extra time. He begged the nurses not to sedate him until he'd seen the end of the match and so he was able to give a cheer when poor Des Walker headed the ball into his own net, to give Tottenham the Cup and Paul a winner's medal at the highest level for the first time in his career. Although the Cup and his medal were brought to his bedside they were small consolation. Ultimately his heart had been set on playing abroad, his heart had stopped him committing himself before the final, and now it appeared to both his heart and his head that there was no justice. A wave of sadness spread across the country felt, not least, by Arthur Cox. 'I knew that if Paul went off at any time, he was injured. He'd play on with an injury rather than come off. The one thing he wanted to do – play football – had been taken away from him.'

John-Paul King went on his own after the final to the Swallow. He bought himself a drink and wandered sadly down to the leisure club where they had experienced so many good times. He went to get the green floating ball with which they'd had so many laughs and it popped in his hand. It was a reflection of all Paul's dreams and ambitions.

For days and weeks after John Browett, the surgeon, had reconstructed the shattered cruciate ligament in his knee, Paul lay helpless in hospital. Arthur Cox had rung him several times. 'Make sure you're a good patient, and do as the specialist tells you. Learn from it.' Cox knew all about learning from injuries. Lazio were almost stubbornly loyal, almost daring the world to say their faith was misplaced. Regalia had stayed over after his pre-final negotiations, thinking to watch Gazza's glory and then take him back to Rome in triumph. Seated at Wembley he'd been horrified by what he'd seen, and his Saturday evening phone call to Gian Marco Callieri was a sad one indeed. Worse was to follow, because on the Sunday Lazio visited Inter Milan and saw their last chance of a UEFA place vanish with a 2-0 defeat.

Callieri, Regalia, Zoff and Manzini all knew the fickleness of the Roman fans, knew they would take neither loss lightly, and decided they had to act positively and speedily. Callieri made three things clear to the waiting Italian public: one, they were not going to abandon Gascoigne in his hour of need; two, they would seek another big-name signing, not as a replacement for Paul but ultimately to play alongside him; and three, that he regarded the media attacks on Paul as nothing less than scandalous.

The telephone lines between London and Rome were red-hot. Back in the office, Stein arranged to meet Manzini on the 23rd and 24th, whilst Solomon had also been talking to the Italians. He was able to report to Scholar and the Tottenham board that two alternative proposals had been mooted. Either Lazio would pay a deposit and then the balance after a transfer in July 1992 (subject, of course, to a medical), or else they would pay a discounted sum in full immediately and

Paul was to join Lazio at the end of the 1991/2 season, again subject to a medical. The rub came when Lazio disclosed the discounted price, £4.825 million, a fairly substantial discount, particularly if they were to get a fully fit player, albeit a year late. Their argument was that they would have to sign somebody else with all the attendant expenses, and further they would lose valuable gate revenue that Paul's presence would have guaranteed. The other sting in the tail of the offer was that if Paul did not pass the medical then Spurs would have to repay the whole of the price, plus interest, hardly a course of action likely to appeal to the bank. Stein and Lazarus had it at the back of their minds that Tottenham had Paul insured for £5.5 million. That sum would have been paid out if Paul was unable to play again; but Lazio's offer created a new scenario. If he didn't pass the stringent Italian medical, but was in fact passed fit to play for Spurs, then the London club got nothing. All they had was a player with a big question mark over his footballing future, a Rolls-Royce that had been in a major crash and might purr or rattle – who could tell?

On 22 May Venables told Scholar he still wanted to buy out both him and Bobroff. By then it seemed he had already had preliminary discussions with a totally surprising individual in terms of football involvement, Alan Sugar. Sugar was (and is) an interesting character, and had their relationship ever been allowed to develop he and Paul would have got on like a house on fire, particularly with their mutual love of tennis. Like Paul, Sugar had left school without any formal qualifications. While Paul had used his natural talent in sport to make his fortune, Sugar had turned his natural aptitude for business from humble market trader to the publicly quoted Amstrad company. He was tough, he was ruthless, yet there was no doubting his scrupulous honesty and his kind heart, which manifested itself in the most generous support and donations to a whole variety of charities. Sugar has a reputation for sticking by his friends if they stay true to him, of demanding the impossible from his employees and obtaining it by a mixture of inspiration, domination and reward. A football *aficionado* he wasn't, yet that was perhaps more a matter of time than a lack of interest.

The Italians were genuinely heart-broken by Paul's injury and clearly felt an enormous sense of personal grief for the lad. On 22 May Manzini and Regalia came to a vital meeting with John Browett, the well-known orthopaedic surgeon who had operated on Paul. At the Princess Grace Hospital they were joined by Dr Claudio Bartolini, the Lazio medical expert and team doctor, and together they were taken to a spare room for what was to prove an X-certificate film show. Knowing how vital was the operation he was carrying out, John Browett had filmed it from the beginning, using a mini-camera attached to the surgical instruments.

Browett seemed confident that Paul would make a full recovery, but was reluctant to predict when he might return to light training, let alone play. The Italians then moved on to Paul himself. It was an emotional meeting with tears on both sides when Manzini and Regalia embraced him like a long-lost son as he lay in bed. They gave him his birthday present a few days early, a Lazio shirt together with a beautiful gold watch engraved with a personal message from the president. Whatever anybody else thought, as far as Lazio were concerned Paul was still an integral part of their plans for the future. All he had to do was to recover.

By the Wednesday after his injury Paul was already making remarkable progress. He had achieved a flexibility of some 70 degrees in the knee and had to be restrained from pushing himself through the pain barrier and beyond. The usual circle of friends had gathered by his side, including Jimmy Gardner. From somewhere or other a pellet gun was produced. Jimmy was asked to lean out of the window to toss water bombs at the journalists camped out on the pavement, and as he leaned out a couple of pellets unerringly found their way into his not insubstantial posterior. The fans too kept up a vigil. Whenever Stein or Lazarus visited they were waylaid by young girls pressing gifts and cards into their hands for delivery to their hero. On the way out they would deliver autographs, and one youngster who'd kept watch for some 72 hours reaped her reward by being given a personal audience with her Gazza.

There were some sterling efforts at subterfuge from journalists to get to Paul, including passing themselves off as long-lost relatives or even doctors. Eventually a list of 'acceptable' visitors was lodged at the hard-pressed reception and a code – 'Kevin Brock' – was instigated for telephone calls. When the former Newcastle player of that name was told of this years later he was puzzled but seemed vaguely flattered.

Stein and Lazarus met with Manzini and Regalia on 24 May, expecting the worst. The papers had already told them of Lazio's reduced offer to Spurs. Were they going to try the same thing with the player? Their fears were groundless. Refusing to take advantage of their strengthened bargaining position, the Lazio officials made it clear that with the exception of a few minor points the original deal stood. Manzini explained that they were very close to agreeing a revised arrangement with Spurs, who were still negotiating through Solomon. However, they were back to looking for some guarantee from Tottenham that if Paul did not pass a medical then all the money Lazio would have deposited, together with all the interest, would be returned to the Italian club. There were now further complications on the timing of the deal. It was clear that Paul would not be fit to play until February 1992 at the earliest – that was Browett's off-the-record opinion. Paul was determined to prove him wrong and make a more speedy recovery, but the interested parties preferred Browett's pessimistic realism.

Under the Italian League regulations, registrations for the season had to be completed by 10 August, with another 10-day window in November. Neither of those was a realistic target so far as Paul was concerned. Lazio had obviously considered the situation in some depth and their view was that Paul would convalesce until February, and then play a few friendly matches before some form of international medical committee decided upon his fitness. If Lazio and the player wanted to progress his rehabilitation in Italy then this seemed to be acceptable. It would give him an opportunity to meet his team-mates and learn Italian. Another redraft of the Heads of Agreement between Paul and Lazio was delivered to Manzini, who agreed that it was vital for the deal to be concluded as swiftly as possible, before anybody changed their mind or had it changed for them.

On 27 May Paul Gascoigne spent his twenty-fourth birthday in his hospital room, rather than being fêted in Rome. His family came down and, their throats lubricated by Newcastle Brown, champagne and whatever other drinks had been delivered to Paul's room by generous donors, gave vent to a typical Geordie sing-song, which gave the other patients in adjoining rooms little choice but to join in. The hospital made a huge cake, Paul was surrounded by cards and gifts from well-wishers, but for him it was a false kind of jollity, a bravado performance, that left him alone when everybody had gone, reflecting through a long dark night on what might have been. He turned to pen and paper for the first time since he'd left school and sought solace in the unlikely therapeutic form of poetry.

> Then do me all a favour.
> Get me fit again.

> Let's all eff off to Italy,
> Get pissed on some champagne.

Despite his outward confidence, if there was ever a moment when Paul feared it might all go terribly wrong it was in the small hours of the first day of his twenty-fifth year. It was all a far cry from the celebratory birthdays of the past, of Teddy Ruxpin and Terry Venables, of hot days in Italy with cake spread all over his face by Waddle. By the 29th things seemed to be improving. He was up to 90 per cent flexibility, Browett had expressed himself more than satisfied with his progress, and Chrysalis TV were deep into their negotiations to film *Gazza, The Fight Back,* including a recuperatory holiday.

James Perry sent through a draft of a deed of release between Paul and Tottenham. He wrote, 'As you will appreciate this Release would be a condition of our deal with Lazio.' From this Stein and Lazarus assumed that there *was* a deal with Lazio, but on the same day Scholar learned that Venables had a new backer, even though he did not yet know that it was Alan Sugar.

Anxious to proceed, Stein and Lazarus pressed Perry for a final meeting in Rome on 30 May. However, he wanted to watch his Torquay play in the end-of-season play-offs, which meant the trip would have to be postponed until the following week.

Time was hanging heavy on Paul's hands. He was working like a lunatic on his exercises, beads of sweat forming on his brow from the herculean efforts that caused amazement and admiration amongst the nursing staff. Visitors broke the boredom and he was never short of company. John-Paul came with Linda Lusardi, whose house backed on to Paul's in Dobbs Weir. He had often used the rear fence as an escape route and had become close friends with Linda and her husband. To liven things up John-Paul smeared his face with jam, swathed himself in bandages and then had Linda chasing him in with a knife in her hand just as a befuddled Gazza woke up. All he took in was a crazed mad woman with a deadly weapon pursuing a man she had already carved. He turned over and went back to sleep, convinced it was all a bad dream.

On another occasion while John-Paul sat with Gazza, Bobby Davro called to discuss a business matter. He was in London and asked if he could come to visit Paul and bring a few cans. As he was on his way the telephone rang again. This time it was Jeff Gold, the manager of the West End Swallow Hotel who had Paul Shane of *Hi De Hi* fame with him, also wanting to visit. Davro arrived first and the plot was hatched. Davro had come and gone before Gold and Shane arrived, then re-entered in a white coat and a mask, with a stethoscope around his neck and an assumed South African accent that would have fooled Nelson Mandela. Gazza said in a reverential tone, 'That's the chief surgeon.'

'I'd like to tell you your operation has been a complete success,' Davro said, 'but I believe you're having trouble with your waterworks. Can I see your testicles?' Then, before Paul could produce them, added, 'When was the last time you passed water?'

Gazza and John-Paul were well prepared. 'It's there,' Gazza said, pointing to a bottle into which they'd poured a mixture of lager and water to give a fair impression of urine.

Davro the Doctor grabbed it and said, 'Right, I'll just test this and come back. What's the time?' he asked with a flamboyant gesture of his arm to look at his watch, spilling the entire contents of the bottle over the expensively dressed Shane and Gold. When Davro pulled down his mask they could all laugh about it, but for Paul the mask could not so easily be removed. He was not just Paul Gascoigne, he was Gazza, and Gazza always had to smile, Gazza was good for a laugh. He had created the character and now he was finding it increasingly difficult to separate the persona.

On 6 June Stein took off for Rome, this time on his own, confident matters were finally to be concluded, and on the following day met with Carla Vissat, Callieri, Regalia, Manzini and Giadoni at the president's new apartment. Manzini explained that there were still problems between Lazio and Spurs, not only over guarantees relating to the money but in connection with the mode of medical examination that would make the final decision on Paul's fitness. Stein left Rome with the feeling there was still some way to go to bring the story to a conclusion, and when he arrived back in England all the concerns that the deal should not be long delayed appeared to be justified. The Sugar-Venables offer had been confirmed to the Stock Exchange, and perhaps even more threatening was the fact that Maxwell had now returned to the arena, declaring that if he acquired Tottenham he would block the Gascoigne deal.

So far as Sugar and Venables were concerned, those around Paul were not to know of a new twist in the story. Although Solomon was still discussing with the Midland Bank the possibility of not selling Gascoigne, according to Scholar in his book the proposal put to him and Solomon by Venables actually contained a clause stating that the offer was *conditional* on the sale of Paul for a figure of not less than £4.5 million. On 10 June Stein faxed Manzini, telling him that Sugar was involved and he and Venables might block the deal. On the same day the Tottenham board met, with Scholar still in attendance, and were advised that a draft agreement prepared by solicitors provided for the payment of the whole reduced price for Paul to be placed in a bank in London, with the interest accruing to Tottenham. Subject to a medical, that meant that Spurs would in July 1992 actually receive about £5.3 million for the player including the accrued interest.

But Maxwell was still playing his own game, and whilst no formal proposal had been made he was still using the *Mirror* to sway public opinion in his favour by his campaign to keep Gazza, as a national treasure, in the country of his birth. Harry Harris, chief football writer of the *Mirror,* was recalled from abroad. Maxwell saw Sugar as having his feet firmly in the Murdoch camp of News International, which numbered the *Sun* amongst its publications. Sugar was inextricably linked to Sky by his ownership of Amstrad and their mutual need to sell satellite dishes. Gascoigne – and Tottenham – had become pawns in a power struggle that had little or nothing to do with football.

Perhaps in his twisted mind Maxwell truly believed that Gazza wanted him to take over and kill the Lazio deal. He was hopelessly wrong. Paul dismissed him as a 'barrel of lard'. It was not a deeply considered description, but with the hindsight of history Gascoigne seems to have had a better grasp of Maxwell's honesty and business ethics than many of the more gullible people who became involved in his nefarious activities. However, despite a last-minute intervention from Maxwell on Friday 21 June, as the clock ticked towards midnight Scholar under pressure from all sides finally sold his shares to the Sugar–Venables consortium. The footballing world held its breath and waited. What would they do about Gascoigne?

20

'THEY TAKE THEIR FOOTBALL SERIOUSLY HERE.'

On 22 June 1991 Venables and Sugar held a press conference to announce formally their take-over of Tottenham. On the subject of Gazza, however, the men seemed at one. Despite his public pontifications, despite the fact that his original bid had stated Gazza should not be sold, now Venables said that he did not know whether or not the club could retain the services of Gascoigne. He was preparing the supporters for the worst, whilst still going through the motions. He phoned Stein and invited him and Len Lazarus to a breakfast meeting at the Royal Lancaster Hotel, the venue for so many crucial meetings.

The meeting was short and to the point. 'I don't suppose I can really stand in his way,' Venables said, 'but I'm not going to give him away.' The threat was clearly there, namely that he did not regard the negotiations with Lazio as at an end. Half-heartedly Venables repeated the vague terms he'd offered before the Cup Final. They had not been acceptable then and they were not acceptable now. Venables knew that. Paul's advisers left feeling less than happy.

Oblivious to it all Paul was enjoying his recuperatory holiday in Portugal. He'd discarded his crutches for the first time and was exercising the damaged knee by daily

(Seated, 3rd from right). Wearing the colours of Redheugh Boys' Club Team.

Butter wouldn't melt in my mouth.

Who ate all the pies? Not me.

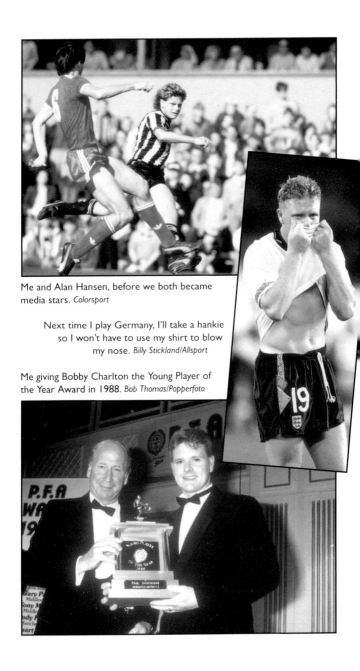

Me and Alan Hansen, before we both became media stars. *Colorsport*

Next time I play Germany, I'll take a hankie so I won't have to use my shirt to blow my nose. *Billy Stickland/Allsport*

Me giving Bobby Charlton the Young Player of the Year Award in 1988. *Bob Thomas/Popperfoto*

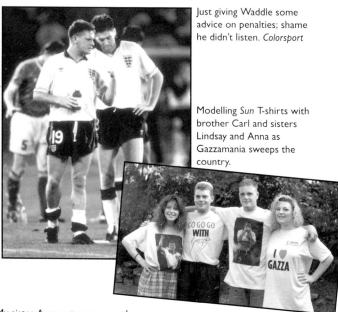

Just giving Waddle some advice on penalties; shame he didn't listen. *Colorsport*

Modelling *Sun* T-shirts with brother Carl and sisters Lindsay and Anna as Gazzamania sweeps the country.

My sister Anna gets permanently engaged at the fan club before she ever meets husband to be, John-Paul King.

Gary Lineker does us all a favour by blotting out most of Peter Beardsley. *Colorsport*

The pleasure and pain of the 1991 FA Cup Competition.
Left *The Sun/Rex Features*, and right *Colorsport*

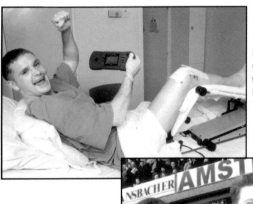

In the Princess
Grace after the Cup
final. Hang on, Lazio,
I'm still coming.
The Sun/Rex Features

Perhaps it was
something I said,
but it was down-hill
from then on.
Colorsport

Champagne for me – tea for the rest of them. A Lazio player at last.

Arriving in Rome. I know I was costing an arm and a leg, but I thought I got to keep my own. *Mirror Syndication International*

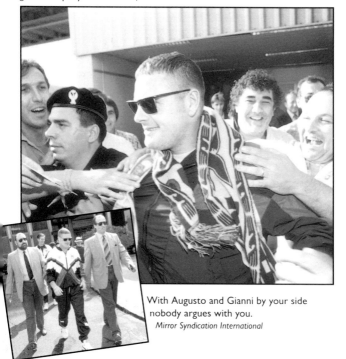

With Augusto and Gianni by your side nobody argues with you.
Mirror Syndication International

Anna looking lovely on her wedding day – shame about Ginga.

I'd just scored a crucial goal in Lazio's derby match against Roma but if I'd known this ugly lot were going to hug me, I'm not sure I'd have bothered. *Colorsport*

He must have been a beautiful baby, but baby look at him now. All sixteen bouncing stones of Fat Jimmy.

A.C. Milan/D.C. Milan. Makes no difference to me, I'm broadminded. *Colorsport*

I've heard of masqued balls, but this is ridiculous. *Bob Thomas/Popperfoto*

Sheryl arrives in Rome to lend her support. *The Sun/Rex Features*

Broken, but unbowed. *Foto Bartoletti*

Yes, it's me! Back in action against Reggiana. *Michael Cooper/Allsport*

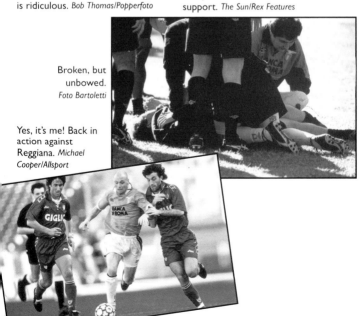

Struggling for fitness and feeling dejected as the England squad prepare for their match against Romania...without me. October 1994. *Martin Beddal/Times Newspapers Ltd*

England v. Brazil, and another new 'look' to keep everyone guessing. *Neal Simpson/Empics*

A dream come true; scoring a goal against Celtic, September 1995. *Alan Ewing*

As I arrived at Ibrox to sign the contract with Glasgow Rangers I was met by over 1,000 fans – some of whom looked just like me! *Popperfoto/Reuters*

swimming, and even managed to play table-tennis. There were frustrating moments for him when the others would play football on the hotel lawns, whilst all he could do was referee. Even then he had to be competitive, urging Jimmy Gardner on to kick John-Paul so that he could have some company in his sessions with John Sheridan. Then there were the nights. At 10.30 p.m. John Sheridan would tap his watch and say, 'Come on, Paul,' and Paul would meekly follow, wobbling along unsteadily on his crutches, whilst the others discussed which nightclub they were going to visit.

They went out fishing from a boat and Paul caught a baby shark, threatened his father with its teeth, then threw it back. There were enough sharks in the muddy waters of English football without him taking another one home. He played brutal practical jokes on everybody, including a televised nightmare for John-Paul. Ginga, holidaying without Anna, slept in a room on his own. At 5 a.m. Gazza arose, got Jimmy to fill a fire bucket with cold water, then tip-toed along the corridor accompanied by a hotel porter with a pass key and the Chrysalis camera crew. Silently they entered Ginga's bedroom. He lay beneath the sheets, quietly snoring. The next thing he knew, he was being doused by freezing cold water, leaping from his bed stark naked, grabbing what he thought was an intruder (Fat Jimmy) and screaming four-letter epithets into an unsympathetic microphone. Gazza and Jimmy collapsed with laughter in the hall outside, Paul with his crutches by his side as if they belonged to another darker life.

Sheridan spoke to Browett regularly. The week before he'd gone to Portugal Paul had difficulty in making a contraction with the leg. Now the muscle was coming back, muscles that had wasted away during the weeks of inactivity. He would measure the knee, work Gazza harder, then measure again. 'He was getting more confident,' Sheridan says, 'but when he'd finished the exercises he'd feel like getting up and walking away. Yet he knew he couldn't do it, knew he couldn't even do it in a month's time.'

One night Paul wandered around a fairground with his travelling companions. They found a small local fair which included a stall with a board containing holes, through which contestants had to kick footballs from about ten yards. Everybody tried and failed, then Paul, leaning on his crutch to support his injury, casually flicked the ball with his good leg straight through the target. It was his first goal since the semi-final, and it was a gesture of defiance, a promise that there would be many more to come.

Paul returned to England with the Lazio contingent hot on his trail. They wanted an update on their injured hero and they also wanted to progress the documentation. Stein and Lazarus had a share in a racehorse which was due to run at Doncaster on 28 June. Arrangements were made for Manzini and Regalia to accompany them on the train to work on the papers, whilst Paul would travel with his dad and Jimmy Gardner to the racecourse. Nobody paid any attention to the four men in the carriage with their papers spread out before them, but the horse duly obliged and the Italians went home with their winnings thinking that perhaps Gazza was a lucky mascot after all.

Whilst Stein visited Rome again at the start of July, Marseille, where Waddle was still a player, suddenly indicated to Spurs that they were prepared to make an unconditional offer of £4 million for Paul. They would then assume all the risks for him, and if it transpired at the end of the day that he couldn't play then that would be their loss. Immediately the offer was brought to their attention Stein and Lazarus phoned Paul. His feeling was that just as Lazio had been loyal to him there was no way he was going to be disloyal to them, even though the Marseille deal might give him greater security. Unless Lazio pulled the plug on the deal, despite the attraction of playing alongside his old friend Waddle, he simply wasn't interested.

Stein told Manzini that Spurs were now also talking to Marseille. Manzini was cynically calm. 'Tapie is buying every player in Europe. Why should Gascoigne be the odd one out?'

Paul had returned from Portugal tanned and walking, albeit still with a substantial limp and on occasions with the help of a stick. However, both Browett and Sheridan expressed themselves well pleased with his progress and there was every chance that he would be back kicking a ball long before Browett's conservative February prediction. He decided to spend the weekend in Newcastle seeing his family and old friends.

On the night of 13 July he was walking his sister Lindsay home. He'd been drinking, but not to excess and he certainly was not drunk. It had been a good night and he felt contented and comfortable, sure of his recovery, but not for the first time unsure that he had done the right thing by leaving Tyneside. He wondered if a Geordie could ever be truly at home anywhere other than within sight of the Tyne Bridge, and the murky river that ran beneath it. He sang a few lines of 'Fog on the Tyne' and his sister joined in. Then stumbling towards him came the figure of a railwayman coming home from a late shift, a few nightcaps already under his belt. At the same time a few aggressive youngsters began to call out to Paul, taunting him for his injury. The bravest amongst them began to push and jostle him, pulling so hard they removed his bright red braces. Paul obviously did not have his usual mobility. It all became confused and then someone, Paul thought the railwayman, punched Lindsay in the stomach. Paul went berserk. He hit the railwayman full in the face and the man fell to the ground to join the winded Lindsay. The youths ran away, and a young Italian waiter came from a restaurant to help, carrying a glass of water. Still confused, Paul flailed out at him as well, at which point somebody called the police.

It was well past midnight when Stein came home. It had been his birthday and he'd been visiting friends locally. The telephone rang. It was a Newcastle police station which had a certain Paul Gascoigne there who would like to talk to Mr Stein. The lawyer thought it was a joke, a typical Gazza prank, but as soon as he heard the player's voice he realized it was for real. 'Mel, they've put me in a cell. I can't take it. You've got to tell them about my claustrophobia. I was just looking after my baby sister . . .'

The voice broke into a mixture of sobs and such broad Geordie that Stein could hardly understand him. He asked to be put back to the police officer who told him Paul had been involved in an affray and subsequently arrested. Stein arranged for a local lawyer to get him out and at 2.30 a.m. Gazza rang Stein again, waking him up to report that he was at home.

Marilyn Stein, on whose side of the bed was the telephone, was not amused. 'It's bad enough he phones to tell you he's in. Why does he have to wake you up to tell you he's out?'

'He thought I'd be worried,' Stein said lamely.

The press had yet another field day. Only the *Sun* gave Paul's side of the story. 'What was I supposed to do? I thought my kid sister was being attacked. She'd already been hit in the stomach. I did what any normal brother would have done. I protected her. If I hadn't stuck up for her I'd have been a coward. They can give me as much stick as they want, but don't involve my family.'

The Italians actually loved it. If he was a hero before, he was now a greater hero, a machismo man gallant towards women.

The responsibility for getting him to John Sheridan's home near Luton usually fell on John-Paul. Gazza was an impossible passenger. 'He's impatient and he'd tell me to drive on the hard shoulder whenever we met a bit of traffic. He'd stay up all night looking at maps to find alternative routes to Luton. I'd be doing 90 mph up the A10 and he'd still be telling me to go faster.'

It was difficult for Paul at the training ground. His team-mates were just a few yards away in pre-season training. He could hear their shouts, imagine what was going on, yet the camaraderie was limited to whoever else might be on the treatment couch. Sheridan had him walking up and down the steps of the treatment caravan at the training ground in the mornings and then doing similar exercises in his own back garden in the afternoon. If he was upset with him, if he felt he was lapsing into bad habits, then Sheridan would simply ignore him. He'd work with him, but there was no conversation. If he let him down really badly then he'd refuse to speak to him on the phone. It was a classic carrot and stick treatment.

The lawyers had brought more complications and problems to the Lazio–Tottenham negotiations. Gazza had become the meat in the sandwich in a struggle between two of the largest firms in the City as Lazio had now instructed Allen and Overy. The Italian club had sought to insert some stringent conditions in the contract regarding the medical tests to be imposed in due course to test Paul's fitness, requiring all the signs of the injury to be 'completely negative'. Without an agreement between Lazio and Spurs, Paul's transfer was again well and truly back on ice.

Stein faxed Manzini in Innsbruck, where Lazio were in pre-season training. He reiterated Browett's view that Lazio's demands for perfection were unreasonable and suddenly, in early August after the fax, things began to slip into place and gather momentum once again.

On 31 July Manzini telephoned Stein. Lazio needed a favour. On the night of 23 August there was to be a friendly match with Real Madrid, in memory of the late Giorgio Callieri, the president's brother. Lazio wanted Paul there even though he was not yet a Lazio player. They felt that if they presented him to the crowd before the match, this would be an enormous boost to the fans for the forthcoming season.

Spurs and Lazio had finally agreed a formula for the medical. The tests would be carried out in the presence of a medical committee which would consist of a representative of Tottenham and one or more representatives of Lazio. There was an agreed definition of 'recovery' and Paul had to achieve average performances for a footballer in various tests. When Gazza learned later what was required of him he smiled. 'No problem. If my speed's above average do I get more money?'

Manzini prepared Paul's arrival in Rome with all the precision of a military operation. The send-off at Heathrow was fit for an emperor about to conquer Rome. Stein, with his family, Glenn Roeder arriving on his own, looking more nervous than on the field, all waited impatiently for Paul. There had been a tearful parting from his new girlfriend, Sheryl Failes. He kept Sheryl outside the terminal and away from the press as he and his father were hustled through the pack of reporters and photographers by a helpful British Airways executive. He had met Sheryl in a wine-bar back in 1991. She had already separated from her estate-agent husband, although that did not stop him trying to cite Gazza in the divorce proceedings. With two children and a middle-class up-bringing, it had at first seemed an unlikely pairing, and indeed when Paul had first spoken to her she had refused to take him seriously; but then he made her laugh and there had been no laughter in her life for quite some time, so the relationship had developed and had blossomed into a romance, without a hint of the violence and agony that ultimately would seem to have destroyed it. On board the plane, Club Class was filled by those connected in some way to Paul: family, advisers, the Chrysalis team, and journalists and cameramen by the score. Somebody commented that Gazza at least was doing his part in fighting unemployment.

As the aircraft came to a halt in Rome, Manzini appeared, overshadowed by the huge form of Gianni. He requested that everyone else be let off, while the Gascoigne party stayed put. Not far behind was Nottage, fussing over anything and anybody she could find. The plane emptied, and as the passengers filed through Italians and English alike wished Paul good luck. In the distance there could be heard a chanting, the sound normally heard walking towards a football stadium just before kick-off. 'There are over 7,000 fans out there,' Manzini said by way of explanation. 'It has not been easy this morning.'

He handed Stein a sheet of paper, headed, 'Program (sic) of the visit of Paul Gascoigne to Italy Thursday 22nd August 1991,' which was all hopelessly optimistic even though it began in an orderly manner. Paul and Stein would go with him in one car, Roeder and Paul's father in another, Stein's family in a third with Nottage, the Chrysalis crew and sundry accredited journalists filling the others.

It began to go wrong in the corridor walking from the plane. Paul was mobbed, everybody trying to get the first autograph he would sign on Italian soil. Customs officers, police, airport employees, all begging him, shaking his hand, just touching him with all the blind faith of pilgrims at Lourdes. Somehow or other photographers had slipped the cordon and Paul found himself relying upon Gianni and a huge bearded giant called Augusto (who turned out to be a former Italian wrestling champion) to push his way through.

Eventually Paul and Stein found refuge in the police room at the airport. A large mustachioed man introduced himself as the Chief of Police in Rome – if Paul needed anything he just had to ask, Gianni translated. They waited for their baggage and the room got hotter and hotter, smokier and smokier. Paul looked around desperately for an escape route. But airports have only one real exit, through the luggage hall, through customs and then out through the public area to waiting cars.

The chants of the fans were now noticeably louder. 'Paul Gascoigne, la, la, la, la, la,' over and over again, an endless litany of promise and belief. Manzini returned hot and panting. Like all good administrators he was upset that his timetable was being abandoned, but he wasn't going to give up without a struggle. 'You have to speak to the press . . . they expect it.'

Paul looked even more panic-stricken. His fear of the press in those days bordered on the paranoiac. Taking a deep breath and holding a scrappy piece of paper upon which Nottage had written a simple Italian greeting in block capitals, he went to face a seething horde of reporters and photographers. It was a scene straight from Bedlam. Cameramen were pushing each other out of the way, even hitting each other. Whilst journalists swapped punches with their comrades, a woman in the midst of it all held up her baby towards Paul as if for a royal blessing. Paul looked around him at the carnage in horror. 'Someone's going to get hurt,' he said, still obligingly kissing the baby for a picture.

Stein grabbed Manzini. 'We've got to get him out of here. Tell them they'll get their chance at the main press conference.'

Gianni and Augusto closed in protectively around Paul, who like Stein had now been draped in Lazio scarves and caps. But Manzini was not done yet. 'Here we have the delegate of the Lazio supporters. He wants to make you a presentation. It is very important.'

The man in question came forward and seriously, with much ceremony, gave Paul a special scarf, posed for a photo, kissed him on both cheeks, and then withdrew in a cloud of garlic. It was time to make a run for it, no easy task for a player with an injured leg.

As the group raced through customs and exited into the main arrival hall the scene was quite fantastic. The crowd was six or seven deep, straining at the police cordon formed simply by the officers linking arms. The noise rose and swelled into an animal roar. One man yelled, 'We want to become a big team with you, right!'

The police did their best, but it was hopeless. One man broke ranks and suddenly everyone surged forward. On either side of him, Gianni and Augusto actually lifted Paul bodily a few inches off the floor. 'Mind my leg,' he said, but they'd already got him on to the escalator. The police threateningly drew heavy riot sticks and beat back the pursuers.

The cars were waiting and the player and his companions were shoved unceremoniously inside, with Gianni at the wheel and a Chrysalis cameraman, who'd lost the rest of his team, at his side. Gianni started the engine, but faces appeared at the window, one young man throwing himself flat across the bonnet. Manzini tried to explain.

'They like you. They love you. They are just trying to show it.' Paul grinned. 'I'd hate to see what they did to somebody they didn't like.'

Gianni decided there was only one way to get through the milling fans. He turned on the siren, signalled to the two police cars that were to be his escort and hit the accelerator. How nobody was killed was a miracle. Pedestrians dived for cover, as oblivious to anything or anybody in his way Gianni headed towards the hill at the top of which was situated the Cavalieri Hilton. Paul, not the most conservative of drivers himself, could only look on in admiration: weaving in and out, ignoring red lights, driving on the pavement when the traffic was halted. Only a nun, knitting by the side of the road, seemed oblivious to their passing. Perhaps nobody had bothered to tell her that the Messiah had arrived.

Roeder summed it up, when the shell-shocked travellers assembled at the hotel. 'They take their football seriously here, don't they?' Paul asked where his dad was. John was fine, if visibly pale. His fear of flying had been put into perspective. Nothing could have been more frightening than Gianni driving him to the hotel.

Everybody gathered in the evening for a dinner at a huge long table, courtesy of Lazio, but with Paul settling immediately into the role of host. He needed no encouragement to try every novel Italian delicacy that was put before him, as course followed course: melon, Parma ham, mozzarella cheese, olives, pasta, cold meats, fish, ice-cream, even Paul was struggling. 'I think I'm going to like it here,' he said.

The following day Lazio had organized, as Manzini described it on his list, 'an escorted sightseeing tour of Rome for the whole party with interpreter and private mini-bus'. As it transpired it was more an opportunity for Rome to see Gazza.

At the Coliseum Paul looked up at the ancient building. 'England supporters been here lately?' he asked. They took him into the main arena for photographs. It was a natural setting for a natural gladiator. Behind dark glasses, wearing a Lazio track-suit, he seemed to swell and grow into the part. He had been there for less than a day and already Rome was his city, there for the taking.

At the Fontana di Trevi he dutifully tossed in coins, assured that he'd be back. Roeder did likewise, standing with his back to the water and throwing them over his shoulder as instructed. Whether or not he would ever return for a holiday, this was to be his only visit in the uniform of Lazio.

At 4 p.m., dead on schedule, there was to be a press conference. Again Manzini had everything neatly planned. It all sounded terribly formal but Paul set the tone when he acquired a pair of false goggle glasses that at first shocked the waiting Italian press, who are not renowned for their sense of humour.

Callieri rose to his feet looking like the cat who had got the cream. He'd done what he'd set out to do. He'd brought the player he considered the best in the world to Rome. It was Paul's turn to respond and he dutifully thanked the president for keeping faith with him and pledged himself to be playing for Lazio within a year.

Then came the questions.

'What do you think of Italian football?'

Paul responded tactfully. 'As a player you always want to play with the best and Italian football is the best.'

'How will you cope with the physical side of the game?'

'Do you like Italian food?'

'Will you learn Italian?'

He kept quiet about that one as his two or three lessons to date had not been wildly successful, not through any fault of his teacher but due to his own inability to concentrate, and his grim determination always to have a ready excuse to cancel any arrangements that were made for him to have further lessons.

Then a pretty woman in the front row asked, 'What do you think of Italian women?'

Quick as a flash Paul responded, 'I'll tell you afterwards.'

The Olympic Stadium, which Lazio shared with Roma, was on the other side of the hill, which involved driving down a twisting, winding road, then up a little on the other side. Oblivious to the cars coming up, Paul was again driven down for the match at a furious pace as if the road were one-way.

There was a good crowd for a friendly in the middle of the holiday season of some 40,000 and there was no lack of noise. Up on the giant screens they showed over and over again a ten-minute film made by Chrysalis as their entrance fee to be allowed to film in the stadium. There was Gazza weaving his way through defences, Gazza singing 'Fog on the Tyne', Gazza baring his chest as he launched into 'Geordie Boys', the huge images on the screen enough to set the crowd roaring, the actual man in the flesh to send them into paroxysms of delight.

Before he went out on to the pitch Maurizio Manzini showed him around the world that existed beneath the stadium. 'This is the team physio, you'll be seeing a lot of him during your stay.' Quite how prophetic that was he could not have envisaged. Incredibly enough after all that had gone before, he was introduced to the coach, Dino Zoff, for the first time. The men embraced, Zoff tossing aside his cigarette. Paul was asked how he felt. He used his hand in a flamboyant gesture that could only be described as Italian. 'Così così', it's good to feel wanted again.'

When it was time to make his entry into the stadium Paul asked if his father could be with him on the pitch, and there indeed was John Gascoigne looking on proudly as Paul came out, the announcement of his name over the loudspeakers drowned by the roar of the crowd. All around the stadium were banners to greet him,

> 'Gazza's boys are here,
> Shag women, drink beer.'

Bedecked in scarves, wearing his Lazio track-suit and cap, he began to jog, but once again the press moved in around him, making it almost impossible to move. He took a microphone in his hand and gave his prepared message in an execrable accent.

'Arrividerci. Al prossimo campionato.'

A few yards behind him, almost ignored, Roeder waved to the crowd, his face impassive, giving no trace of what he actually felt.

Back in the tunnel Paul was breathless and red-faced. 'Unbelievable. It's electric. I can't wait to get out there and play.'

21

'ONE DRINK AND WE'RE OUT OF HERE.'

On the night of Saturday 28 September Paul Gascoigne, in Newcastle for the weekend, decided to go into town. Roeder had been the last person outside the North-East to speak to him before he embarked on his own personal day of reckoning. 'He'd told me he was going up to Newcastle with one of the young Spurs players, Tony Potts, who was injured. I heard the warning bells go off in my head. I told him to make sure he stayed with his family, to go to the Excelsior, but to stay away from the town. He said he would, he promised he would . . .'

But Paul was to break that promise with disastrous consequences. Quite what possessed him to put everything at risk the day after everybody had finally reached agreement even Paul himself does not know. 'I'd been to Walker's night-club often enough in the past. When I'd been playing up there it was the place the lads all went to on a Saturday night. I thought I'd be safe there, but once we'd got inside I realized it had changed. I should have left there and then, but I didn't.'

They arrived at Walker's at 10 p.m. None of them was roaring drunk, but they had been asked to leave one of the pubs when Jimmy Gardner became a little rowdy and tried to dance with an unwilling customer. Gazza had been showing his city to Tony Potts with pride. Now he looked around for familiar faces, for fellow professionals, but none were to be seen.

'OK,' he said to his brother Carl, 'one drink and we're out of here.' They ordered, Paul drank up and told Carl he was just going to the toilet and then they'd leave.

He walked along the narrow, dark corridor. From the shadows a voice called 'Gazza'. Another autograph he thought resignedly as he turned. The rest was a blur. A fist slammed into his jaw and he literally took off, slid along a nearby counter western movie style, and crashed unconscious to the floor, falling as dead weight onto his knee.

His companions brought him round. One of them, his 'uncle' Ian, who had been a constant provider of sweets in Paul's childhood, decided to get him out as quickly as possible before the press got there. That was also too late, and as Paul was helped to a car supported by his friends there was a cameraman. The photograph and the story began to buzz down the wires.

The first Stein knew of it was a telephone call from a journalist on Sunday morning at his office. It was a north-eastern writer politely enquiring about a 'night-club incident which took place last night resulting in Paul being taken to hospital'. Stein stonewalled, then immediately phoned Paul at his parents' house. He was nearly in tears.

'I was just about to phone you,' he said.

'What happened? How serious is it?'

Paul told him. As to the gravity of the injury he just did not know.

'Have you told the police?'

'No.'

'Paul, we have to. You get yourself down to London to see Mr Browett. I'll call the police.'

Stein then spoke to Carol Gascoigne, who was virtually hysterical. The Newcastle underground telegraph had been busy. Nobody could take a swipe at their local hero and hope to get away scot-free. But the news that it brought was not reassuring. She knew for certain who had hit Paul. He was a local lad with a terrible reputation for violence and a criminal record to go with it. He'd just been released from gaol after serving a lengthy sentence for grievous bodily harm and a message had filtered through: if Paul went to the police his family would not be able to walk the streets of Newcastle without a bodyguard at their backs. Stein tried to persuade her that it was all bluff, that the police were there to give protection in such circumstances, but she was unconvinced. They were 'her bairns' and like any good mother she was fearfully protective of anything that might happen to her young. As it transpired she was right and Stein was wrong. Some months later the individual concerned, involved in a local drug battle, found himself assaulted in the apparent safety of a hospital bed, then eventually was stabbed to death in a gangland revenge attack.

Meanwhile the media seized upon the mystery assailant. Cartoons appeared linking Paul to pink spotted elephants and the general consensus was that he had done it again, that he'd had a few too many drinks, stumbled and fallen, and the 'attack' was just a cover story.

Once they'd got beyond that stage it was a question of how bad was the injury. The answer was very bad. By lunchtime he'd reached London and seen John Browett, who told him he'd fractured his knee-cap in the resulting fall, an injury which was in its way far more serious than the cruciate. Browett was asked to prepare a report for all the interested parties, but his initial reaction was that there was certain to be a delay of a couple of months in Paul's recovery. Manzini, and doubtless everybody else at Lazio, was in a state of shock. Alan Sugar was more vocal; he was furious. He'd based his whole entry into the Tottenham situation upon the imminent sale of Gazza. A week or so before, when Paul had been photographed standing on the terraces at St James's Park like any other fan, he'd erupted and phoned Stein. 'What would have happened if the crowd had pushed forward? Is your client a complete idiot? Doesn't he realize he can't do that sort of thing any more?'

It was a very subdued and chastened Paul Gascoigne that Stein and Lazarus visited in hospital on 30 September, the day his transfer was to have been concluded. It was his third operation at the Princess Grace in the space of five months. Nobody could have been more upset than John Sheridan, although there was some consolation because the graft from the original operation was fine even though it had suffered a tremendous trauma. Paul was inevitably in tears as his advisers sat by his bedside. 'That's it. I'm never going to a night-club again. I realize I can't be one of the lads. Tell Lazio I'll stay home every night.'

'We'll tell them, Paul, but why should they believe us?' Stein and Lazarus felt in a brutal mood. They'd worked for nine months on this deal and now it seemed as if it might have been tossed away in one day of foolishness.

The Italians, having thought they'd paid their last visit to London in respect of the transfer, made their arrangements to travel again in a state of disbelief. On 2 October most of the main players assembled in a small consulting room at the Princess Grace. Callieri, to Paul's great disappointment, was in the process of selling his interest in the club to Sergio Cragnotti, a merchant banker. Cragnotti was a far different proposition to his amiable predecessor and had appointed Lionello Celon as chief executive of the club. Now to Celon, Manzini, Bartolini, Venables, Sheridan, Colin Sandy (Sugar's finance director), Stein, Lazarus and Lazio's lawyers, Browett's report sounded like an obituary:

'On Saturday p.m. he had a hard blow to the left side of his jaw which knocked him out and [he] fell on to the right knee from a standing position. He's a heavy man and this led to a heavy fall which fractured the patella . . .' The faces of the men in the room were solemn, but in the same funereal tone he continued in a more optimistic vein: 'There should be no problem with the healing. The surface is all intact and it's looking very encouraging, although it's very frustrating and annoying and clearly will delay things.'

At least the cruciate had held firm, had been put to the ultimate test and had passed. The priority was to get the broken bone to unite. He would leave the wiring in for four or five months. It sounded like eternity. There would be stiffness and the quadriceps would waste. That would be something for Sheridan to work upon in physio later, but as he was to note, 'There was wastage in the muscle, but it would have been a lot more if the knee had been put in plaster.'

The crucial date in the transfer was 31 May 1992. That was the end date that Lazio had given Tottenham for Paul to pass his medical. It was in Lazio's gift to extend the date, but they showed no sign of doing so at this meeting. Browett sighed. If 31 May was decisive, then they must strive for it and he would hope Paul would be fit by that date. He was looking at eight weeks for the bone to unite, but ultimate strength would take longer. If one was talking about six months then Browett was sure the patella would be strong enough, but earlier . . . ? They discussed the removal of the wire, the laymen leaving it to the doctors. Browett said that if the wire were removed about May this could lead to further delays in Paul's recovery and might well jeopardize the 31 May date.

The Italians moved up to see Paul. It was yet another emotional meeting, with even Celon, who hardly knew him, embracing his stricken player, or nearly player.

Manzini looked sadly on. Once again fate, and Paul himself, had conspired to knock the celebratory chalice from his hand. Eventually they all went their separate ways leaving only Paul and Stein. Again the player asked the question to which there was really no answer. 'It's all going to be all right isn't it?'

The angry words that came to the lawyer's lips were bitten back. 'Yes, Paul, it's all going to be all right.'

22

'WE DON'T HAVE TO SELL PAUL GASCOIGNE TO SURVIVE . . .'

For Roeder, though, it was not all right. On Monday 7 October he phoned Stein's office. It was a sad conversation. 'I've thought about it long and hard,' he said. 'I've discussed it with Faith and I'm not going to Rome. Paul promised me not to go into the town. He broke that promise and look what's happened. I just can't expose my family to those sort of risks. It's cost me a lot of money, and I know it's going to cost me more, but I can't do it.' There was no point in seeking to persuade him otherwise.

On the same day Lazio's Italian lawyer, Giuseppe Biolato wrote: 'Lazio regrets that Tottenham is not able to exercise any kind of control on the player, who at this time is still in its employment, with the consequence of exposing him to accidents that undoubtedly affect his ability to recover well from the first accident suffered.'

It was a far cry from the hugs and kisses that had accompanied the Italian visit. Biolato copied Stein in on the letter. Was this a genuine threat, or was it more bluff to put the Italian club into a better position to renegotiate with Tottenham? There was no doubt that an element of acrimony had crept into the relationship between the two clubs. At first the conflict had been with Scholar, but now that he was gone it was Venables who was seen as trying to strike a hard bargain; but

Venables's trump card, the early recovery of the player, had fallen from his hand. Lazio now had all the aces, the first decent hand they'd been dealt, and Biolato wanted to make sure they took full advantage of it.

Stein went to see Venables, the two men united in adversity. Sitting at Scribes, Terry's club, they pondered the problem caused by their wayward genius. Venables was less than pleased with Lazio's letter. It was, of course, absurd to suggest that Tottenham could monitor any player's activities twenty-four hours a day. Venables suggested those around Paul should exercise more control over him. Stein laughed. Some days he, or Jane Featherstone, Paul's personal assistant who had replaced Renée Menir, would make six phone calls just to find out where Paul was. Yet Biolato had not been far off the mark when he blamed Spurs. The fact was that once Spurs had signed the initial contract with Lazio, then, apart from supplying John Sheridan and paying Paul's wages, it seemed in the opinion of Paul and his advisers that they had washed their hands of him. Paul actually wanted to be with his team-mates, to stay with them in hotels, to travel with them on match days, even to sit on the bench and act as some kind of third coach. But the Tottenham management had denied him all this, and indeed had at least once requested he keep away as a disruptive influence. Disruptive – it was a nonsense. Gazza, even an injured Gazza, was great for morale, inspirational for dressing-room confidence.

Venables and Stein agreed that initially Paul would be housebound when he left hospital. Browett had already put the fear of death into him in that respect and John-Paul had volunteered to keep him company. After that Sheridan would get his hands on him and then he'd have imposed upon him all the discipline of a full first-team member. It was closing the stable door, but Browett's prognosis gave him some hope that the horse had not yet bolted beyond recall.

Whilst Stein tried to pour oil on troubled waters in correspondence with Biolato, the *Sun* carried an alleged statement by Dr Bartolini that Lazio's interest in Paul was cooling. Bartolini denied saying any such thing but Lazio's lawyers refused to write to the newspaper to set the record straight. Although Lazio claimed to have issued only a general press bulletin, without commenting on Paul's medical condition, their doctor's track record of talking to the press, coupled with the club's reluctance to take any remedial action, did upset those around Paul.

Meanwhile Paul left hospital and sat quietly at home growing a beard. Stein had, in collusion with John Browett, given John-Paul his instructions, which were to keep him quiet and calm and not let him move. It was easier said than done.

On 24 October Alan Sugar decided to flex his muscles. Every company in which he had been involved had been operated hands on, and Tottenham was to be no different. He wrote directly to Stein, suggesting: 'It is an implied term of Mr Gascoigne's employment with Tottenham that he will exercise reasonable care in the performance of his duties. These include duties to have due regard to the necessity of maintaining a high standard of fitness and to refrain from indulging in activities or practices that might endanger his fitness. I regard Mr Gascoigne's involvement (and the injuries sustained) in the recent incident as a breach of the duties referred to above and as a consequence I believe that Mr Gascoigne is liable to indemnify Tottenham in respect of any losses which it might suffer as a result.' Then as an afterthought he wrote in manuscript, 'PS Would you please copy your client with this letter.'

It showed how little he knew Gazza if he thought he would read it. Stein, Lazarus and Paul discussed it at length. Paul's reaction was short and to the point, basically consisting of a four-letter epithet followed by the word 'him'. His advisers were more restrained, but the letter had to have a reply.

By now, out of the blue, two witnesses had come forward supporting Paul's version of the night-club incident. They were 17-year-olds who had actually written to Venables after reading the lies about Paul in the press. Stein pointed this out to Sugar, but assured him that Paul had no intention of attending clubs of this nature ever again. He also made one highly relevant point clear in connection with an insurance policy that Spurs had been seeking, to protect their position should Paul not pass his medical. 'As I told Terry Venables, the only possible beneficiary of that policy is Tottenham Hotspur. Should Paul fail his medical in May and find his career at an end he will not benefit from any of the money payable under the policy nor will he receive the financial rewards he would have gained in Italy. He would be faced with a situation where he would have one year left of his contract with Tottenham and therefore would face an extremely bleak future.'

John-Paul and Anna were doing their utmost to ensure that Paul did not go out of the house, let alone go night-clubbing. John-Paul can now look back on those difficult days with a smile although nobody saw much to laugh about at the time. 'We decided that to make life easier for him, we'd bring his bed downstairs. It took me and John Coberman two hours to demolish it, and put it in the lounge with the television and loads of videos we'd got for him. While he was in hospital all he kept asking was whether the house was tidy. He came home, saw the bed and went crazy, telling us it belonged upstairs. He'd direct the cleaning of the house as he lay on the couch. "I think we'll polish the brass", or "Today we'll wash the windows". What he meant was that Anna and I would do it.'

He was always trying to persuade them to take him out, but his minders hardened their hearts, whatever might be the personal price they had to pay. One day he suggested doing some shooting. They opened the French windows, and with Paul seated on the sofa John-Paul went to the bottom of the garden to set up the targets. As he bent over, Paul promptly shot him with an air-gun in the backside. So much for gratitude.

Paul had difficulty sleeping but he never allowed it to get him down, nor did he complain about the constant pain. If he was up then he was going to ensure that everybody else was as well. He had acquired a starting pistol with blanks and every morning at 6 a.m. he would fire it in John-Paul's ear, adding, 'Morning, Ginga, the day starts now.'

He was learning the keyboard and guitar, and within minutes of waking he'd be on the phone to people with a cheery 'Good morning,' and a version of 'Coming Round the Mountain' which was the only piece he could play. In desperation John-Paul bought him a mouth-organ, thinking this would be easier to learn. It was a bad move as throughout the day he had to listen to the blues man coming out in him. Finally John-Paul hid it. The listening public would be spared 'Gazza Sings Bob Dylan'.

He was house-bound for a month and it felt like a lifetime. Things came to a head with the visit of a man with a huge X-ray machine which spilled oil all over the carpet. He went absolutely wild, insisted on a leg brace being fitted, and he was out on the road having served his term. For the first time in his life he'd not been moving at 100 mph and it had done him the world of good, even though he may not have appreciated it.

Yet his first trip out nearly ended in disaster. Anna had appeared in a Pet Shop Boys video and had been invited to their end-of-tour party. She took her brother and boyfriend as her guests, or rather they took themselves. Everybody who was anybody in the world of pop music was there – Bros, Duran Duran, Spandau Ballet, even Sinead O'Connor on the bouncy castle. Paul obviously could not dance and sat on the lawn, quite happy with a drink in his hand. Up came Janet Street-Porter, who both Anna and John-Paul thought would be a good contact to further their careers.

''Allo, Gazza, Janet Street-Porter,' she said in her broad cockney accent.

'Well you can just bugger off,' Gazza replied, hardly bothering to lift his head.

'Well, I'm just— '

'F—off. I'm trying to enjoy my drink.'

She went. John-Paul was horrified. He'd never seen Paul behave like this before. 'Why did you do that, Paul?'

'She just breezed up to me and said she was a reporter.'

'No, Paul, it was Street-Porter.'

He began to frequent the Swallow Leisure Club again, working himself as hard as he could. He would do bench presses, with John-Paul holding his leg while he pressed. He still had the leg brace, but he was determined that next time he saw the Italians it would be off.

At the beginning of November Benfica showed an interest in Paul. But the player showed no interest in them, he was committed to Lazio. Then came the oddest event of all. Venables phoned to say that Tapie and Marseille had contacted him again to see if the Gascoigne deal had been concluded. He'd said it was not. They therefore wanted to meet with the representatives of both Paul and the club and would fly into London for that purpose. Stein and Lazarus were both cynical and unexcited but eventually were persuaded to meet Tapie at Luton Airport where he would land in his private jet, and arrangements were made to collect both Stein and Lazarus from their respective homes.

At about 8.30 p.m. Venables called from Luton to say that the plane had landed and a driver was on his way. Nothing happened. At 11 p.m. Stein decided he was going to bed. Just then Venables called again. 'You're not going to believe this,' he said. 'We've just gone out to see what happened to you and we found the driver who was coming to collect you fast asleep in his car. Tapie's got fed up waiting and has gone home.'

It was like something out of a farce. 'Oh well, if he's that interested he'll come back,' Stein said, relieved that he'd not had to attend a futile meeting. He never did come back.

It now seemed clear even to Tottenham that it was to be Lazio or nothing. Some months later, at a charity dinner, Sugar met up with Stein and Lazarus and came across to chat. 'I hope your boy is going to pass his bloody medical,' he said gruffly. Whatever anybody has ever said publicly there can be no doubt that the Gascoigne money was absolutely vital to the Sugar-Venables takeover.

Arguments raged back and forth between Spurs and Lazio over the required insurance policy, but on 13 November after phone calls between London and Rome it looked as if Paul would just have to pack his bags to be on the plane to Italy. Stein and Lazarus arranged to be with him and to wait for the phone call to say everything was finalized. It was the day of the England – Poland European Championship match. The three of them watched the game together in London and saw England get the point they needed to qualify, then waited for the phone call to tell them everything was finalized. Almost inevitably it didn't come.

By December, although Paul was working hard with John Sheridan within the limitations set down by the doctor, there was a silence from both Tottenham's and Lazio's lawyers which was bordering on the ominous. Stein telephoned James Perry, who politely apologized for the delay and said there were some direct discussions going on between Sugar and Callieri (who was still involved, despite the pending sale of his interest) with a view to bringing the transfer forward. On the following day, 18 December, Carlo Regalia and Lionello Celon visited England and, accompanied by John Campion of Allen and Overy, went to see Stein. They still wanted to conclude the transaction by the end of the year, but they too had become frustrated by the delays in putting the policy in place. Now they were checking out the cost of insurance to enable them to insure Paul themselves, actually to buy him and then lend him back to Spurs, or possibly a Swiss club where his rehabilitation in Italy would still be possible.

Again the Gascoigne camp was lulled into a false sense of security. On 12 December, earlier than originally planned, Paul had seen Browett again. 'He was strongly motivated and we had to hold him back. I knew as soon as he got the green light, he'd go. I "gated" him for a few weeks and said he could start gentle jogging very soon, and put him back on weights straight away.'

On Christmas Eve the *Sun* ran a feature headed 'Tel Fury at £4m Lazio Rip-off Deal for Gazza'. In the article Venables claimed that Lazio had tried to cut the fee for Paul to £4 million, and maintained that unless Lazio confirmed the agreement for £5.5 million by 1 January the deal would fall through. He claimed, 'They are trying to get Gazza on the cheap. They think Spurs are in a weak financial position, that we are a soft touch. Well, they've made a big mistake. They have until 31 December to stand by our original arrangement. If I don't hear from them by then, the transfer is off. We don't have to sell Paul Gascoigne to survive and I have maintained throughout that I want him to stay with Spurs . . .'

January 1 came and went. Venables's deadline ultimatum passed without anybody withdrawing from the deal. They couldn't; with or without the policy there was a binding agreement. On 3 January 1992 John Campion wrote to Stein on behalf of Lazio stating that correspondence between his firm and Spurs' lawyers showed that the Tottenham understanding of the new Lazio proposal was somewhat different from that which had been intended, and it had now been withdrawn. Everybody would just now have to wait until 31 May, or whatever earlier date might be decided upon for the medical. It was disappointing news, but at least everybody knew where they stood, even if they stood in no man's land.

The big question on the lips of every Tottenham fan was whether or not they would ever see Gazza in a Tottenham shirt again. Venables had fuelled the hope, which had fanned some life back into the season, but most sensible fans realized it would be a foolish act of sentimentality to risk him in a competitive game before the transfer actually went through.

Paul was single-minded about the work involved in his rehabilitation. Everything else went by the way. Commercial engagements were kept to a minimum, just enough to fulfil contractual obligations; language lessons were missed with alarming regularity. Lazio were looking for monthly medical examinations and the first of these was held on 28 January at the Princess Grace. The usual Italian delegation arrived, Manzini, Regalia, Bartolini, only this time without lawyers. Browett had seen Paul the day before in anticipation of the meeting. The player was now running at three-quarter speed and it looked encouraging; the knee was stable and generally looking good. Browett was now planning to remove the wires at the end of March, earlier than anticipated, but felt Paul would need another couple of months to allow the wound to recover from the operation. 'In a way the fracture had been a good thing as it had allowed the cruciate injury even longer to recover.'

Without the setback Paul would already have been playing, and knowing his patience threshold that return would inevitably have been earlier than Browett would have wanted. As far as the surgeon was concerned he would prefer Paul to play no contact football until the summer.

The Romans asked Paul if he would attend the Lazio-Roma derby on 1 March as they felt it would be good for him, the club and the spectators. Eventually Venables agreed, provided Sheridan sent a work schedule for Paul to follow. Even before he left for Italy he was running at the training ground and, more important, turning with ease if not without pain. Dave Butler put him through his paces, watching with amazement as his times tumbled down towards those of his former team-mates.

He still found time for two important social functions. *Dream On,* a film starring his sister Anna, was being premièred in Newcastle. Paul arrived at the cinema looking quiet and dignified in a dinner suit and bow tie. He couldn't restrain himself for long. Introduced to the Lord Mayor of Newcastle bedecked in his gold chain, Paul winked at the cameras and mouthed 'Mr T', referring to the huge black star of *The A Team*.

It was an improvement on his last effort to support Anna's career. She and John-Paul had been appearing in pantomime, and persuaded Paul to come to a matinée. The big mistake was going for a pre-performance drink, after which Ginga put Paul in his seat some half-way down the stalls. One of the stars, Bernie Clifton, came on stage with a big sausage, which he would throw and would normally see passed around the entire audience. On this occasion it got as far as Paul and no further as he refused to let it go. While Clifton was still negotiating its return, John-Paul came on stage dressed as a Chinese policeman. All he could hear was a guttural chant of 'Ginga', followed by, 'He went that way.'

Worse was to follow. Anna came out dressed in a harem outfit as the slave of the ring. She had to stand there for three minutes and just listen to the rest of the dialogue, but she had something else to listen to as well. From the moment she appeared Paul chanted his pet name for her, 'Spenna', followed by 'Look at the size of her boobs.'

By the interval the cast was exhausted with worry. The script was in shambles, as was their timing. Suddenly Paul remembered an urgent engagement and departed. A relieved voice came over the backstage tannoy, 'Ladies and gentlemen of the cast, Mr Gascoigne has left the building.'

Then on the weekend of 8/9 February he attended Paul Stein's bar mitzvah, his thirteenth birthday and coming of age in the Jewish religion.

Paul Stein recited his portion of the law and it was then the turn of Rabbi Yisrael Fine to talk from the pulpit. 'There are wicked tongues in this community,' he said. 'It is rumoured that Paul Gascoigne sees more of my congregants on a Saturday than I do . . .'

On the Sunday Spurs had to travel to Nottingham for the first leg of their Rumbelows Cup semi-final. Gazza went with them to lend his support and then hurried back to attend the bar mitzvah party. Joining in the Israeli dancing, which involved the separation of men and women, he whirled around. Stein and Lazarus exchanged glances. 'Great. I can see the headlines now. Gazza's career cut short by injury sustained in Israeli dancing. Let's stop him now.'

On 19 February England played France at Wembley. Chris Waddle was by now firmly out of favour and had been asked to commentate for Sky. The mad brothers from the Café de Paris had come across for the match and everybody met up at the Hard Rock Café for lunch. Paul was in great form, his problems seemingly forgotten. The following day it was off to the North-East for the press showing of the Chrysalis film. It made gory viewing as the camera focused on the surgical instruments but Paul sat quite happily in the front row with his family, cracking jokes as if what was happening on the screen had nothing to do with him. It was also the first public appearance for Sheryl Failes, although he glared angrily at any photographer who flexed his camera-finger in her direction. Available for questions he made it clear that while he was happy to deal with anything appertaining to his career or the film, he would walk out at the first enquiry regarding his personal life. Journalists generally are not very bright, and when one local writer asked if 'there were any wedding bells in the air' he found Paul meant exactly what he said and the press conference was at an end before it had really got going.

Before he went to Italy he received a royal summons to meet Cragnotti in London. The banker had now fully completed his purchase of Callieri's shares and, as Stein said in a note to Jane Featherstone asking her to make the arrangements, it was 'an offer he couldn't refuse'.

The meeting took place at Cragnotti's office in St James's. 'Nice of him to change the name of the area to make me feel at home,' Gazza said. A preliminary meeting with Celon attempted to deal with one or two matters that were still outstanding and Celon, who had proved difficult in the past, was now as meek as a lamb, doubtless subdued by the smart surroundings. Cragnotti himself appeared like a Venetian prince, immaculately dressed as usual, grey hair swept back, a minimum of affectation and a maximum of style. His English was perfectly adequate to speak to Paul, who made no effort to try out his minimal Italian and had used the waiting time to make a rubber-band sling and a series of paper pellets which he promptly let fly in the general direction of the new president. Cragnotti, to his credit, did not flinch. He merely smiled politely as if he were entertaining an unruly nephew to tea, then told Paul exactly what he expected from him in a Lazio shirt. There was something impressive about Cragnotti, but there was also something frightening. He was not a man to cross and even Paul Gascoigne in his heart of hearts realized that.

23

'I'M BACK.'

It was a motley crew which assembled in Rome on Sunday 1 March. Paul and Jimmy Gardner, Stein and Lazarus, George Constanti (a North London garage owner who'd helped Paul out with cars and who was celebrating his birthday), Sheridan, who'd come with a view to chaperoning Paul on to Feyenoord where Spurs had a Cup winners match on the 4th, Nottage, and John Gascoigne who had decided to drive with a friend rather than suffer the agonies of flying.

Manzini met them as usual at Rome Airport and reported that there were thousands of fans again. Paul went white; he remembered the last time. Manzini had produced another military-style schedule. They had hoped that Paul would do a lap of the stadium to show the fans he was back to running, but both Roma and the Italian FA had objected, feeling it might give Lazio an unfair advantage. What he therefore had in mind was for Paul to greet the crowd from the stand.

When they arrived at the Olympic Stadium it was virtually full. One end looked like a blue cornfield, the other a bank of poppies. Manzini grabbed Paul and started to drag him to the top of the stand to wave to the crowd. Paul looked around, appealing for help. Gianni beat a way through the crowd to cover one flank whilst Augusto took the other. Manzini manfully battled past the press area to the very end of the stand, with the crowd now moving forward anxious to see or touch their new-found hero. Having got up there Paul dutifully waved, bedecked in his Eagles scarf.

'Why am I up here?' he asked plaintively. Nobody could give him a sensible answer so he went down again, life and injured limbs at risk as the crowd moved in on him. As he took his seat in the directors' area there was an enormous roar as the Lazio half of the stadium took up his name in a frightening rhythmic chant. The game itself ended in a 1–1 draw, yet another in a long sequence for Lazio. The Italian press were eager for Paul to comment on the match but he kept tactfully silent.

There was barely time to wash and change after the match before the party was swept away to Tele Monte Carlo for Paul's first television appearance in Italy. The driving was as manic as ever and Paul casually leaned forward and asked, 'Where did you learn to drive – BSM?'

The show was introduced by a young lady called Alba Perrietti, a former topless model who had cut her broadcasting teeth in a local chat show. As Paul took his place on stage, alongside Giorgio Chinaglia, the old Lazio hero, Alba moved towards him. Her legs were endless, topped by a small dress which paid lip-service to her waist and ended somewhere before her cleavage. She leaned towards him with the microphone from a high stool and Paul simply did not know where to look. He was genuinely embarrassed, worried what Sheryl would think back home. He had started to become intensely jealous whenever she even spoke to another man and in order to compensate for that he was trying very hard to keep his distance from other female company. He knew when the photos got back to England he was going to have a hard time on the phone.

At a birthday meal after the show George Constanti was to make an offer he would live to regret. Whenever he was in England, Paul shouldn't hire a car but borrow one of his. Whether it was because he'd had too much to drink or because he had not known Paul as long as everybody else, George was quite insistent on the offer. Paul, for his part, was only too happy to accept, and when he returned to England he took collection of George's pride and joy, his beautiful red Porsche. It was a disaster. For reasons best known to himself Paul, with the assistance of Gardner, decided to test the motor's emergency stopping abilities, and was amazed to find the steering wheel in his hand – not attached to anything, just in his hand. After a few more scrapes and several weeks of worry for George he finally gave the car back. Reluctant to see the lender face to face he had the vehicle delivered with a simple message written in the dust that covered its paintwork, 'Sorry George!'

On 16 March Paul was back at the Princess Grace. It was time to remove the wire, the last obstacle to his playing a competitive game of football. A few days later Browett was able to report that the fracture had mended completely. The surgeon sent Paul home advising him to rest for ten days, keeping the leg up in the air as much as possible. Ten days, the end of March, another ten days nearer the 31 May deadline. The period was one of increasing frustration for everyone, but once the wound caused by the operation had healed then Paul could resume full training. The only permanent reminders of the injuries would be the scars and a slight, but noticeable limp. The limp has in fact been advantageous. Deceptive in pace at the best of times, the imbalance makes him even more difficult to read on the field.

The Italians were more than encouraged by the latest report and decided they would pay another monitoring visit on 1 April, a suitable date against the background of the transaction. They came, they saw, they were satisfied, and on 8 April the transfer took another step nearer to completion when they wrote to Venables trying to finalize arrangements for the medical.

Whilst the nuts and bolts of the transfer deal went over his head, something in which Paul did want to get involved was the Tottenham Hospital radio service. This had for years provided commentary on Spurs matches for patients in a whole string of North London hospitals, but under their new administration, as part of a cost-cutting exercise, Tottenham were withdrawing their financial support at the end of the season. Paul's reaction was immediate, he'd pay for it himself. Tottenham's reaction to Paul's reaction was similarly immediate. Jonathan Crystal, a barrister and friend and associate of Venables, was on the phone to Stein like a shot. It was, of course, all a misunderstanding, and eventually it was agreed that Spurs and Paul would meet the cost equally for the rest of the season.

Paul had committed himself to appear at Ian Macdonald's testimonial at Woking on 21 April. Macdonald had never been a big name in soccer. Now 39, he'd played for Barrow, Workington, had a spell at Liverpool without ever being given a game, moved on to Colchester, York and Mansfield before ending up at the hapless Aldershot, who were to vanish from the League in the middle of the 1991/2 season. With his wages unpaid for weeks he was now working as player-manager at Woking and the testimonial match was the one chance he was likely to have to secure his future. It didn't matter that Paul had never met him, he was a fellow professional in trouble and if Paul could put some numbers on the gate by turning up, then he would do so.

By mid-April, after the removal of the wires, Paul had stepped up his training schedule to masochistic levels. He was in the sauna by 7.30 a.m., then off for a swim, running, doing leg work, 300 sit-ups, warming up with the rest of the Spurs lads, then more running when they had all gone home. Day after day the same routine, working harder than he had ever done before in his career. Under Dave Butler's watchful eye his speed tests were down to 31 seconds compared to the 30 he'd achieved when fully fit. He was nearly there, but not quite.

The Italians had written to Venables confirming the arrival of Celon, Dr Bartolini and a certain Professor Macotti at the end of April for a further examination. Venables arranged an internal practice match against a mixture of reserves and youth at the training ground for the 28th, but unfortunately the Italians arrived too late to see it.

For Paul this was the peak he had set himself to climb. 'I looked at the team sheet pinned to the wall. Nayim, Paul Walsh (I thought that was nice because he'd been sub for about four years) and then finally Gascoigne. It did my heart good to see it in black and white after all that time.'

The match was played in appalling conditions. John Gascoigne stood on the touchline, huddled beneath an umbrella, whilst the Chrysalis camera crew did their best to film Paul wading through the deep puddles. It had to be said that the tackles that went in on Paul were half-hearted – nobody wanted to be the one to make any headlines the following day – but the headline was to be written by Paul himself. He left it late, but a few minutes from the end he got the ball mid-way into his opponents' half, beat one man, beat two, then with all his old skill and dexterity slotted the ball into the corner of the net. Triumphantly, arms raised, he slid towards the cameras and mouthed the words, 'I'm back', then punched the sky in triumph and ran half the length of the field before diving into a huge puddle like a playful puppy. It was the first real goal he'd scored since his semi-final effort against Arsenal. That had been in front of a gigantic crowd at Wembley. This was before a sparse scattering sheltering from the torrential rain, but in its way it was just as important.

The Italians arrived not best pleased they had missed it, but fortunately Chrysalis were able to supply a video, and Venables after a little discontented grumbling agreed to arrange another practice session at Tottenham the following day. The press turned up in droves and all those journalists who'd been sharpening both knives and pencils for months (the one to plunge into his back and the other to enscribe the last rites of his career) had to admit that Paul looked good, if a little over-weight, a little slow. Yet there was enough of the old Gascoigne magic to satisfy – a twist, a turn, a dummy, an accurate pass. There was still a lot of work to do and as Sheridan watched, chewing his pipe, he knew his job was still not over. The medical had now been agreed for 26 May in Rome, a sensible compromise, just about a month away. It was time for the final push.

A flurry of correspondence began moving towards what was intended to be a critical meeting on 18 May. Paul had now decided that as Roeder was out of the picture he would like his brother Carl to accompany him to Rome. Carl is a quiet, thoughtful boy, whose talent at football has been lost within his introversion. There is much of Paul in him in looks, but they are very different people. As his mother Carol once said of him not unkindly, 'His ideal job would be testing mattresses.' His life until then had been sadly lacking in direction and Paul wanted to give him the opportunity to earn a bit of money and invest in a small business for the future. Carl was unlikely to talk to the press, and the least likely person to whom the press would want to talk; basically he wanted a quiet life, and for what Paul had in mind for him – gofer, driver, eating companion, friend – he was perfect.

The Italians duly arrived on the 18th and again watched Paul in a practice match. He was looking better by the day, slimmer, faster, his confidence growing with every kick, every tackle. With the medical just over a week away there was every reason to believe the deal would finally go through. Gino Santin, an Italian restaurateur, was now dealing with Lazio on Tottenham's behalf. The Gascoigne camps did not want Santin. He seemed oblivious to the amount of blood, sweat and tears that had gone into the transaction already. It may well be that he had some earlier involvement, but it was not until mid-May 1992 that Paul and those around him knew anything of his intervention. Yet although he may have come to the party late, he still wanted to be the star guest. On the flight to Rome on 22 May there were not enough seats in Club Class for everyone in the party. Santin was insistent that he fly with Paul and sit next to him. 'Spurs have entrusted Paul to me and I will deliver him personally,' he said, sounding like Clint Eastwood dealing with an escaped prisoner.

At the meeting on 18 May it was down to basics. The end of the Italian season was not until 30 June and therefore no licence could be issued for Paul until after that date. To allow a little leeway it was finally decided that Paul would not look to be registered as a Lazio player until 6 July. However, on that date Lazio would be touring Brazil and they wanted Paul to join them there accompanied by Nottage. Given the length of the flight and his proposed travelling companion, Stein and Lazarus knew that Paul was really going to love that trip. As Stein told him on the phone later, 'There's good news and bad news. The good news is that everything is moving forward smoothly; the bad news is you're going to Brazil – you'll feel at home there, it's where the nuts come from.' Paul had never seen *Charley's Aunt* but he got the joke. He asked how long the flight was and groaned when Stein told him. But he had to go. There were times when it was best to be firm.

For some extraordinary reason Spurs did not wish to have any medical advisers present at the final examination in Rome, or perhaps they just didn't want to pay for one. It was therefore left to Paul to pay for Browett's attendance, whilst Lazio had decided to back up Bartolini with the American Jim Andrews, the surgeon first mentioned by Browett and from whom he acknowledged he had learned his technique for the operation. On 22 May Nottage, Santin, Paul and John Gascoigne and Sheridan set off; Browett would join them on the 24th, and then everybody would reassemble in London on the 26th to conclude matters.

The actual medical was a non-event after its massive build-up, and anybody who had paid for admission would doubtless have demanded their money back. Paul passed with flying colours.Then, on the morning of what was intended to be the completion meeting, the Italians dropped a bombshell. They wanted to turn the documentation on its head, notwithstanding the agreement that had been reached. Rather foolhardily Paul had been told to be at Finers' offices at 3 p.m. to sign off, and he and Nottage had already had their vaccinations for the Brazil trip. However, without a signed final agreement with Lazio neither of them would be boarding any plane.

Paul arrived at the offices in good humour, thinking he would be in and out in five minutes. After two hours of waiting, he and Jimmy Gardner were fretting. They'd amused themselves as best they could within the constraints of a solicitor's office: they'd tossed half-full Coca-Cola cans off the mezzanine balcony on to anybody unlucky enough to be passing by; they'd tried photocopying Jimmy's bare bottom; they'd rearranged all the potted plants in some gigantic game of draughts; and finally in desperation they'd mooned through the unfrosted glass in the upper part of the windows of the conference room where the meeting was taking place. Paul then turned his attention to a pile of books consisting of copies of his own pictorial biography, *My Life in Pictures*. One by one photos were torn out and thrust under the door with ever more threatening messages, including one picture of Stein and Lazarus with the words 'You're fired!' scrawled across it. By the time things got to the stage of asking him to consider signing something he'd had enough and gone.

The Italians were rattled. The impression they got was that Paul had taken umbrage at their attitude, at their desire to spend hours churning over matters that he'd thought agreed long ago. Could it be that after everything he was going to refuse to sign? Stein and Lazarus tried him on his mobile, but he was too experienced to leave that switched on, but when they finally caught up with him at Sheryl's house he was unrepentant. 'I thought you'd realize that I was just giving them a bit of a fright.'

The meeting broke up, with the parties agreeing to meet again the next day. It was calmer, more business-like. Celon, who had got most agitated, had gone to Amsterdam, as it transpired to complete the comparatively simple signing of Aron Winter. It was agreed that Stein would redraft the agreement once again, and there would be a completion meeting the following Tuesday, 9 June, subsequent to a proposed completion with Tottenham.

The parties reconvened once more in the early afternoon of the 9th and at 11.30 p.m. they were still there, Celon having walked out at least once, and Lazio were quite unjustifiably threatening litigation when it was they who had sought to overturn the original deal. It took a lot of tact and a lot of control on the part of the Gascoigne representatives to calm things down, particularly as there had been a major misunderstanding over the trip to Brazil. Having got herself ready to leave, Nottage spoke with Manzini and then told Stein she had been told that Paul need not go. It had been decided in view of the delays that it was a long way to go for only part of the trip. Stein in turn told Paul, who then promptly took off to Newcastle for the weekend. It then transpired Lazio *did* want Paul to go, but by the time Paul could be contacted it was too late. Celon was less than happy.

After the eight hours of negotiations and recriminations on the 9th, the parties got together yet again on the 10th, this time with Paul present. As the documents whirled off the word-processor, Celon finally permitted himself a smile. He was obviously under enormous pressure from Cragnotti and the task allotted to him had not been easy. Suddenly it was realized that nobody had thought to bring a camera. Urgent calls were made to the *Sun*, the *Mirror* and the *Express*, not to sell the story but just to get a professional photographer along to record the event for posterity. Incredibly enough they were all too busy. All their resources were committed to England's European Championship game against Denmark in Sweden. This was it, the Gascoigne deal was being concluded, and after all the ups and downs, after all the months of media pursuit, nobody wanted to know.

'Perhaps we should have asked for £50,000, so that they thought they were getting an exclusive story,' somebody said cynically. John Coberman was despatched to a local Boots to buy a camera, and as the champagne corks finally popped the only pictures taken were with a £30 instamatic. Stein and Celon put their arms around each other and then raised their glasses in a mutual toast. 'To Lazio.'

24

'I'LL GET THESE BUGGERS LAUGHING.'

While Paul jetted off for a long-delayed holiday in the United States the papers pursued him mercilessly. He had not helped his cause or lowered his profile by shaving his head and those of his other male travelling companions before he left. As it was, they photographed him looking like a beached whale and then touched up the pictures to make him seem fatter. They photographed Sheryl reading a book as if it was headline news that somebody connected with Paul should be literate, they photographed them kissing, and they photographed them arguing. The relationship was becoming tempestuous. Paul always had to be on the go. He couldn't conceive somebody just wanting to sit and sunbathe. He was beginning to feel that Sheryl sought her space because she didn't love him enough to want to follow his lead blindly all the time. He was wrong, but by the time he realized that it was probably too late. If he suggested something to Jimmy, or Cyril, or Ian, or indeed to any one of his friends, they invariably agreed and followed him. So why didn't Sheryl? Everywhere that Paul went the cameramen went too. 'If I went to the loo I expected to see one of them alongside me unzipping his fly. I pleaded with them, offering to pose for a picture if they just left me alone. It was really getting to me. After all I'd been through I just wanted a quiet holiday with my girlfriend and my folks and they were ruining it for me.'

Back home loose ends had to be tied up to ensure that all Paul had to concentrate upon once he had stepped on to Italian soil was football. Arrangements had to be made for him to stay at a hotel and the one selected by the Italians was Degli Aranci. It was Celon who made that decision and he somewhat bluntly told the rest of the travelling party, including Paul's father and brother and Jimmy Gardner, that they would have to make their own arrangements. Whilst an 'armoured car' would collect Paul from the airport, he would travel alone and the rest could grab a taxi. The honeymoon seemed to be over before the marriage had even been consecrated.

Unwilling to upset Lazio, who generally speaking had been more than fair, Stein responded to Celon noting the arrangements, but requesting that Paul at least be allowed a couple of familiar faces with him in the car from the airport. The mercurial Celon relented, and in fact the whole Gascoigne party would be accommodated, even the Chrysalis crew.

Everybody was making every effort to get all the rest of the detailed documentation in place – various guarantees to be given by Lazio and the clearance from the Italian FA which would enable Paul to play for England whenever chosen. In fact a much wider clause had been negotiated on Paul's behalf, releasing him for all internationals whether competitive or friendly, and even all England get-togethers. There was nothing now that would stand in the way of Paul's departure except some further act of folly.

Paul did his level best to oblige. A farewell party arranged for him in Newcastle was to be a send-off to end all send-offs, a family affair with nobody from outside the North-East welcome, not even Stein and Lazarus lest their middle-aged professional staidness put a damper on the celebrations. Chrysalis, whose cameras had been ever present since the injury, were unfortunately replaced by a local photographic firm. Without having the small print checked it was no great surprise when photographs followed hard on the heels of rumours about the event into the tabloids. They made neither pleasant reading nor viewing, and were immediately seized upon by the Italian press as evidence that Lazio had not signed a footballer but had done a deal with Attila the Hun. Paul had clearly decided this was his final binge, but a binge in the safety of the surrounds of his own people. Lindisfarne provided the music, which was perfectly in order, but some strippers provided the entertainment, which was not. The photographs of a half-naked Paul Gascoigne, his bare torso still showing the excesses of his summer holiday, his hair still giving him the appearance of a Nazi stormtrooper, did nothing for the family image that his advisers had struggled so hard to promote. Whatever else Paul may have done in his Tyneside days, nobody who attended his farewell party was ever likely to forget it.

The pain for Paul in flying to Italy on 7 July came with parting from Sheryl. They remained in the car outside the terminal not sure whether to argue, laugh or cry, and eventually settled for a mixture of all three. Until that moment neither Stein nor Lazarus had realized what she had come to mean for him. Jimmy Gardner in all his glory was no compensation. As the plane landed it was a case of *déjà vu* – there were Manzini, Gianni, Augusto, Nottage. Only Roeder was missing. Plus five or six thousand fans.

Backed against a wall Paul did his best to answer questions, kissed what appeared to be the same baby he'd met on his first coming, then, watching the police separate fighting paparazzi and journalists, decided it was time to leave. Somehow or other the group collapsed into one of the waiting cars, the wall of noise still ringing in their ears. Paul looked in dismay at his new silk shirt which had been ripped from top to bottom. 'Next time I come I'll dress from Oxfam,' he said.

At the hotel there was another crowd, although a heavy police presence saw them comfortably through the gates. Paul looked around the hotel, and asked where the swimming pool was. 'It hasn't got one,' Manzini replied, 'but it has a beautiful orange tree.' Paul was not impressed.

He went to his room and immediately phoned Sheryl. It was the start of a major boom for the Italian telephone service. He needed immediate reassurance that she was at home, waiting for his call, and he confided to Stein, for the first time, that he wanted her out there with him as soon as possible. It didn't take long for Paul to make his presence felt. Looking down into the courtyard he saw an unsuspecting Chrysalis cameraman and promptly emptied a jar of water on his head. He was raring to go and within half an hour of arrival was asking to be taken to the Hilton for a swim and enquiring the whereabouts of the nearest tennis courts.

By the late afternoon of 8 July there was nothing more that Stein and Lazarus could do. It was all over. The carousel had finally stopped and Paul had stepped off to become a Lazio player. He would join up with his new team-mates within the week at their pre-season summer training camp in Austria; he would be hearing, if not speaking, a strange language, eating strange food, playing his football on a strange stage. It had been a long journey with many diversions and both the professional advisers felt curiously empty, flat, almost drained.

'Is that it?' Stein asked.

'I think it is,' said Lazarus.

They turned to Paul. 'Will you be all right?'

Paul hugged them both. They were all close to tears. 'Thanks for everything,' he said, 'I couldn't have done it without you.'

Nobody knew quite what else to say. 'We'll call you every week and be back in a month. You know where we are if you need us. Be good.'

Paul grinned. 'I'll get these buggers laughing,' he said. He'd watched them training back in August and, accustomed to Venables's joke-a-minute style, had been appalled by the lack of humour.

'I'm sure you will,' Stein said. It was time to go.

There was no real chance of Paul being bored. Everybody wanted to meet him, to be his friend, to do him favours. But Paul is never lightly taken in by people. He has some in-built radar that tells him whom to trust, whom to pull closely to his side and whom to reject or keep at a distance. Gianni was to become his closest confidant in Italy, proving to be not only a bodyguard, but a friend and adviser.

Paul's radar about Nottage was far more accurate than that of Stein and Lazarus. They believed she should be given a reasonable crack of the whip, but perhaps they too should have spotted the danger signals. Her first task was to find Paul a villa. He did not really want to make a decision on the villa on his own and Sheryl came out to assist him. Paul had been very specific as to his requirements in relation to a home; he wanted space, he wanted privacy, he wanted a pool, preferably a tennis court, sufficient guest rooms to entertain the various members of the Geordie army he'd invited out on a general basis, and he wanted to be able to move in without any need to decorate. Instead of going out on her own reconnaissance Nottage made the mistake of leaving the search to agents. Estate agents are the same the world over, they live in a permanent haze of hope and optimism. If their brief is to find a client a bungalow they'll take him to see a three-storey building and try and persuade him the stairs don't exist. So it was with the first few properties Nottage took Paul to see. Finally she claimed that he would find nothing in the price range he'd given her, so Paul increased her parameters. Then she came up with the villa into which Paul ultimately moved. When she told Stein and Lazarus how much it was going to cost there was a sharp intake of breath in stereo. It sounded like a fortune. 'Well, that's it,' Nottage said, as if she could not face pounding the pavements any longer in her search. 'He won't find anything else.' They took it. It was only later that both Manzini and Gianni told them that they had vastly overpaid.

The house did have many advantages. It was at the end of a quiet unmade road, surrounded by high walls with an automatic security gate; the pool was large, the grounds spacious with their own orchards. Beyond stretched open countryside containing kennels, some farmland, but without a neighbour in sight, and perhaps best of all it had a huge snooker table in the basement which had previously belonged to the king of Italy. But the problems were never ending. The security gates regularly jammed, and Lazio would have been horrified to see £5 million worth of investment scaling the walls and then leaping down some six feet just to gain entry to his own property. The plumbing, too, had a mind of its own, and over the period of his stay Paul developed an interesting relationship with his local plumber.

Then there were the dogs. What the owner had not told Paul was that at least three Alsatians came with the property, and Paul's fondness for animals did not extend to creatures who barked all through the night at every grasshopper who threatened their space. Eventually their number was reduced to one, a dog who growled fiercely at Paul and his guests but who appeared to have rolled over to allow his tummy to be tickled when the villa was burgled.

One image persists in the mind. Back in London Paul had gone out on the town with Danny Baker. They had gone into an expensive cigar shop and Paul had ordered twenty of 'whatever Russ Abbott buys'. Baker had then decided it was time for a brandy. Off they'd gone to Champney leisure club in Piccadilly where he showed Paul how to pour a glass of brandy and warm it in his hands. One day, soon after Sheryl's departure, Paul phoned John-Paul from Rome. 'I'm sat on my balcony,' he said, 'I've got a cigar. I bought a bottle of vintage brandy for £200. I'm mixing it with Sprite because you can't get lemonade in Rome. I wish you were here.'

Paul was finding that it was one thing to pass a straightforward medical on his knee and quite another to get match-fit, not just to English standards but to the enormous demands made upon Italian professionals. Up in the mountains of Austria he found himself in a totally different regime from anything he could have expected, a regime based upon super fitness, super professionalism, total dedication to the task in hand. He also found himself wrapped in cotton wool. Dr Bartolini was far more involved in club affairs than his counterpart in England. He kept a daily eye on Paul's progress, the measurements on his quads, his weight, his diet, his pulse, his heart rate. Everything was noted amidst a mass of statistics, and worse still everything was discussed with the press, who'd moved in a pack to join up with the club in their summer quarters. It was like an old-fashioned army on the move – generals, soldiers, medical staff, camp followers, war correspondents. Every word was hung upon, taken, examined, held up to the light, then twisted and turned into a whole article. And the microscope was focused most often on Paul Gascoigne. As far as Lazio watchers were concerned he was the only big news.

Paul and his new Lazio team-mates returned to Rome on 10 August. The Italian season was due to start on 6 September, but still Paul's training and rehabilitation was kept under tight control. As part of the final deal between Lazio and Tottenham two friendlies had been arranged, the first in Rome in August, the second at Tottenham. As soon as it became clear that in Bartolini's view Paul would not be sufficiently match-fit for the first game, it was rearranged for 23 September.

In early August Stein and Lazarus came out to visit Paul for the first time, and he appeared to have settled down remarkably well. Sheryl was spending a considerable amount of time with him, virtually commuting between Hertfordshire and Rome but the relationship still had its difficulties. Paul was showing signs of the violence that would erupt by the end of the year and neither Sheryl nor his family were prepared to stand for it. Time and again, arguments would end in her leaving, or Paul storming off. Each time Paul would beg her to return, asking third parties to intervene on his behalf, and each time she was eventually persuaded that his regret and love were genuine. In his naïvety he thought he could compensate her for the way he'd treated her by buying her expensive presents, taking her on fabulous holidays; but she had seen one relationship founder and end in acrimony and what she was seeking was kindness and romance. He was still avoiding every effort to have formal Italian lessons, but he'd picked up enough to communicate with his team-mates and his sense of humour was sufficiently international to bridge the culture gap. As they sat by the pool of his villa, with Sheryl's children Mason and Bianca happily playing in the garden, the horrific events of the past eighteen months seemed to belong to another world. He said that he was happy but they wouldn't let him play.

By the time they returned to Rome at the beginning of September the mood was shifting. Sheryl had felt isolated and exposed, while the children needed to get back to school. Paul was growing almost obsessively jealous ar.d she would find no space to breathe in Italy. She had to get back to England if the relationship was to have any chance of survival. Without her calming influence Paul himself felt edgy and unsettled. Despite Carl's presence he also felt more than a little lonely, and Nottage had become a point of conflict and aggravation. He had become accustomed to the gentle, coaxing approach of Jane Featherstone in the UK, but Nottage was far more assertive. She simply could not accept working within the idiosyncratic framework that had been established by trial and error over the years, and Paul liked neither her visits to the training ground nor her own wish for personal publicity. It became a simple clash of approach and personalities. Even those closest to him accept Paul can be aggravating and frustrating when he has to do something, but Nottage never came to terms with that. Then there was also Lazio itself. They still had to comply with certain terms of the agreement, some financial, some just petty, and each meeting with them was becoming a little like drawing teeth. They had appointed a new general manager in the shape of Edoardo Bendoni, a charming man who had been Nottage's immediate boss in the 1990 World Cup. On 7 September Paul's advisers met with him, Celon and Biolato to endeavour to resolve the outstanding differences, some of which were beginning to affect Paul's attitude to the club. Part of the problem lay in the accounting methods of Italian clubs. An English footballer is accustomed to receiving his wages slip or packet at the end of each month. However, in Italy the August salary is paid at the earliest on 10 September and sometimes even a little later. It was just another cultural difference that Paul was going to have to accept.

Whilst all this was going on for his benefit, Paul flew off to Spain with the England team for a friendly. There was no real chance of him playing but he was pleased to be part of the squad again, even though he was policed by the Lazio doctor. England lost 1-0, and if there was need of further evidence of how much his talents were missed, then that match provided it. It was clear that with a fit and available Gazza, his name, together with that of David Platt, should automatically go down on the team-sheet, and as for the rest it was a case of perming any nine from about thirty.

From Rome, feeling that with Bendoni in charge the problems were as good as solved, Paul's advisers went off to Venice to meet with Edoardo Artaldi of Lotto. Even though Paul had not kicked a ball in anger for some fifteen months, the boot company recognized the potential of a Gazza endorsement.

Paul himself was less than happy. Even without fully taking part in the training sessions, he had not yet been able 'to make them laugh'. It wasn't the work that bothered him, 'I just felt that training ought to be fun, and this lot weren't even smiling, let alone laughing. Zoff never cracked his face and it was tough going. It was all a matter of life and death for them.' That wasn't to say that Paul did not care, nor that Spurs had not taken their training and matches seriously. It was just that the pressure on everybody in Italy was so much greater. 'I felt I was ready from the off, but they just kept putting it back, and I was running and running while all I really wanted was a ball at my feet.'

Lazio had lacked a killer instinct the previous season, and it looked as if they were going to go the same way this time. On 6 September they drew 3-3 at Sampdoria, with Beppe Signori scoring twice, the first clocked as the fastest authentic goal of the new season although Diego Fuser had already put Sampdoria ahead with an own goal. Signori received 700 bottles of wine for his effort and Paul, watching from the sidelines, said, 'Blimey, he's going to need some help in drinking that! I'd never heard of Signori before I arrived in Rome, but after watching him in a couple of matches I rated him as one of the sharpest strikers I'd ever seen.'

The following week Paul's name was yet again not on the team-sheet as Signori found the net once more in a 2–2 draw with Fiorentina. 'I thought I had a genuine chance against Cagliari, but again Zoff left me out. I was beginning to lose my patience. I knew I was fit, but I couldn't get match-fit unless I played in matches.' Another 1–1 draw against Cagliari, another Signori goal. Four games, four draws, and it was to be against Tottenham, in the full glare of the TV cameras, that Paul was belatedly to pull on a Lazio shirt in public.

If Paul had not been fit for the friendly against Tottenham it would have been like staging *Hamlet* without the Prince. In the afternoon before the match Stein and Lazarus had a meeting with Artaldi of Lotto on the balcony of Nottage's flat. It began in bright sunshine but gradually the sky clouded over. The detailed proposals for the Lotto contract were on the table when a sudden gust of wind picked them up and blew them into the courtyard of the house that backed on to Nottage's apartment. Everybody looked aghast. All it needed was for the occupant of the courtyard to realize what he had, take it to the papers, and every detail of Paul's proposed contract would be plastered over them all.

They set out on their retrieval mission. A bottle was tied to the end of a piece of string, and having lowered it gently down they managed to scoop the papers into the neck. The string then promptly broke. Artaldi was despatched to see if he could ascertain which house contained the relevant courtyard. He couldn't. A patio door was open in the courtyard and so they decided to try and attract the attention of the occupants. There was a little table set for a meal which did suggest that someone was at home or likely to arrive soon. They scoured Jane's flat for ammunition – bottles, cartons, anything that would make a noise. They had been joined by an accountant called Kevin Valenzia, and he must have wondered what he was letting himself in for as four grown men threw rubbish from a fifth-floor balcony into an empty courtyard below. It was all to no avail. 'We need Gazza here. He'd have just climbed down and got it,' someone said.

It may well be to this very day that an Italian family has no idea why their patio was filled with rubbish when they got home from work, and as for the message in the bottle, if anybody wants to know the details of Paul's Lotto deal, then they only need to find it.

As the players came on to the pitch at the Olympic Stadium the barrage of sound and fire-crackers that greeted them belied the half-empty stadium. As if in a greeting from the gods thunder rolled over the Roman hills and forked lightning split the sky. Even the weather had contrived to make Paul feel at home, but it did little to help the fans stuck in a grid-locked city and still arriving at half-time to catch a glimpse of their new hero. Inevitably Paul rose to the occasion. One tackle went in on him from a Spurs defender which he rode majestically, but after that it was fairly noticeable that nobody wanted to get near enough to hurt him. The first goal was his, he had decided that long before the match started. He ran punching the sky to the fans jumping up and down on the high-banked terrace. The stadium reverberated to the chants of 'Gazza, Gazza,' the accents Italian, the sentiments the same, the sound making the distant thunder seem as nothing in comparison. Even his former Tottenham team-mates did not appear too unhappy at going a goal down, and Lazio then proceeded to take a young and inexperienced Tottenham side to pieces. Playing in second gear for much of the second half they ran out easy 3-0 winners. Paul came off on the hour to a tremendous reception. 'The knee felt great. I scored and I feel great.'

After the match Paul invited Stein, Lazarus, Nottage and Fernando Orsi (the reserve team keeper, known as 'Nando') back to the villa for a barbecue and, as he put it, 'a knees-up'. The rain had now passed and with that sudden change of temperature so typical of Rome, the night was warm and cloudless. Paul's mum and dad sat at a long table, Sheryl, whom he'd persuaded once again to return to him, busied herself in the kitchen, Paul put a rock and roll tape in his machine, then took his mother in his arms and danced with her across the patio. He gave a cheeky grin, hurried inside and played 'Fog on the Tyne', then asked Stein if he could get him a few more copies of the record. 'The lads are driving me mad for it.'

That was Paul in a nutshell. He'd flatly refused to allow the record to be released in Italy because he wanted neither the pressure nor the embarrassment, but for the lads . . . well, anything.

25

'F* * * OFF NORWAY.'

Having come through the friendly with just a few aches, the question on every Lazio fan's lips was whether Paul would make his Serie A début against Genoa. As Paul said on his Gazzetta programme the day before the game, 'I've made Zoff tea, cleaned his shoes and his boots, done everything he wants in training. If *that* doesn't work then I'm going to go on a sea food diet. Every bit of food I see I'm going to eat.'

The threat was unnecessary as he did finally make his début at home to Genoa on 27 September 1992. It was hard to believe he'd not played a competitive match for sixteen months, as he slalomed his way through three or four tackles from the Genoese defence. There was every reason to believe he was back. The age of miracles was not past. Then the whole of the Olympic Stadium and the millions watching on TV, both in Italy and England, held their breath. Paul went into a fairly innocuous challenge with Marco Bortalozzi, a slightly built playmaker and certainly not known as one of Italy's hard men. Paul went down and stayed down, clutching the famous knee. It was just before half-time, and when he did not appear for the second half there were some who feared the worst. However, it was merely a 'dead leg' arising from a knock on the nerve and by Tuesday he was back in training.

At least Paul knew how to get to the training ground by now. On his first day he'd got hopelessly lost and ended up on the motorway heading north. He'd stopped another car, tried to ask the way in Italian, failed miserably, but the other driver then recognized him and did a 30-mile detour to escort him in. That was better than the day his car had refused to start. The owner of the villa had left behind an old motor-bike which Paul had got going. Kicking the car in temper, Basil Fawlty style, he leapt on to the bike, roared it into life and took off for the training ground like a TT rider minus a crash helmet and any insurance. Manzini nearly had kittens when he saw the arrival of his star on the frail machine and promptly arranged a lift home for him.

Paul worked harder than ever after the Genoa match, which had ended in yet another draw, determined to keep his place for the game against Parma in the first week of October. He started the match in scintillating form, inspiring the midfield, and Lazio ran out 5–2 winners over the Italian Cup holders, who were also to end as runners-up in the European Cupwinners' Cup. Signori benefited from Paul's incisive passing to get his first hat trick in Serie A and, as Paul said afterwards, 'There can be no more doubts about my knee. I'm fit enough. It's perfect. I'm back.'

Graham Taylor had not only watched Paul in Serie A action but, unknown to both player and club, had sneaked over on a private visit, paid 40,000 lire admission and seen Paul play in a three-team friendly tournament. He had been sufficiently impressed to include Paul in the squad for the crucial World Cup qualifier against Norway at Wembley on 14 October.

'I felt much closer to Paul,' Taylor recalls. 'I'd spent a couple of days with him in Rome in August and told him I wanted to build the side around him. It was the first time we'd been able to be together away from everybody and I think we were beginning to understand each other.

It has to be remembered that he'd not played for me since a friendly against Cameroon back in February 1991, and even that game he didn't finish because of his hernia problem. We had a lot to catch up on.'

It was not the smoothest of build-ups to the match. Paul was asked to say hello to Norwegian fans by an Oslo camera crew, did not realize the camera or mike were live, and said, 'F*** Off, Norway,' with a big grin. Lawrie McMenemy tried to make light of it and explained that Paul was only joking, asking in vain for the comment to be kept confidential. Gazza himself turned back and said, 'Only fun, what can I help you with?' It was too late and Paul became a target of a hate campaign in the Norwegian media. Yet he rose above it and Taylor was able to keep him on for the whole match. Although England could only draw 1-1 Paul did enough in patches to show exactly what England had been missing in his absence.

Back in Italy Paul felt more than a little home-sick after his few days with the England team. The whole atmosphere was a million light-years away from the discipline and obsession of the Lazio camp, and at least he'd been able to have a few laughs with his old friends. They had their memories to bond them together; with Lazio he had only the future.

The immediate future was in the shape of AC Milan away in the massive San Siro Stadium. Milan, the champions, were protecting an unbeaten league run that stretched back forty matches. Paul knew he would be under the microscope yet again. How much more did he have to prove? The game was to be shown live on British TV as well as in Italy, and turned out to be a wonderful advertisement for Italian football. Milan played total soccer of such brilliance and perfection that they seemed to have learned the game on a different planet. Eventually they ran out 5-3 winners, a goal glut virtually unknown in Serie A, and although Paul was substituted yet again before the end of 90 minutes, he felt he could have gone on longer.

On 20 October Paul returned to Tottenham for the second fixture between his old and new clubs. Lazio won easily and as the Lazio captain lifted the London Cup, the trophy prepared for the encounters, Paul ducked behind him and pulled down his shorts in front of the cameras. He may have left the court, but the jester still regarded it as his territory. The winning run continued back in Italy. A 3-0 victory over Atalanta saw Lazio move up to sixth in the League, just four points behind Milan, although they still had the problem of only being able to play three of their four foreigners. When those imports were of the class of Doll, Riedle, Winter and Gascoigne it was inevitable that, when they were all fit and available for selection, the one left out would be disenchanted. Winter had of course been bought when Paul's return had been delayed, but he had scored twice from midfield while Paul had yet to find the net. As November approached and the leaves fell from the trees to fill his swimming pool, it began to appear that despite his return to fitness Paul could be looking at a winter of discontent.

Throughout November the form of both Lazio and Paul was fitful. Some weeks he was substituted, others injured, and the club scraped a draw at lowly Udinese, then lost at home to Torino and worse still 2-1 at Foggia. Only Signori was scoring and they had slipped to tenth in the table, a poor return for their huge investment.

Paul missed out on the Torino game. Depressed and disillusioned, still unnecessarily insecure in his relationship, he decided to take Sheryl and her children to Euro-Disney. Despite Bendoni's good intentions Lazio had still not dealt with several of the outstanding contractual points and it was necessary for another meeting to be called to clear what was becoming clouded air.

The team was due to fly out to Spain on the Wednesday and Paul's advisers made it quite plain that if matters were not resolved he was not only not going to Spain, he wasn't going back to Italy either.

The meeting began at a hotel near to Paris's Charles de Gaulle Airport at 11 p.m. on Monday 9 November and finished at 6 a.m. the following morning. Paul waited by the phone at his hotel for instructions. Finally he'd fallen asleep, and Stein and Lazarus had to get a porter to wake him up to be told he *was* going on the tour. Everything had finally been resolved. While Bendoni did not approve of his actions he could understand them. There was never any question, as Nottage suggested in her book, of Paul asking for more money before he would play in the match. His advisers were merely trying to obtain things to which he was contractually entitled, and which had become long-running sores on the surface of his relationship with Lazio. There had been a lot of plain speaking. It was accepted on Paul's behalf that he must work on the language problem. As he was to say later, only half-jokingly when he'd become virtually fluent, 'They'd shout right in Italian and I'd go left.'

The meeting was a turning-point in his career in Italy and he returned more determined than ever to achieve the sort of heights he'd scaled at Newcastle and Spurs. On 14 November he was back in England again, this time not as a refugee but as part of the England squad and to be best man at the wedding of Anna and John-Paul. He'd been given special permission by Graham Taylor to travel up to the North-East on Saturday morning, although Lawrie McMenemy was designated the task of accompanying him as his unofficial 'minder'. Taylor was taking no chances on anybody taking a pot-shot at his star this time around.

The ceremony was at the local church and the whole of Dunston seemed to turn out to line the streets alongside a fair percentage of the world's press. Paul took it all in his stride, looking as comfortable in his smart blue morning suit with grey waistcoat and bow tie as he did in a football shirt and shorts. 'I was dead worried that I'd steal the limelight from Anna. She was the star of the show, not me, but she looked just beautiful and I thought to myself, if they take pictures of me rather than her, then they're madder than I took them for.'

Paul managed to raise a laugh even in the church by pretending to have forgotten the ring, but as the bride came out to flashing cameras he quickly left centre stage to her and hurried off into one of the waiting cars. He hid his own heartache at the absence of Sheryl with whom he'd had yet another spectacular row which had ended in one of the most physical clashes to date.

The speeches were hilarious, John-Paul's in particular. 'I've always wanted to take revenge on Paul for throwing that bucket of water over me in Portugal. We were up at the Spurs training ground in Mill Hill and there's loads of press about. So Paul gets into the boot of the car and I smuggle him out as usual. I hear this muffled voice, "Have we passed them?" "Yes." "Let me out." "Good luck," I said. We drove around and around. He uses his mobile to call his mum. "Ginga's kidnapped me." We must have driven half-way around London and he's tearing up all my map books. The only place we didn't get as far as was Gatwick Airport. The police that day were looking for £5.5 million of dope. And I had him in the boot of my car.'

If the love affair with Lazio was not blossoming in the way that he'd hoped, at least Graham Taylor still had a place for him in both his heart and his team, and as England took on Turkey on 18 November at Wembley there was a resolve and purpose about Paul that Taylor had not seen for a while. Within a quarter of an hour he had scored and was once again the darling of the fans.

Before half-time he'd helped Shearer to a goal, Pearce got a third on the hour and Paul his second a minute later. He tried manfully to get his hat trick, but even without that he'd done enough. 'I was proving a point not just to the journalists in England who'd written me off, but also to the Italians who seemed to think I couldn't last ninety minutes.'

Paul received the man of the match award and airline tickets worth £8,000. He immediately donated them back to the team pool. 'It was a team effort that won the match, not just mine.' Whilst Turkey were not the strongest of opposition it was a convincing victory.

It was back to reality for Paul in Italy. Sheryl was again home in England, and when Lazio lost to Foggia on 22 November he was feeling down again. Yet what kept him going was a burning desire not to let his critics have the last laugh. The following week was the local derby against Roma. 'It really was a matter of life and death to these people, and it spilt over to me. I was left hoping I'd still be alive after the game.'

When Roma were ahead with three minutes to go, Paul was thinking about the best way to get out of the stadium in one piece. Then Lazio were awarded a free kick just inside the Roma half on the right-hand side. Instead of running to take it, something told Paul to get into the penalty area and leave it to Signori. He put a long looping ball into the box, Paul connected perfectly with his head and there was the ball miraculously nestling in the back of the net. He started to run towards the crowd, but never made it as he disappeared under a sea of players, substitutes, ball boys and even officials. He walked away in tears, his hands together in a silent gesture of prayer. 'I'd never been so scared of losing. It was no use telling the Lazio fans that we'd get a result next time. They didn't even think about next time. I came in absolutely drained, slumped down in the dressing-room and all I could say was that I never wanted to play in another derby match as long as I lived.'

Suddenly Paul was the flavour of the month again. Rome is a beautiful woman and in the days after his equalizer she was proud to claim Paul as her lover. It did wonders for his confidence. One goal, three minutes of football and it all seemed to be slipping back into place. Just as in November he'd seemed to be slipping into the dark abyss, now in the cold of December he was coming into the light. On the 6th Lazio went to Pescara and won 3-2 with Paul scoring an outstanding goal, selling dummy after dummy, drifting past defender after defender, before slotting the ball past the keeper, a goal that was to be a candidate for the Italian Serie A goal of the season.

Just as his season was picking up momentum Paul picked up another little injury, but although he missed out on the Inter Milan match, the team was still on a high and won 3-1, with Signori taking his tally for the season to thirteen before the Christmas break, an outstanding accomplishment in the Italian League.

The break in the season took a bit of getting used to, but Paul could now feel happier with life. With 14 points Lazio were equal fourth in the table, and if they maintained this form they were in line for a UEFA Cup place.

Somehow, Paul was never able to achieve the perfect balance between happiness in his professional and personal lives. The relationship with Sheryl, which had smouldered on and off, now burst into flames. She had a life to live in England with her children but Paul needed her with him. When she was with him he could not cope without her undivided attention, his jealousy at times extending to the children, who for the most part he loved as much as he loved their mother. It was a terrible conundrum, but Sheryl did what any compassionate mother would do and put her children first. Paul was desperately in love with her, but found it difficult to accept that she was different from his home-town lasses. She was a sophisticated woman of the world, who'd been married, had a decent education, a comfortable middle-class upbringing, and whose idea of a good time was to go to the theatre or ballet rather than a smoky bar. Paul followed her back to England. Before she had left he had raised his hand to her yet again and this time she was leaving for good. He phoned his mother, he phoned Stein and Lazarus, he phoned anybody who could plead his case for him, a case he simply could not plead himself. There had been too many broken promises. Eventually Stein and Lazarus went to Dobbs Weir, not to advise on legal or financial matters, but to put Paul's case to Sheryl, who had every justification not to listen; but she was eventually convinced, particularly when Paul swore to seek help from a sports psychologist. It was at the time a turning-point in their relationship and in Paul's life. He went up to Newcastle, not to stay but just for the day, delivered his presents, and then returned to Sheryl. The two of them took off together for a romantic New Year at the Lygon Arms in Broadway, a pretty village deep in the heart of the Cotswolds. Cromwell is rumoured to have stayed in the sixteenth-century coaching inn, but even he could not have attracted more attention than Paul.

As they saw in the New Year, all the old ladies, the country gentry with their purple-tinted hair, wanted to dance with Paul, taking the risk of him stepping on their toes. Good-naturedly he entered into the spirit of the occasion, signed innumerable autographs, but felt happy and relaxed in the peaceful country setting. On New Year's Day the two of them walked hand in hand, peering into the windows of antique shops, buying little presents for the children, looking for all the world like any other happy young couple.

It was with the greatest reluctance that Paul tore himself away from the idyllic rural setting to fly back to Italy, but there was still business to be done. As he and Sheryl parted it was with genuine regret on both sides, and with a fresh renewed commitment between them that would keep the telephone lines between Rome and London constantly engaged.

Paul returned to chaos. Gianni had gone up to the villa to feed the dog and found the place had been burgled. It was hard to tell exactly what had been stolen as Paul never knew quite what he had, but one thing was for certain, his entire wardrobe of clothing, much of which he'd bought only a week or so before in a shopping spree, had disappeared. Left behind though were valuable stereos and irreplaceable trophies. 'I think they just admired my taste in clothes. I don't know why they didn't ask – everybody else did.'

After the burglary Paul himself began to spend less time at home, preferring the noise and bustle of the Hilton to the echoing solitude of the villa. Fortunately he had the distraction of getting back to playing football. Lazio had picked up in January where he'd left off in December, as indeed had Beppe Signori. The team won 3-0 on a visit to Ancona, with Signori claiming one, then both in a 2-0 victory at home to Brescia. After a slight hiccup with a home defeat against Napoli they then faced mighty Juventus on the 24th – without Paul, who'd picked up yet another slight injury. Lawrie McMenemy had come to watch his two England stars, but needn't have bothered as Platt, too, was missing for Juventus. It was a hard life being the assistant England manager.

On 26 January 'Belchgate' hit the headlines. The Lazio players had been operating a united press blackout since the heavy (and they felt unjustified) criticism to which they'd been subjected back in October. The pressures on Paul to speak to the press were even greater than anybody else. Walking along, with David Platt at his side, both had been subjected to enormous harassment to speak to the reporters. Twice a microphone was stuck under his nose, twice he pushed it away with a 'no comment', but the third time when asked if he had anything to say, he simply burped into the microphone, a sound that was to reverberate, not only around Italy but the whole of Europe.

The incident made the front pages of the British papers, prime-time news and was even raised in the Italian parliament as an alleged insult to the Italian people. 'It was totally crazy. It was just a joke. The MP must have needed a bit of publicity himself. I found it incredible that a parliament that contained a self-confessed porn queen should be having a go at me for belching.'

Lazio were incredibly supportive. He'd been wearing Lazio uniform and they could easily have taken a different approach, but they merely told him to get on with his game. Nottage was less tolerant, complaining to Stein on the phone about how difficult it made her job. The lawyer suggested she get Paul an endorsement for indigestion tablets, but the lady was not amused, although that did not stop her using the line during one of her later interviews to promote her book. She would have been even less amused if she'd realized her days were numbered.

Stein and Lazarus had gone out to dinner with Sheryl and Paul on the weekend of the Juventus game and had discussed long and hard the state of play in the management of Paul's commercial affairs. Whilst both lawyer and accountant were irritated at times by Nottage, they did not feel unkindly towards her at the time and indeed they had shared many moments of laughter with her on the seemingly endless trail to Rome. She had a kind streak, but also had, like most people, a devil within her that would make her say and do things which she later regretted. They felt she should be allowed to see out her contract simply upon the basis of 'better the devil . . . '; but Paul and Sheryl were adamant. They clearly did not like her, and both felt (with some justification as was later proven) that she was indiscreet and unreliable. It was the first time in the relationship that Paul had actually opposed his advisers' views and, as it transpired, Paul's instinct was absolutely right. Stein was instructed to give her the required notice and to let her down as gently as possible; even if she was not to work for Paul any more there was no point in hurting her pride. The solicitor did his best, but there is no kind way of telling a woman she's sacked.

Whether it was then she decided to break her silence and write her book or whether that had been in her mind all along who can say? What she did do at the time was to bond Paul and Sheryl even closer together. She genuinely cared for him and he for her, and not only her but the children. Paul had a ready-made family, and if he wasn't quite ready to start his own as yet they were the next best thing. 'I came to look on them as my own family. Mason called me dad, and in fact I was the only dad he really knew. Bianca was a bit distant at first, but I think I won her over and I treated them as if they were mine. They loved my version of Peter Pan when I'd do all the voices and had them terrified of Captain Hook.' It was a face of Paul that the public rarely saw, the home-loving, caring face for a woman and two children who, until they'd met him, had not had the rub of the green in their lives.

By the end of January 1993 Lazio's star was really in the ascendant, not least due to Paul's improving form. There were times when he could not understand his substitution, on occasions as early as half an hour before the end; but as long as the results panned out well he was not desperately unhappy. 'I get paid the same money for ten as for ninety minutes,' he joked. Yet Sheryl was once more the target for any frustration on the field and, by the end of January 1993, the relationship seemed to be finally at an end. He still loved her, felt enough obligation to her and the children to help buy them a house, but he could not control himself when he was with her.

After a 1-1 draw at home to Juventus, Lazio beat Sampdoria, the unhappy Des Walker and all, 2-1 and by the end of the month had moved in to joint third place with Juventus, only headed by the two Milanese giants. Inter and AC were having their own private battle for the title, but with AC eight points ahead Inter's chances looked hopeless unless their neighbouring rivals suffered an incredible loss of form.

Another cause for celebration was the success of Paul's Channel 4 programme, *Gazzetta Italia*. Chrysalis and Channel 4 had gambled and won in their decision to screen live Italian Serie A matches on Sunday afternoons. The games were peaking at audiences of 3 million, while even the Saturday morning show which Paul hosted was attracting 800,000 viewers, huge figures for a minority channel, and in the race for a live football audience both Sky and the regional ITV stations were being left far behind.

After the Sampdoria match Neil Duncanson of Chrysalis went out for a meal with James Richardson, the presenter of the programme, and his girlfriend, Paul himself, Anna, three itinerant Geordie friends of Paul, Stein and Lazarus, and Rob Shepherd of *Today* newspaper. When it came to the bill Paul first offered to pick up the tab, but Duncanson and Shepherd said it would be fairer to divide it into three, a reaction upon which Paul had been banking. Still seeming generous Paul said that as he'd had more guests (seven compared to Chrysalis's three and Rob's one) he would take care of two-thirds and the service charge and the tip for everybody, and then went off to sort things out with the proprietor in his, by now, quite fluent Italian.

Duncanson groaned at the size of the bill, as did Shepherd. Paul went out to the car with a grin on his face, and later admitted that he'd got the restaurant to charge him 10,000 lire (about £5), and the rest had been divided in two. Nobody should ever underestimate Paul Gascoigne when it comes to financial matters.

On 7 February Lazio won at Fiorentina, but with Paul summoned for the England match against San Marino they lost at home to Cagliari, seemingly a surprise setback although Cagliari, so well known to Paul from the summer of 1990, were having a great season and were just outside the top six.

Paul had thought a month earlier that he couldn't live with Sheryl, but it now seemed he couldn't live without her either. A joint *Sun/News of the World* team of journalists and photographers went to see them in Rome. The couple posed for pictures and suddenly Paul darted into the bushes and came out with a paparazzo clenched in his fist. Richard Pelham, the *Sun* photographer, leapt to Paul's assistance, but unfortunately the 'paparazzo' turned out to be an undercover policeman who'd been peacefully eating his lunch. At that point some genuine paparazzi appeared and Paul went crazy. He launched himself at one of the photographers to seize his film, but the man ran to his car and locked his camera in the boot. Paul suggested to Rebekah Wade of the *News of the World* that she 'nick his car keys', which she did, at which point Gianni appeared, smuggled Gazza and Sheryl away, and left the British journalists to their fate. Hauled off to the police station, the car keys returned, they were finally released several hours later. Curiously none of the tabloids reported the incident in any great detail. Rebekah was to reap her reward in July 1994 when Paul chose her of all the journalists he'd dealt with as the most trustworthy and opened his heart to her regarding the violent side of his relationship with Sheryl.

Meanwhile the Italian Cup had reached the quarter-final stage. In the first leg against Torino Fiori in goal had made an error to surrender Lazio's one-goal lead, and although Paul had given one of his finest exhibitions since his arrival Lazio flew to Turin level 1–1 on paper, but with Torino having the advantage of the away goal. The second leg in fogbound Turin was a fiasco. The stands were invisible from the pitch by the time of kick-off and the start was delayed for an hour or more while the referee trotted on to the pitch, ran from end to end, gave an interview to the waiting reporters, then hurried off again. Eventually he decided to allow the kick-off to the accompaniment of howls from the crowd behind one goal of the Italian equivalent of 'We can't see a f****** thing.'

The normal smoke-bombs tossed on to the pitch by the same supporters who'd complained they couldn't see merged with the fog and blotted out the view for everybody for the first few minutes. Then Lazio had a man sent off, went a goal down, equalized, went 3-1 down, pulled a goal back, and finally lost 3-2. Another route to Europe had been closed to them and now it was all down to finishing sufficiently high in the League.

It was easier getting into Turin than out. The airport was fogbound and when Gazza and his team-mates arrived for their noon flight to Rome they found Stein and Lazarus still waiting for their 9 a.m. flight to London on a plane that hadn't yet arrived. Eventually the Lazio plane took off before the London flight and Paul was torpedoed into yet another controversy. An Italian journalist accused him of breaking wind at him in the hotel in Turin. Even if it had been true it was hardly something to get excited about, but Paul hotly denied it. Witnesses had seen (and heard) the incident and Paul claimed the only noise emanating from his lower regions was a rumble of hunger from his empty stomach. However, by the time he got on the plane filled with players and journalists it was clear that the latter group had their combined bits between their Dracula-like teeth and were looking for blood – English blood.

This time the suggestion was that Paul had staggered on to the plane roaring drunk and had actually assaulted one of the newspapermen. Again it was pure fiction. Stein and Lazarus had been talking to him until he passed through airport security and he was perfectly sober then. As for the assault, his team-mates swore that the journalist had just gone down without being touched, but with a dramatic groan that would have earned him nine out of ten for artistic impression.

26

'UNFIT AND OVERWEIGHT.'

On 17 February England entertained San Marino at Wembley, and although they won 6–0 Paul knew he'd not played well, and the press were not slow to confirm his own opinion. Nothing annoys him more than to fall short of his own high standards, and after the San Marino match, when he'd been subdued by a part-time player who was also the postman for one of his Lazio team-mates, he was so upset that he actually demanded a meeting with Graham Taylor and Lawrie McMenemy. The manager and his assistant closeted themselves with him for nearly half an hour and once again he was the tearful schoolboy, needing comfort, to be told that he would and could do better, and that he'd be given another chance to prove it.

At the following day's press conference Graham Taylor took the bull by the horns. Gascoigne had not been right in himself either physically or mentally. The journalists swooped in on the words. Everything else about the performance became irrelevant, Ferdinand's goal, Wright's failure to score, Platt's four-timer. As ever it was Gazza, Gazza, Gazza they were after. There can be no doubting the special place that both Taylor and McMenemy had in their hearts for Paul; he was as much Taylor's talisman as Bobby Moore had been Alf Ramsey's. If Gascoigne is there then all will be well, and a fit Gascoigne will always be there.

The Taylor press conference lit the fuse, and then came the explosion. Taylor called Mel Stein to explain what he had said and why. Stein accepted that the message had been given in all good faith and there was no doubt that Paul was *not* happy with himself. He felt continually guilty over the way he treated Sheryl, continually frustrated that he could no longer control his darker side. Mr Hyde was beginning to win the battle with Dr Jekyll. He had failed to live up to the impossibly high standards he had set himself, and inexplicably he looked less than fit. Even when he'd joined up with the squad Taylor had commented that he did not think his physical condition was as good as when he'd last been with him. Then twenty-four hours after the match everything became clear. Paul began to run a high temperature during the night, and by the time he boarded the plane Stein had telephoned ahead to Lazio so that Manzini and the club doctor could meet him off the flight. He was whisked off to his villa, found to have a temperature of over 100 and put straight to bed. Perhaps another player would have surrendered to the illness before and cried off, perhaps Paul could have been accused of putting the team at risk by playing, but Paul is never one to look for excuses. All the old headlines were dredged up. 'Overweight', 'Unfit', and the Italian press joined in the clamour, concentrating more on his alleged failure to set Lazio alight, forgetting the fine matches he'd had so soon after his recovery from a career-threatening injury.

There was speculation about his early return to England. Blackburn's name inevitably arose, with Dalglish such an admitted admirer, the revitalized Newcastle, Tottenham still claiming their unenforceable first option, and unlikeliest of all Chelsea. But Paul was determined to see it through in Rome rather than be labelled a failure if he came back to England before the expiry of his five-year contract. He had also not yet achieved his ambition of bringing laughter to the Lazio training sessions, although he was getting there. The unfortunate John Coberman accepted an invitation to stay at Villa Gazza, as it was known, and was plied full of drinks by a group of itinerant Geordies. They then solicitously tucked him into bed, only to return when he was in a deep alcoholic sleep to shave off his hair and eyebrows. Looking like something out of *Star Trek* and feeling as if he had collided with a Klingon warship, John arrived at the Lazio training ground. Expertly coached by Gazza the players chorused in Italian with varying degrees of success, 'You bald-headed bastard.' Zoff tried to keep a straight face, failed, and collapsed with laughter alongside everybody else. He was, after all, only human.

In the last week of February Lazio won at Genoa, but at a price. Paul tangled with Marco Bortalozzi, the same player who'd put him out of the game in his début back in September. It was all very innocent and mild by English standards, but as the Genoa player fell to the ground the referee was already feeling in his pocket and to Paul's astonishment produced a red card. He'd felt he was getting on well with Italian referees in general. One man in black had given Paul a stick of chewing gum to shut him up, rather than a card, but today there was to be no spearmint, just the lonely walk to the touchline. 'I couldn't believe it. I'd been in those sort of incidents a hundred times. You reach down, pull your man up, pat him on the head and it's off again.'

But even with ten men Lazio won.

At the end of February Lazio were clear third, 12 points behind AC Milan but now only 2 points behind Inter, and the runners-up position in the League seemed a perfectly feasible target. March blew in like a lion. A 2–1 defeat at Parma was no disgrace, and Lazio followed that up with a 2-2 draw at home to AC Milan, who had finally been beaten in the preceding week (albeit in the Cup) by Roma. Paul scored one of the goals, then headed another in a commendable 2-2 draw away to Atalanta, before departing to join up with England for their World Cup trip to Turkey. In his absence Lazio destroyed Udinese 4-0 and were still in third place at the end of the month. Europe with all its rich pickings beckoned.

Although England won 2-0 and Paul scored it was not over-impressive. He was tired. Getting back after the double injury was one thing, getting fully fit was quite another. But whilst Milan's lead at the top of the table began to erode, the gap between Inter and the rest, headed by Lazio, began to widen. In April Lazio were back to their most irritating form with three consecutive draws ending in a dull and ill-tempered 0-0 with Roma.

The World Cup game against Holland at Wembley on 28 April brought its own traumas. Of all the World Cup qualifying matches this was considered to be the most vital. Trips to Norway, Poland and Holland themselves were still to come, and although the win in Turkey had put two points in the bag, it had not been unexpected. As ever Graham Taylor not only had to deal with the opposition but with the pressures of the English season. Ian Wright had broken a toe, Alan Shearer was struggling to recover from a cruciate operation, David Hirst was still some way off full fitness, and then to cap it all Gazza arrived from Italy with an injury – not just any injury, but an injury to 'that knee'.

For the press it was more manna from heaven. They'd called him unfit, overweight, there'd been suggestions of excess drinking, training rows, of Lazio looking to dump him, but they'd never been able to find any hard facts to back up the allegations. It all started innocuously. During the Lazio–Roma match the previous

Sunday Paul took a knock in a fairly harmless tackle, but naïvely he headed off to England and Sheryl rather than the Lazio treatment room. By Monday morning the knee was swollen and tender and he was beginning to panic. Lazio would not be happy that he'd gone off to England, but then he'd never really thought it was anything but a slight knock that would wear off. By late Monday something had to be done. Paul was terrified to turn up at the England camp with no chance of playing and reluctant to make the sort of fuss that would guarantee headlines.

There was yet another consideration. Lazio had for reasons best known to themselves agreed to tour Japan – this in the midst of the Serie A season with their European place hanging in the balance. The highlight of that particular trip was a head-to-head confrontation with Grampas 8, Lineker and all versus Gascoigne. Under both FIFA rules and Paul's contract Lazio had to release him for the Dutch match and had actually sent Zoff's number two, Oddi, to shepherd Paul and Aron Winter (who was playing for Holland) on to the midday flight to the Far East on Thursday. Paul realized that much of the attraction of the tour centred on him. His own licensee Basic had filmed an advertisement for mail-order sales in Japan and there were financial penalties in Lazio's tour contract in the event of Gascoigne failing to appear.

Paul arrived at England's hotel in the middle of the night. Sensibly Graham Taylor had already arranged a visit to a London specialist to set Paul's mind at rest, and before the press could write their headlines he'd been smuggled there and back. The injury was trivial and there was no reason why he should not be fit to play. The drama appeared to be over, but it was merely the end of the first act.

It was the match everybody wanted to see, the two heavyweights in the group locked together for the first time since the ignominy of Düsseldorf when a Van Basten hat trick had wiped Bobby Robson's team off the European map. For once Paul was not the most pressurized England player. John Barnes, the gentlest of men if also one of the most laid back, had been the target of England boo-boys in the draw against Norway. Originally discarded for the match against Turkey, injuries to almost all of his rivals had forced him back into the team, and his performance there had been just good enough, given the unavailability of Wright, Shearer and Hirst, to justify Taylor selecting him for the Holland game. The media were unanimous: this would have to be his last chance.

Within minutes of the start of the game, before the boos for Barnes had a chance to take shape in the throats of the idiot minority, England were awarded a free kick just outside the Dutch penalty area. It was much the same position from which Paul had scored in the 1991 Cup Final. He lined up now alongside Barnes, dummied away and Barnes scored with a clinical shot that might just have been saved by a better and more experienced keeper. Len Lazarus leapt to his feet in the stands. A great one for backing hopeless causes he'd put £10 on Barnes at 12-1 to score the first goal.

England took the match by the scruff of its neck. Every time Gascoigne got the ball the Dutch looked nervous. A powerful run took him towards their goal and was only halted by a violent tug on his shorts; a delightful ball along the bye-line that only half a dozen players in the world could have achieved in such a tight position, and a great through ball, ended with Platt scoring England's second goal. The Dutch were on the ropes. Gullit was invisible and on the rare occasions he touched the ball was risibly jeered with the chant of 'Get your hair cut'. Aron Winter, so influential for Lazio, was pushed back into a defensive role, leaving a huge hole through which Gazza, Platt and even Carlton Palmer poured at will. Then a few minutes before half-time the ill-fortunes of Gazza and Taylor combined. Gascoigne had moved forward menacingly and went for an aerial ball with Jan Wouters, the tough Dutch defender. The two men were no strangers to each other, Paul had been vociferously critical of him in their last encounter and there had been rumblings of revenge from the Dutch quarter. Wouters's elbow crunched into Paul's cheek and he fell to the floor in obvious distress. Paul can never be accused of feigning injury; if he goes down it's because he's hurt and he has to be seriously hurt not to rise again. He got to his feet, a little unsteadily, seemingly bloody but unbowed. The half-time whistle blew and the crowd rose to their feet to give England a rare standing ovation: 2-0 up against the much-feared and respected Dutch, a lead that could easily have been greater and 45 minutes of the best football ever played under Graham Taylor.

Fifteen minutes later the crowd was more muted. Gascoigne was off and Merson was on. Even the Arsenal supporters, usually so ebullient when one of their players pulls on an England shirt, were not celebrating. The radio commentator said that X-rays were being taken, and as England continued their all-out onslaught to no great avail the mood gradually shifted both on and off the pitch. Barnes faded, Merson flattered to deceive; nobody put his foot on the ball or hit the telling defence-splitting pass. In a way it was no great surprise when Holland scored, a brilliant individual effort on the turn by Bergkamp. The equalizer had no hint of brilliance about it. Des Walker, normally so reliable in defence, so speedy to spot danger, was caught napping and in the midst of a brainstorm pulled back a Dutch forward when there was little or no chance of him scoring. It was undeniably a penalty, which was coolly converted by Van Vossen to level the scores and with five minutes left England were left trying to save a match they seemed already to have won.

The news about Gazza was unclear. He should have attended an after-match function sponsored by Mars with the rest of the team. As Stein and Lazarus walked across to the conference centre they bumped into Jon Smith of First Artists, the commercial managers of the England team, who reported that Paul was very groggy and not sure to be attending. The rest of the team came across, but minus Barnes and Gazza. Barnes was giving an interview but Paul was in pain. Several of his team-mates were very angry over the elbow incident. Lawrie McMenemy, as ever, was a calming influence, saying that he'd just taken a bit of a knock, but it had been X-rayed and there was no fracture, perhaps some mild concussion.

A few minutes later there was an urgent message for Stein. It was Sheryl on the phone, in the car with Paul and being driven by John Coberman. She said he was in a terrible state and could barely talk. Then Paul came on the phone sounding slurred and confused. 'Can you talk to Lazio?' was the first request, which had a familiar ring about it. He quickly explained that although no fracture had been found he had a splitting pain in his jaw and head. It was gone eleven at night but Stein found Manzini's mobile number and made two quick decisions. First, there was no way Paul could undertake the long flight to Japan in the morning, and second, he had to see another doctor in a hospital with more sophisticated equipment than had been available at Wembley.

Stein spoke to Manzini from his car driving home. The Lazio team manager was desperate. He'd seen the match live on TV, seen the incident and had already woken up Marilyn Stein twice. She may not have been a happy lady but Manzini was even more unhappy when he was told that Paul would not be on the plane with Aron Winter and Oddi, the assistant coach. At 1 a.m. on Thursday Stein and Manzini spoke for the last time and the lawyer promised to call the Italian in the morning to tell him what he'd been able to arrange.

Stein's wife worked as a pharmacist at Holly House, a private hospital in Buckhurst Hill, Essex. Their principal maxillary surgeon was James Evans. A call was put out to him and Paul, by now in great pain, set off on his trip to Essex driven by Sheryl. Manzini had discovered another flight on Friday which would have got Paul there for both the matches, including the Grampas 8 showpiece with Gary Lineker. Mr Evans, however, had other ideas. X-rays revealed a fracture of the zygomatic arch, too close to the eye for comfort, and he advised immediate surgery. The operation was simple and brief but it had to be done. Paul went white in disbelief. Before his double hernia in April 1991 he'd been virtually free of injury, but in the two short years since then he'd spent almost as much time in hospital as he had on the football field.

Familiarization with anaesthetists and the surgeons' knives had not made Paul any more comfortable with them. Evans gave him the choice of having the operation either on Thursday night or Friday morning and with his usual stoic courage in situations like this Paul opted for the later date and decided to use the rest of Thursday to go fishing. The troubles of the world could descend on the shoulders of his advisers; they were used to it. He just wanted some peace and quiet.

All the press wanted to know was whether Wouters's elbow in Gazza's face was deliberate and if it constituted an assault for which Paul was going to take legal action. In fact the thought of suing a fellow professional never crossed Paul's mind. 'These things happen in football. You have to take the knocks with the smooth.'

Lazio were not taking the knocks lightly, however. They felt both helpless and distanced. Manzini was in

Japan by now and Stein's office faxed Bendoni asking Manzini to call them. At 11 p.m. Tokyo time he duly called and was told that the operation would take place the following day. Then Stein received another call, this time from Gianni who had been despatched to London with an Italian doctor to report at first hand. He was desperate: he'd taken a taxi from central London and it was still cruising around the wilds of Hertfordshire and had so far run up a fare of over £200.

The operation duly took place on Friday morning. The press at first were completely mystified. Where was Gazza? A few of them camped hopefully outside the Princess Grace, but this time there were no water bombs or air-rifle pellets to greet them. They'd been out-flanked. Inevitably it was the *Sun* who found him first and journalists descended *en masse* on Buckhurst Hill. The hospital, unused to being in the spotlight, coped manfully. Jim Evans walked past the hordes of photographers and journalists unrecognized and unhassled. A short and simple statement was put out to the press: the operation had been successful, had taken a little over a quarter of an hour, and Paul would be discharged either later in the day or the following morning.

Gianni, with little to do all day but read magazines, fretted over an escape route. For Paul just to walk out through the front door, get into a car and drive away was not sufficiently dramatic for his Latin temperament. Finally he had a brainwave. Ambulances were coming in and out all day. He'd put Paul in the back of one, he, Gianni, would take the wheel, and the local public and hovering pressmen would be treated to a view of the first ambulance ever to break the sound barrier. He explained his plan to Marilyn Stein who thought that neither the hospital nor the owners of the ambulance would be too keen.

Paul eventually made his exit into a waiting car, then simply confounded everybody by having the vehicle driven out of the gate marked entrance. By now he had also been examined by the Italian doctor sent over by the club in the absence of Bartolini in Japan. Together with Gianni he had tried to persuade Evans that Paul could still hop on a plane to Japan and at least wave to the crowd, if nothing else. Evans stood his ground, a brave thing to do when confronted with a man the size of Gianni. His patient wasn't fit to travel.

27

'PHANTOM OF THE OPERA.'

On Monday 3 May, the bank holiday, Paul had agreed to stand in for Alan Shearer as the surprise guest at an all-day charity football marathon at Wingate in aid of Ravenswood. Paul arrived in less than good humour, muttering about reprisals against Jane Nottage as a result of an interview she'd given the *Sunday Mirror* in which she had been highly critical of Sheryl and which had led to the headline 'Gazza's women at war.' But within moments all of his personal problems were forgotten. Ravenswood has developed from being a small Jewish charity to a national organization centred on the Ravenswood Village where people with learning difficulties are taught to provide for themselves and to live within a community. On this day, not only was there fund-raising for the charity, but a team of villagers had actually been brought to take part in the event.

They all instantly recognized Gazza, which took him a little by surprise. At first he felt a little awkward and ill at ease, but when one by one they were introduced to him, when the most effusive of them threw his arms around him and clung closely like an affectionate child, all his reservations were gone. He signed T-shirts for them all individually, posed for photos with them, then patiently agreed to have photographs taken with any member of the crowd who was prepared to donate

£5 to the charity. A brief half-hour visit turned into a couple of hours and ended with him recording a message for a sick lad in hospital. No complaints, no boorishness, just a big chunk of his day dedicated to bringing happiness to others.

There was another up side to the day. Glenn Roeder and Paul had neither met nor spoken since Roeder's decision to turn his back on Lazio. Glenn was already at Wingate by the time Paul arrived. The two threw their arms around each other, and Gazza suggested a meal that night, as if they had seen each other the day before rather than eighteen months ago.

Lazio were not to be won over by Paul's charitable exploits in England when they would rather have had him filling their coffers in Japan. The tour had not been a great success and they had even contrived to lose to Grampas 8. No Italian team ever plays a genuine friendly, and the Roman sports papers had been less than kind to them. As far as Paul was concerned there were still a few nasty innuendos in the press to the effect that his failure to travel had been as much a result of some self-induced injury to the knee as to the genuine injury to his cheek.

In any event Lazio had expected him back for training by Thursday morning, when in fact he did not arrive until late on Thursday night. By that time Manzini's phone was red-hot with his efforts to try and trace Paul's whereabouts. In typical Gazza fashion he had disappeared. He wandered cheerfully into training on Friday morning, only to be told that the club intended to fine him £25,000 (a figure which seemed to contain an element of Japanese penalty) and would not permit him to return to England the following Monday for the London 5-a-sides, which was a long-standing commitment for him. Paul shrugged and phoned Stein who was by then ill at home, an illness that was a few days later to see him admitted to Grovelands Hospital in Southgate for a total rest from all the stress and strain that surrounded him. Paul discussed the situation briefly with Stein, then sensing that he was not himself thoughtfully told him he did not want to put him under any pressure and would resolve the matter himself. He tossed back a couple of brandies and confronted Bendoni.

'Look, Bendoni,' he said, slipping into the Italian habit of calling everybody by their surname, 'I know I've not had the greatest of seasons, but it's been difficult for all of us. Let's just put the year behind us, make sure that we qualify for Europe and I promise you next year you'll see the real Gascoigne and we'll win something.'

Bendoni was virtually won over by the Gazza charm. It had worked on the likes of Jackie Charlton, Arthur Cox, Venables, Scholar, Robson and Taylor, so why not on Lazio's general manager. He still thought they should fine him for turning up late for training, however.

'Nah,' replied Gazza, 'I can't afford it.'

The meeting ended with mutual embraces, with no fine, and with Lazio's blessing for Paul's return to England not on Monday morning, but on Sunday night. Lazio played Inter Milan on the Sunday without Gascoigne and duly lost, while Paul flew to England and duly attended the London 5-a-sides.

The following day Paul was back in Rome and training harder than many of the uninjured players. Jim Evans had told him that he must avoid contact sports for at least three weeks, ample time for him to recover to play in England's next two qualifiers away in Poland and Norway, but a deadly blow to Lazio in their effort to qualify for Europe. Zoff saw how sharp Paul was in training, hammering in two spectacular goals in a competitive match. He spoke to Dr Bartolini, who in turn spoke to Evans. It was agreed that if in some way the left side of Paul's face could be protected then he could make a surprise return in the home fixture against lowly Ancona. Eventually they came up with a mask that made Paul a natural for the starring role in *Phantom of the Opera*. It came as a total surprise to the fans when Paul trotted out on to the field heavily disguised. The referee's approval had been sought and given and Paul once again hauled himself up and away from the criticism by turning on his best-ever display for Lazio in a 5-0 thrashing, including laying on two of the goals.

The rumours still began to gather strength that Paul's days at Lazio were numbered and that his return to English football was imminent. Even the *Daily Telegraph* joined in the speculation, although their stab in the dark was wilder than most. On 19 May Peterborough wrote in his column: 'A notable fixture yesterday at Simpson's in the Strand – Graham Souness, manager of Liverpool Football Club, was seen lunching Mel Stein, adviser to Lazio's Paul Gascoigne. Their conversation remains a mystery, but it may be worth monitoring the movements of Gascoigne, who has already cast doubt on the posssibility of his rejoining Tottenham.' That brightened the day of Stein and his fellow patients at Grovelands Priory where he was still undergoing treatment, and made him wonder if he was suffering from schizophrenia having been in two places at once.

There was no keeping Gazza out of the headlines. Somebody had broken into the Lazio training head-quarters and stolen his carbon-fibre mask. *Corriere Dello Sport* was convinced that the culprit was a fan overcome with joy after Gascoigne's brilliant display in the previous Sunday's 5-0 win over Ancona. It was 'not an act of violation, but of love'.

It had been that sort of week.

Until May 1993 Lazio had been more than accom-modating regarding international releases for Paul, even when it meant him missing a competitive league or cup match. An excellent relationship had developed between the England officials and the Lazio management, illustrated by the warm welcome always extended to Graham Taylor and Lawrie McMenemy. The England assistant manager, in particular, would chat regularly with Manzini, and Taylor was invited to watch training sessions when there had been any doubts about Paul's fitness.

Yet a slightly bitter taste was left after the facial injury, which had in turn led to a loss of face by the Italians in failing to produce Paul in Japan. Despite the impending World Cup matches against Poland and Norway Paul was requested to play for Lazio away to Brescia on 23 May. He wore his mask, convinced it was a good luck charm, but this time it failed to conceal the defensive frailties of Lazio outside the Olympic Stadium. They lost 2–0 and slipped to fifth in the table, their UEFA Cup place in the 1993/4 season under threat. Lazio were desperate to qualify and needed just two more points from their last two games to make that virtually certain.

Paul would be in transit between Poland and Norway for their penultimate match on 30 May, and assuming he stayed injury-free was likely to return exhausted for the final game of the season, away to Inter on 6 June. That was not likely to be an easy fixture as Inter had hauled themselves back into the title race, a challenge that might go right to the wire.

Lazio floated the idea that Paul should play against Poland on the 29th, return to Rome and play for Lazio on the 30th, and then rejoin the England party in Norway on the Monday for the Norway match the following Wednesday. 'I'm surprised they don't want me to run a marathon, take part in the world snooker championships and try and qualify for Wimbledon in between.' It was asking too much of a player who was still a fraction off peak fitness after the turmoil of the previous two years, and the idea was politely rejected.

Taking all that into account, it was perhaps not unreasonable for Lazio to refuse Graham Taylor's request for him to play in the US Cup the week after the Norway match. Just before Stein had been taken into hospital Taylor had rung him at home to tell him the situation. Stein, in turn, told him of the very wide release clause in Paul's contract. Taylor was loath to rock the Lazio boat.

Paul's main concern was his further visit to Jim Evans and being passed fit to play for England in the two strenuous matches to come. The masked raider was determined to strike again. Having got the all clear he travelled to meet up with the England squad bound for Poland. Katowice is not the most welcoming of places. The centre of Poland's iron industry, it provided the England party with its best hotel, an establishment that with a lenient inspector might have scrambled one star in England. Taylor and his men were fortunate compared to the Polish squad, who seemed to have been allotted the local YMCA.

As ever Paul Gascoigne was the centre of attention. The mask was an issue of continuing controversy. Neither the England management nor Paul himself wanted it to be worn, although Paul was only aware of it for the first ten minutes or so of a game. Lazio were as ever over-protective. It seemed to them that every time Paul left to play for his country he returned somewhat the worse for wear; they were taking no chances.

Interviewed before the match, Paul was accused of blowing hot and cold for England during the season. Asked which he was that day, he replied that he was roasting, hair grotesquely sleeked back for battle. And battle it turned out to be, both on and off the pitch. Within two minutes Poland missed an open goal, and three minutes later Paul was flattened when in possession for the first, although certainly not the last, time in the match. By the thirty-fifth minute the Poles were in front. Every time an England player (and Paul in particular) looked dangerous, he was viciously fouled. Apart from one yellow card the referee seemed oblivious to it all – he was Swiss and probably neutral. Yet fouls apart, Poland having knocked England out of their stride were the faster, friskier side, hardly surprising when for a player such as Carlton Palmer this was the fifty-eighth game of a seemingly endless season.

At half-time England were still a goal down. Ince had been booked, thus earning an automatic suspension for the match against Norway, and the umbrella that was supposed to have permitted Gazza a free role had been blown away by the Polish storm. Taylor and McMenemy were angry men. They felt England had been drawn into the war and too many players had lost their concentration and positional sense in their rush to retaliate. Gazza was exempt from this criticism. 'If there's one thing playing in Italy has taught me it's not to retaliate. But in that Poland match I was pushed to the limit to hold myself back from laying one on some of the Poles, not just because of what they were doing to me but what they were doing to my mates.'

The second half began a little more promisingly. Suddenly Paul got the ball on the right-hand side of the pitch and set off on one of his surging runs. He burst past two Poles, then two more cynically hacked him down. He rose unsteadily to his feet, watching with disbelief as his sock turned red. He hobbled off the field for some emergency repairs, returning some five minutes later in some distress. With about twelve minutes to go Taylor decided he had taken enough punishment. The Number 8 card was held up and Nigel Clough took his place. Unlike the Holland game Paul was not to be moved from the bench, despite his urgent need of treatment. Ian Wright, having had one effort saved, banged in the equalizer for a final score of 1-1, a point grafted out in adversity by endeavour and courage rather than skill and inspiration.

Paul's reward came in the shape of five stitches in a leg wound that had gone right through to the bone. He had done his best, but that was not enough for some of the press. Whispers were also coming from the England camp that there would be changes for the match against Norway. Walker and Barnes had their respective heads on the block, but what about Gascoigne? Initially the injury to his leg had made him a doubtful starter, but when Graham Taylor said that he would not hesitate to replace anybody if he thought the replacement could do a better job, the papers started putting two and two together and came up with the Number 8. The impossible was about to happen – England were going to drop Paul Gascoigne.

Taylor spoke privately to Paul and told him that whatever he might read, whatever the papers might say, he was never going to leave him out. Paul, as ever, ignored the turmoil around him. He knew he'd not played brilliantly against Poland, but he'd not played disastrously either.

News from Italy augured well for the next season. Lazio had beaten Napoli 4-3 to guarantee them a place in Europe via the UEFA Cup for the first time in sixteen years. Zoff had achieved the first step in his long-term plan to restore the club to its former glory. Paul, for his part, had already gone public when he was with the England team at Burnham Beeches, stating that he was happy in Italy and had no intention of returning to England whether that be to Newcastle, Tottenham, Blackburn or Barnet. Now that he would be playing in Europe there was also little or no chance of him joining another continental club. He had gone to Lazio because they had convinced him that they had ambitions to win a domestic and European trophy. Now he had the opportunity to fulfil those ambitions.

28

'AM I PLAYING CRAP, OR IS IT ENGLAND?'

It was hardly likely that the Norwegian people were going to hang out the flags for Paul after his ill-considered, impetuous remarks prior to their visit to England. However, Paul has a way of winning people over even after doing the most outrageous things to them. Whenever the chips are down he is usually able to dig deep into his resources and pull out something special. On that first day of June 1993 there was no doubting that something special was needed.

There was some fairly blunt talking by the England manager. 'Over the past two years we have developed a degree of honesty and I have to confirm that the Gazza who made his comeback against Norway in October is not the same Gazza preparing for 90 minutes against Norway now. It's there for a lot of people to see – it can't be hidden. People have to see it for themselves, you can't actually hide it. You've got to have a degree of fitness to last 90 minutes and that is a problem. The lad knows it.'

The lad did know it, but he also knew the reason, and despite what everybody was suggesting his weight had nothing to do with it. As he had explained to Bendoni just a few weeks before, it had been a year of settling in, a year when everything had been strange, from language to training sessions, from food to the pace of the game. His emotions were as troubled and turbulent as those of any adolescent. His season had been one of constant interruption, even once it had undergone its delayed start. He had been forced to wait months before he was permitted to play through a whole match, and then he found himself bouncing back and forth in aeroplanes – to London for the friendly against Spurs, to Spain for the friendly, back to England for the home matches against Norway, Turkey, San Marino and Holland, then to Turkey itself, to Poland and finally to Norway. It was an exhausting schedule, and added to a series of niggling injuries involving operations, stitches and further periods of enforced rest, he had never been able to settle to the rhythm to which he had become accustomed in English football.

During training on the day before the Norway game Paul was heckled not just by the Norwegian supporters, but by a minority of English fans. Gazza swapped insults with them, and having brought a smile to their faces then proceeded to drive in one of his 30-yard free kick specials past Chris Woods. Turning to the spectators, Paul gave them a one-finger gesture, a big grin and received a huge cheer in return. The naughty schoolboy had won yet another round.

It was Tottenham all over again. They'd known he was not fit to play the full semi-final against Arsenal, any more than he'd been fit to play the sixth round against Notts County; but Venables had taken a gamble and on each occasion a piece of Gazza magic had seen them scoop the jackpot.

Rather than getting behind the team and the manager before such a crucial match, the media still trowelled around for dirt. On the morning of the match itself, the *Sun* claimed that Paul's problem was an alcoholic one. They even went so far as to get a so-called expert dietician to set out a liquid menu for Paul to follow. In a press conference the previous day Paul had honestly admitted his performances were not up to his usual standard; he did not feel there was any realistic chance of being dropped but accepted his passing against Poland had not been of the highest quality, and he desperately wanted the chance to put it right against Norway.

Paul disclosed, half-jokingly, that Dr Bartolini had initially told him to drink wine, but had then changed his mind and told him to get back to beer. Inadvertently Graham Taylor gave the press some new Gazza head-lines. The man was (and is) genuinely fond of Paul, but there was a certain naïvety about his openness with the media, as if being honest with them would make them love you more. 'There is something Paul has to come to terms with,' he said, 'it's how you refuel yourself between training sessions and how you feel. There is only one person who can influence Paul's situation and it isn't me. There comes a time when a player has to take the responsibility on himself.'

Graham Taylor is an honourable, decent man whose vilification, particularly at the hands of the *Sun* during their 'turnip' campaign hurt both him and his family deeply; but on this occasion his well-intentioned words did Paul no favours. 'Refuelling' as far as the British and Italian press were concerned could mean only one thing. 'As far as I was concerned I used the word refuelling in the athletic sense,' Taylor says, 'what you eat, how you live, what you drink, how you exercise. It never occurred to me not to play Gazza even if he wasn't as fit as he should have been. I was convinced in my mind that whatever they might say publicly the Norwegians were scared of him.'

If the build-up to the match was problematic, it was as nothing compared to the nightmare of the game itself. Taylor had made some adventurous changes, for once claiming he had picked a side specifically with the opposition in mind. But in the midst of chaos Gascoigne ran about aimlessly looking for space that he never found. It had started with a hint of promise: Paul was fouled and took a snap free kick that nearly caught his former Spurs team-mate, Thorstvedt, napping. But that was about it for the first half. There were a few harsh challenges on Gazza, there did appear to be two men on him whenever he got the ball, but even in one-on-one situations he rarely came out the winner. When Norway scored just before half-time it was no great surprise. Des Walker was to blame for Norway's second goal, just as he'd been culpable for the first, and it was merciful when Clough replaced him in the sixty-third minute, but still neither Paul nor England could get back into the match.

Paul tossed his mask away in temper but no new Gascoigne was revealed. He still seemed ill at ease with himself and his team-mates and it was not until ten minutes from the end, when the game had long gone from England's grasp, that one 20-yard diagonal pass, and one shimmy that took him past two Norwegian defenders and ended in a cross, gave any hint of huge natural talent.

There was no respite that first weekend in June. Lazio's tour to Canada, which had been the main reason they'd withheld him from the trip to the USA, was cancelled as they had now committed themselves to the pre-season Makita tournament in London. Technically therefore Paul was available, but Taylor quite properly, having named his squad, could not very well drop somebody in favour of Paul.

The newspapers saw it differently. Colin Malam in the *Sunday Telegraph*, usually the most reliable of reporters, got it as wrong as anybody else. 'Paul Gascoigne is the first victim of England's shameful World Cup qualifying performance in Norway. Significantly manager Graham Taylor has declined to add the £5.5 million midfielder to his squad for the US Cup '93 . . . It is pretty obvious that he has decided to wash his hands of Gascoigne for the time being. The rejection could last for the rest of Taylor's threatened reign too, if the player does not succeed in reversing the perceived decline in his general fitness.'

Taylor was again lured by the press and his own frankness into controversy. 'I can't allow myself to record publicly exactly what I think all his problems are. If I did all hell would be let loose. What I find difficult is that there are people who know, but they want me or someone else to say what is wrong. However, I cannot and will not go all the way down the line . . . I thought he was capable of having a superb game against Norway. As he has proved with Lazio he digs them out from somewhere. But he didn't deliver the goods and the more that happens I think he'll start to worry.'

Privately Taylor did what he could and flew to Rome to talk to Paul personally. Paul was not ungrateful. 'I know he cared. I took everything he said on board and even though he's gone I'd like him to know that.'

All that had really happened was that he had pushed his tired body and mind just about as far as they could go. The boy was exhausted. He needed a holiday and was only too pleased not to have been included in the party for the United States. He would go to America, but only to holiday at the Florida Keys with the blessing of Zoff and Bartolini. In their final match Paul had been substituted 25 minutes from the end and Lazio went down 4-1 in Turin to Juventus. However, the game meant little or nothing to the Romans, whilst Juventus had been told by their management that if they lost they'd be fined £20,000 a man!

Despite the miles between them the Gascoigne–Taylor saga refused to die a death. The press would not permit it. The *Sun* ran a phone-in as to whether or not Taylor should have publicly criticized his star and having done so whether the player should be axed: 82 per cent said Taylor was wrong 'to publicly criticize Gazza' (the *Sun* were clearly *Star Trek* fans in relation to split infinitives), 76 per cent did not believe Paul to be overweight, and 72 per cent thought he should be retained in the side. The Great British public in the shape of *Sun* readers had spoken. In Boston the hounds cornered the hare and Taylor hotly refuted the latest fantasy that Paul was abusing himself with drugs. It was all getting wilder and wilder.

'I am sick and tired of being grilled about Paul Gascoigne. If anyone has supported him it is me. I refute any suggestion that I'm about to drop him because what I want is a fit and eager Gascoigne for our match against Poland in September. In the last six months if there's anyone who has supported the man through the good and the not so good times it's me. I'm the one person who has been prepared to grasp the nettle and I'm suffering because of it. I want him fit to play for England. He has shown strength of character to come back after two serious injuries and I don't want him to throw everything away. We have seen what's happened with talented players before and we don't want it to happen to him. This is not something I have just started saying. In England I detected problems with Paul were about to start. It was me who said, "Please God, nothing happens to him." All I can say now is, "Come on, I'm waiting for you for that match in September."'

It showed how little was understood about Paul when Michael Hart reporting from Boston said he was surprised at the level of support Paul commanded from his team-mates. Wherever he has played Paul has received total loyalty and respect from those around him on a day-to-day basis. Paul's confidence in the summer of 1993 was at its lowest ebb. In three years he had experienced the heights and plumbed the depths. He felt worse than when he had hobbled out of the Princess Grace on crutches. Then his injury had been self-inflicted, now the wounds were to his back, from all quarters. He was in such a state that for several days he could not even bring himself to telephone Stein, thinking he'd depress him yet further. He was beginning to cut himself off from reality, his moods shifting from anger to morose disbelief that had never before been a part of his personality.

His old friends were the most supportive. John Coberman called just to tell him to keep his chin up. Despite the treatment meted out to her, Sheryl never lost faith even though she too was drawn into the 'let's write anything about Gazza' syndrome. The *Daily Express,* which probably should have known better, bought a so-called exclusive from Colin Kyle, Sheryl's ex-husband, when he claimed that Paul had not only stolen his wife but had now stolen his children. There was just so much Paul could take. He rang his old friend Waddle seeking reassurance, but he was on holiday in Cyprus and all Paul got was the answerphone. 'Am I playing crap, or is it England?' he asked the recorded message. It was a question he would never usually have needed to ask.

He rang Stein the morning after the USA game not even knowing the score. Paul Ince had been made captain, the first black player ever to lead an England team, at football, cricket or rugby. It was not going to be a night to remember for anything else. The final score was a historic 2-0 win for the States. Paul asked Stein to go out and buy the tabloids, then phone back and leave the headlines on his answerphone. The best of them was 'Yanks 2, Planks 0'. As for Gazza he was going fishing. The *Titanic* appeared to have sunk and he was relieved that just for once he'd missed the boat.

In the last show of his *Gazzetta Italia* series on 12 June Paul appeared relaxed and far from overweight, lounging in the garden of his villa. He had spent the last few days 'refuelling' mentally and admitted to feeling much better, his first public admission that the furore had actually got to him.

On the weekend that the dishevelled and shattered England were due to play Brazil, Paul was back in Hertfordshire yet again. Sheryl had to return for the children's schooling and with time on his hands he flew back to keep her company. That was typical: the insecurity, the loneliness, things he could not cope with on his own even for a day. This time he was able to watch the England game on TV and his feelings were totally different. He saw the way the Brazilians played, the easy rhythmical flow of their passing, almost in time to the constant beating of the drums, as beautiful as the girls in yellow and green who danced bikini-clad throughout the whole match. It was his kind of football and he now desperately wanted to be part of it, to be an Englishman playing the Brazilians at their own game. Without Paul it was beauty and the beast and the beast nearly won. The midfield without Gascoigne looked ponderous and uninventive. Nothing had happened, nobody had suddenly appeared to put Paul's place at risk. Once again he had been proved irreplaceable.

As Paul took off for holiday he was able to look at his life in more perspective. Despite everything that had been said, despite the dirt that had been hurled at him, he could regard his first season in Italy with quiet satisfaction. For the first time in nearly 20 years Lazio were back in Europe, they'd finished fifth in Serie A, their highest position since 1976/7, and perhaps most important of all they'd become a club that stars wanted to play for. The pride had been reinstated. They were the top club in the city of Rome.

Taylor, unable to speak to Paul, phoned the recuperating Stein again. He'd returned from his own crucifixion in the States and wanted to be sure Paul was not upset at some of the quotations and comments that had been attributed to him. 'You know what it's like,' he said. Stein did indeed. 'Just tell him his place is safe for the Poland game.' Graham sounded anxious, almost as if he was scared that his mercurial star was angry with him. 'I've left messages, but he hasn't called me back . . .' 'Don't worry,' Stein replied, 'he doesn't call anybody back.'

29

'HE WAS NOT THE USUAL GAZZA. HE WAS SAD.'

As Lazio assembled in Austria for pre-season training at their camp in Seefeld they were joined by a fair proportion of the world's sporting press. The *Sun* led the way with a photograph of Paul running with the rest of the team under the headline, 'Fattaboy Gazza'. His performances in the early friendly matches did little to lighten the gloom. Paul's response was unemotional. He'd heard and read it all before. 'So what? That's what pre-season friendlies are for – to get fit. I don't know why they bother to write the same stuff each year. They might as well bring out the old cuttings, shove them in a computer and sack all the journalists.'

He was in much better shape by the time the Italians met Karlsruhe. Although Lazio lost 0-1 he was far and away their best player. He'd put in a lot of hard and determined work, spending at least an hour a day running up the side of a mountain, then returning to the hotel's sauna to metamorphose his fat to muscle.

Lazio flew into England to take part in the Makita tournament, which was also to feature Tottenham, and inevitably Paul arrived in the face of yet another row. The Makita organizers had set up a press conference at Gatwick Airport at which Paul was billed to star. Unfortunately nobody had bothered to ask

Paul or his advisers or they would have been told that Paul had been so upset by the articles that had been written about his weight that he simply did not feel like talking to the same journalists who had caused him so much personal anguish. Paul flatly refused to attend, leaving an embarrassed Zoff and Manzini in his wake to attempt an explanation.

The following day all was forgotten as Paul ran on to the Tottenham pitch to salute his old fans, stopping on the way to shake hands with John Sheridan. All suggestions that he was fat were rebutted by his very appearance, his body lean, his face almost gaunt, yet softened now by the mass of curls he'd grown in the close season. He approached the match as if it were a championship decider, demonstrated all his old skills, and as Lazio lost 3-2 he left the field arguing violently with the referee. 'I'd asked him how long to go and he'd said seven minutes. He played two at most and then blew up for time. If I play in any match winning means everything to me.' The words had an ominous ring about them.

On the Sunday football was forgotten yet again as all hell broke loose. Without permission, consultation or notice Nottage had written a book concerning her 'year' with Gazza which was about to be serialized in the *Sunday Mirror*. The exaggeration of her time with Paul was the least of the problems the publication brought with it. Nottage had made some extraordinary and ill-founded allegations – Paul was 'bulimic', he binged on food then made himself sick, he was on laxatives to lose weight, was potentially suicidal if Sheryl left.

Rather than taking legal action Paul and Sheryl hit back immediately through the *News of the World*. They spoke to their good friend Rebekah Wade: 'I'm furious about these slurs. She's trying to ruin my life and my life with Sheryl. I know why too, it's because I sacked her. She doesn't really have a clue what I'm like . . .

If Jane's seen me being sick it's only because I'd just seen her face. It's ridiculous my suffering the same disease as pencil-thin Lady Di . . .'

It was strange that Paul should refer to Princess Diana. Outsiders could see just how much the two had in common. Both were often accused of courting publicity, but in fact the media was the suitor, not the intended. Just a few days before the Princess had snapped and angrily confronted a cameraman. Now Paul was nearing breaking point as well.

If Nottage succeeded in anything, it was to push Paul and Sheryl closer together, as Sheryl said, 'I feel sick and gutted. Jane has betrayed us all and I feel sorry for a woman who has to stoop so low to attack Paul in public.'

Paul's friends rallied to his side. Jimmy Gardner proudly stated, 'If Paul's bulimic, then I've got AIDS.' Dino Zoff was equally astounded, 'These problems don't exist for him . . . I judge him only on what he does on the football pitch and what I see is very satisfactory . . . All the great players have broad shoulders . . .'

Lazio clearly had big ambitions for the season. They had bought an astonishing seven new players at a total cost of £15 million, including, most significantly, Luca Marchegiani, the world's most expensive keeper. Even he, though, could not prevent Lazio being well and truly beaten by Ajax of Holland in their final game of the Makita. Less than happy in defeat Paul stormed off the pitch, yet even in his anger did not forget his younger fans. A child came up to him and asked for his autograph. Paul quickly peeled off a sock and gave it to him. Another youngster ran over and received a shin-pad for his trouble. For them it might as well have been a million pounds; for Paul it was a naturally generous gesture.

He went and sat down in the Tottenham restaurant, and tucked into a meal of steak, chips and fried onions, and followed that with a chocolate dessert and a pint of beer to wash it all down. An hour later, having digested his meal, he decided to head for home. Bulimic? It was a joke.

Back in Italy, the nation was purging itself commercially and politically. Paul and his advisers had seen how corruption worked, and had they been willing to pay bribes could have obtained several sponsorships that otherwise passed them by. A wave of arrests and suicides seemed to have passed Lazio by as well, but then came the body blow. Their president, the ultra-smooth Cragnotti, was arrested at the beginning of August, just as the club faced Olympique de Marseille in another friendly. One would have liked to have been a fly on the wall as the beleaguered Bernard Tapie, still president of O M, gave Cragnotti advice on how to deal with a police investigation.

Lazio's continued pre-season build-up was a disaster. In Spain for a tournament involving São Paulo of Brazil and La Coruña of Spain, they lost to the Brazilians and drew with the Spanish side, leaving them without a win against first-class opposition on all their travels. The Brazilian game was little short of war, with three red cards and four bookings. Paul had been substituted and was safely out of it on the bench when one of his team-mates, not known for his gentleness on the pitch, was tossed into the fray. 'Go on,' said Gazza, 'see if you can get a yellow card!' Within five minutes the player was back at Paul's side, having gone one better and received a red one. 'Was it one lump or two you wanted in your coffee?' Gazza asked innocently.

On the England front the news was encouraging. Graham Taylor called Stein to see how he was, and at the same time told him to believe nothing that he read, only what he heard directly from the England manager's lips. More importantly he confirmed once again that Paul's place in the England squad was perfectly safe.

Meanwhile Bartolini, the Lazio club doctor, was not doing a lot for Paul's confidence. 'He cannot play two consecutive games because he doesn't have the strength . . . the Gascoigne of today is only at 50 per cent. In the two weeks which separate us from the start of the season we are counting on bringing him up to at least 70 per cent.' When the doctor's words of wisdom hit the Italian press Paul took immediate action. He identified Bartolini's car at the training ground and let down all its tyres.

Lazio seemed genuinely concerned about him. Manzini recalls, 'He was not the usual Gazza. He was sad.' On 18 August, after another three-team tournament in Rome, Cragnotti and Bendoni took Paul out to dinner, anxious to get to the root of his problem. 'We really cleared the air that night and I think they understood that I wasn't superman. I'd do my best in every game, but I couldn't guarantee it would work.'

Yet a week is a long time in football and by 24 August, just five days before the start of the Italian Serie A season proper, Lazio faced Inter Milan in their final warm-up match. Taylor flew to see it and to make his peace with Paul after some damaging comments attributed to him in Nottage's book. He could not have picked a better moment. Paul, looking strong and fit, was involved in everything. With the score at 2-0 in Lazio's favour he was brought down in the penalty area, took the spot kick himself and missed. Nonplussed, he just pushed his game up that extra little notch, scored a fine header, and then to his surprise found himself substituted after 70 minutes. It was almost as if the Lazio medical team were scared he might prove them wrong by lasting out the full 90 minutes on a hot August evening.

Taylor returned to England a happier man, and confident that he could name Paul in the England squad on 30 August for the match against Poland in the knowledge he would let nobody down. He felt no need to attend Lazio's first game of the season against Foggia, which was fortunate for him as it ended in a dull goalless draw. Paul, however, received a magnificent reception from the Lazio fans, and playing to his audience clenched his fist and punched the air. It was a declaration of intent for the coming season, a season that was to end in tragedy. Although the result was disappointing, Paul had a solid match, keeping his position and passing accurately. He was brought down brutally, made to pursue his attacker, then grinned at Zoff, smiled at the referee and took the free kick.

At his post-selection press conference Taylor refused to answer any questions regarding Gazza. He was perfectly within his rights, having learned the bitter lesson that whatever he said was likely to be turned and twisted until it bore no resemblance to his original comment. It was an interesting footnote that once the subject of Paul was closed the conference took only seventeen minutes.

As it was, for once Taylor and Gascoigne were to have the last laugh. On 8 September a trim Gazza, both in hair and figure, stood in the England line quietly and self-possessed. A smile for the camera, but no evidence of a stuck-out tongue, no larking around with officials. This was the World Cup and this was for real.

From the kick-off he looked on top of his game. Within seconds he was at the thick of things, racing on to a ball on the left with all his old pace, then putting in a shot that the Polish keeper kept out with his legs. A 40-yard pass to the left wing was followed by one to Platt, then on to Ferdinand who scored after pulling the ball down superbly. Paul orchestrated the crowd and they rose to him and the team, all the disappointments and embarrassments of the American tour now forgotten.

The Poles were a disgrace, rolling over in agony at the slightest touch, and there was an inevitability that

Paul would get involved. Sure enough a robust challenge on the Polish number 3 on the touchline saw Gazza booked. 'I didn't realize at first it would mean I'd miss the Holland game. I knew I'd been booked against Norway, but that had been three months before and it seemed like it belonged to a different season. When I was told at half-time I was gutted.'

As England came out for the second half, again Paul got the crowd on its feet without delay. Ferdinand won the ball in the air majestically, Paul swivelled in the box and scored with his right foot. It was a goal only Gazza could have scored, his sixth for England and probably his best. The virtuoso performance was not yet complete. There was a free kick from Paul's favourite Wembley position, just outside the penalty area. The Poles clearly thought he'd take it, but they were in for a surprise. Platt touched the ball to Gazza, he put his foot on it, and there was Stuart Pearce after an eight-month absence cracking the ball home.

The Wembley crowd broke into a moving version of 'Swing Low, Sweet Chariot' as the rain sheeted down, and a minute from the end Gazza set off on yet another run, as if to make the point to his Italian employers who thought him incapable of completing 90 minutes. As the final whistle blew he was reluctant to leave the field, saluting the crowd as they saluted him in song. The noise swept over him, the sweet sound of success that had so long eluded him and England.

30

'IF I KEEP AT IT THE PAIN WILL STOP.'

While Paul basked in the sunshine of England's success, and even the *Sun* promoted Taylor from turnip to tulip, there were storm clouds gathering in Italy. Cragnotti was unhappy that Paul would not talk to the Italian media and wanted to know the reason why. Then Paul managed to report back a day late for training after the England game, and all of that, added to Lazio's first win of the season against Parma without Paul, started the transfer rumours rolling once again. Cragnotti was alleged to have said, 'This is a year of destiny for Paul. If he does not succeed we are sure there is still a market for him in England.'

On 10 September despite all the headlines, Paul was in the starting line-up for the visit to Cremonese. He began where he'd left off for England, hit the bar with a crashing free kick, and by half-time with Lazio well on top he felt better than he'd been for months. He came out for the second half all ready to deliver the killer punch. It took just 12 minutes for it all to go wrong. He got a sharp pain in his leg, hobbled about for a moment, then withdrew with a split muscle. Without Gazza Lazio went to pieces and lost 1-0.

He missed Lazio's first UEFA match against Plovdiv, which they won 2-0, but hard work saw him back for the match against Inter Milan on 19 September, although not before his name had been quite innocently linked with two sleazy stories that broke in the British press. A *Panorama* special shattered Terry Venables's image of *bonhomie* and seemed to have put a permanent end to his ambition to be England manager, whilst Nottage's affair with Andy Roxburgh, the married Scottish team manager, was yet another story hung on the hook of Gazza's name.

The Inter Milan game ended again without goals and Paul was substituted to a chorus of whistles, not aimed at him but at the decision to take him off. As rumours grew of Paul's imminent departure from the club, the Lazio switchboard was jammed with protests at the possible loss of their hero. Again Cragnotti met with Paul and this time two positive statements came out of the discussions. Paul would be staying at Lazio and he had agreed to talk to the press.

However, his fitness was a continuing problem; the pulled muscle in his thigh had cleared up, but now his Achilles' ligaments were troubling him. And if he was troubled, Dino Zoff was even more pressurized. Without Gazza, and Signori injured as well, Lazio went down 4-1 to Cagliari and despite all the millions spent they were just one point above the relegation zone.

Paul's desperate luck continued. He got himself virtually fit to face the mighty AC Milan but just missed out, then fell awkwardly in training and damaged his knee, the left one this time. Bartolini was quick with the ready quote – 'a twisted left knee with slight damage to the rear ligaments. His recovery will take around three weeks give or take the odd day.'

As Paul nursed his latest injury both of the teams to whom he owed allegiance suffered disasters. Lazio lost the first leg of their Italian Cup match 2-0 to a Serie C (third division) side, Avellino, and then on 13 October England met their nemesis in Rotterdam. Paul was determined to be there but Lazio would not have it. He was injured, they needed him fit and every day was vital to his treatment. He would have to support them from a distance. On the morning of the match Paul rang Stein, still recuperating at home. 'Listen mate, do us a favour. I've forgotten to send the manager and the lads good luck telegrams. Do it for us will you, and don't forget to say the bastards here won't let me go.'

England lost 2-0, and could justifiably claim they were hard done by when the referee failed to send off Koeman for a professional foul. Their hopes of qualifying for the World Cup were now in Never-Never Land – if Poland beat Holland at least 1-0, if England beat San Marino 7-0, if pigs could fly. It was hopeless and everybody knew it. The next World Cup would be in 1998 and Paul would be 31 by then. It all seemed a long way ahead.

Paul's way back in Italy was not going too well either. He missed the second leg of the Cup tie against Avellino, when Lazio could not pull back any of the two-goal deficit and exited from a tournament that could have offered another doorway to European competition. The fans were not amused, arriving at the training ground in numbers and smashing up the players' cars. Although Paul's was not touched he expressed his intention of trading it in and buying a Fiat 500 if things got any worse. They were certainly not getting any better for him, particularly when the club signed Alan Boksic from Marseille, another foreigner and another rival for Paul.

Paul pushed himself even harder and did play at least a half against Piacenza. However, the tendon began to trouble him again and he had to signal to Zoff to take him off. It was more than frustrating: if he rested the injury it felt perfectly comfortable, then as soon as he played the pain became unbearable. He was worried. He sat out the Rome derby, then in desperation Lazio agreed that he could return to England to see Sheridan and Browett. Before he left yet another warning shot was fired across his bows when Cragnotti stated: 'Next season we are gong for the title and we cannot wait any longer to see if Gascoigne is going to find his form . . . we expected so much from him . . .' That was part of the problem – everybody expected so much from him. But he was only one lad and there was only so much he could do, so far he could push himself. And Paul, for one, was never prepared to accept that he was only human.

In London there was good news and bad news. On the positive side Browett felt that no immediate surgery was necessary, but the injury would need three weeks' complete rest to avoid the risk of serious damage to his inflamed Achilles' tendon. After that he'd review the situation. Three weeks – he could forget all about the San Marino match on 17 November. It was just one thing after another. He'd survived the psychological devastation of two serious injuries by concentrating on his obsession to play football and now he was stopped in his tracks by a whole series of niggling injuries.

While Paul was in London, Lazio beat Udinese 2–1 and presented Alan Boksic to the crowd before the match. Boksic himself was full of praise for Gazza: 'He'll be my fortune. Nobody's better than him. Every attacker in the world would like to play in front of him.' He was tactful too: when asked how he would cope now that Lazio had four foreigners, he pointed out that at Marseille they had five on their books. That day Lazio had played with only Doll and Winter in the side. There was room; but would the room be for Boksic or Gazza?

Worse was to follow for Paul, working hard with Sheridan in London. Lazio took a narrow 1-0 UEFA Cup lead to Boavista in Portugal and went down 2-0, to end their European campaign before it had ever really begun. The financial ramifications were obvious and it did not need a crystal ball to realize that Zoff's job was on the line. Despite their communication problems Zoff was a fan of Paul, but who was to say that his replacement would feel the same way?

Yet the Lazio players dug deep into their reserves of character, travelling to a hostile Naples and beating Napoli 2–1. Suddenly they found themselves only three points off the top of Serie A and were clearly back in the hunt for a UEFA place the following season. Paul just could not think that far ahead. On Sunday 7 November Taylor phoned Paul's advisers to enquire as to his health. It was merely a courteous formality: four games played, none of them completed, more time spent on the treatment couch than on the pitch. Yet again England would face a World Cup match without Paul Gascoigne. 'I was very down. I knew England would beat San Marino with or without me, but even if this was going to be the end of the road for both the team and the manager I wanted to be a part of it. The dream of playing in Europe for Lazio and in the States for England had been what had kept me going, and I'd seen them both disappear.'

Sheridan travelled back to Rome with Paul and found the Italians desperate to get their star back on the field. He recommended a particular machine for treating Paul's injury and Lazio did not hesitate to buy it.

Although the England–San Marino match was played in Bologna, Paul could not bring himself to make the trip. As it happened those who stayed away were the lucky ones. England were caught absolutely cold and went a goal down within the first minute, and although they ran out 7–1 winners on the night, the result was irrelevant once Holland had beaten Poland. 'I felt dead sorry for Graham Taylor. Nobody should have had to take the stick that he did. I had to ask myself if I'd done enough to help him keep his job and I couldn't help thinking about my below-par performance against Norway. I tried to tell one of the Sundays how I felt and I must have got the message across, because he actually phoned me to say thank you.'

It was a mutual admiration society. 'My main regret as England manager was the short amount of time I had with Paul. Three and a half games and then I lost him for eighteen months. He was always under such pressure, always having something to prove. People don't realize how sensitive he is, how his confidence always needs building up. Yet at the end of the day he is simply the most gifted individual player that I've worked with.'

Lazio's up-and-down season continued. Boksic on his début put them ahead against Torino but they still lost 1-2. They needed a fully fit Gazza and they needed him quickly. Sheridan persevered. He and the doctors had set themselves a deadline: if Paul could not be back in training by the end of November, then an operation would be needed on the Achilles' tendon, an operation which would put him out of the game for some three months. With that sort of absence he could well become the forgotten man of European football.

Paul was not about to let anybody forget him, and with super-human effort he drove himself back to fitness and into training. 'It was hurting me, but I didn't let on. I thought, I've beaten worse than this, if I keep at it the pain will stop. And it did.'

A virulent press campaign was gathering strength, fuelled by rumours put out by greedy and ruthless agents seeking to drum up business. It was suggested, quite incorrectly, that Paul had come down to a hotel foyer naked, that he'd urinated in Zoff's car, that he'd insulted Cragnotti, and that Lazio had put up with enough. Now they were looking to rid themselves of their overweight, overpaid liability.

Another scandalous rumour was about to break regarding so called 'illegal' loans made by Spurs to Paul under the stewardship of Scholar and Venables. Everything Paul had earned, every benefit he had received, had been declared by Tottenham to the Inland Revenue, and if the Football League had not been advised of the same then that was the responsibility of the club and not the player. However, none of that made any difference to the tabloids. Finally Len Lazarus could stand it no longer. As the papers reported that Santin had offered Paul on behalf of Lazio to Newcastle, Manchester United, Leeds and Blackburn, and with both Howard Wilkinson and Kenny Dalglish expressing an interest, he arranged with the Italian club to issue a press statement: Paul was not for sale to anybody at any price. As for Santin, as Bendoni said to Lazarus, and indeed wanted to put in the press release, 'Let him concentrate on running his restaurant.'

Paul was equally dismissive. 'I don't go around trying to sell his restaurant behind his back so why's he trying to sell my backside behind my backside?'

The penultimate match before the Christmas break was against Juventus and Paul beat the odds to be back in the side. Boksic put the ball through to him, a little turn in the box, a left-foot volley saved, and then he was on to the rebound to put Lazio one up. After a Juventus equalizer Boksic made it 2-1. Then two minutes into stoppage time Paul sprang the offside trap, the keeper saved his first shot and he swooped on to the rebound to make it 3-1. As Lazio moved up to sixth place Gazza moved from 'burnt-out has-been' to the 'saviour', conquering the city he'd seemed about to lose. 'I was just pleased I'd let nobody down. I felt terribly tense. It wasn't the press I cared about, it was the fans.'

A win against Lecce meant they went away for the holidays on a roll. Paul was asked what he wanted for Christmas. He hesitated for a moment, then with a broad grin replied, 'Half of President Cragnotti's money, new boots to make me run quicker, a diet sheet from Jimmy Gardner and the ability to keep laughing like Zoff.' As 1993 ended 1994 looked full of promise.

31

'IT'S AS IF THERE'S A CURSE ON HIM.'

Paul's New Year resolution to pick up no more injuries did not last beyond the first match after the break, against Sampdoria on 2 January 1994. With the score at 1-1 he turned sharp left, caught his foot in a hole and freakishly fractured a rib. He went off in agony to a great ovation and immediately was given six pain-killing injections in his back. Strapped up and fitted into a plastic girdle, he was determined to be fit for the next match at Foggia. 'The strapping was so tight I could hardly breathe, but it didn't half make me look slimmer.'

Despite the incapacitating injury Paul was made man of the match, but Lazio went down 4-1. Cragnotti was furious and gave the whole team a verbal lashing. He had paid them huge sums of money and they'd rewarded him with early exits from Europe and the Italian Cup, and now it looked as if they were out of the race for the League as well. Manzini came round with pieces of paper to sign and told Paul it related to new legislation to curb Sunday driving on the autostradas for conservation reasons. Paul signed, then signed another sheet that Manzini thrust at him.

On Thursday night at 10.15 he received a call from the team manager, checking if he was at home. Manzini explained that he'd committed himself to a 10 p.m. curfew every night except Sunday and Monday, when he could stay out to midnight. Paul countered the ruse by leaving his answerphone on all night. If Manzini wanted to know where he was then he'd have to come calling personally.

Whatever Cragnotti had said seemed to have worked. Gazza and Boksic combined superbly in a 2-0 victory over Reggiana, to complete the side's third win in five matches and put them firmly in the frame for a UEFA place, even though the title looked out of their reach. On 23 January Lazio were due to travel to Parma and Paul was about to make his sixth consecutive appearance for them, incredibly the longest run he'd had in any team since he'd completed a nineteen-match unbroken run for Tottenham on 26 December 1990. But there was no fairy-story end to the match: Lazio lost 2-0 and slipped back to sixth.

In England, meanwhile, there had been an astonishing turnaround in the fortunes of Venables. If Keegan might come out of the Tyne with a salmon in his mouth, Venables had emerged from the mire of his Tottenham dismissal and his trial by television with the England job firmly clenched between his teeth. Paul was unhappy with his performance against Parma, but delighted with Venables's appointment. He'd dreaded the thought of getting to know a new England manager and here was the man he knew almost best of all. 'It was up to me to prove that at 26 I had learned a lot, even though I knew I still had a lot more to learn under Terry.' He gave Venables the best message he could by playing superbly in a 4-2 win over Cremonese.

Gazza's name echoed around the stadium and then, as Cravero was substituted, Paul pulled on the captain's armband for the first time in top-class professional football. Could it be that the rehabilitated England manager was about to appoint his own personal black sheep as the leader of the national side?

Off the field Paul had not done his captaincy prospects a lot of good. Out shopping with Sheryl near the Spanish Steps, they were pestered by a paparazzo who must have taken fifty or sixty photographs. Eventually Paul had had enough. He offered the photographer five minutes if he would then leave them alone. 'And what if I want ten minutes?' the man rudely replied. Paul asked him to leave, at which point he was grabbed around the neck while his assailant's friend suddenly appeared to take a photo of Paul locked in combat. Enough was enough and Paul lashed out, bloodying the first man's nose. Everybody ended up at the police station and soon the wires were buzzing to London that Venables's potential captain had just got himself arrested. Eventually Paul was released with the help of Gianni and no charges were made, but it had been an unpleasant and frightening incident.

On 6 February Paul was suspended and missed out on Lazio's 1-0 defeat of Inter Milan. As he put it, 'The yellow cards were given out like espressos in the local restaurant. I was playing my natural game, playing some of the best football of my career, let alone my time in Italy, but I'd picked up three consecutive bookings. I was beginning to wonder if I was playing in the right country.' On the 13th Venables was in Rome to see his erstwhile star for himself. Paul as ever rose to the occasion and curled a superb free kick into the net, past astonished Cagliari defenders and keeper alike. Lazio ran out 4-0 winners and Paul swung from the crossbar at the end like an excited child who has just pleased a proud parent. Venables was more than proud, he was delighted. 'He played as if he was happy. They clearly love him, he likes them and the crowd responds to him.'

He might just as well have been talking about Paul at Newcastle and Tottenham. His moods were mercurial to say the least. If he was on top of his game, fit and well, then all was right with the world; but it only needed something small to tilt the balance. He had pulled out all the stops for Venables without losing the element of court jester. For one magical afternoon Paul Gascoigne had met Gazza and the two of them had got along extremely well.

The following day Venables took the extraordinary step of holding a press conference with just one of his players and, perhaps even more extraordinarily, indicated that he intended to build his England team around Paul Gascoigne. 'Every footballer in the country wants to captain his country, but I don't need the captain's badge to prove that I want to win for England.'

At last everything seemed to be clicking into place for Paul in England and in Italy. Pannini, the giant distributor of football stickers, gave a voting slip with each pack sold in Italy. In the resulting poll Gazza won comfortably, beating Roberto Baggio and Franco Baresi into second and third places. It was a great tribute to a man who had played only forty or so first-class games in the past three years. Yet just when it seemed it was not only safe to go back in the water, but positively recreational, Paul was injured once again. Lazio lost a vital game at home to AC Milan 0-1 and he picked up a bruised right thigh as well as his sixth booking in the last nine matches. Fortunately, this time the knock appeared to have been shaken off and on 27 February he was able to play a vital part in his team's 2–1 win at Piacenza. AC Milan, inevitably, were running away with Serie A and with 40 points had a 6-point advantage over Juventus in second place; but Lazio were tucked in nicely in fifth, only 3 points behind and with every chance of grabbing the runners-up position. It was all to play for.

But there were more tears in store, more dramatic pictures and headlines. As Paul had already discovered there was nothing like a Rome derby to set the city's adrenaline coursing through its veins, and for once he was actually looking forward to the match on 6 March. It was a match he would not finish. In the first half he tried to prevent a diving header from Roma's Giannini, was stamped upon by Lanna for his troubles, and had to be helped from the pitch by Signori and Dr Bartolini. At first it was thought he had fractured an arm and a rib, but further examination revealed only severe bruising. He was patched up at hospital in time to return to the Olympic Stadium to see Lazio run out 1-0 victors and to hear the crowd chanting his name as if it had been he himself who had scored the winner.

As he boarded the plane for London to join the England squad for the friendly against Denmark, the pain was acute and breathing was difficult, but this was Paul Gascoigne and he knew that Gazza's laughs and smiles would somehow see him through the pain barrier. David Platt had been named captain, and whilst he could see the logic of that he still felt a twinge of disappointment, which was nothing compared to the pain in his ribs. He spent hours with an ice-pack held against his chest, and finally twenty-four hours before kick-off felt able to tell Venables he felt fit to play. 'If desire has anything to do with it, Paul will play,' Venables had said.

With hindsight Paul accepts he should not have played, but considering the restrictions placed upon him by his injury his performance was more than acceptable. He spurned two chances he would normally have put away with ease, but he lasted 66 minutes, by which time England were 1-0 up and cruising, and his job was done.

As Venables had acknowledged for Tottenham, and now for England, an unfit Gascoigne was better than no Gascoigne at all, not just for his influence on the field but for his confidence in the dressing-room. Darren Anderton of Spurs, who had such an impressive début, said afterwards, 'Gazza took me to one side and was brilliant. He told me I was in the team because I was good enough, to believe it, to express myself, be confident and most of all to enjoy it.'

Paul, his ribs still sore, was due to return to Italy on Thursday night and present himself for treatment and training on Friday morning. He'd asked Lazio if he could stay until Friday and they had refused. He knew why he wanted to stay but did not want to tell the Italians, who found the greatest difficulty in keeping a secret. On Thursday evening he ordered a limousine and had the rear seat strewn with roses. He took Sheryl to see *Carousel,* then swept her off to Le Gavroche for a meal. She noticed he looked nervous, that he wasn't eating with his usual appetite, but put it down to the discomfort of his ribs. He complained of the heat and kept taking his jacket on and off. Then a waiter was asked to bring a bottle of their best champagne to the table. It arrived and following hard on its heels came a cake. Iced upon it were the words, 'Will You Marry Me?'

As Sheryl says, 'I burst into tears. It was just about the most romantic thing that had ever happened to me. And when he started to recite a poem he'd written himself I was so choked I could hardly say yes. I think in the three years we'd been together he'd been saving up all the romance for just this one evening.' He'd promised again there would be no repetition of the violence. He had seen a psychologist and had felt he was cured; but it was one thing to be alone with a beautiful woman in a restaurant, quite another to be away from her. He had to know where she was all the time, who she was with, what she was doing. It had been like that with Gail when they were both kids, but Paul was now nearly 27 and Sheryl was an experienced, intelligent woman with a mind of her own, who wanted some kind of life of her own, a life that would not necessarily be lived in the permanent cruel eye of the all-seeing camera; but the camera did not see all. Nobody would see all until Paul chose to reveal all in a desperate effort to purge his conscience of guilt. And so the romance of the night was not to last. There were just too many pressures on the pair of them, and finally neither could live with them.

The Italians were not so swept away. Romantic Latins they might have been, but when Paul flew back on Friday night and was clearly not fit to play on the Sunday they blew their tops and promptly fined him. Perhaps if the team had won without him they might have joined in the good wishes, but a 2–2 draw at lowly Udinese on 13 March kept them in fifth place, whilst a win would have seen them move up to third.

The two weeks that followed were to be almost the stormiest since his arrival in Italy. On Monday Paul trained for about ten minutes, then withdrew still feeling the pain from the injury received in the Roma match. He arrived at the training ground on Tuesday in a very emotional state. 'Somehow I felt the club just did not believe that I was genuinely injured. Anybody who knows me well would know I'd never fake an injury. I'd walk over broken glass to play football. It was really getting to me and I'd never felt more depressed or lower.'

The Italian press were not slow to sense that there was a major problem. 'Lazio and Gazza. The Love Affair Is Over,' trumpeted *Corriere Dello Sport*.

On Sunday 20 March he was omitted from the team to play Napoli. Was he injured or had he been dropped? 'I wasn't fit physically or mentally to play. I felt I was coming to the end of the road in Italy. I had to be happy to play my best and I certainly didn't feel that. I knew I was being played in the wrong position, just behind the front two. I'm a central midfielder, and I was old enough to decide that I didn't want to play for anybody unless I got that position.'

Paul did not help his cause by refusing to turn up to watch Lazio beat Napoli 3-0. The fans missed him even though the result suggested his team-mates did not. Cragnotti's patience was being sorely tested. 'Gascoigne, that's enough,' he declaimed through the papers. 'He is no use to us like that. I intend to talk to him severely . . . if I can find him.'

Paul was not hiding, and turned up for training on Tuesday 22 March all ready for a confrontation. Within a few moments of training beginning he could feel the pain again, and it all proved just too much for him. He left the pitch in tears, returned to the locker room and began to vent his rage on anything he could find. Manzini and Zoff tried to calm him down, tried to understand his frustration. The coach and the player embraced, linked by a mutual misery. Just that week Zoff had learned that his days in charge of the team were numbered; he was to be replaced by Zeman, the tough coach of Foggia. His reputation preceded him and he would have none of the banks of historical emotion to draw upon in his relationship with Paul.

Lazarus, still working on his own in Stein's continued incapacity, flew to Italy. Given what he'd heard through the media and read in the papers the attitude of Lazio came as a great surprise. They were desperate to keep him, dismissed all thoughts of selling him, and told him that the one or two overtures they'd received from English clubs, such as Leeds, had been promptly rebuffed. Their main problem was trying to ensure that he came on a club tour to South Africa when Venables might want him for some England inter-nationals. As a clear-the-air exercise it was totally successful and both club and player felt much more comfortable with each other.

On Sunday 3 April, with all his problems seemingly behind him, Paul played well enough in a 1-1 draw at Genoa and then returned to Rome to look forward to Easter with his family. Sheryl was there with the children, and his mother and his sister Lindsay had also come out for a holiday. There was so much to talk about – the wedding, family gossip, the future of Mason and Bianca, Sheryl's children, his own future with England. Sitting in the sunshine of the garden at his villa, basking on a Roman beach, it was hard to believe that only a few weeks before he'd been so depressed that he'd actually tried to phone some English managers himself.

Thursday 7 April was a warm, bright spring day in Rome, a day that gave no hint of shadows or storms. Paul invited Sheryl and his mother down to the training ground; he wanted to show off his club to his family, and he wanted to show off his family to his club. It was just an ordinary training session culminating in a practice match against the junior side. The game was just coming to an end and Paul was thinking where he should go for lunch when he launched himself into a tackle on the 19-year-old reserve Sandro Nesta. Neither man was wearing shin-pads, and as Paul crossed in front of Nesta the two shins collided with a frightening crack that brought a chilling silence in its wake. As his team-mates tried to lift him to his feet Paul screamed in agony. Sheryl ran to his side in anguish as Manzini called for an ambulance. He was rushed to hospital, where a double fracture of the tibia and fibia was quickly diagnosed and a heavy plaster was tossed on to the leg – the right leg, the same limb which had suffered so many traumas in the past.

The news broke in England in the late afternoon. Stein, still not back at work, was driving back from a trip to a bronchial physiotherapist in Leamington with his son, Paul. Radio 4 actually interrupted its programme for a news flash about the injury, and within seconds his car phone was ringing even though he'd not been available to the media for nearly a year. He referred them to Lazarus, then tried to get through to the accountant himself. The two men spoke, both close to tears. 'It's as if there's a curse on him,' Stein said.

Lazarus was asked by Lazio to contact Browett, by now a professor, and arrangements were made to fly Paul home with a view to him operating on Saturday. Nobody knew the leg as well as he did and the Italians themselves were keen that he should take control of the patient. Everybody, Paul included, were like children grasping at straws, looking for some good news amongst the tragedy. Sheridan was perhaps the most devastated of all; it was as if somebody had destroyed the masterpiece that he had taken years to paint. 'That knee injury was worse. If he came through that then I'm certain he'll pull through this latest setback.'

The journey back to Heathrow was an agonizing nightmare. Accompanied by Bartolini and Sheryl, Paul tried to stretch out the damaged and plastered leg over the spare seat that had been provided for him. The rest of the Club Class cabin was occupied by the British press, many of whom had flown over in the morning just to be able to return with Paul in the afternoon. It was obvious he was in great pain. He told them he'd give them a few minutes for photos, gave a short TV and radio interview and then expected to be left alone to his misery. It wasn't to be. He had a brandy on the doctor's advice to help subdue the pain that the sedatives were just not reaching. Seeing him with a drink in his hand was a signal for another surge forward of the photographic vultures, and it was hardly surprising when Paul was goaded into tossing a drink at them. They had their story, but to their credit several of the journalists apologized at the end of the flight for the behaviour of their fellow reporters. Paul for once was lost for words. 'I was gutted not just for me, but for my country. I thought then, on the plane, that it would be six months at most before I could pull on an England shirt.'

Browett had other views and there was no easy way to tell Paul. 'It will be ten months if you're very lucky, but you have to be looking at a year.' The operation took more than four hours. Sheryl loyally slept by Paul's side on a mattress on the floor.

Bryan Robson, who had spent so much time on the sidelines, was one of the first to phone him and assure him that hard work would see him back as good as new, and after that the phone did not stop ringing. There was a hint of humour when the hospital again introduced a code to enable his family and close friends to get through. It was decided that only those closest to him would know that John was his middle name and consequently the question was posed to every caller. A lady claimed to be his grandmother but said she'd forgotten her grandson's middle name, and the phone was promptly put down by the nursing staff on the old lady. A few minutes later Paul's sister called telling him that his nan was outraged that she'd not been allowed to speak to her favourite grandson just because she'd not had his birth certificate at hand, and she doubted if he knew what her middle name was.

Chris Waddle and Chris Woods, down in London for the PFA Award Dinner, were his first visitors, staggering in at 6 a.m. on Sunday morning somewhat the worse for wear after a night on the tiles. 'Shall I get out of bed and let you get in, Waddler?' Gazza asked with all his old humour.

Cragnotti, too, came to see him, immaculately dressed as ever, able to pass for a successful surgeon rather than the merchant banker that he was. He assured Paul of Lazio's loyalty; they would be waiting for him. On Sunday 10 April Lazio won 3-1 at home to Atalanta. Signori scored a hat trick and immediately dedicated it to Paul. The fans sang his name throughout the match, leaving nobody in any doubt as to how much they loved him.

Stein and Lazarus came to see him on the Monday. He was down but determined, surrounded by fruit and flowers, countless cards and goodwill messages. The hospital fax machine had been jammed by greetings coming in from all over the world.

'I'll be back.'

'We know you will, Paul.' Stein felt his own problems fading into insignificance. They kissed the stricken player and made their farewells.

On Tuesday he was up on crutches, able to get to the bathroom. A few small steps for Paul Gascoigne but a giant step for the future of English football. On the Wednesday afternoon, 13 April, Paul Stewart and Steve Sedgley, Stewey and Sedge his old Tottenham team-mates, came to visit him. Sheryl, grateful for some fresh air, got up and left them to it. As she was closing the door she heard Paul say, 'Frightened any patients, Sedge? You're still as ugly as ever.' The three players talked and joked as if they had never been apart, men linked by a common language, a common love, the never ending affair with the fickle woman that is football.

Later, left alone, Paul felt better for their visit. Paul Gascoigne had taken too strong a hold on him and they had helped to release Gazza, and Gazza had raised a smile, been able to laugh when Gascoigne could only cry. The machine beneath his right leg rose and fell in a gentle rhythm. The painkillers began to take effect, and as he gradually fell asleep he repeated over and over again his comforting mantra, 'I'll be back, I'll be back, I'll be back . . . '

He was out of hospital within a week, a day earlier than expected, already anxious to be ahead of the game. He felt he could not stay still. He flew back to Italy, then returned to England, before he and Sheryl took Concorde to the United States; but New York had no magic spell to weave over them. The rows and the violence began again, nurtured by the months of frustration that Paul knew he had once more to live through. They returned to headlines and rumours, then issued their own dignified press statement. 'With much sorrow and regret' and 'after considerable thought' the couple had 'terminated their engagement'.

Friends came and went through Paul's Dobbs Weir home, and then with some two dozen journalists camped out on his front lawn he had endured enough, and used his old escape route through the home of Terry Bailey and Linda Lusardi. He went fishing in Scotland, shooting in Berwick, until finally he returned to Newcastle for his twenty-seventh birthday. Sheryl phoned him as a friend to wish him many happy returns, the family fussed about him, his friends rejoiced to see him. For the moment, the Geordie boy had returned home, but for how long nobody knew.

Then on Friday 3 June 1994 came the news that Newcastle United had been nominated to fill the UEFA Cup place left vacant by the problems in Yugoslavia. Lazio had already qualified by virtue of their Serie A position. A fascinating new prospect was opened: Lazio v. Newcastle in a competitive European tie. If they should meet up it was a conflict that Paul did not want to miss. If he needed any incentive to accelerate his recovery then this was it; the chance of returning to St James's Park in the blue and white of his Italian club, to run out into the state-of-the-art stadium he would hardly recognize and to hear again the roar of the Tyneside faithful, 'Ha'way the Lads,' a war cry and an anthem. Wherever he played, and whoever he played for, he would always be one of those lads.

32

'WHEN HIS FOOTBALL'S RIGHT THEN EVERYTHING ELSE WILL BE RIGHT . . .'

Without Sheryl, Paul was finding it impossible to sleep through the night. He would wake at two and three in the morning, soaked in sweat, fresh from reliving the nightmare that was also the secret truth. He had been blessed with the love of a beautiful woman and he had destroyed it. The words of the old Dr Hook song echoed through his mind, 'When you're in love with a beautiful woman, it's hard.'

For him it had been too hard, another examination he had not passed. The jealousy he had felt had not only consumed him, it had consumed the relationship as well. He had to do something about it. He did not want to trouble Mel Stein, he knew he was still not fully recovered from his own mental anguish of the previous year. If he contacted Len Lazarus then he was convinced he would do everything he could to stop him. In despair he telephoned Rebekah Wade, the Features Editor of the *News of the World,* a long time confidante of both he and Sheryl since Stein had introduced her to them.

The previous Sunday he'd seen Sheryl when he'd gone to collect Mason and Bianca to take them out for Father's Day. They had been begging their mother to allow them to see the man they called Dad and she had finally relented. It was never going to be that simple for her and Paul to part. Their lives had become too intertwined.

When he arrived at Sheryl's house he had been shaking, once again a schoolboy hauled up for some misdemeanour, an apprentice about to be hauled over the coals. That outing had been the final straw. He could see all too clearly what was missing, the close family life with children he had so longed for yet could not deal with when it was presented to him. He'd fled to Henlow Grange Health Farm and it was to there he summoned Rebekah. He blurted out to her the whole story of the relationship, of his guilt at the way he'd treated Sheryl, of his regret at every harsh word he had used to her and the children. He broke down more than once during the hours it took to complete the rambling confession, but throughout he made her promise not to tell anybody of the story that was about to be revealed. It was his story, and his alone, and it has to be seen as such. He received no money for the exclusive. He had replaced his psychiatrist with the *News of the World* and had invited half the British Public to witness his confession.

When he had finished he felt cleansed. He knew it was not over, that a new life would begin for him, a life where he was no longer Gazza, the Geordie lad who was always good for a laugh, but Paul Gascoigne an injury-prone athlete who took out his frustrations on a woman who was no match for his strength and violence.

Arthur Cox among others worried for him. He phoned Paul, but Paul did not return his call. He returned no calls during those traumatic days between the tormented disclosures and his journey back to Italy and Lazio.

'All his then problems seemed to me to stem from the fact he hadn't got his football,' his old mentor said, 'that's all his life is. When his football's right then everything else will be right and his whole life will fall back into place. He wasn't born to be a celebrity or a comedian or a singer. He was born to play football.'

So why did he do it? Was it an act born out of frustration? Was it a cry from the heart, a plea for forgiveness, not just from Sheryl but from every woman in the country? Was it a public plea for Sheryl to return to him? He phoned both Stein and Lazarus on the morning of 3 July. He knew he owed them both an explanation, but he found it hard to put into words. He felt a more honest person. He had ceased to live a lie and now he wanted to get on with his life. If it was to be a life that Sheryl could share some time in the future then so be it, then at least he had exorcised his guilt and could sleep again.

It was another trauma in a life of traumas. His father's blood clot, the family friend lying dead in the road, the yellow card he had received in the World Cup in front of millions and the tears that followed, the horror of Wembley, of Walker's night-club, of the crack of bone at an Italian training ground. The face of the child had for too long been exposed to the dogs of war.

The words of Dennis Tuohy spoken during the edition of 'This Week' at the height of Gazzamania were coming back to haunt him.

'How long before the music stops?'

It had stopped, but it had not died. Paul Gascoigne and his partner Gazza were no longer Jekyll and Hyde, Hyde it was who had died, his death celebrated on the front pages of the Sunday tabloids. He re-entered the Princess Grace on Monday 4 July, after spending the night at the Dorchester in a vain attempt to avoid the Press. Chris Waddle had understood when he had noted that after a few months of living in the eye of the camera that Paul wanted it to stop dead, not tail off, but just to come to an emergency stop there and then. Paul wanted that now some four years later more than ever, but it was the impossible dream. Whatever he did, wherever he went, he would be news, a public property that any attempt to self-protect would be news in itself. John Browett removed two screws from his leg. Independence Day, 4 July, the music had begun again, faint and distant, inviting Paul Gascoigne to dance to a different tune.

33

'I CAN'T SEE YOU PLAYING AGAIN BEFORE NEXT SPRING.'

Having been there before did not make it any easier to return. It was almost unbelievable. March 1994, a few months off his twenty-seventh birthday and it was back to the tedium of crutches and therapy, of watching rather than playing, of once again being the outsider, tolerated rather than welcomed at the training ground. The only difference to 1991 was that he was stranded in a foreign country. How would Lazio react? Would they abandon him in the same way that Tottenham had done and leave him to his own devices? It was a frightening and lonely prospect.

The prognosis when it came was depressing. Flown back to England in agony, his plastered leg spread across three airline seats, gripping Sheryl's hand to ease the pain that came with every jolt of the plane, he felt confused, felt that just when he seemed to have lifted himself permanently from the depths that he was now plumbing even deeper waters. John Browett was the one doctor in whom he had faith, but what he had to say was like another prison sentence. 'It's a serious break. I can't see you playing again before next spring.'

Next spring. They might just as easily have said next decade. It took all of his will-power to produce a spark of the old Gazza. 'I'll be back by Christmas, just you watch.'

It wasn't Christmas, but he was a lot closer than the doctors thought. In October 1994 his recovery was so well advanced that Venables felt sufficiently confident about his future to invite him to join up with the England party at Bisham Abbey for the friendly against Romania. As Andrew Longmore wrote in *The Times* he 'looked on forlornly, like a schoolboy waiting to be picked for the playground team'. That, and a photograph of him standing in isolation, leaning against the post of a deserted goal, were evocative and saddening images. Vicious and untrue was the suggestion in one Sunday paper that some England players did not want Paul at training. In many ways his presence was more beneficial to the rest of the squad and the team spirit than to his own well-being. 'I knew Terry was trying to help me by getting me along with the lads, but it hurt just the same. Being a part of it, but not being a part of it, knowing you don't have to bother to look whether or not your name is on the team-sheet,' Paul recalls.

Venables was more than supportive. 'Paul Gascoigne needs to be involved. I will select any players I feel respond to that involvement. In a few months he'll be fit. He might not think too kindly of us if we ignored him until that moment and then said to him, "OK, we need you now." He's a genuine world-class player and I will always be biased towards people with his talent. There's no sentimentality about this.'

His involvement in the training was limited to a few wistful headers, a glimpse of what might be possible. Whilst in England he should have had the metal rod removed from his leg, but even then there was a delay and he had to return to Italy knowing that another visit would be necessary for what he hoped would be the final operation. Bartolini, the Lazio doctor, ever ready with a quote said with imponderable wisdom, 'We have emerged from a tunnel of doubt.'

Eric Cantona, himself, could not have done better. A few weeks later, on 7 November, Paul's twelfth operation in two years did indeed take place at the Princess Grace and the twelve-inch rod was removed from his right leg. Browett's statement and prognosis were more enlightening than those of his Italian counterpart. 'Everything went perfectly well. The bones have healed and joined together as we would have hoped. With careful rehabilitation the leg will recover fully and I hope this will be his last operation. We will make further checks over the next two days before sending him back to Italy. All being well, I expect him back in action next spring.'

Paul said with some relief, 'I can't wait for the New Year when I want to be running around like a big kid. I've had enough of crutches.'

Once again the light-fingered villains had not had enough of Gazza in Italy. He flew into England to appear on his old friend Danny Baker's show and they promptly raided his home, removing most of his recently purchased designer clothes. It was almost as if they knew whenever he went on a shopping spree.

As early as December, however, he could forget about formal clothes and get back into his training kit as he was doing some light jogging. The impatient photographers at last got the shot they had been waiting for. It was strange. With Gazza injured there should have been a dozen young pretenders coming forward to seize the crown, but any one of them who momentarily caught the public imagination flattered to deceive. It was as if the footballing world was holding its breath, waiting for Paul to return. Almost every article that spoke of the state of the footballing nation had something to say about Paul. Yet, for every journalist suggesting that the future of Venables's team rested on one player alone, there was another hack suggesting that the dream was over, that the bubble had finally burst and this time the troublesome youth had gone for good. In a way they were right. The youth had gone, never to return. The more thoughtful man who emerged was different; the only problem was going to be convincing everybody else what he now truly believed.

Not that he had been ignored by the press whilst recuperating. The on–off relationship with Sheryl still kept the tabloids going and back in August, when he had hired a fleet of limousines to meet her at Heathrow Airport, it was yet another desperate attempt to rescue a relationship that he needed even more than his career. It wasn't necessary, but Paul could not see that at the time. Sheryl, for her part, simply sent the cars back and took an anonymous mini-bus for her returning party. In October he flew to Euro-Disney with her and the children, yet a few weeks later the paparazzi were pursuing him again, suggesting he was out on the town with a 'stunning raven-haired girl'. In fact, the woman in question had merely followed Paul into a Rome restaurant where there was also a dance floor. Even though he didn't even know her name, this didn't prevent the papers from putting two and two together and coming up with anything other than four!

Apart from Sheryl, the main thing that kept him going was the challenge of winning something with Lazio, of once more being a part of a successful side. New coach, Zdenek Zemen, had taken them into second place in Serie A and had kept their hopes alive in both the Italian and UEFA Cup competitions. There was no guarantee of a place in the team for even a fully fit Paul Gascoigne. When the parting from the Italians finally came, Paul's greatest disappointment was the feeling that he had been used, that whatever he might or might not have achieved on the road to recovery, there was never any real prospect in the minds of those who ran Lazio that he would ever again be a permanent part of their spearhead challenge for European honours. The thought that it might happen had always been at the back of his mind. As he'd come out of hospital he'd commented rather more openly than usual to a journalist, 'Things haven't gone well in Italy. I always said I wanted to achieve something out there and I don't think I've achieved anything apart from being injured. If I think I'll be happier back in England, then that's what I'll do.'

It was not a thought that gave him any pleasure yet, for the first time, he had had the courage to put it into words.

As early as November 1994, when it appeared Paul was still some way off fitness, Len Lazarus received a call out of the blue from a UK football agent who was, he claimed, jointly instructed by Lazio and an Italian agent, to sell Paul Gascoigne. Sergio Cragnotti, the Lazio President, wanted a meeting. He wanted to know where Paul would be prepared to go and ideally was looking for a club to take him there and then – and also to assume the risk that he may never be the same player again. They would not be difficult about the fee; £3 million pounds would secure him and even then they would probably be prepared to take a down payment of £1 million, with the balance being paid on a match-by-match basis. There was, however, one catch. Lazio were aware of the favour Paul had found and retained with the fans despite his limited on-field success. They could not be seen to be selling him against his wishes. If anybody asked, they would deny they had started the ball rolling, deny that they wanted to recover a part of their heavy investment, deny that the meeting had ever taken place. It was agreed that the English agent and Lazarus would ask around informally to see who might be interested and the parties would generally keep in touch. That was the scenario as 1994 turned into 1995. There was, however, a major problem. Nobody had sought Paul's approval of the script.

34

'THE OLYMPIC STADIUM HAS REDISCOVERED ITS IDOL.'

As had happened so many times before, Paul's grit and determination would confound the doctors and cynics alike. English journalists had flocked to the flag in the campaign to write off Paul Gascoigne once and for all. This was the injury that would finally bring both player and Gazzamania to a permanent and precipitous end. Yet, by March he was back in virtually full training. He had lost some three stone in weight and it was a new slim-line Gazza who performed for the world's media. 'I feel good, I look good and in a couple of weeks I reckon I could get the all clear to play again,' he told anybody who was prepared to listen. There was no denying that, as time and time again he curled the ball past the keeper in training as the press looked on with mixed feelings. Gazza's recovery was a story, but probably not as good as the one they thought they would write – about his 'demise'.

His old friend Maurizio Manzini monitored his progress with paternal pride. 'By March he looked the best he had ever looked during his time with Lazio. He was working morning and afternoon, running with binliners to sweat off any excess weight, putting in extra hours in the gym. There was nothing more we could ask of him. As for his future, I always knew that was for the coach and President to decide. As far as I was concerned he had a contract until 1997 and the most important thing for him and the club was to get him playing again.'

The serious training in no way affected his love of practical jokes which, to the casual observer, at times bordered on all out war. Aron Winter was the latest target as Paul happily filled the Dutchman's shoes with shampoo, 'Just to give them a bit of a clean, like.' Winter was unimpressed and his retribution was to steal Paul's car keys and to keep him a prisoner at the training ground. That was enough for Paul to concentrate his efforts on Winter's Porsche. He let the air out of every tyre, first having ensured that all possible means of pumping them up again had been carefully concealed. When the news that he was to leave finally leaked out, there were one or two sighs of relief from his regular victims.

Paul's continued march towards full fitness was reflected by Venables's invitation to him to join up with the England squad who were preparing for their match against Uruguay at the end of the month, quashing all rumours that he was unwelcome by the rest of the players. Although Lazio allowed him to travel, they would not clear him to partake in the training sessions with the England side even though he was training regularly at home. They gave the excuse as 'insurance problems', but who could really blame them for hesitating to put their expensive recuperatee back in the firing line when there were no medals to be gained?

David Platt, at least, could see the reality of his Italian compatriot's comeback. 'He's looking good for the European Championships. A player of his ability will help us in '96.'

If he was welcome before the match he was even more lauded after it. The game was a drab goalless draw, carved out by an uninspired England side, which showed just how far Venables still had to go to create a serious challenge for European honours. Michael Herd, writing in London's *Evening Standard* summed it up when he wrote, 'For all his shortcomings, Gascoigne, at the top of his game, provides the creative impetus that was so sadly lacking . . .'

Venables was not slow to divert attention away from the players who had played and on to the one who had not. 'Gazza can fit into any system. Once he's match fit he's going to be a big plus to the squad. When he's back to his best he will help the cause because he can give us something different.'

Sunday 9 April was the day for which Paul and English football had waited so long. 'I felt a kid all over again. It was like being back at Newcastle seeing if my name was going to be on the team-sheet. It was only against Reggiana, who were next to bottom in the league, but as far as I was concerned it was one of the biggest days of my footballing life. Just to be involved again, to be in the dressing room knowing you're going to get out on the pitch. In Italy, if you weren't playing you couldn't even sit on the bench and I'd had enough of watching from the stands however comfortable the seats might have been, however nice the coffee and cakes at half-time. I just wanted to play.' And play he did, not just as substitute, not just for a nominal half hour, but for the full ninety minutes – and in eighty degrees heat.

It wasn't only his weight he'd shed, it was his hair as well, and the streamlined skinhead showed enough touches in the 2–0 victory to delight the 40,000 Lazio fans in the stadium and his millions of friends watching on television. In the 75th minute he even nearly carved out a storybook ending to his return. He spread the ball out wide to Beppi Signori, summoned up his tired legs to race through for the return cross and then put his header just wide. It didn't matter. *Corriere dello Sport* welcomed Paul's return with the headline, 'The Olympic Stadium has rediscovered its idol'.

Venables had been there to witness the rediscovery. 'He has shown that his spirit cannot be broken. Even against the odds he is prepared to fight the impossible. He has a big heart and a lot of guts.' As to his performance, he was slightly more restrained, 'He played with a lot of common sense.'

It was a far cry from Bobby Robson's description of him as being 'daft as a brush'. Had he finally left behind the image of the man who would pour shampoo into his team-mate's shoes, the man who would tip spaghetti over a sleeping diner's head, who would eat ice cream covered with salt by his good friend Jimmy Gardner? The Italians might not have known the phrase but, both on and off the pitch, the lad was back.

35

'VILLA, LEEDS, QPR, CHELSEA . . . OR RANGERS?'

Despite the meeting between Cragnotti and Lazarus, Paul could still not fully accept that the Italian dream was really over. He still felt that a fully fit Gascoigne, together with the kid's winning smile, would turn it all around and he would be welcomed back as the prodigal son. But the new coach, Zeman, was not Zoff. He had his own plans and it soon became abundantly clear that many of Zoff's acquisitions, including P. Gascoigne, did not figure in them. Even with the comfortable win over Reggiana, Lazio were still only fifth in Serie A, fourteen points behind Juventus, who had already broken away from the pack. What was worse was that they were behind Roma. It might only be a point behind, but it was enough. There was a clear-out in the offing akin to a fire sale and only a demonstration of supporter power stopped the unthinkable sale of Beppi Signori himself. It suddenly dawned on Paul that rather than working towards the role of the prodigal son, he was, in fact, being prepared as the fatted calf. On the last Sunday in April he came on as a midfield substitute against Cagliari and played poorly by his own standards, even experiencing the fickle jeering of a few fans who had greeted his return with such enthusiasm just a few weeks before. Looking back, he could understand what was going wrong. He could see the few games he had been given in whole or part were not to restore his confidence, not to get him match fit, but rather to showcase the wares on the way to market. Even then it was not a satisfactory mode of exhibition. 'Zeman seemed convinced that my best position was on the left side of midfield whilst I knew I was much more effective playing down the middle. I wasn't being big-headed, I'd just had more experience of my own play than he had.'

He felt that he had been abused, gulled, cheated, that all the hard work he had put into the recovery, the monumental efforts he had made against all the odds, were purely for Lazio's benefit, for Lazio's gain. It was at that moment, and that moment alone, that he decided if Lazio wanted to sell him then it would not be made easy. He had not asked for a transfer, he had been fully prepared to see his contract through and to fight for his place in the team. He knew how fit he was, knew that all he needed were a few matches under his belt to be back as good as new, and if Lazio did not want him then he would have the pick of teams. He would go where he wanted to go, not where Lazio would necessarily make the most money. As it transpired, although he could not have known it there and then, Rangers in Glasgow were to satisfy both criteria.

Once it was clear that Paul Gascoigne was fit and was not being considered for selection in Lazio's push for a UEFA place, then the race for his signature was on. By early May Paul had demanded and got a direct man to man talk with Dino Zoff. It transpired they had already visited London and spoken with Chelsea, but Zoff also told Paul of the interest being shown by Leeds, Coventry, Villa and, in particular, Rangers in Scotland. Mel Stein was back at work, at least part-time after his lengthy illness, and there followed an interchange of phone calls between him, Lazarus and the UK agent. Would Paul join Villa? Was he interested in Coventry? Did Leeds figure in his plans?

QPR were about to sell Ferdinand and were looking for a big-name replacement; could Gazza fill the gap? Wilkins had already made some enquiries about loaning him when he'd thought he was just about fit. Glenn Hoddle at Chelsea knew the player, warts and all, so would he be the manager to bring out the best in Paul at what should be the peak of his career? There was also talk of a move to another country; Portugal, Spain and Turkey were all floated as possibilities, possibilities soon to be discounted.

The crucial factor in the transfer, as it transpired, would prove to be a holiday that Paul had enjoyed in the States in 1992. There, relaxing on the beach in Florida, he had heard a Scots accent, which proved to belong to Walter Smith, the manager of Rangers. There was an immediate bonding between the two men and indeed, Walter's family as a whole. Nothing he had heard about the wayward and troublesome English star prepared Smith for the pleasant and friendly young man who never tired of entertaining the Smiths' young son. He grew to like and admire the Englishman over the few days they spent together, although from time to time the mischievous streak that on occasions could prove so dangerous would surface to give an indication of what it might be like to have Paul around on a permanent basis. There had been a ball game going on around the edge of the water involving Paul and Smith junior. Suddenly, Paul threw the ball so that it landed violently on a scantily clad American couple who, to say the least, were not amused by the incident. Walter's son looked around appealingly to Paul to accept responsibility and to get him off the hook. He was to be sorely disappointed. Gazza had disappeared, as he had done so often in the past when trouble was around. This time he had immersed himself under water, and the lad was left to face the wrath of the couple on his own.

It was during their last evening together when Paul and Sheryl joined Walter and his wife for a drink and a meal, that the Scottish manager first allowed the thought to cross his mind that one day he would like to have this player in his team, not just for his playing responsibilities, but also for his personality. In spring 1995 that day seemed to have dawned and Smith decided on speedy action when it was apparent that there was going to be a stampede for Paul's services. He and David Murray, the Rangers Chairman, arrived in Rome; one to speak to Paul, the other to open negotiations with the Club. But, one task proved easier than the other. Paul was receptive to Smith's overtures, although he made it clear that any negotiations would have to be left to his advisers who might well want to hear what everybody else had to offer. Lazio had clearly been surprised by the amount of interest shown in a player who they felt still had to prove his fitness and return to form. However, their own lack of faith did nothing to reduce their financial awareness of their position and the £3 million in stage payments that had previously been mooted as the price they required, had now magically become £5 million, cash down. After some haggling, Murray came away from the meeting with the firm impression that he had an agreement, subject only to the player being happy with the terms. Inevitably, it was not going to prove anywhere near that simple.

Cragnotti was holding court in London and Rome, interviewing potential applicants for the post of principal employer of Paul Gascoigne, Esq. At the end of the round of discussions Colin Hutchinson of Chelsea, Doug Ellis of Aston Villa and Bill Fotherby of Leeds were also similarly convinced that if they could only agree personal terms with Paul's advisers, then the player was theirs. Whether this was prudent business on the part of Lazio or simply Machiavellian tactics will never be known. There did not appear to be any great effort to conceal from each of the parties the identities of their rivals, yet it does appear to be a rather singular commercial achievement to convince four separate parties, all seeking to purchase the same commodity, that they, and only they, are favoured to secure it.

As far as Paul's advisers were concerned the position was somewhat simpler. The four clubs had spoken to Paul who had confirmed that he was prepared to consider each of them as they all had something to offer him. With Rangers it was their successful reputation, the manager and the chance of playing in the Champions League as the Scottish title-holders; at Chelsea there was Glenn Hoddle, whose play and personality he had long admired and whom he knew well through their mutual friendship with Chris Waddle; at Villa there was a Geordie manager in the shape of Brian Little and a Chairman upon whose yacht he had been a guest in Italy back in 1990; and the history of Leeds and the potential shown by their late run into Europe in 94/95 (at the expense of Newcastle) gave him the chance of facing up to Lazio in the UEFA Cup.

In fact, Leeds had been the first to arrive at the party, Bill Fotherby having contacted Paul's advisers back in September 1994 to ask about Paul's availability. He continued to phone Len Lazarus from time to time and was confident that he too had an agreement with Lazio, although at a price of only £2 million. Somebody else had rung at the doorbell in the early days, namely Alan Sugar of Spurs, who had spoken to Len Lazarus and asked to be kept posted as to developments. Yet, when the time came for action, for money to be put down on the table, they were nowhere to be seen. All talk of the so-called option to buy Paul back, the same option of which Terry Venables had made so much when Paul was sold, was forgotten. Perhaps Paul's hasty and ill-considered comment earlier in the year that he would rather join Grimsby than Tottenham under Sugar's control had something to do with it! It was only when the ink was about to dry on the terms agreed between Paul and Rangers, that Lazio almost half-heartedly mentioned that they had to give Spurs notice. As previously mentioned, Paul was not a party to that 'option' agreement anyway, but later, as Klinsmann, Barmby and Demetrescu led the talent charge out of White Hart Lane, Tottenham fans were bound to ask and wonder why no effort appeared to have been made to bring Paul back to North London after that initial enquiry. The rumour was that the powers that be regarded Paul as a disruptive influence at the club and at least one Director was heard to make that statement publicly. But as Spurs faded into the shadow of Arsenal's glamorous signings of Bergkamp and Platt their fans, at least, would have welcomed the kind of disruption Gazza's return would have brought with it. By the beginning of May, however, it was time for all the skirmishing to end and the real talking to begin.

36

'NO-ONE, PARTICULARLY LAZIO, WILL CHOOSE MY NEXT CLUB FOR ME.'

On the 12 May 1995, after a series of telephone conversations with Rangers Chairman, David Murray, Stein and Lazarus embarked upon the third round of contract negotiations in their decade of representation of Paul. Newcastle to Spurs, Spurs to Lazio and now Lazio to who knew where. All they did know was that there would be twists and turns in the path. In the world of Paul Gascoigne, only the unexpected was expected.

They had asked for their meeting to be strictly confidential and honouring that request, David Murray arranged for them to be met at Edinburgh Airport and brought to his impressive offices a short distance away. Murray was an interesting character, an impressive addition to a collection of chairmen that included Scholar, Callieri and Cragnotti. If and when Gazza ever wrote a book entitled 'Chairmen I Have Known,' it would have guaranteed bestseller status. The Rangers Chairman had bought the famous old club in the 1989/90 season and had brought about a revolution. The best of traditions had been retained; the old oak panelling in the Board Room, the Victorian entrance hall with its broad sweep of a staircase, the famous Blue Room in which every major signing had been unveiled. But beneath the traditional veneer, Murray introduced new technology, a new marketing approach and, most important of all, a burning desire to make Rangers the best club side, initially in Europe, but ultimately in the whole world.

Murray had overcome personal tragedy in his private life. Despite the loss of both his legs in a car crash in his twenties, his determination had meant that his mobility had not been completely impaired, and the death of his wife at a young age from cancer had ensured a fierce dedication to his children and family values. And that was how he perceived Rangers – as a part of his family. Yes, he had bought the Club with the fortune he had carved from metals, rather than conceiving it, but the new Rangers, twenty-first century style, was his creation. His ambition was to create a dream stadium and by 1995 that dream was well under way. Only the corners needed to be filled in to complete an all-seater, 50,000 capacity, state-of-the-art theatre in which the team that he was compiling could ply their trade. He wasn't seeking to buy Paul to fill the ground, he made that perfectly clear. Every game was sold out, there was a waiting list for season tickets, and he already planned to build another tier to accommodate the fanatical demand that the city of Glasgow (or at least half of it) had for the Protestant section of 'The Old Firm'.

He and manager Walter Smith made an interesting combination. There could surely have been no greater contrast between Smith and his controversial predecessor, Graham Souness. Smith was a Rangers man through and through, an expert at handling the football media, a quiet man, who could inspire by leadership rather than a flamboyant personality. At the meeting there was an immediate empathy between the four men, the high-flying chairman with a faint air of loneliness about him, the manager whose concern did not go beyond football, the accountant and the solicitor, who knew that this time round it had to be right for their client both on and off the pitch.

The two Scotsmen clearly felt that the meeting was a formality, that they had their man, and were a little taken aback when Stein and Lazarus told them that they felt they had to talk to everybody else, that they would report back to Paul, and then, and only then would they make the final decision. They also made it clear that everything was conditional upon the terms for Paul's departure from Lazio being agreed. Rangers, as the buyer, found that far easier to accept and understand than Tottenham had ever done as the seller back in 1991/2.

Of the chasing crew Doug Ellis of Aston Villa was by far the most persistent. His club had experienced a nasty shock the previous season, having been fancied for the title but ending up as real relegation prospects. Ellis was accustomed to getting what he wanted, but at the tail-end of the season, with the Endsleigh First Division beckoning, had found it hard to attract top-class players to the Midlands. Now, with Premiership football guaranteed at Villa Park, he realized he needed a big name signing to show the fans that he meant business for the forthcoming campaign. And he, at least, realized, there were no bigger names than Paul Gascoigne. He had already met with Mel Stein in March and following that meeting, had flown to Rome to meet Paul himself. The two men had met for a lengthy breakfast and had found that time had done nothing to destroy the feel-good factor between them. There was no doubt that Villa were serious players in the game.

Knowing that Paul had already met the Scottish and Midlands contingents, both Chelsea and Leeds were keen not to be left behind in the game. Colin Hutchinson, the Chelsea Chief Executive, came to Lazarus's office to meet with him and Mel Stein and it was agreed that arrangements would be made for Paul to meet with Glenn Hoddle in Rome. Hoddle was planning to be in Italy for another major signing, incredibly enough

Ruud Gullit. With Gullit and Gascoigne in the squad there could be no doubting that Chelsea were likely to be serious contenders for major honours *and* the focus of media attention. It was a bold ploy and one that was to have a 50 per cent success rate. Hutchinson also promised confidentiality, although when he signed the Dutchman and failed to get Paul that did not stop him from claiming that Gullit spoke about football whilst all that seemed to interest Paul was the money. There was an element of sour grapes about the disclosure as Paul could hardly have been expected to discuss the niceties of tactics with a man who had never played the game at any serious level. Fotherby, on behalf of Leeds, continued to phone to ask when Paul would be able to meet with himself and Howard Wilkinson, and it was becoming increasingly clear that although Paul no longer figured in Lazio's plans, he was still much loved in Britain.

There were one or two surprising omissions from the list of Gazza's fan club. Arthur Cox at Newcastle had indicated that Paul's home town team could hardly fail to be interested in a fully fit, fully committed Gascoigne, but Keegan (and perhaps more surprisingly, and more publicly, Sir John Hall) did not seem to share that enthusiasm. Kenny Dalglish, who was on his way to the Championship with Blackburn, also appeared to have lost his passion for the player that had so entranced him some four years earlier, although this lack of interest may be explained by the fact that at this time Dalglish had given up the day-to-day management at Rovers. Alex Ferguson at Manchester United had apparently not forgotten what he had taken as a snub when Paul had chosen White Hart Lane in 1989 rather than Old Trafford, and the message came down through the channels that Old Trafford was not about to welcome Paul Gascoigne. Paul was hurt by that, just as he was hurt by what he perceived to be a public snub by Sir John Hall, a man he had willingly helped in his first abortive effort to gain control of Newcastle some years earlier. Yet, when interviewed by Gary Lineker on the BBC in September 1995, Paul was man enough to admit that if he had come back to England and had his choice of clubs, Manchester United would have been top of his list.

But United weren't in the race. Doug Ellis left with Villa for their pre-season tour of the West Indies, vowing to return at the merest hint that Paul was possibly going to sign. Hutchinson at Chelsea continued to phone, and poor Bill Fotherby at Leeds was feeling perplexed and concerned that his rivals had had the chance to speak to the player whilst he was left waiting patiently and politely for his opportunity. Which left Rangers still as the front runners.

Despite all the efforts at secrecy the *Sun* still carried the headline on Friday 13 May, 'GAZGOW RANGER' and accurately reported the meeting with Murray and Smith but incorrectly suggested that, 'Gascoigne and his advisers gave the club a binding undertaking on Thursday night'. On 17 May Stein and Lazarus flew to Rome to meet first with Paul to discuss his options and then with Cragnotti to finalize the terms of Paul's departure. It was Gianni who met them at the airport, the gentle giant somewhat subdued by the inevitability that he and Augusto would be losing their troublesome, but much loved, ward. He took them to Paul's villa where the Chrysalis camera crew were already waiting to film Paul's interview for the forthcoming weekend's *Gazzetta*. It began to rain, a miserable cold rain more reminiscent of London in winter than Rome in spring, but quite in keeping with the predominant mood.

Paul arrived late and virtually unrecognizable. Everybody else might have been taking the situation seriously but Paul had had his hair cropped and dyed blond for the occasion. He had no idea that it was to be a hairstyle that would take Britain, and Glasgow in particular, by storm. They sat around the table, Paul,

Stein and Lazarus, oblivious to the Chrysalis cameras, to Jimmy fussing in the background. Paul munched happily on plain beigels that his advisers had brought from London, listening to the various options being presented to him. Although he appeared surprised that none of the really big English clubs were interested, he still appeared to favour Rangers.

On his *Gazzetta* programme of Saturday 6 May, Paul had already made his feelings quite clear, 'No-one, particularly Lazio, will choose my next club for me. I'll do that. Who knows, I might even decide to remain in Italy.' That was something that Lazio certainly did not want. The thought of Gazza turning up at the Olympic Stadium in the colours of another Serie A side was daunting to say the least. The man had the annoying habit of proving his detractors wrong and they genuinely feared the wrath of their fans. If they could convince them that Paul had returned to Britain because he wanted to leave Italy then they could get away with that; but that story simply would not fly if he joined a rival side.

There were rumours that the England Manager was also trying to influence Paul's future playing career. The *Sun* had already run one story describing Venables, somewhat inaccurately, as 'Mr Fixit' with regard to the transfer deal and suggesting by innuendo that he would prefer to see him playing in England, and particularly for Villa, where Doug Ellis was an old friend. Yet, on this occasion, Paul was still determined to be his own man. He had already taken the bold step the previous week of asking not to play against Juventus. 'I was training with them and here they were, trying to sell me behind my back. It made it very hard for me to get myself into the right frame of mind to actually play for them in a competitive match. I have to admit that one of the things uppermost in my mind was what would happen if I got injured again. Lazio certainly didn't want me, and nobody else would want somebody with my track record.'

When Paul met with Stein and Lazarus his main concern was the seemingly spiralling transfer fee that Lazio were demanding. If they were looking to sell him on the basis that he was fully fit and back to his best then they were also going to have to compensate him for cutting short his contract when he had worked so hard to get ready to play for them again. Lazio had asked Paul's advisers to attend a meeting at their new offices in the heart of Rome at 2.0 p.m. With a return flight booked for 6.15 p.m. it did not give a great deal of room for error. By 3.30 p.m. it was clear that the waiting Chrysalis film crew would not be capturing the completion of the deal and that Stein and Lazarus would not be returning home that evening.

37

'IF GASCOIGNE LIKES FISHING SO MUCH THEN THAT IS WHAT HE CAN DO FOR THE LAST TWO YEARS OF HIS CONTRACT.'

The meeting began with an exchange of pleasantries and compliments. Paul had enjoyed his stay at Lazio; he liked Cragnotti personally and the decision to leave was not his. However, if they wanted him to go then he would not linger where he was not welcome, and if he was going to go he would join a club of his choice and not one Lazio selected simply because it was the best deal for them. All of that appeared to be straightforward and accepted by the Lazio contingent, consisting of Cragnotti, his local lawyer Biolato and his group lawyer Bianchini, a new addition to the party and clearly a heavy weight. Unfortunately Manzini, with his command of English and pleasant negotiating manner, was out of the country, and at first Paul's advisers' request that no agents be present at the meeting seemed to have been honoured. Quite why a club of Lazio's standing, with its President's access to top legal advisers, should have needed agents to negotiate and conclude the deal was not clear, but even as the two sides spoke agents were hovering in the background.

Paul's men tried to clarify the position. They had been told that Leeds felt they had reached agreement on a price as long ago as March, that both Villa and Chelsea thought they had written confirmation that their offers had been accepted, and Rangers firmly believed that their offer was larger than the others, which had the effect of leaving the field clear for them. Cragnotti shook his head. He had no idea how the English clubs could have reached such conclusions. Lazio had a deal with Rangers. The Scottish club's manager, Walter Smith, was waiting in a hotel around the corner. Surely Paul was not going to be difficult and turn down the opportunity of signing for the great Glasgow club. They would send for Smith and the deal could be concluded that day.

Stein and Lazarus tried to explain that Paul had not yet made up his mind and that in any event, he would go where he wanted to go. If that was to be Rangers, then fine, but he was not going to be ridden out of Rome on a rail. The mood of the meeting changed when the Italians realized that the signing for Rangers was not going to be a mere formality. Smith was summoned and suddenly the pace of the negotiations quickened. On Walter's arrival Stein and Lazarus brought him up to date with developments. He was more than a little puzzled. He had been brought to Rome believing that Rangers had the field to themselves and that there were no real obstacles in the way of Paul signing there and then. The trio were then joined by two agents. One of them claimed to have brokered the deal between Rangers and Lazio, the other, ('Vinny' to his friends) maintained that he had been instructed by Lazio to represent their interests. Whatever might have been the position of the two men it was quite clear that their main concern was to ensure that Paul Gascoigne joined Rangers and that they profited by it to their maximum advantage. Paul's advisers were underwhelmed by their presence and flatly refused to discuss Paul's financial position in their presence. That brought Cragnotti back into the room without his lawyers, a President who was clearly losing both his patience and his cool with the situation. Gascoigne had been an expensive and trouble-some investment which had paid no visible dividends. Why could he not now go, and go quietly? After a few more moments of negotiations Cragnotti exploded; if Gascoigne did not want to take what was on offer from Lazio and Rangers then that was fine, but he would never play for the Italian club again. 'If Gascoigne likes fishing so much then that is what he can do for the last two years of his contract,' he said and stormed out of the room, leaving his representatives to pick up the pieces. The various parties continued their discussions but Signor Cragnotti had left the auditorium, pausing only to hold a brief press conference on his way out to disclose to the waiting Italian journalists a somewhat one-sided version of events. As somebody said, 'There is no point in trying to speak to him again just now. Wait a week or so and maybe he will have calmed down!'

Somewhat depressed by the whole day, Stein, Lazarus and Smith repaired to the Cavallieri Hilton to meet up with Paul. Gazza himself had been quite happily attending a birthday party, confident that everything would be sorted out to his advantage. Reluctantly, he agreed to prise himself away and meet up with his advisers and manager elect. He could hardly believe that matters had been left where they were, although his disbelief did not prevent him from ordering a couple of bottles of champagne on his lawyer's room number. He might not have anything to celebrate as yet, but at least the drink would put them in a better mood for the night of discussion that lay ahead.

Smith and Paul went up to Lazarus's room and began to talk. It was quite clear that the Scottish club were determined to get their man although that did not mean they had a bottomless financial well upon which to draw. Yet as the night wore on, and despite Cragnotti's difficult attitude, the transaction began to take a more positive shape. Smith spoke to his Chairman, Paul's men spoke to Vinny, Lazio's agent, Gazza spoke to Sheryl and by 3.0 a.m., when everybody staggered exhausted into bed, it looked likely that one more meeting might be sufficient to secure a deal and that some time before the start of the new season, Paul Gascoigne would be buying a one-way ticket from Rome to Glasgow.

The day before the meeting *La Gazzetta dello Sport* reported, '*L'unica cosa certa e la partenza di Gascoigne che va ai Rangers*'. The day after the confrontation its rival, *Corriero dello Sport*, trumpeted, '*Gazza-Lazio lite finale*', and displayed a photograph of a troubled looking Paul with the caption, '*L'ultima follia di Gazza; i capelli blondo platino*'. What would have passed as another hilarious Gascoigne prank when he was taken to the heart of the city was now dismissed as the final folly. If Paul had not yet received the message that it was time to move on, then this was it, signalled loud and clear. He had lost the power to amuse.

38

'THE NEXT TIME WE SEE GASCOIGNE IN ROME HE WILL BE A TOURIST.'

It took many phone calls, letters and faxes but on 24 May the parties finally reassembled at Cragnotti's London office to see what could be done to settle their differences, bridge the gaps between them and ensure that Paul signed for Rangers. The Italian psyche was again illustrated when Cragnotti arrived in the best of moods – totally oblivious to the fact that his outburst may have left a sour taste in the mouths of the Gascoigne camp. He was accompanied by his lawyers Bianchini, Riccardi and Biolato and his son-in-law, who seemed less than enamoured with the continuing negotiations. Rangers, hopeful of a conclusion, had sent Campbell Ogilvie, the Club Secretary, to accompany Walter Smith.

After the meeting in Rome the Italians had tried to play hard-ball with Paul. On 18 May Lazio had a meaningless friendly against Grosseto in Tuscany and it suddenly seemed vital to them that Paul should play. Under the circumstances it was hardly surprising that Paul did not agree and failed to show up at the training ground as instructed. Manager Zoff declaimed to the eager media, 'The matter will be investigated by the club and appropriate action taken.'

Paul was at his lowest ebb. 'Tell them I'll not play for anybody for two years. Tell them I'm giving up football,' he told his advisers and at that moment he meant every word of it. Yet again it was Sheryl who got him back on an even keel. 'You've worked like hell for six months in the gym and now you're going to pack it all in? Football's your life,' she told him.

Paul had generally resisted a war of words through the papers, but when he had flown into London on 22 May he could not bite back the angry words, 'They've hurt me and now I'd like to turn the situation around a little bit. It's as simple as that. If they'd come up to me and said that as things weren't working out because of injuries, perhaps I should consider going back to England, I'd have accepted that. But it was all the things being done behind my back. I just felt sorry for the fans. In three years I'd only played about forty games and yet they were still chanting my name even when they knew for certain I was leaving.'

On 23 May Paul flew to Newcastle for his grand-mother's funeral. He had just paid for her to go on holiday, a holiday she would never take, and as the inevitable cameras caught his tears at the graveside it was obvious that his grief had focused his attention away from his own immediate problems. Death, the great equalizer, which so terrified Paul in all its cunning guises, made him realize that his own situation had a solution. For his beloved grandmother there would be no more choices. Perhaps it was then that he finally decided that Rangers represented the best option for him. There he could be close to his family, and could see far more of them before any future tragedies struck.

In Cragnotti's London office the mutual acrimony seemed forgotten. Over the weekend, whilst Juventus had secured the Italian Championship, Lazio had beaten Sampdoria, guaranteeing themselves a slot in the UEFA Cup the following season. The optimism and general bonhomie in the Lazio camp was demonstrated by their intention to be away by lunchtime in order to reach Vienna in time to attend the European Cup Final between Ajax and AC Milan. As lunch came and went the plane was cancelled and they ordered a large television set to be brought to the offices so that they could at least view the game.

Stein had been equally optimistic. He had theatre tickets booked for the evening, and had arranged to meet his wife at the National Theatre. He had reason to be hopeful when Paul himself arrived and confirmed that, subject to agreement on a few outstanding terms, he had decided he would sign for Rangers. He seemed more at peace with himself as soon as the words were out of his mouth. As ever, he had not wanted to upset anybody, had wanted to be friends with everybody, but had finally faced up to the harsh reality that in any race there had to be losers and there was always the possibility that the losers in this game would not take it graciously. Once he had made his decision he just wanted to be away, to get on with the daily training he had promised Venables he would undertake before and during his holiday. This time, whether it was to be for Rangers or England, there was no question of him returning looking like a sumo wrestler!

By 7.0 p.m. it looked as if sufficient progress was being made for Stein to leave Len Lazarus with his assistant and go off to meet his wife as planned. As he raced out of the building and hailed a taxi he was surrounded by a horde of pressmen. 'Has he signed? We don't even want to know who he's signed for, just tell us if he's signed,' they yelled.

'Sorry, boys, I'm off to the theatre and if I'm late my wife will kill me,' the lawyer said as he leapt into the sanctity of a taxi. It was one of the few occasions when the papers accurately quoted him. Yet, when he arrived at the theatre as the curtain rose, he couldn't settle, couldn't concentrate. His long-suffering wife saw his discomfort. 'You want to get back, don't you?' she said.

He nodded and they left after half an hour. Gazza had something else to answer for in the Stein household!

Back at the meeting all was not going well. The Italian lawyer was being difficult; Zoff and Cragnotti were watching football – and Smith and Ogilvie were becoming increasingly disenchanted. By 10.0 p.m. everybody had had enough. There had been enough all night sessions in the Paul Gascoigne Story already and this was not to be one of them. The parties had gone sufficiently far in their negotiations to be satisfied that the transaction would almost certainly go through. Cragnotti, never short of words said, 'The Gascoigne era for us is over. The next time we see Gascoigne in Rome he will be a tourist.'

It was time to go home. When Stein got back to North London at 11.0 p.m. he had just missed a phone call from Paul. He had been sitting in a restaurant with Sheryl, obviously well pleased with the day's events, despite the few problems yet to be resolved.

'Listen,' he said to Marilyn Stein, 'I don't think I thanked Mel and Len properly for all they'd done for me. I know Mel's been under a lot of pressure lately, but I want him to know I really appreciate everything.' There could be no doubt, as the lad headed for his holiday in Mauritius and his twenty-eighth birthday on 27 May, that he was finally growing up. John Sadler, writing in the *Sun*, for so long firm supporters of the troubled star, gave it to him straight. 'The modern, re-modelled, mended Paul Gascoigne has to prove he can STILL play the game for which he was blessed with such sublime talent . . . Italy owes him nothing. England owes him nothing. The fans don't owe him a thing either. But Paul Gascoigne owes everything to himself . . . Those who yearn for an exciting England side should recognize the mighty burden he carries and wish him . . . Happy Birthday.'

39

'IS HE STILL ABLE TO ACCELERATE PAST PEOPLE?'

It rained in Mauritius and Paul and Sheryl decided to move on to Florida. As they went shopping Paul asked if they'd forgotten anything for the move to Glasgow. 'Yes,' she said, 'a cot.'

Paul looked at her in astonishment. He'd always wanted a family of his own and ever since he had met her he had wanted Sheryl to be the mother of his children. Yet now the moment had arrived, now she was actually pregnant and had plucked up the courage to tell him, he could hardly believe it. And when he did believe it, at first he found it hard to come to terms with. And Sheryl found his attitude even harder to understand. She thought she was giving him what he wanted and here he was not only pushing her away, but also distancing himself from her children who he had treated as his own.

'What, are you pregnant then?' Paul asked. Sheryl nodded, but instead of hugging her he simply carried on writing his list on one of his endless scraps of paper. 'Cot, Sheryl pregnant,' he wrote, and then it was back to his plans for Scotland – and then silence. It was not the happiest of parties who moved on to the second stage of their holiday.

Looking back, Paul accepts that it was fear that made him react the way he did. It was one thing acting as a surrogate father for Bianca and Mason, and quite another to be faced with the responsibilities of real parenthood. It was, he swore to himself, to be the last time he would act badly towards Sheryl. Yet again he was pushing her to the brink not realizing that it was his own future happiness he was moving ever nearer to the precipice.

Whilst their relationship did not make for the best of holidays, at least this time around Paul neither ate nor drank to excess. He worked out daily, feeling for the first time that at least in the footballing sense he had something to strive for. He used the daily exercise to try and exorcize from his mind all the external pressures and left his future playing career in the hands of his advisers. His parents' marriage had finally come to an end amidst an unwarranted amount of publicity with the Gazza tag once again being the peg around which the stories were built. His father's health was giving cause for great concern and although he had come through one operation to ease the pressure on his brain, there were far more serious operations ahead, so serious indeed that the surgeon wanted to see all the family to explain the situation before these were undertaken.

Back in Rome, the pieces were slowly but surely falling into place and Lazio certainly regarded Paul as having already departed. They announced that as far as they were concerned Rangers could have him. The 'and welcome to him', was suggested but left unsaid.

Stein spoke to Villa manager, Doug Ellis, who took defeat manfully and gracefully wishing Paul all the best but still feeling he had taken the easy option. He was convinced that the English Premier League was somewhere Paul could really test himself, could really extend his talents. Neither Chelsea nor Leeds were as gracious. Chelsea consoled themselves with Gullit, whilst Leeds still felt, somewhat justifiably, hard done by that they had not even had the chance to talk to the player.

On 30 May Paul joined up with the England squad, this time not as a spectator, but as a player who had every reason to believe he would play for at least part of the four nation Umbro Tournament between England, Brazil, Sweden and Japan. Venables was suitably cautious. 'I'm really looking at what he can give us on the ball. He's dead keen, but we'll find out whether he's capable or not in the four days we're together before our first match. Is he still able to accelerate past people which he used to do so well, and what's his strength like while he's doing it? You know the desire is there. Sometimes when someone gets these serious leg injuries the desire is only 60 or 70 per cent, but with him the full 100 per cent has always been there.'

Venables was wrong. The desire was 110 per cent.

The desire of the media to question him at the first press conference was 150 per cent. It was as if neither Venables nor any of the other players existed. Yet, if they thought they were going to get sensational copy, or Gazza the joker, they were to be most disappointed. There were no funny faces, no tongue poking out; he was serious, reflective, even a little philosophical. 'If I stay fit, this will be a fresh start. I'm very hungry, but in the past I've been too hungry. I rushed things, brought injuries on myself. When you're injured you want to come back so much. Now I need to be involved. I need to be winning. Going to Wembley on Saturday (for the match against Japan) will be an emotional time for me. Just to be here with England is a bonus. Football is all I know. If I haven't got that, I haven't got anything. What kept me going through all of this is the fact I will never let anybody, or anything, beat me.' That determination showed itself during training. He asked for and gave no quarter, never flinched from a tackle, even on that damaged leg, even from the likes of David Batty. 'They treated me as any other lad and I was grateful for that. I'd had enough of being treated as an invalid.'

405

England put up an awful display in the opening match of the Umbro Cup against Japan on 3 June. The biggest cheer of the night was reserved for Paul who came on as a substitute in the 68th minute to help England turn what looked like being an embarrassing draw into a narrow 2–1 victory.

After the near embarrassment against Japan there was much discussion as to whether Paul should be in the starting line-up for the match against Sweden on Thursday 8 June at Elland Road, Leeds, but Venables was never one to be railroaded by the media or public opinion and once again Paul took his place on the substitutes' bench. It did not take long to realize that the England Manager had probably done him a favour by relegating him to the sidelines. Within 36 minutes England were 2–0 down and although Sheringham pulled one back just before half-time, it could have been worse. After just 23 seconds of the second half it was. Sweden's Andersson lobbed the ball over the England keeper Tim Flowers to put the match seemingly out of the home nation's reach. By then the crowd were booing poor John Barnes almost every time he touched the ball and baying for Paul to be brought into the fray. In the 63rd minute (some five minutes earlier than in the previous match) they got their wish. A telling Gazza pass to David Platt laid on England's second goal and then, with only a minute to go, Gascoigne, with all the enthusiasm of a teenager making his international début, raced to take a free-kick from the left. The clock was turned back to the World Cup match against Belgium some five years before. Paul hit the ball long and Platt, instead of swivelling to volley, headed the ball home for the equalizer.

Almost inevitably there was controversy. In a battle for the ball, just a moment before the last gasp equalizer, Paul had accidentally clashed with Sweden's Magnus Erlingmark. The tough Swedish player, who had looked able to give as good as he would get, had come out of the tussle with a broken nose and claimed he had been hit by Paul's elbow. Paul was devastated that his otherwise successful come-back should be clouded by such a suggestion. 'I was gutted. I've never elbowed anybody in the face deliberately. I immediately went to look for the fellow to say I was sorry. In some ways, the manner in which the incident was reported was a warning to me. The papers were never going to be satisfied with concentrating on the positive things I did on the field. They were always going to look for the dirt, always going to probe for the angle.'

It was hardly surprising that the press failed to praise Paul's contribution to a remarkable team recovery against top-class opposition and the headline, 'Gazza Bust My Hooter,' was fairly typical of the tabloid coverage.

And so to Sunday 9 June and Brazil. Again Paul hoped he would start, again he was to be disappointed. By the time he was brought on, less than 15 minutes from the end, England had been taken apart and were 3–1 down. If Venables was hoping for another miracle, he was to be disappointed. For most of the second half the cries of the crowd for Gazza seemed only to make him the more determined *not* to bring him on, to show them that he was boss and that he would make the decisions. Yet again, the decision, right or wrong, worked in Paul's favour. In the short period of time allotted to him, he showed that he stood head and shoulders above anybody else on the England side in his ability to match the Brazilians for close control and vision of the game. He made one stunning run, leaving three Brazilians trailing in his wake, and generally did enough to make the crowd wonder what might have been if he had played the whole game. He left them hoping, as Paul himself had said, that the best was yet to come. Three appearances as substitute, less than an hour of football, but what he had done had all been good. There could be no doubt that as long as he retained his fitness his claim for a guaranteed place in the England starting line-up was irresistible.

40

'PRESSURE, EXPECTANCY. I'VE LIVED WITH IT SINCE I WAS 18.'

Eventually the date was fixed for Paul to sign for Rangers, 10 July, but first he had to tidy up his affairs and make his farewells in Rome. He went to the training ground and said goodbye to the players and Zoff. That part, at least, was none too painful. Of the playing staff who had been there when he had first arrived in a blaze of glory and hope only about three still remained and the relationship with Zoff had become ever more distant since he had given up the day-to-day training. He hardly bothered to speak to Zeman, the new coach. The man had had little enough time for him as a player when he was there and Paul was never one for false emotion. He saved his real emotion for his parting from Gianni and Augusto. They had been introduced to him as minders and they parted as family. Even at the end it was Gianni who helped him pack up the villa, Gianni who spoke to the owner to iron out the inevitable problems, and Gianni who took him to the airport. He delivered the letter that Carla Vissat, the Italian lawyer, had arranged for him to give to the police at the airport to signify that he was leaving Italy for good. There were tears in his eyes as he boarded the plane, tears for a lost opportunity, tears of frustration that he had not been able to make good his promise to succeed when everybody had said he would fail. He was determined not to make the same mistakes in Scotland.

Yet there was still something to make him smile as he flew back. As he left the training ground for the last time, a man on a motorbike had spotted him and given him a victory salute. Paul had waved back, but even as he did so, he saw the man heading towards the back of a truck, his eyes on Gazza, oblivious to the danger ahead. 'Even as he hit it and flew off his bike, he was still waving,' Paul mused afterwards. It was right and fitting that the Rome adventure should end upon a note of farce.

Glasgow in July 1995 may have been three years and several thousand miles away from the greeting he had received in Rome, but it seemed that 'Gazzamania' had struck again. Perhaps it had never died and was only sleeping, but there could be no disguising the wave of near hysteria that swept through the city to welcome Paul Gascoigne.

The crowds on the pavement may not have amounted to the thousands who had assembled at Rome Airport, but the noise levels were the same or even greater. Blond dyed crew cuts were the order of the day, as was anything that the fans could have gathered together, to celebrate the coming of what many saw as the final piece in the jigsaw of the great side being assembled by Walter Smith and David Murray. Many of the crowd had bought a flag with a portrait of Gazza printed upon it, a product manufactured in blatant breach of the registered trademark and which, it appeared, had already been on sale with some success at the Orange Day Parades a few days earlier. Stein and Lazarus were unimpressed. Paul's company had spent a considerable sum of money in protecting the 'Gazza' trademark, not just for financial interests, but also to protect an unsuspecting public from the purchase of unauthorized, sub-quality goods. They had battled to preserve the image on Tyneside, in North London and in Rome with some success and they were not going to give up the fight lightly in Glasgow. Rangers' representatives told them with a slight hint of fear in their voices that these items were almost certainly being made by certain local gangs who did not take too kindly to interference with their illicit money-spinning activities. The club was already suffering from pirate merchandise and was taking the appropriate action through the Trading Standards Officers. Gazza's advisers vowed to do the same, only more so.

Ken McGill of Chrysalis had been with Paul to film his arrival in Scotland and when they'd flown into Glasgow airport he recorded the incredible contrast with the scenes that had greeted Paul in Rome. Only Walter Smith was there to greet him although a few of the ground staff gave him a ripple of applause.

'Where's Sheryl?' Walter asked.

'I thought I'd get up here and settle down first,' Paul replied.

As Paul returned from his first training session with the club all personal and commercial matters were pushed into the background; the privacy of his arrival almost forgotten. The noise reached sound-barrier levels and he was hustled inside, pausing only to wave at the door to his new found worshippers. Paul was to enjoy the morning training session far more than the formalities of the signing and press conference that were now in store for him. Before he'd gone to the training ground he had been incredibly nervous, shaking like a leaf over breakfast at the thought of meeting his new team-mates. Ken McGill, who had by now become more of a friend than an all-seeing eye recording every event, tried to calm him down. 'What are you so nervous about? They're your peers. They'll be nervous about meeting you. You're Paul Gascoigne.'

Amongst the faces he saw was that of Gordon Durie who'd played alongside him at Tottenham on the few occasions he'd been fit. To Paul's astonishment the first sight that met his eyes at the training ground was Durie on the treatment table. 'Still f***ing injured, I see, Gordon,' Paul said with a smile.

There was another reunion, this time with Ian Ferguson, the Rangers' defender he'd last met up with when the pair had hit the headlines for fighting on the pitch during a pre-season friendly between Spurs and Rangers back in 1990. The two men eyed each other with some caution yet were destined to become the best of friends. Ally McCoist also approached the new signing cautiously. He had a hard-earned reputation for being both the star and joker of the team and was not about to give up either without a fight. Ian Durrant also had a reputation as a prankster and immediately nick-named Paul 'refresher mouth', claiming his mother must have given him refresher sweets to suck instead of a dummy.

If Paul had experienced any doubts about the wisdom of choosing Rangers over any English clubs they soon evaporated when he saw the camaraderie and skill in the side even in early pre-season training. Brian Laudrup could make the ball talk, Stuart McCall he remembered from his Everton days as was the case with Gary Stevens. Mark Hateley he knew from the England squad, although his presence was not to extend beyond the end of September when he was transferred to another Rangers, this time QPR in West London. Although Richard Gough had never played alongside him at Spurs, they had enough mutual acquaintances from their White Hart Lane days to make immediate conversation, whilst Andy Goram in goal showed Paul enough skill in stopping his shots during training to signal that he was going to be hard to beat all season. Some of the skills of the youngsters were encouraging as well

(Charlie Miller in particular) and the way that they immediately looked up to Paul. This gave him a new sense of responsibility that augured well for the future.

What had impressed Paul the most, however, was the friendliness yet absolute professionalism of the squad. They all seemed to have an excellent relationship with the manager who gave them licence and rope, yet seemed to have no need to tug it in. The players themselves knew just how far they could go without abusing the trust he put in them.

Back at the club after training, David Murray looked out of the window at the crowds below, who broke into excitement every time they saw any kind of movement at a window. 'We've had a few signings since I've been here, but I've never seen anything like this,' Murray said.

McGill could see the differences in this 'Second Coming' more than most. 'At Rome there was mayhem, a passion that hurt your eyes. This was just as passionate, but not so frightening. After all, there weren't any baton-wielding carabinieri.'

Murray tried to appear calm, but it was hard to avoid the impression that here was a kid who had been given exactly what he wanted for Christmas. Murray had insisted that the press conference took place in the Blue Room, where every important event was held that had ever occurred at Ibrox. It was going to be bursting at the seams with journalists, photographers and camera crews, but that could only add to the atmosphere.

To a stranger in town it would have appeared that the creature the media had come to see was from another planet, that it had never been viewed before, that here was something totally unique in the history of reporting. Paul was totally unfazed. He had seen it all before.

David Murray had everything organized with military precision. The cameramen were given the first five minutes, then they were shooed out of the room to make way for the journalists, who sat with pencils poised or tape recorders whirring, hoping upon hope that somebody would say something that would give them the chance of an unusual headline. Outside in the street, the crowd continued to chant Paul's name. They already had their hero, they did not need any newspaper reporter to tell them what that meant to at least half of Glasgow.

Paul at long last signed the contract to play the next three years of his career with Rangers and walked through the door of the ante-room to join Walter Smith at the top table. The Chairman introduced the man who needed no introduction. 'To save you wondering, let me tell you the fee was £4.3 million and he's signed a three-year contract.'

Now that they had him at their mercy the pressmen seemed curiously reticent about asking any embarrassing questions. He was asked about the sort of pressure he was likely to feel. 'Pressure, expectancy? I've lived with it since I was eighteen. I've lived in the bright lights of London and with the demands of Rome. I can handle Glasgow.' The question was not raised as to whether or not Glasgow could handle Paul.

'Don't you think it's rather a lot of money to pay for somebody who's had your sort of injury record?' somebody boldly asked. Instead of taking offence the calmer, maturer Gazza simply grinned and nodded in the direction of David Murray. 'You'd better ask him, he's paid it, not me,' he replied.

Again, the Murray guillotine came down on the proceedings and it was off to the pitch for another photo session and some one-to-one interviews with the local radio and television stations. It was not the first time that Paul had stepped onto the Ibrox turf since he had decided upon his move north of the border. On one of his visits to the city he had gone to Ibrox on his own, secretly and privately. Walking out onto the empty pitch had been an almost eerie experience. 'There was no-one around, just me, and the silence was frightening. It seemed a very big stage and I felt very small.'

There was no chance of him being alone today. It was clear to those who knew him that Paul had had enough. His gaze was wandering, the answers were becoming ever shorter. He had come to Glasgow to play football, not to be part of a media circus. Yet he still found time to don a T-shirt bearing the motto, 'The Breath of Life Challenge', in aid of the British Lung Foundation of which he had agreed to become a Patron. Needless to say, that was part of the day's events that was studiously ignored by the media. Finally, he escaped down to the main entrance hall. Nobody had left from the throng outside and he was encouraged to go to the door and give them a regal wave. Three fans begged to give him a presentation. It was Lazio all over again, only this time instead of scarves and plaques he was given a suit made out of a specially designed 'Gascoigne Tartan'. 'I never knew I had any Scottish relatives,' Paul said, laughing, and strangely touched by the gesture. At that moment every man, woman and child standing on the pavement, still chanting Gazza's name, felt they were related to him.

41

'GAZZA TO BE A DADDA.'

Not all the headlines on 11 July 1995 were about Paul Gascoigne. If he was under pressure, some of it at least was released by the simultaneous return to England of his erstwhile Italian compatriot, David Platt. Curiously, nobody suggested Platt's time in Italy had shown him to be a failure, although his time with various clubs had brought him as little reward and success as Paul had achieved at Lazio – and that without the added burdens that Paul had suffered due to his crippling injuries. It was all about perception and it was fortunate indeed that Paul was able to look forward, and not back, without any bitterness towards those who earned a living by writing about the likes of him and David Platt.

Paul took to Glasgow with ease. He strolled the streets, proudly wearing his tartan suit and topped off by the blond crew cut that had become almost the norm for any teenage Rangers fan. It had been a long time since his days were spent training with a hope of actually playing. He moved into the Cameron House Hotel on the banks of Loch Lomond and soon made the high-class establishment the headquarters for the usual Gazza camp followers. If the management required any advice as to how to handle it they need only have made one phone call to The Swallow at Waltham Abbey. Then, even before he could kick a ball in anger, two stories broke which threatened to ruin the honeymoon period he seemed to be enjoying with the media. The first seemed innocuous enough, celebratory even. The Editor of the *Sun* phoned Mel Stein and said, 'Congratulations.' Stein wasn't too sure what he had done, but it soon became evident that the good wishes were for Paul and Sheryl. At long last the tabloids had discovered that Sheryl was pregnant.

'Gazza To Be A Dadda', proclaimed the *Sun*, who, like every other publication, were desperate to get a direct interview with what they perceived to be the happy couple. The only problem was that the couple were still not happy. Paul, who had for so many years longed for a child of his own, was now faced with the reality of fatherhood and simply could not cope with it. 'Looking back on it now, I was a real selfish bastard. I didn't think about how Sheryl was feeling, only about myself and how this was going to affect my life. I was awful to her and even worse, I was a nightmare for Mason and Bianca, who I already regarded as my kids. I can't say why I reacted like that, only that I did. Sheryl would have had every right to tell me to get lost for ever and bring the kid up herself.' And that was what she nearly did. The publicity did not help. Once again journalists camped on her front lawn, rang the doorbell, posted notes and offers through the letterbox, whilst those who had the phone number called at whatever time of the day or night suited their deadline. The first indication to the public that this was anything other than a storybook upturn in Paul's personal fortunes was when a couple of papers carried the story that Sheryl had rejected Paul's latest offer of marriage. But by 20 July it was clear that this was more than just another blip in what had never been the smoothest of relationships. Sheryl was adamant. It was over and Paul was left begging her to return. It was not the best background for the start of his playing career at Rangers.

The attitude at the club was more prosaic. John Greig, one of the past heroes of the club said drily, 'I hear you've been busy. Where did you conceive it?' Paul just looked a little sheepish.

The telephone lines between Denmark (where Rangers had jetted off to for their pre-season tour) and Essex were red hot as Paul tried manfully to concentrate his efforts on the field. Len Lazarus acting as an intermediary managed to get the star-crossed lovers talking again and perhaps that helped Paul to find the net in his first public match in a Rangers shirt against Brondby. The Scottish club eased to a 2–1 victory and Gazza's marker, Kim Vilfort, had nothing but positive things to say about him. 'He was very good and I'm sure he'll be happy he got that goal. If he continues to play the way he played tonight he'll be a real asset to Rangers. There's a lot of aggression in his play, but it's all done in a football way.'

Walter Smith was also delighted with his acquisition although he had some reservations because he knew that Paul still needed to get match fit. The only way he could achieve that was by playing matches and that was exactly what Smith would give him the opportunity to do. He'd already had a few practice games against opponents behind closed doors and had scored twice. He'd found the net three times and July was not yet over. If only he could get his personal life on an even keel . . . if only.

Curiously enough it was a journalist who helped mend the bridges. Rebekah Wade, now the Features Editor of the *News of the World*, spoke to Paul and Sheryl and finally got them speaking to each other to such an extent that in the edition of 23 July she was able to announce that they were back together. 'I was so pleased about the baby,' Sheryl said, 'but when I told Paul about it he clammed up. I was hurt. I only wanted a hug.' Paul was openly, and yet again, publicly contrite.

'I'm so sorry for the way I behaved. Now I couldn't be more pleased. Boy or girl, I'll buy it a football.'

Football, that was what Paul now had to concentrate upon and indeed, he produced a magical display against the Danish side, Hvidovre, which included a brilliant 25-yard free-kick that could be compared to his semi-final goal against Arsenal. This one hit the post, but Paul then grabbed the ball when Rangers were awarded a second kick from a similar position and this time he made no mistake. The critics, who had been sharpening their blades and poison pencil points would have to wait a while. Not that some of them had the patience to wait. James Lawton, who had been around long enough to know better, wrote one of the most unpleasant little pieces that had been seen in Paul's playing career, headed, 'Enjoy Gazza freak show while it lasts'. In it he alleged, without any justification whatsoever, 'Gascoigne's . . . yearning for personal publicity, which is frequently denied but slavishly sought . . . long ago outstripped his performance on the field [and] has found an ultimate market place'. It was when Lawton went on to suggest that there had been a 'profound decline in his powers' that one was left wondering if he had actually seen any of Paul's games for Rangers during his period of rehabilitation and indeed, whether the professional suffering the decline was the journalist himself, rather than the footballer.

What had been written was rubbish, vitriolic rubbish, and it hurt. Yet, as Rangers returned to Glasgow to host what had, to an extent, been hyped as the Ibrox International Tournament, Paul knew that was the sort of media pressure he was going to have to endure. Yet again, the game was on to prove all the critics wrong and to make them eat their words.

Gazza began the 'forced feeding' in the pre-season tournament, where he was surrounded by old friends. Spurs, Sampdoria and Rangers, together with Steaua

Bucharest, made an interesting combination, which saw Tottenham outclassed in the very first match against Sampdoria – and left Paul feeling satisfied that they had not shown any real interest in taking him back to White Hart Lane. With Klinsmann's departure, accompanied by a chorus of insults from that well-known football aficionado, Alan Sugar, and Barmby about to choose Middlesbrough over London, it looked at the time as if it might well be a difficult season.

Rangers played some irresistible football in their game against the Romanians and romped home 4–0 winners, with Paul scoring his first goal at home. It was a goal that was going to cause more grief than any goal he had ever scored before. For the moment, though, he could look forward to a final between his new team and Sampdoria which saw the home side run out easy 2–0 winners. Paul himself played some dazzling football during the 70 minutes he was on the pitch and felt that Rangers would be fully up to the challenge of the European Champions League which had been such a tempting factor in seducing him north of the border. He'd survived the greater part of two matches in 24 hours to add to the half a dozen matches he'd already had under his belt in the blue of Rangers. 'I felt really good, although I knew I could get even better. I'd settled in quickly to Rangers' style of play and if I'd had any doubts about the move, they'd vanished by then.'

During the tournament Paul had an unlikely confrontation with Sean Connery, the original 007, James Bond. A huge shadow fell across the pitch as Paul warmed up hours before a match. Gazza rushed to shake his hand and asked if he could talk to him. Here was Paul Gascoigne super-star in total awe of a super-star from the silver screen.

'You're bigger than I thought,' Paul said.

'I always am, laddie,' Connery replied. 'I always am,' his Scottish accent stronger than ever.

'What do you think I ought to watch out for up here in particular?' Paul asked, anxious for advice.

'You'll get a lot of rabbit,' Connery said, and he was right.

As the actor left, Paul turned to Ken McGill who'd filmed the episode and said, 'I shook his hand. Just imagine how many pairs of beautiful boobs they've held.' Later though, Paul was to stand up both Connery and David Murray for a dinner date, fearing the inevitable media attention such a gathering would attract. Connery dropped a line in what was hopefully mock pique saying, 'You Geordie bastard, where were you?'

At the end of the tournament the 20,000 Rangers fans who turned up to witness their team lift the first (albeit somewhat meaningless) piece of silverware of the season cheered him to the echo, 'Glasgow belonged to Paul Gascoigne and he belonged to Glasgow'. James Lawton may have thought it a freak show, but nobody present at Ibrox on that desperately hot summer's afternoon would have agreed with him.

No sooner had the dust settled on the result than a whole new storm erupted over Paul's celebration of his goal. A team-mate, who for obvious reasons wished then and for ever to remain anonymous, had suggested that a way to win over the hearts of the hard-core Rangers' fans would be to 'give them the flute' when he scored his first goal. Unfortunately, and foolishly, he failed to tell Paul the significance of the gesture, or the likely outcome of his giving it. The flute, as a musical instrument, has a special place in the history of the Orangemen, the Protestant sector of Glasgow, who form the bedrock of Rangers' support in direct sectarian conflict with the Catholic support of Celtic.

To add fuel to the fire, BBC Scotland bought the tape of the match from Rangers and broadcast the footage on the following Tuesday, 1 August, thus stoking up the controversy over an incident that would have been put down to innocent naïvety in anybody except Paul Gascoigne. *The Times* was able to report on 3 August that Rangers had actually banned the BBC over their showing of the incident. David Murray was, to say the least, sensitive about anything that might suggest that his club was still living in the dark ages of sectarianism. He had already had cause to fall out with a Dutch TV company who had focused a documentary on the Protestant–Catholic divide and felt that much of the effort he had invested in making Rangers a team that was not merely inter-faith, but above faith, had been sacrificed for the sake of a cheap story.

Gazza was bemused and contrite. He had learned his first footballing lesson in Glasgow. There was no such thing as a joke, even in a match which was little more than a friendly. His next game, however, was to be anything but friendly. Much to their annoyance, Rangers had been forced to play in the preliminary round of the European Champions' Cup, whilst the English champions, Blackburn Rovers, had been given a bye until the actual money-spinning league situation. They were drawn against the Cypriot champions, Anorthosis Famagusta, and were on a hiding to nothing. 'I thought they were some kind of disease when I first heard the draw,' Paul recalls, 'but they turned out to be anything but mugs.'

That was the harsh lesson that British clubs were to learn in their 1995/6 European campaign; there were no such things as mugs anymore, at least not when they were faced with British opposition.

On Wednesday 9 August the weather in Glasgow was more suited to the visitors from Cyprus than the home side. A shirt-sleeved crowd filled the ground, despite the holiday season, to see their side give a footballing lesson to the no-hopers; they came to see Paul Gascoigne perform for the first time in a competitive match in a Rangers shirt; they came to see a goal deluge – and in every way they were disappointed.

Before the match Paul met up with a youngster called Zach who was suffering from a rare form of leukaemia. Despite the pressure on the player he took the boy into the dressing room and out onto the pitch and gave him the run of the club shop at his own expense. The youngster, decked out in his new Rangers shirt had an evening he would never forget and Paul's only condition was that there would be no publicity. It was only in October, when he heard the lad had died, that Paul broke his silence and was prepared to make any sort of comment. So much for the allegations that he was a self-styled publicist.

The match seen by Zach and the rest of the crowd turned out to be an ill-tempered affair. The Cypriots were quite aware of their own footballing inferiority and were fully prepared to demonstrate the physical side of their game to keep the match level. Indeed, on the break there were times when they looked the more likely to score. Only some fine goalkeeping from Andy Goram kept out the Bulgarian trio in the Cypriot side. It was not until the 68th minute that Rangers finally broke down the stubborn visitors and then it was a piece of Gascoigne inventiveness that gave the crowd some relief. Paul angled a pass around the defence to reach Stuart McCall, who in turn laid the ball off to Gordon Durie to score. 1–0, hardly a comfortable cushion for the visit to Cyprus, particularly as there were grave rumours as to the unpredictable nature of the playing surface in Famagusta. David Murray, who had calculated that the League section of the European Cup was worth some £6 million pounds, was left to worry.

Yet, before the visit to Cyprus Paul had still to have his induction into the joys of the Scottish Premier League. Saturday 19 August saw the visit of Greenock Morton to Ibrox, not perhaps the most exciting of fixtures, but it still brought an incredible 42,949 spectators into the ground, of whom the odd 949 may have come to support Morton. On the same day in England, Liverpool attracted 40,000 for their match against Sheffield Wednesday, and at Aston Villa, 34,000 for the visit of Manchester United. Once again it was brought home to Paul what a huge club it was that he had joined.

A comfortable 3–0 win, with Paul scoring the third in stylish manner, may have lured the Englishman into thinking that he was in for an easy ride at least in the League, but it would not take too long for him to discover otherwise.

Certainly in Famagusta there would be no easy ride. The Cypriots' coach set out his stall in no uncertain manner. 'Some players you have to keep an eye on and put them under pressure. That's exactly what we intend to do to Gascoigne. We will do it within the rules, and perhaps a little more, and see how he reacts.'

As it happened, they had to do very little. After just 5 minutes Paul told captain Richard Gough that he thought his thigh muscle had gone and after a brief struggle to run off the injury he limped off in the 25th minute. Once again, as he trudged dejectedly to the bench, there were tears in his eyes, but this time they were tears of frustration.

'I couldn't believe that this was happening. Inevitably, now whenever I get an injury I think the worst. I suppose it was to be expected that I'd pick up some sort of knock or strain. I'd played no games for about eighteen months and then it seemed like I'd played eighteen games in a month.'

As it transpired Paul had no cause to cry and no real cause to worry. Rangers battled out a goalless draw to take them through to the Super League section of the competition and the ice-pack Paul held on his thigh throughout the second half of the match was most of the treatment he needed.

Inevitably, the media seized upon the injury as another disaster in a career of disasters and one tabloid, to its later embarrassment, even suggested it threatened his whole season. Brian Woolnough, who never seemed to miss the chance to create a Gazza drama, even went so far as to suggest that Paul remained, 'only half the player he was'. That was always the way. There could be no middle ground as far as Paul's exposure to the public was concerned. It was all highs or lows and there were times when he longed for a plateau.

Yet, Terry Venables remained true to his man. Whatever accusations might be levelled against the England Manager, both in his private and professional life, nobody could accuse him of being anything other than undyingly loyal to those players who he believed had served him well. When the England squad was announced on 29 August for the friendly against Colombia to be played at Wembley the following week, he seemed to have no doubts or hesitation about naming Paul in his squad. 'The Boss phoned me to ask if I'd be fit and I didn't need to be asked that question twice. Whatever work I needed to put in I'd do, even if I had to go for it all night.'

Through to the next challenging round in Europe, a goal under his belt in his first league match and now once more a part of the full England line-up. At long last Paul Gascoigne had something he could look forward to with genuine optimism.

42

'GIFTED AND BLACK, IF NO LONGER YOUNG, PAUL GASCOIGNE PUT THE HOPE BACK INTO ENGLISH FOOTBALL LAST NIGHT.'

In the build up to the match against Colombia, yet again the focus was on Gazza rather than the England team as a whole. Up until the day before the game there was still some doubt as to whether he would be in the starting eleven, and Paul himself under interrogation at the Press Call said, 'I'd like to think I could be as good as I was in 1990. It won't happen in the next two months but it will come.'

There was a quiet certainty about that comment, a certainty helped by the fact that he had been told that he would be given the chance of playing 90 minutes against the Colombians. It would be only the second time that Venables had been able to pencil him in from the start of a match, the first occasion having been in his very first international in charge against Denmark back in March 1994.

'It seemed that every time I had a chance of playing for England I'd hurt myself the week before. Back then they'd thought I'd fractured my ribs and my arm against Roma, but I made it and here I was having made it again.' It might have been merely a friendly against a team who had wildly disappointed in the World Cup, but for Paul the game against Colombia was far more important than that. He had to take it seriously because every match for him at this stage was serious, whether it was a friendly or not. To show just how seriously he was taking it, he decided upon a new image. The blond look was gone and when he took the field to great acclaim on the night of 6 September his hair was a dark, sombre colour.

Paul knew he was under pressure, but then that was nothing new to him. All his old critics had had their moments of pontification. John Sadler wrote, 'We have reached a stage when Paul Gascoigne has to be included or discarded . . . the nation has waited long enough for confirmation that England's most talented footballer can rediscover enough of his old magic to make him a worthwhile proposition'.

'Long enough', the poor man had returned to first-class football after an eighteen month lay-off in July. It was now just September, he had worked himself silly, but for the sake of a story this was the moment of truth. And what made matters worse was that the readers believed it.

Fortunately he let nobody down, least of all himself. 'Gifted and black, if no longer young, Paul Gascoigne put the hope back into English football last night,' wrote Martin Samuel, who the Gascoigne camp had never regarded as a friend. Coming from him that was praise indeed.

On the night Paul carved out chance after chance, linking up so well with young Steve McManaman that they might have been playing together for years. Within 7 minutes Paul had sent Shearer through with the best defence-splitting pass of the night, but the Blackburn striker's goal drought persisted and he was unable to convert the chance. Then in the 26th minute Paul went through himself only to see his vicious shot hit the near post and ricochet out to give McManaman a chance to open the scoring. Paul was also involved from dead-ball situations, twice coming close with swerving free-kicks from outside the penalty area. Yet for all his fine work it was Rene Higuita in the Colombian goal who shared the headlines with Paul. After 22 minutes of the first half Higuita dived forward to save a 20-yard drive from Jamie Redknapp. The ball fell behind him and whilst in mid-air the keeper flicked his legs up to donkey-kick the ball away from danger. Gazza, the arch-joker himself, was both bemused and amused. 'I couldn't believe the guy. It was like something out of a circus. What with his kick and Valderrama's hair, they made me feel quite normal. I was really pleased with my own performance, but I was also delighted for the likes of the youngsters, Redknapp, McManaman, Steve Howey, Gary Neville, Graham Le Saux and Nicky Barmby. Nicky had been a junior at Spurs when I was there and I'd always felt he had a big future ahead of him. With all those kids in the side it made me feel quite old.'

And perhaps that was no bad thing. Black hair, great control, wonderful self-discipline, a new elder statesman had been born.

There were some half a dozen friendlies to come before the European Championships and on that September night Paul was determined to play in every one of them. How could he have known that once again the injury jinx would strike and he would miss the very next one? What was clear was that with every game played, with every hurdle cleared, he was getting stronger and stronger. His confidence (never the weakest facet of his character) was also returning. On at least a couple of occasions he had waltzed past not just one, but two or three opponents with the old Gazza arrogance and flair. Each time he had felt hungry to try it again, like a man who has not swum for a long time pushing himself to do another length of the pool. Joe Lovejoy, writing in the *Sunday Times*, perhaps summed it up best when he said, 'What was a real boon after all those injuries was the return of that missing yard of pace which some of us feared was gone for good. O ye of little faith. Here . . . was the Gazza of fond memory, gliding past opponents with a touch on the accelerator complementing that mesmeric close control.'

It was all Paul wanted to hear and it was what he deserved to hear. Those who had written him off remained silent, nurturing their poison for the next occasion, confident that they would not have long to wait.

43

'I DON'T THINK I EVER CLAIMED TO BE A MONK, EVEN THOUGH I MIGHT HAVE HAD A HAIRCUT LIKE ONE.'

On 10 September the Sunday papers were able to report another convincing victory for Rangers following their 4–0 win over Raith Rovers. Going from the cauldron that was Wembley to the likes of little Raith was something that Paul would have to get used to. Something else that he should by now have become accustomed to was the blaring headline in the *News of the World*, 'Gazza's Foul Play With A Married Blonde'. Paul was unimpressed. 'Me make a pass at Karen? She looks like Shergar.'

Paul might have shrugged it off but Sheryl was less than amused. She was four months' pregnant and could well do without this type of story surfacing about the man who was to be the father of her child, even if they were of historical curiosity value. Again the pressure was on Paul. He might have reached the stage where he wasn't putting a foot wrong on the pitch, but off it there was still ample opportunity for him to put his foot in his own mouth.

In that odd roller-coaster ride that was his life, the next competitive match which promised so much turned into a gigantic disappointment.

When Rangers had hosted Steaua Bucharest in the pre-season friendly tournament, and beaten them at a canter, they could not have envisaged meeting up with them again so soon. Yet, for their first match in the Champions League, off they went to meet the Romanian champions – and this time to be beaten by them. Paul had failed to impose his authority on the match but Rangers made a valiant attempt to hold off the opposition until Alan McLaren was dismissed. Just eight minutes later, the Romanians grabbed the only goal of the game. Paul had a generally unhappy night and was kicked whenever he threatened. One particularly nasty tackle left him writhing on the ground thinking his leg had been broken yet again. 'It was terrible. I felt a whack, then searing pain and all I could think was here we go again. Fortunately it was only the initial impact and I was able to run it off, but I'm not sure I could have coped with another lengthy lay-off.'

It wasn't all one way. Paul was booked for a flying tackle and as he left the field at half-time, still bitterly arguing over a fruitless penalty appeal, he dropped his shorts to his knees. 'I know it was daft, but to me it showed that I cared. If there was one match I wanted to win it was this one.'

An away defeat was not the end of the world, but it was an inauspicious start to the campaign. Until that match Paul had felt he had complete empathy with the fans, but he had underestimated their patience. One of the Glasgow papers, *The Record*, opened its phonelines to angry fans and Paul seemed to bear the brunt of their frustration. It was unfair. For the most part they could only have seen the game on TV and the cameras had failed to pick up the effort Paul had put in off the ball and the nudges and kicks that at times bordered on assault. Walter Smith, under fire himself, came to his rescue. 'Paul is just back from a lengthy lay-off and we are trying to fit him into a team with new players. He's not at the stage in his career where you tell him how to play.'

The pressure was coming from all sides. Yet another girl from the past was coming out of the closet to haunt Paul, although to be fair to her, this time it was not she who initiated the sale of her story but one of Paul's so-called former friends. All sorts of unsavoury allegations were made regarding what occurred with one Tricia Dolan following a drinking session at the local in Dobbs Weir. 'Again, I couldn't understand why anybody would be interested. Yes, we'd had a fling together, but so what? Sheryl and I were apart at the time, I wasn't married and I don't think I ever claimed to be a monk, even though I might have had a haircut like one.'

He might try and laugh it off but Paul knew that Sheryl was hurting at seeing his former love-life, and by inference her present life, aired in public. Once again their relationship was under threat, fuelled by a third party's greed for money and publicity, fuelled by the media who never seemed to care what damage they might cause in their search for an easy story.

Walter Smith guessed, quite correctly, that Paul might need a break before facing up to Celtic in his first Old Firm Derby. Rangers travelled to Falkirk without Paul, and won 2–0 which kept up their 100 per cent record in the league. But everybody knew that the real test would come on the following Tuesday when they'd been tossed in against Celtic in the Coca-Cola Cup. Paul was careful to defuse any animosity he might have stirred up with his flute-playing antic at the start of the season. 'It was just a bit of fun. My dad was born a Catholic, whilst my mum's a Protestant, but as far as I'm concerned they're both Christians, or perhaps even more important than that, they're both human beings. I've never been a great believer in public religion. I've got my own beliefs and they're between me and God. That's how I think things should be, but as long as you don't hurt anybody then everybody should be

432

left to themselves.' Yet on the night of 19 September Paul did cause hurt; he hurt every Celtic supporter packed into Parkhead when, in the 75th minute of a closely contested game, he sent over an inch-perfect cross that teased and tempted the Celtic keeper before finding contact with Ally McCoist's head to give Rangers victory. The Celtic fans may have sung, 'Gazza, Gazza, who the f*** is Gazza?' but now they knew.

'I'd expected something a bit special. Newcastle–Sunderland, Arsenal–Spurs, Lazio–Roma, I'd played in them all, but somehow this one was different. I've never heard such a wall of sound. You felt you had to fight your way through it to get to the ball. It was as if the football was secondary.' Ken Gallacher writing in *The Herald* in Scotland said, 'Paul Gascoigne, the player whose temperament was supposed to crack in the white-hot heat of an Old Firm clash, provided the answer to his doubters last night. Reviled by the Celtic support throughout the game . . . he produced a piece of magic which silenced his persecutors.'

That was what it was coming to. No longer did he have critics, he had persecutors and once again he had taken all they could throw at him and thrown it back in their faces.

44

'WATCH YOURSELF GAZZA, BECAUSE WE'RE WATCHING YOU.'

He was enjoying life in Glasgow, but there was also a dark side to the city. He'd not expected to be universally loved, that had not even happened in his native Newcastle, but then again, he had not anticipated receiving death threats either. On the way to a game a car had pulled alongside him, a window had come down menacingly and a voice had said with stunning venom, 'Watch yourself Gazza, because we're watching you. One mistake and we'll slit your throat.'

Then there was the hate mail. After the death of his paternal grandmother, one so-called Protestant wrote stating that he couldn't believe Paul had gone to the funeral because she had been 'a Catholic bastard . . .' Her death had been, as far as this correspondent was concerned, 'the best thing that ever happened' and 'one less for the Protestants'.

The only upside to this campaign of hatred was that Paul has never been tempted by Glasgow nightlife. He had begged and pleaded with Sheryl to join him in the beautiful setting of the Cameron House Hotel, but given the tabloid stories of his indiscretions he could hardly feel aggrieved at her hesitation. He still had something to prove as far as she was concerned. And so he settled for the comfort of Jimmy Gardner's company once again. Jimmy was gaining cult status himself with

434

TV offers pouring in, including one where he would be giving guidelines on etiquette to the unsuspecting British public. When Len Lazarus told Paul of the offer for Jimmy he insisted it be accepted without even telling his fat friend. 'Yeah, go ahead, it'll do him good.' It was like lighting the fuse on a firework and then tossing it into a crowded room.

On 23 September it was back to the mundane business of the Scottish Premier Division but a shock was in store for Rangers who went down 0–1 at home to Hibernian, with Paul's old Newcastle team-mate, Darren Jackson, getting the only goal of the game. What was worse was that Celtic thumped Hearts 4–0 to go top of the league.

For once, however, Paul had other things on his mind apart from football. Sheryl's 30th birthday was on 24 September and Paul knew exactly how he intended to celebrate it. He bought her a watch that any woman in the world would have killed for, and booked a room for them at the romantic Danesfield House Hotel. Then, after a delicious lunch, went down on his knees in a crowded restaurant and for the second time in their relationship formally proposed to her. He waited for what seemed like an eternity on the floor until, doubled up with laughter, she said, 'Yes, all right then.'

Before the story had broken about Paul's brief indiscretion with Tricia he and Sheryl had been getting on far better than at any time in their tempestuous relationship. Paul was fascinated by the child that was growing within her and solicitous to the point of driving her crazy. He had stood by aghast at the threat that had come from left field in the shape of the sensational newspaper stories. Now this was his last throw not only to get her back but to get her for ever. When Rangers faced up to Borussia Dortmund in the next European challenge on 27 September he could afford to relax knowing that she would be watching proudly from the stand, and assured in the knowledge that when the game finished they would be able to leave the ground together as a couple.

This confidence showed in his play if not in the result. A goal down early in the match, Paul refused to panic and looked comfortable and dangerous whenever he received the ball. In the 52nd minute the crowd gasped as he first controlled the ball on his heel, then flicked it inside only to see Gordon Durie shoot against the German keeper's leg. Ten minutes later, he swept a perfect free-kick into the box and there was Gough to level the scores. Yet, Paul could not be everywhere and within a matter of five minutes the defence had leaked another goal. One could almost see Gazza rolling up his sleeves as he settled to his task once again. In the 73rd minute Paul took a pot shot that caught out the defence and the deflection ran kindly for Ferguson who equalized 2–2. On its own a commendable result against a fine footballing side, but realistically, one point from two matches in a league that also contained Juventus was simply not enough. The European dream was slipping from Paul's grasp as he headed down to London for the launch of his new boot contract with adidas.

Gradually, he seemed to be winning over his critics. Rob Hughes writing in *The Times* noted that Paul had 'skinned three or four opponents in his surging runs, his touch was always of a more certain nature than those around him and despite his petulant arm-waving and obviously foul language, there was much to suggest that come next summer he may indeed be a player fit for the European Championship'.

Yes, there was aggression, but that was Paul. Sanitize him and he became a different player, a different man. He could be changed, he wanted at times to be changed, but not to the point where he became less effective on the field. And adidas were justifiably proud of their new recruit. In the Predator boot they had one of the most revolutionary pieces of footballing equipment since laces were removed from footballs.

The contract between Paul Gascoigne Promotions Ltd and adidas had been negotiated over a period of months. M Dreyfuss, the President of the company, was a Gazza fan. They had tried to prize Shearer away from Umbro and failed but in many ways Gazza was a bigger catch, a bigger attraction. He didn't just score goals, he made them too, and there was no doubting the size of his personality. If there was any catch then it was just that. They had made a policy decision to concentrate on the product rather than those who wore it and questioned if Gazza might threaten to be bigger than the Predator. That, together with the flaws that had occasionally been exposed in the past in relation to other sponsors, was the potential drawback. However, by the end of the discussions, both sides were confident that they could move forward positively in an exciting partnership.

That wasn't good enough for some elements of the media. At the Kensington Roof Gardens on the 28 September adidas proudly unveiled their new signing to the expectant hordes of journalists and photographers. They threw the forum open to the reporters, but the most controversial question was whether Paul had used meditation on his road to recovery. Paul peered carefully through the subdued lighting at the female questioner and said with a smile, as if he'd never heard the word before, 'Meditation?' (pause . . .) 'Nah.'

The organizers took him outside for a photo session and he obediently obliged, posing this way and that. Then individual reporters tried to corner him, whilst TV cameras and radio mikes were thrust under his nose. It had been almost an hour under the spotlight and still they did not think they had been given enough. It was not a question of getting their money's worth, because they had paid no money. Yet, by the end of the session there were some amongst them who did not think they had a story – and by that they meant there was nothing negative they could write. They had come, given of their time, drunk the free booze, eaten the free food, and there had to be a story. If there wasn't one, they were going to manufacture one.

Brian Woolnough, that dangerous creature, an intellectual journalist, cornered Paul McCaughey, the senior adidas representative on the scene. Having elicited from him how long the negotiations had taken, he then put a question to him which seemed so absurd to Paul that he could only laugh. 'What would adidas do if Paul farted in front of the Queen?' 'Well, it's hardly likely, but we wouldn't be very pleased,' was McCaughey's somewhat naïve response, but it was all Woolnough needed to hear. He had his story. The fact that he had written just the night before, 'Gazza Is Magic As Rangers Hang On,' did not stop Woolnough from following that up with a nasty little piece under the headline, 'Blow Up And You Get Boot, Gazza'. According to Woolnough, adidas 'reckoned he was such a gamble they spent months researching Gascoigne before offering him a five-year package'. He claimed that Paul McCaughey had said, 'If he farts in front of the Queen we're in trouble. We get blemished . . . It is safe to say more research went into Gascoigne than any other player.' The only constructive thing Woolnough could find to say was that Paul had worn his new boots the night before against Borussia Dortmund and had 'produced his best display of the season.'

McCaughey called to complain the next day but to no avail. 'You didn't give us enough time with Gazza,' was the only excuse.

Fortunately Paul was truly able to let his boots do the talking the following Saturday against Celtic. Yet again, Rangers visited the old enemy and it was their new recruit who was to prove the telling factor. 'Celtic undone by Gascoigne,' wrote Joe Lovejoy in the *Sunday Times*, and he was right. 'Paul Gascoigne rounded off a resurgent week for himself and his club by scoring a coolly taken, if controversial, goal to set the seal on an Old Firm win which sees Rangers displace the old enemy at the top of the Scottish Premier Division.'

Paul was happy, to say the least. He was coming to terms with what it meant to beat Celtic; he'd scored again and, perhaps most important of all, he had come through the full 90 minutes of two taxing matches within the space of four days. For his goal, after an alleged hand ball by McCoist, Paul had raced half the length of the pitch to latch on to a telling pass from Salenko. His joy as he turned to the massed banks of Rangers supporters behind the goal was unconfined.

He was named, almost automatically and without qualification, for the international against Norway which was due to be played on 11 October and could feel with some justification that his rehabilitation was almost complete. But the dawn for the umpteenth time proved to be false.

The night after Venables had announced his team Rangers played Motherwell in what appeared to be a less than challenging conflict. For Paul, however, there was no such thing as a friendly, let alone a meaningless league game and he was clearly still inspired by his success over the weekend. He seemed prepared to take on the opposition almost single-handedly and within ten minutes he had mesmerized the defence on several occasions and actually scored the goal that put Rangers into the lead. Yet, the evil fairy who dogged his footsteps, who was determined to roll him down the hill just as fast as he neared the top, struck again. Almost a quarter of an hour into the second half he pulled up as if shot and could only leave the field with the help of Gordon Allison, the Rangers physio. Closer inspection showed that he had pulled a muscle.

It was another protest by a body that was unaccustomed to such consistent usage. Almost inevitably there followed another two weeks out of the game and another international in which he would not be playing.

45

'IF YOU DON'T FEEL RIGHT THEN YOU DON'T HAVE TO PLAY TOMORROW.'

It was not until Saturday 21 October that Paul was fit to pull on the blue shirt of Rangers again. It had been only eighteen days compared to eighteen months, yet every day lost to him was painful. He did not yet feel old, but he knew he was no longer young, at least not in footballing terms. He missed a 4–0 thrashing by Juventus in the Champions League in Italy on a night when not even his talents could have rescued the situation. In fact, the situation in Europe was so desperate that immediate measures needed to be taken in order to keep Rangers' hopes alive and Paul, in turn, was desperate to be part of the battle. He worked hard on the injury, he was used to that, but he also felt the need to have some fun as well. His brother-in-law, John-Paul King, came to stay with him at Cameron House, a restraining influence perhaps compared to some of his other companions, but still ever ready for mischief.

The news came through to the two men that Walter Smith and his wife were in the health club at the hotel and they were warned that they should be on their best behaviour. That was probably the worst thing to say to P Gascoigne.

Gazza went off to sit with his manager and his wife by the side of the pool and at a given signal John-Paul, who had never met Smith, appeared in the guise of the football supporter from hell. Like all good comics he started slowly. He went up to Paul and asked for his autograph, and then did the same to Walter. He explained away his Mancunian accent easily enough, then to their horror pulled up a chair and began to point out to Smith exactly where he thought he was going wrong in his tactics. Too polite to be abusive to the man in front of his wife, Smith had to sit there and take it all, with only the occasional comment to Paul as part of his armoury.

'Don't you get upset with strangers taking up your time?' Smith said to his player. 'No,' Paul replied, 'you've got to give your fans a bit of your time.' It was two hours later that the two pranksters finally cracked up and Paul introduced his brother-in-law. 'You bastards,' was all Smith could say. It had taken a while, but even he had become a Gazza victim.

Hearts on 21 October were victims too. Somebody was going to pay for the time that Paul had been sidelined and it took him just 110 seconds to score in a 4–1 victory. Unfortunately, his enthusiasm got the better of him and he found his way into the referee's book as well as onto the scoresheet. He was getting perilously near to a suspension, something he had to avoid at all costs. All of his critics had said that the cloggers in the Scottish League would test his temperament to the full. So far he had avoided being dismissed, but any time out of the game for disciplinary reasons would be playing into their hands.

Tuesday 24 October should have been a night of triumph. Rangers had already seen off Celtic's challenge in the Coca-Cola Cup and a semi-final at home to Aberdeen should not have prevented them from going through to the final, a guaranteed place in Europe, and Paul's first medal since the one brought to him on his hospital bed after Tottenham's FA Cup victory back in 1991. It was, in fact, a night of nothing but disaster. Paul seemed almost as hyped up as he had been under Venables over four years earlier and spent the first twenty minutes chasing, pushing and kicking everything in sight *except* the ball. It was no great surprise when he was booked for elbowing Billy Dodds and indeed, he was fortunate to remain on the field after another wild challenge. What was even more frustrating was that it was all to no avail. Aberdeen went two goals up and although a late effort by Salenko gave some impetus and excitement to the last five minutes, neither Rangers nor Paul himself could have any complaints about the result.

Rangers against Raith Rovers just a few seasons ago would have been considered a David and Goliath confrontation that could only happen in cup competitions, but Raith had come a long way since then and perhaps Rangers had not come as far as they might have liked. Indeed, Raith had put up a far more impressive struggle against Jurgen Klinsmann's Bayern Munich in their European campaign than Rangers had achieved against Juventus. It was no great surprise, therefore, when they actually took the lead at home to the injury torn Rangers, but this time Paul rolled up his sleeves and began to take control of the game. With pin-point accuracy his free-kick went to Richard Gough who equalized; then a corner from the right found Petric and Rangers were in front. Paul was running riot, his surging runs were leaving Raith defenders trailing. He slalomed by three, then four players like the Gazza of old, got to the bye-line, centred, but even as the ball hit the back of the net it was ruled to have gone over the line. It didn't matter any more than the Raith equalizer which was almost incidental; it didn't matter that it was against Raith rather than Juventus. The pace, the control, the inspiration were all there and Paul knew it, felt it in every sinew of his battered body.

In fact he didn't have to wait long to try to prove that he could do it against the likes of Juventus as well. Wednesday 1 November saw the return fixture at Ibrox, a packed Ibrox that was willing its players to erase the memory of the embarrassment of Turin just a couple of weeks before. Yes, they still had an injury list that read like something out of *Casualty*, but Gazza was back and surely that would make all the difference, wouldn't it?

'This one's for the Boss,' Paul said before the match. After it, he said nothing, merely hung his head in shame. His presence had made no difference and the score-line was the same all over again, 4–0 to Juventus. There had been a brief flurry in the second half when, with a little bit of luck, two efforts would have gone in rather than hitting the woodwork, but at the end of the day the Scots lost to a better team. It was no consolation that, with the exception of Nottingham Forest, the entire British European campaign was ended. Theoretically, Rangers still had a slim chance of progressing. They had two matches left. If they won them both, and if Juventus beat the same teams, then Rangers would come second in the league and stay in the competition. It was unlikely, but Scottish optimism being what it is they had not given up hope.

Yet the question had to be asked as to why, as *The Times* put it, 'Paul Gascoigne disappeared in pained insignificance'.

The answer was not long in coming. Once again Paul had allowed his personal life off the field to affect his concentration upon it. On Thursday, while the sports reporters were completing Rangers' epitaphs, the tabloid journalists were getting news of an incident that had occurred in London's Quaglino's restaurant on the previous Saturday night. An attractive blonde had come over to the table where Paul and Sheryl were dining, had paused to talk to Paul and, moments later, Sheryl had walked out in anger. It was another time for the intellectuals amongst the tabloid writers to pull out their abacuses and ensure that two plus two added up to five. The girl herself was Sarah Heaney, inevitably a model, who was based in Glasgow and was engaged to the Aberdeen player, John Inglis. What added a bit of spice to the story was that she had also been linked in the past to Rangers' Chairman David Murray. The innuendo that Paul was in any way involved with the girl was as inaccurate as was the suggestion that Sheryl had acted unreasonably or hastily. Paul had indeed met the young lady, for all of five minutes when she had been introduced to him as he was leaving a social evening. Her appearance at the table was the final straw in an evening which had started off so well and had then descended into acrimony as, for no apparent reason, his mood with himself and Sheryl darkened.

Later, he was to admit publicly that he had behaved appallingly and boorishly and that with or without the presence of young Miss Heaney, Sheryl was perfectly entitled to have upped and left. Unfortunately the story had by then escalated to something approaching earthquake proportions that could be measured on the Richter scale.

'Chat's it, Gazza . . . Sheryl dumps him . . .' screamed the *Sun*, accompanied by a photo of Sarah in a revealing swimsuit on the front page and even more revealing lingerie on page three.

It wasn't like that, but nobody wanted to listen. A couple of adults had rowed in public; there was a problem in their relationship. Left to themselves they could work it out, but the only trouble was that nobody was going to leave them to themselves. Yet again, Paul Gascoigne had to bow to the inevitable fact that Gazza was public property, and that made anybody in any way associated with him, particularly the woman who was expecting his baby in February, public property, too.

On the morning of Friday 3 November, as he awoke to the furore in the hotel, Paul had had enough. He spoke to Mel Stein on the phone and told him he did not even feel he could go to training. Stein spoke to David Murray and Chris Waddle. The Chairman was sympathetic, and Chris as a fellow professional who had experienced more than his fair share of an amoral media, fully understood. Eventually, Paul was coaxed down to the training ground where he had to run the gauntlet of reporters for the umpteenth time in his life. 'If you don't feel right, then you don't have to play tomorrow,' Walter Smith offered generously, referring to the match against Falkirk. 'We've got Kilmarnock on Wednesday, leave it till then.'

It was a wise and considerate decision and Paul returned to the hotel to rest. The reporters were still there. Sheryl herself was in a terrible state. It was bad enough to be several hundred miles away from her fiancé when six months' pregnant, but now she had the whole of the southern tabloid press camped on her front lawn, whilst Paul had their northern compatriots at his hotel. He did his best to explain the situation, to justify Sheryl's reaction, but it was nowhere near as good a story as the one that had been conjured up twenty-four hours before. It was certainly no longer front-page news. The newspapers had done their mischief, had done their best to ruin the relationship, and not for the first time it was left to the couple themselves to try and see what could be salvaged, not just for the sake of their own relationship but for the sake of the infant who would always be known as Gazza's son or daughter. It was not so much a question of being born with a silver spoon in its mouth as an albatross around its neck.

46

'HE'S ALWAYS PLAYED WITH HIS ELBOWS OUT.'

Gradually things began to return to what passed for normal in the life and times of Paul Gascoigne. By Thursday 9 November, not only were he and Sheryl talking to each other again, but *The Times* was able to carry the headline, 'Gazza Inspires' in describing Rangers' 2–0 away win at Kilmarnock. Although he did not score, one swerving run from the half-way line was particularly memorable, with only a fine save from the home keeper denying him a spectacular goal. Yet, amidst all the fine football Paul was booked again, his fifth of the season, and now was really teetering on the brink of his first Scottish suspension. However, his club were six points clear at the top of the Premiership and he could afford to draw breath and try and put the nightmare of the previous couple of weeks behind him.

He flew to London to join up with the England squad and after a couple of days' training was on his way to the airport to jet back up to Glasgow on the Friday to join up with his club team-mates for the match against Aberdeen on Saturday. He had virtually reached the airport when he was called on his mobile to be told that Venables wanted him back with the England side, that he had got the wrong end of the stick, and was leaving a day earlier than was permitted. It was hard to understand the logic behind the England manager's decision. Presumably he already knew whether or not Paul would start the match against Switzerland the following Wednesday and the match itself was only a friendly. He of all people knew the mental and physical pressure that Paul had endured yet he expected him to train on Saturday morning and play on Saturday afternoon after a dash to the airport and a tiring flight. Venables may have felt the need to flex his muscles, but it was an odd way to do it.

As it was Paul only lasted 63 minutes on the field and was somewhat fortunate to have got that far in the game. Early on in the match he appeared to cannon his head into John Inglis's chest and then a flying elbow caused Paul Bernard to have five stitches in his chin. Even the referee received the sharp end of Paul's tongue, yet by some miracle he escaped a sixth booking that would have seen him out of the Glasgow Derby that was to be played the following Sunday. Paul was tired and when he got tired he got irritable – and it showed. Yet, as the game finished in a tight 1–1 draw, Paul's thoughts turned towards Wembley and the forthcoming international. They certainly did not turn to a potential prosecution.

There could be no doubt that tempers had flared in the Aberdeen match, but the referee had not seen fit even to book Paul, and it was left to the referee's supervisor to make his report. This he duly did and by the following Tuesday the newspapers had their headlines. 'Police to investigate Gascoigne incidents,' said *The Times*, whilst the *Sun*, as usual, was more dramatic *and* pessimistic. Their headline read, 'Gazza Prison Threat'. The main article began with the words, 'Paul Gascoigne could be facing THREE YEARS in jail'. It was a nonsense, of course, but it didn't make pleasant breakfast reading.

The truth of the matter was that the Procurator Fiscal had asked Strathclyde Police for a report on 'incidents which allegedly occurred' during the 1–1 draw, and then, and only then, would The Crown decide whether any charges should be brought. It was not proving to be Paul's week. Even his selection for the England team was in doubt after he received a knock in training.

Whilst Paul had never claimed to be an angel either on or off the field there was considerable merit in what he had said before he knew that the incident was about to become a matter for public concern. 'Nobody took any notice when I was spat on. Nobody bothered with the fact that I was punched in the ribs so badly that the doctor had to look at me after the game. It's a regular occurrence for me. I'm not saying I'm victimized, but sometimes I feel I need a bit more protection.'

Venables immediately sprang to his favourite player's defence. 'He's always played with his elbows out. It's part of his screening and lots of players do that very well. Even when he's standing still you cannot get to him. You should screen with your elbows out.'

The comparisons with Duncan Ferguson, the ex-Rangers player who was already serving a three-month jail sentence for an assault by way of a head-butt, were inevitable. Yet, nobody bothered to point out that Ferguson's past record was a larger contribution to his incarceration than the head-butting incident itself. As far as Paul was concerned there had been a multitude of bookings, intermingled with very few dismissals, but for the most part they were for niggling tackles or for not knowing when to shut his mouth in front of the referee. It would have been difficult to find another professional who considered Paul Gascoigne to be a genuinely dirty player who went out to injure opponents.

It was hardly the best of preparations for a match against Switzerland, a team still managed by Roy Hodgson, an Englishman who had only recently been invited to double up as the Inter-Milan coach in Italy's Serie A. Platt, until the start of the season a member of that very team, could not force his way back into the England side and it was clear that Venables had chosen a side that would rely heavily on Gazza's inspiration from mid-field. It was to be hoped that the pressure would not prove too much. 'I was really beginning to feel that I was taking on too much,' Paul recalls. 'I'd played on Wednesday against Kilmarnock; then I'd flown to London to join up with the England squad, put in some hard training, got injured, received treatment; then I'd flown back to Glasgow, played against Aberdeen, then back to London again to all the fuss and bother, and all that doesn't take into account any of my commercial obligations, my house-hunting, my dad's ill-health, and the fact that I was only a couple of months away from being a father myself.'

Put like that it was a wonder that his battered body and mind could keep going at all. Yet, it did. Rob Hughes writing in *The Times* perhaps summed it up best when he said, 'What of the talisman, Gascoigne? He looked almost frenetically busy, determined when he had the ball to impress on this game, on the doubting critics, that he still has the pace to get away from cloying markers, the creativity to deceive and perplex them.'

For just six minutes during the game Paul seemed to strike up a real understanding with young Jamie Redknapp who was playing alongside him in mid-field. But then the Liverpool player had to leave the pitch with a pulled hamstring and a reshuffle brought into the fray the prematurely balding figure of Steve Stone of Forest. Stone had been a Newcastle fan all of his life, and now here he was playing alongside his old Tyneside hero. It was the stuff of which dreams are made and he deservedly received the Man of the Match award in a 3–1 England victory. Paul for once had to take second place, but his contribution was still important without ever being dominating. A curling free-kick here, a powerful run in the 27th minute, a one-two with

Sheringham and then there was Paul bearing down on the keeper with the crowd on its feet anticipating a goal. As it was the goalie made a fine save, but Paul was sufficiently encouraged to charge through five minutes later, shrugging off the challenge of a Swiss defender through sheer strength, and finally forcing another excellent save from the keeper. Again, as Hughes in his *Times* report said, 'Still, in this England side, Gascoigne is a talent'. That may have been damning with faint praise, but at least it was praise rather than condemnation. The only disappointment was the public criticism by Venables, who may have felt that he was justified after the years of defending Paul's maverick behaviour. 'When we went ahead Gazza was all over the place instead of bossing the midfield.' Indeed, one of his mistakes had nearly led to a Swiss goal, but he had got his head down after that, concentrated and battled on. He felt hard done by as far as the England chief was concerned, and again the feelings of persecution were never far from his mind.

Someone else *was* also praising Paul Gascoigne, albeit cautiously. Glenn Hoddle, caught in the cross-fire in the battle for Chelsea between Ken Bates and Matthew Harding, had believed Paul needed to be taken out of the cauldron that was Glasgow and had actually phoned Rangers to see if he could take Paul on loan. Whether or not this was a political move inspired by Harding or whether Hoddle genuinely thought he could do for Paul what he felt Walter Smith had not yet achieved, we will never know. As ever, the truth was probably somewhere in-between. In any event Hoddle wanted to take a long hard look at Paul before making a bid to secure him on a permanent basis, always presuming that Harding would make the money available. The Premier League rules allowed for three-month loans for Scottish players but Rangers turned Hoddle down flat. As far as he was concerned that was the end of the matter, even if it wasn't the end as far as the tabloids were concerned.

'Gazza Can Go! Rangers to flog Paul and end a nightmare,' was fairly typical of the coverage. Yet again they had got it wrong. Rangers were at the top of the Scottish Premier League; they had lost in the semi-final of the Coca-Cola Cup but could still progress in Europe if results fell their way. Paul was a fixture in the England team, and best of all he was playing regularly and steering clear of serious injury. Yes, he still had to face the music on the Aberdeen incident, but compared to some of the disastrous years in the past, he was almost in heaven!

As it was, nobody from Chelsea ever spoke to his advisers, and as far as Paul was concerned, he had only completed four months of a three-year contract. Instead of looking South his attention turned inwards to another Old Firm Derby, Rangers against Celtic on Sunday 19 December 1995.

47

'TAKE THE UNPREDICTABILITY AWAY AND YOU LOSE THE REAL GAZZA.'

Paul Gascoigne was never going to be the most popular figure with the Celtic fans and his early booking for a fairly innocuous challenge brought the biggest roar of the afternoon from their huge contingent of fans. Paul said nothing, but realized he would now be facing a suspension. To the neutral observer it appeared that this particular referee had decided that the best way to get a grip on the match was to book Gazza at the first opportunity. Yet, with hindsight it seemed that he may well have done Paul a favour. Rangers having gone a goal down, suddenly found Paul on a run into space, and as he elegantly passed the ball across Celtic's back-line there was Laudrup to hit it into the far corner.

Celtic restored their lead through a penalty, but then, in the 63rd minute, there was Gascoigne again with a teasing, tantalizing free-kick that found the reliable head of Ally McCoist. Seven minutes later Rangers were back in front, but within a couple of moments Celtic had made it 3–3, a result that kept Rangers just four points clear at the top of the table.

They were certainly not top of their European Champions' League. Quite the reverse, in fact, with only one point from four matches after the two crushing defeats by Juventus. Yet, a win at home to Steaua Bucharest, linked to a predictable victory by Juventus over Borussia

453

Dortmund, would still give them a life-line. They would need to beat Dortmund and hope that Juventus defeated the Romanians. In every pub in Glasgow hopes ran as high as the piles of dirty glasses.

For half an hour Paul and the rest of his team-mates put in a strangely subdued performance, given the importance of the occasion. The crowd at first tried to lift them, then turned on them in frustration. It was left to Paul to bring a sense of majesty to the evening. The Steaua defence moved out in a mass attempt to play Laudrup off-side, and when Paul collected the ball from him in midfield the route to goal looked as irresistible as a gap on the rails that would have tempted the Lester Piggot of old. Paul was away like a shot, gathering speed as he ran to beat Stelea in goal with a low, rasping shot from some twelve yards. Incredibly enough, at twenty-eight years of age, it was his very first goal in a European competition.

Time and time again, Rangers threw men forward to increase their lead, a feverish effort given the bad news from Turin that Juventus had fallen behind to their German visitors. The Scots contingent had feared the worst when they learned that the Italians were resting some of their key players in the knowledge that they were already certain to qualify, but a Scotsman never believes the worst until it actually happens.

Then it did happen. In the 55th minute Steaua equalized and shortly afterwards Dortmund went 2–0 up against Juventus. Although the Italians pulled one back, the dream was over. The *Guardian* headline summed it up. 'Gascoigne goal is not enough'.

Paul was bitterly disappointed. He had really believed that Rangers could be a force in Europe and here they were, like all the other British teams, with the exception of Nottingham Forest, sent packing to do some more revision before they would be allowed to resit their exams the following year. That was always assuming, of course, that they won the title again. The following autumn seemed a lifetime away.

There was no time to dwell on what might or might not have been as Paul rose early on Thursday morning to catch a flight to London to film a Walker's Crisps advert with Gary Lineker. The venue was Queens Park Rangers' ground at Loftus Road, and inevitably, the script called for Lineker to steal Gazza's crisps and reduce him to tears. Lineker, older, wiser, greyer, and now an established media star, greeted Paul fondly.

'How you doing, Gazza?' Paul asked Lineker, imposing his own nick-name on his erstwhile team-mate. They sat and chatted as they were being made-up, like the old friends they were. They may have been a million miles apart in attitude but they were linked by that indefinable bond that links all professional footballers.

'He was still the same Paul,' Lineker says, 'a bit more mature, but never boringly predictable (like me). But take that away from him, take the unpredictability away, and you lose the real Gazza.'

Paul seemed to have put behind him an ominous summons from the Scottish Football Association. He was to appear, along with three other players, to explain the maelstrom that had been the Aberdeen–Rangers match. That was to be the following Thursday and was to result in a one-match ban to add to the match he would already have to miss following his cumulative bookings. In typical Gascoigne manner he could relegate that to the recesses of his mind. That was tomorrow's problem, for the moment he could only cope with today.

Gascoigne and Lineker walked across the pitch towards the cameras, still deep in conversation. Behind them, almost unnoticed, the Chrysalis cameras continued to roll. The two players were in a world of their own. Back on a football pitch together five years after the drama of the World Cup semi-final in the heat of Italy. Then Lineker had signalled to manager Bobby

Robson that he thought Gazza's head had gone. Now they were both older and wiser. Lineker had endured and survived the illness of his son, the ignominy of being substituted by Graham Taylor in his final international, a miserable time with injuries in Japan. Nothing remained the same. Taylor himself had resigned from his job at Wolves just two weeks before, and Lineker and Gascoigne could not turn back the clock; they would never play together again in a competitive match.

The stand was filled by extras. The cameras began to roll. Drops were put into Paul's eyes to make him cry, the *Spitting Image* eyes were produced to spout tears, the crowd spontaneously burst into applause as Paul got it right first time, reducing the watchers to helpless laughter. Tears and laughter. What had Paul put into the eyes of the nation all those years ago to make them cry? What had he done since then to make them laugh? That was part of the problem. What did the future hold for Gazza, laughter or tears?

PAUL GASCOIGNE CAREER RECORD TO DECEMBER 1995

MILESTONES

SENIOR DEBUT:	Newcastle Utd v QPR (sub.)	April 1985	at St. James's Park
FULL DEBUT:	Newcastle Utd v Southampton	August 1985	at The Dell
FIRST GOAL:	Newcastle Utd v Oxford Utd	Sept. 1985	at St. James's Park
INTL DEBUT:	England v Denmark (sub.)	Sept. 1988	at Wembley

HONOURS

FA CUP	WINNER	1991
FA YOUTH CUP	WINNER	1985
PFA YOUNG PLAYER OF THE YEAR		1988

ENGLAND UNDER 21

	13 APP	6 GOALS
1986 – 7	v	Morocco	USSR	Portugal
1987 – 8	v	W. Germany	Yugoslavia	Scotland
		Scotland	France	France
		Switzerland	Mexico	USSR
		Morocco		

		ENGLAND FULL	35 APP	6 GOALS (to December 1995)
1988 – 9	v	Denmark Chile	Saudi Arabia Scotland	Albania
1989 – 90	v	Sweden Denmark Eire Belgium	Brazil Uruguay Holland Cameroon	Czechoslovakia Tunisia Egypt W.Germany
1990 – 1	v	Hungary	Poland	Cameroon
1992 – 3	v	Norway Turkey Norway	Turkey Holland	San Marino Poland
1993 – 4	v	Poland	Denmark	
1994 – 5	v	Japan	Sweden	Brazil
1995 – 6	v	Portugal	Switzerland	Colombia
		ENGLAND 'B'	4 APP	1 GOAL
1988 – 9	v	Switzerland	Iceland	
1989 – 90	v	Italy	Yugoslavia	

458

PAUL GASCOIGNE CAREER RECORD TO DECEMBER 1995

SEASON	CLUB RECORD	LEAGUE		FA CUP COPPA ITALIA		FL CUP SC. LG. CUP		EUROPE		TOTAL	
		APP	GLS	APP	GLS	APP	GLS	APP	GLS	APP	GLS
1984 – 5	Newc. Utd (Div.I)	2	0	0	0	0	0	0	0	2	0
1985 – 6	Newc. Utd (Div.I)	31	9	1	0	3	0	0	0	35	9
1986 – 7	Newc. Utd (Div.I)	24	5	0	0	2	0	0	0	26	5
1987 – 8	Newc. Utd (Div.I)	35	7	3	3	3	–	0	0	41	11
1988 – 9	Tottenham (Div.I)	32	6	0	0	5	1	0	0	37	7
1989 – 90	Tottenham (Div.I)	34	6	0	0	4	1	0	0	38	7
1990 – 1	Tottenham (Div.I)	26	7	6	6	5	6	0	0	37	19
1991 – 2	Tottenham (Div.I)	0	0	0	0	0	0	0	0	0	0
1992 – 3	Lazio (Se. A)	22	4	4	0	0	0	0	0	26	4
1993 – 4	Lazio (Se. A)	17	2	0	0	0	0	0	0	17	2

COURTESY OF P. JOANNOU 1996 REV A

459

1994 – 5	Lazio (Se. A)	4	0	0	0	0	0	0	0	4	0
1995 –	Gl. Rangers (PL)	14	6	0	0	3	1	7	1	24	8
TOTALS	(to December 1995)	241	52	14	9	25	10	7	1	287	72

OVERALL CLUB AND INTERNATIONAL TOTALS

		APP	GLS	APP	GLS	APP	GLS	APP	GLS	APP	GLS
1984 – 8	Newc. Utd	92	21	4	3	8	1	0	0	104	25
1988 – 92	Tottenham Hot.	92	19	6	6	14	8	0	0	112	33
1992 – 5	Lazio	43	6	4	0	-	-	0	0	47	6
1995 –	Gl. Rangers (PL)	14	6	0	0	3	1	7	1	24	8
	England (Under 21)	13	6	-	-	-	-	-	-	13	6
	England (B)	4	1	-	-	-	-	-	-	4	1
	England (Full)	35	6	-	-	-	-	-	-	35	6
TOTALS	(to December 1995)	293	65	14	9	25	10	7	1	339	85

460

INDEX

474

477